D0294817

Michael Heseltine

BY THE SAME AUTHOR

Militant
Scargill and the Miners
The March of Militant
(*with David Smith*) Manchester United:
The Betrayal of a Legend
Jeffrey Archer: Stranger Than Fiction
The Complete Manchester United Trivia Fact Book

Michael Heseltine
A Biography

Michael Crick

HAMISH HAMILTON · LONDON

To Sheila Dunn

HAMISH HAMILTON

Published by the Penguin Group
Penguin Books Ltd, 27 Wrights Lane, London w8 5tz, England
Penguin Books USA Inc., 375 Hudson Street, New York, New York 10014, USA
Penguin Books Australia Ltd, Ringwood, Victoria, Australia
Penguin Books Canada Ltd, 10 Alcorn Avenue, Toronto, Ontario, Canada m4v 3b2
Penguin Books (NZ) Ltd, 182-190 Wairau Road, Auckland 10, New Zealand

Penguin Books Ltd, Registered Offices: Harmondsworth, Middlesex, England

First published 1997
1 3 5 7 9 10 8 6 4 2
First edition

Copyright © Michael Crick, 1997
The moral right of the author has been asserted

All rights reserved.
Without limiting the rights under copyright
reserved above, no part of this publication may be
reproduced, stored in or introduced into a retrieval system,
or transmitted, in any form or by any means (electronic, mechanical,
photocopying, recording or otherwise) without the prior
written permission of both the copyright owner
and the above publisher of this book

Set in 11½/14pt Monotype Ehrhardt
Typeset by Rowland Phototypesetting Ltd, Bury St Edmunds, Suffolk
Printed in England by Clays Ltd, St Ives plc

A CIP catalogue record for this book is available from the British Library

ISBN 0-241-13691-1

Contents

List of Illustrations

THE HESELTINE FAMILY TREE

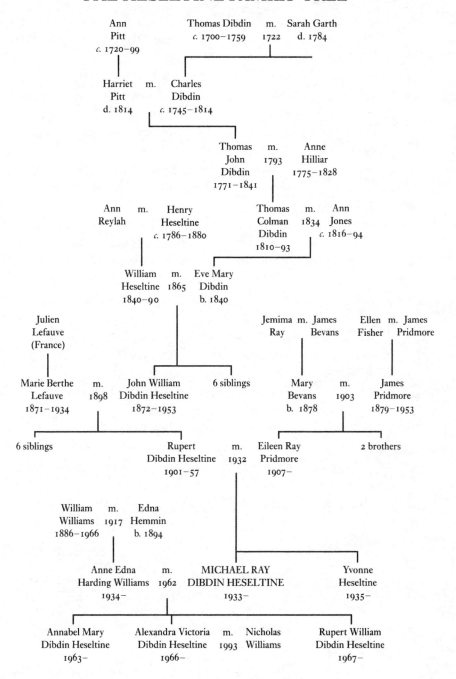

Ann Pitt
c. 1720–99

Thomas Dibdin m. Sarah Garth
c. 1700–1759   1722   d. 1784

Harriet m. Charles
Pitt   Dibdin
d. 1814   c. 1745–1814

Thomas m. Anne
John   1793 Hilliar
Dibdin   1775–1828
1771–1841

Ann m. Henry
Reylah   Heseltine
         c. 1786–1880

Thomas m. Ann
Colman 1834 Jones
Dibdin   c. 1816–94
1810–93

William m. Eve Mary
Heseltine 1865 Dibdin
1840–90   b. 1840

Julien
Lefauve
(France)

Jemima m. James
Ray   Bevans

Ellen m. James
Fisher   Pridmore

Marie Berthe m. John William   6 siblings
Lefauve   1898 Dibdin Heseltine
1871–1934   1872–1953

Mary m. James
Bevans 1903 Pridmore
b. 1878   1879–1953

6 siblings

Rupert m. Eileen Ray   2 brothers
Dibdin Heseltine 1932 Pridmore
1901–57   1907–

William m. Edna
Williams 1917 Hemmin
1886–1966   b. 1894

Anne Edna m. MICHAEL RAY   Yvonne
Harding Williams 1962 DIBDIN HESELTINE Heseltine
1934–   1933–   1935–

Annabel Mary   Alexandra Victoria m. Nicholas   Rupert William
Dibdin Heseltine   Dibdin Heseltine 1993 Williams   Dibdin Heseltine
1963–   1966–   1967–

Preface

It was October 1979 and I was anxiously hosting my first debate as president of the Oxford Union. Michael Heseltine was one of my two 'star' guests, on his way home from his latest triumph at the Conservative Party conference in Blackpool. I didn't appreciate it at the time, but Margaret Thatcher's new Environment Secretary was returning to the Union almost twenty-five years to the day since his own first debate as president of the Society – when he had held a similar motion of 'no confidence in Her Majesty's Government'. Surprisingly perhaps, I remember nothing of what Michael Heseltine said that night in 1979, though he certainly didn't disappoint the vast crowd which always attends the first debate of the academic year.

My most powerful memory, in fact, is how difficult Heseltine was to talk to, both over drinks beforehand and then during the customary pre-debate dinner. It surprised me, for Heseltine was on familiar territory; one might have expected him to inquire after the health and fortunes of the Union, or to ask, for instance, what my colleagues and I intended to do with ourselves after Oxford. I assumed he must have more pressing matters on his mind. Later my brother-in-law related how he had found the same coolness when he had welcomed Heseltine to another student meeting in Oxford some years later. It seemed such a surprising shortcoming for a politician, particularly one who was supposed to be so charismatic and ambitious.

In January 1996 I reminded Michael Heseltine of that first encounter – though not of his cold manner – and we discussed how his victory in the debate had been the last time for sixteen years that the Tories had won a Union 'confidence' motion. I had written to the Deputy Prime Minister telling him that I had been commissioned to write this biography, and suggesting that as a goodwill gesture it might be worth having a brief chat. Eventually, the call came through to 'come and see the DPM' at the Cabinet Office in Whitehall.

I had made it clear in my letter that I was not looking for Michael

xi

Heseltine's cooperation or approval for the book. I would never have expected it, and it's not my style. Biographers can sometimes get too close to their subjects; it is all too easy to be charmed and come to feel indebted, with a consequent loss of impartiality. It's far healthier, I feel, for a biographer to remain independent; to get as close as possible through friends and colleagues without active assistance from the subject. Equally, one hopes the subject won't put too many obstacles in the way.

Barely had I sat down in his office before Heseltine announced he would not cooperate with my plans – despite the fact I'd expressly stated I wasn't seeking his help. He claimed to have said exactly the same thing to previous intended biographers (though I later discovered he'd given quite a lot of assistance to a book which Linda Christmas and Hugh Stephenson started during his 'wilderness' period in the late 1980s but subsequently abandoned). Our encounter seemed perfectly amicable, however. Keen to know whether I could expect any obstruction, I inquired what he'd say to friends who asked him whether they should talk to me. 'If they ask,' he said, 'I shall say, "No."' The tone of his response left me quite cheerful; there seemed to be a touch of emphasis on the word 'if', suggesting that he rather hoped they wouldn't consult him in the first place. When I asked if there was anyone he'd prefer me not to approach, he said, 'No.'

With a general election in the offing, and Michael Heseltine set to play a key role, I was perhaps being a little optimistic. Fairly swiftly the word went round Whitehall that the Deputy Prime Minister would prefer it if people didn't talk to me. Within Heseltine's old department, the Department of Trade and Industry, a memo was even circulated telling senior staff that 'a biography of Mr Heseltine' was being prepared by 'Professor Michael Crick of the Institute of Contemporary British History at the University of London'. I was delighted, of course, to be elevated to such high academic rank (in fact I am simply a journalist and an ordinary, subscribing member of the ICBH, which has no formal attachment to London University). 'It is not appropriate,' the memo continued, 'for civil servants to offer views, whether on or off the record, on their working relationship with a Cabinet minister and would be against the general principles of conduct and breach the duties and obligations of members of staff ... You should, therefore, politely decline any invitation to contribute to the research.'

Fortunately for me, dozens of government officials and former civil servants did accept my invitations to discuss Michael Heseltine. In many cases their insights were far more illuminating than those of politicians.

The attractions of Heseltine as a biographical subject are obvious. At the simplest level, it's a tale of thwarted ambition. But for a few famous lapses of judgement and the flaw I briefly glimpsed at the Union debate in 1979, he probably would have attained his goal of becoming Prime Minister. Even now it would be rash to write him off, a mistake that commentators and colleagues have often made in the past. Heseltine has outlasted all his colleagues from the original Thatcher Cabinet of 1979, and many more have come and gone since then. Just as in 1977 and 1987, Michael Heseltine is still being mentioned as a possible next Conservative leader: at the start of 1997, the bookmakers William Hill quoted him as 9/2 favourite to succeed John Major, though that seemed rather generous (to Heseltine).

His career has been strewn with regular controversies, scrapes and confrontations, not least, of course, his overthrow of Margaret Thatcher in 1990. But alongside the colourful episodes and famous Heseltine ambition lies a substantial record of ministerial activity; though he's no great intellectual theorist, he loves playing with practical policy ideas. To the observer, the fascination has lain in Heseltine's efforts both to confront what he has seen as the excesses of the prevailing Thatcherite orthodoxy, but also to build on its more positive features.

On top of Heseltine-the-politician comes the story of the self-made multi-millionaire. Few men in recent British history have both reached the front rank in politics, and also amassed a considerable personal fortune from almost nothing. In building his Haymarket business, Michael Heseltine was a leading pioneer in magazine and careers publishing; many of the people and ideas he encouraged in the 1960s remain an important influence in the industry thirty years later. Yet behind the publicly recognized politician and successful businessman lies a very private individual – Michael Heseltine the tree-planter and country gentleman.

It is now almost ten years since Michael Heseltine's lifelong friend and Tory colleague Julian Critchley first published his 'unauthorized' biography. Witty and irreverent, Critchley's book was largely an affectionate memoir and left plenty for others to explore. For a figure of Heseltine's importance in contemporary history and continuing stature in British politics, a more detailed examination is long overdue.

Inevitably, given the circumstances in which this book was written, many of those who discussed their experiences of Heseltine wished to remain anonymous. I am grateful that they were willing to talk at all. The research has involved many hundreds of interviews; the difficulty in thanking people is deciding where to draw the line: helpful conversations can range from just a few seconds on the telephone, to several face-to-face sessions lasting many hours.

I express my gratitude both to those I cannot mention and to those who spoke 'on the record'; I hope those who are already cited in the footnotes will forgive me if I do not repeat their names here. Many others who gave interviews are not quoted directly in the text, but nevertheless provided useful background material; these include Ken Aldred, Bernard Barnett, Tom Baron, Lord Bellwin, Peter Boston, David Bradley, Lord Briggs, Peter Brown, Colin Bruce, Paul Cherrington, Sir Frank Cooper, Philip Critchley, Phyllis Dalton, Christopher Dobson, Sir George Edwards, Harry Edwards, Peter Elman, Graham Elsom, Sir Christopher France, Harold Gatehouse, Sir William Harris, Bob Hastie, Sir Michael Heron, Sir Robert Hicks, Peter Hillmore, Sir Derek Hornby, Tim Horton, Nan Howard, Tony Hutt, Leonard Hyde, John Illman, John Izbicki, Michael Jameson, Richard Jameson, Lord Jellicoe, Julian Kavanagh, Ian Kerr, Peter Krivinskas, Neville Labovitch, Elizabeth Leigh, Tim Lewis, Gerry Loughlin, Pat Macmillan, Philip Manzano, Lord Marlesford, Sir Ronald Mason, Alan Mitchell, Sir James Molyneaux, Christopher Monckton, Sir Hector Monro, Christopher Morgan, Richard Needham, Ronald Nicholls, Wally Olins, John Osborn, Olive Page, Sir Dan Pettit, Michael Pickard, Clive Ponting, Stanley Price, Sir Timothy Raison, Richard Raven, Bill Robinson, Ruth Rosenthal, Sir Hugh Rossi, Ron Rulton, John Saunders, Stuart Sexton, Alan Sked, Jackie Smith, Evie Soames, William Solesbury, Ralph Steadman, Lord Stoddart, Richard Storey, Graham Stringer, Sheila Thompson, Diana Tole, Sir David

Trippier, Peter Unwin, Reg Ward, Kenneth Warren, Cecil White, John Wilkinson, Peter Williams, Rusty Wood, Colin Woodhead and Ivan Yates.

Some people went to quite extraordinary lengths to assist me. Michael Charlesworth and James Lawson helped with Heseltine's days at Shrewsbury. Robert Unsworth delved into material assembled for his planned history of the *Cherwell* newspaper, and Gerry Woodcock showed me his unpublished political history of Tavistock. Barrie Macdonald of the ITC library never seemed to tire of my quest for details of Heseltine's TV career. Peter Gillman generously supplied copies of interviews he conducted for a 1990 profile of Heseltine the businessman, while Ivan Fallon lent me relevant notes of interviews done for his book on the Saatchi brothers. Paul McQuail was a constant and ever-patient guide on Heseltine's three spells at the DoE, and Professor Michael Parkinson shared his observations of his role as Minister for Merseyside. Tony Barker of Essex University also dispensed regular information and advice, while Philip Cowley assisted with his work on the 1990 and 1995 Tory leadership elections. Peter Catterall and the ICBH kindly supplied both expertise and temporary accommodation.

Others who helped in significant ways included David Alden, Andrew Alexander, Rodney Atkinson, Michael Barber, Robert Barrett, Hilary Bevan, Lord Blake, Don Bridge, David Butler, Francis Carline, Travers Cosgrove, Camilla Costello, Lord Devonport, Anne-Lise Gotzsche, Peter Hennessy, Martin Holmes, Robin Jackman, Bill Kirkman, Steve Leach, Simon Lee, Daksha Patel, Dan Plesch, David Rogers, Jan Rockett, Trevor Taylor, Lionel Trippett and Roger Young. Vernon Jackson showed me round Stockbridge Village. Vi Bellamy of Companies House was a model of cheerful and constructive service.

Several publications carried appeals for information, which often prompted quite fascinating responses: these included *FDA News*, the *Kentish Express*, the *Mourne Observer*, the *Oldham Evening Chronicle*, *Oxford Today* and the *Oxford Times*. The *Liverpool Post and Echo*, the *Reading Evening Post*, the Reading Newspaper Company, the *Henley Standard*, the *Oxford Mail and Times*, the *South Wales Evening Post* and the *Tavistock Times* all granted access to their libraries. David

Sheppard of the *Daily Mail* picture library also went out of his way to help.

I am grateful to the staff of Ashford and Tenterden councils, the Bow Group and the Oxford Union for access to their archives, and to Martin Maw who looks after the Conservative Party papers at the Bodleian. Sue Robinson supplied details from the files of Granada TV. One day I shall dedicate a book to librarians: from Swansea to Ashford, Chipping Norton to Tavistock, Kensington to Coventry, this project depended on their guidance. Time and again, however, I returned to the reading room I first used as a schoolboy. If there's a better public reference service in this country than Manchester Central Library, I have yet to find it.

I am, as ever, grateful to Bill Hamilton of A. M. Heath. Andy Curry, Bob Davenport and Andrew Stephenson did much to improve the manuscript in their own individual ways. Keith Taylor skilfully guided the ship into port.

This book could never have been completed without substantial contributions by my research team. Amina Wright was painstaking in her inquiries into Heseltine's family history and his property interests. My mother, Pat Crick, explored Heseltine's French ancestry and compiled the index. Sean O'Grady worked doggedly in pursuit of political material. Tom Fairbrother researched large parts of Heseltine's ministerial career; at the age of only twenty-one he showed a remarkable knowledge and understanding of British history and politics, and it was a privilege to have the services of one who is obviously destined for a glittering career as a historian. I must also thank Sean McDougall and Tom Happold for their research work, and not least my wife, Margaret, who compiled the photographic sections and also conducted numerous interviews.

Michael Crick
Swerford, Oxfordshire
20 January 1997

1. *Family Furniture*

One December morning more than a hundred years ago, a businessman walked into a solicitor's office in Lincoln's Inn Fields. When nobody was looking he took out a loaded revolver and shot himself in the head. He died instantly. He was William Heseltine, the great-grandfather of the Deputy Prime Minister.

In the autumn of 1983 Michael Heseltine began making private inquiries about some of his extraordinary ancestors. At a time when the nation might have expected the then Defence Secretary to have weightier matters on his mind – such as the imminent arrival of cruise missiles – he got his personal secretary to write to Hubert Chesshyre, who bears the title of Chester Herald at the College of Arms in London.

Chesshyre assumed that Heseltine was interested in finding out if any of his ancestors was distinguished enough to entitle him to a family coat of arms. That, after all, is why most people ask the College of Arms to help with genealogical research. Chesshyre made preliminary inquiries, and traced the Heseltine tree back to the late eighteenth century, but it didn't look promising. Further research would cost Michael Heseltine £350, and the matter was quietly dropped.[1] Instead of a coat of arms above the gates of their Northamptonshire country home, the Heseltines have made do with the simple characters MAH, entwined in wrought iron and denoting, presumably, Michael and Anne Heseltine.

In Conservative circles, Michael Heseltine has been the victim of some snobbery about his background. 'The trouble with Michael is that he had to buy all his furniture' is the widely quoted jibe. It's often attributed – wrongly – to Heseltine's former ministerial colleague Alan Clark. But in his diaries Clark credits the 'snobby, but cutting' remark to the former Chief Whip, Michael Jopling.[2] In fact Michael Heseltine's forebears actually achieved considerable fame and wealth in their time.

Michael Heseltine is often described as Welsh. Indeed, commentators have occasionally tried to explain his odd fiery moments – such as the time he picked up the Commons mace, or his sudden walkout from the Cabinet over Westland – as being due to Celtic corpuscles rushing through his veins. But his Welsh blood is actually rather diluted. The fact he was born in Wales, he once asserted, 'doesn't make me Welsh. I have at least as much French blood in me as Welsh blood.'[3]

Others assume from his Nordic appearance and the surname 'Heseltine' that there must be some north European background: Scandinavian, perhaps, or German. In fact 'Heseltine' is a very old-fashioned English name – a variation on 'Haseldine', 'Hazelden' and more than twenty similar versions, all of which originally meant someone who lived in a hazel-dean, or a valley of hazel trees. Even today, inspection of the phone directories shows a strong concentration of Heseltines, Haseldines and Haseldenes in North Yorkshire. And that is where Michael Heseltine's family originates from.

Michael Heseltine's great-great-grandfather, Henry Heseltine, was born around 1790, in the vicinity of the city of York, though he ended up as a tailor in Huddersfield, in what is now called West Yorkshire. His son, William Heseltine, Michael's great-grandfather, had a far more successful business career, although he died in tragic circumstances. William was born in 1840; by the age of twelve he had finished his schooling, and by his early twenties he had moved to London. There he became a clerk in the tea trade, working for E. Tetley & Sons, run by one of the two Tetley brothers, who also came from Huddersfield.

By 1872 William Heseltine had become manager of Tetley's, though he wasn't a partner. Then in 1876 he took a decision which not only would change his life but also helped transform the whole of British food retailing.

One of his staff at Tetley's, Hudson Kearley, who was only twenty – sixteen years younger than Heseltine – decided to branch out on his own. Kearley had found that there were hundreds of small grocers who wanted to sell tea but weren't big enough to order from a wholesaler as substantial as Tetley's. Kearley therefore planned to become a middleman, ordering from Tetley's and supplying such businesses. But he explained to William Heseltine that he needed capital to start up. Heseltine said he knew a man who 'might be interested', and, as Kearley relates in his memoirs, 'Next day Mr Heseltine informed me that the person he had had in mind was none other than himself, and that he was prepared to invest five hundred pounds in Kearley & Co. if I was prepared to devote my whole time to the business.'[4]

Within a few months the enterprise had taken off, and Heseltine soon left Tetley's to join it. Heseltine & Kearley, as the partnership was initially called, was later joined by a third colleague from Tetley's, called Tonge.

Kearley was keen to expand, and before long the partners had opened their own grocery shop, in Brentford, west London. By 1880 they had ten outlets around the Home Counties. Hudson Kearley would later claim to be a 'pioneer' in 'the reorganization of the marketing and distribution of the world's food supply', and, although Kearley was probably the most dynamic partner, Michael Heseltine's great-grandfather can also claim a part in the Victorian revolution in retailing.[5] Until the 1880s, grocery chains were uncommon, and those that did exist tended to specialize in particular types of produce. Heseltine, Kearley & Tonge sold food right across the range, and also experimented in what would now be called 'vertical integration', expanding into manufacturing and food-processing. By 1885 the firm had 100 shops around the country, mostly trading as International Stores. Within just five years these had grown to 200 – far more than any rival group.

William Heseltine became rich in the process. He and his family eventually acquired a substantial house, 'The Turret', which had just been built on West Heath Road in fashionable Hampstead, overlooking the Heath. But in 1887 William Heseltine suddenly sold his share of the partnership to Kearley and Tonge. Why he left is not clear – Kearley writes of 'Heseltine's retirement', yet Heseltine was only forty-seven at the time. But relations between the two men had never been warm. In his memoirs Kearley accuses William of 'a shabby trick' over his original appointment at Tetley's. Having agreed to increase Kearley's pay to £60 a year after a three-month trial period, Heseltine, he says, then reneged on the promise.[6]

Whatever his motives for leaving the company, William Heseltine must soon have realized it was a dreadful mistake. Although he had easily become the equivalent of a millionaire by modern standards, he had thrown away the chance of an even greater fortune, for Kearley and Tonge's International Stores went from strength to strength (and later evolved into Gateway supermarkets – now part of the Somerfield chain). Kearley & Tonge still exists as a subsidiary company, but 'Heseltine' was dropped from the name more than a hundred years ago.

In 1895 the business he had created went public, and his old partner reached new heights. In 1890 Hudson Kearley was elected a Liberal MP; he later served as a junior minister at the Board of Trade under both Lloyd George ('a family friend') and Winston Churchill, and as Food Minister during the First World War, ending up with a heredi-tary peerage, as Viscount Devonport.

Today, more than a century on, Michael Heseltine behaves as if he has learnt the lesson of his great-grandfather's calamitous misjudge-ment in quitting the business. Recently one of his Henley party officials, Christopher Quinton, explained to Heseltine how he himself planned to build up his computer software business and then sell it: 'He got absolutely shocked and said, "What do you want to do that for?" And I said, "Well, don't you want to sell your businesses?" He said, "No, never." I said, "Why not?" And he said, "Because it's mine." '[7]

What subsequently happened to his great-grandfather may also explain Michael Heseltine's strong feelings about selling a successful enterprise. William set up two new ventures: the Indian Empire Tea Co., which had about ninety shops around the country, and William Heseltine & Son Ltd, a tea blending and dealing firm based in the City. But William soon fell into bad debt – not just through his businesses, it seems, but also because of the unsound way in which he reinvested the rest of his fortune.

In December 1890 William Heseltine arranged to see a friend called Wladyslaw Gutowski at the office of Gutowski's lawyer. Gutowski wanted Heseltine to make an arrangement to repay £380 he had lent him – which was then a considerable sum. He would later report that Heseltine 'was much agitated', and had thanked him for the loan, explaining how it had saved both 'his life and his family from disgrace'.[8] It was while both Gutowski and the lawyer were distracted that Heseltine suddenly shot himself dead.

William's eighteen-year old son, John Heseltine – Michael's grand-father – testified at the inquest three days later that his father had been in financial difficulties. 'A company in which he was interested had wound up, and in consequence the deceased had lost all his money.'[9] Heseltine had lost £35,000 in the firm – the rough equivalent today of about £2 million.

The Heseltines were left in a parlous state. John, his mother – Eve – and his five younger brothers and sisters quickly had to leave their smart Hampstead address. For a while the family seems to have split up, with Eve looking after the youngest children while John was left on his own caring for the older siblings. But after a few years the family came together again sixty miles up the Great North Road near Huntingdon, in Hemingford Grey – which happens to be the village where John Major first lived when he became the local MP nearly ninety years later. The Heseltines were given room at the Manor House, a run-down, ramshackle building, most of which dated back to Norman times, and which had no running water, only an outside well. The house was later immortalized as 'Green Knowe' in the famous children's stories by Lucy Boston, who herself lived there from the 1930s until her death in 1990.

As well as perhaps providing the entrepreneurial streak in Michael Heseltine's character, William Heseltine may also have recruited another strand of his great-grandson's personality, through his marriage to Eve Mary Dibdin.

Michael Heseltine, his father and his grandfather have all carried 'Dibdin' as one of their middle names, and so, too, do all three of Michael's children. In fact, at one time Michael's father used to write his signature as 'R. Dibdin Heseltine', as if 'Dibdin' was part of his surname, and his father, John Heseltine, did likewise.[10] It was a proud reminder of the family's distinguished artistic ancestry. Over three generations during the late eighteenth and early nineteenth centuries the Dibdins contributed three outstanding figures to English cultural life – two composer/dramatists and a painter.

The most illustrious of them was Charles Dibdin, Michael

Heseltine's great-great-great-great-grandfather. As a singer and actor, a comic and mimic, and the writer of patriotic songs and operettas, he achieved as much celebrity in his day as perhaps a pop star in modern times, though he reaped few of the financial rewards. At the age of only seventeen, in 1762, Dibdin was performing at Covent Garden in a two-act opera he had written and composed himself; at twenty he was working with David Garrick, the greatest English actor of his age. An operetta which Garrick commissioned Dibdin to perform – *The Padlock* – went on stage at Drury Lane in 1768 and became one of the most popular shows of the eighteenth century.

But Charles Dibdin was also a quarrelsome character. By his own admission he was 'extremely fond of folly', and he eventually fell out with Garrick, even though he had been a most valuable patron.[11]

Despite Dibdin's considerable talents and charisma, theatre managers were soon reluctant to work with him, and he was forced to tour the country performing one-man shows of songs, stories and jokes. A contemporary print shows him as a stout, almost porcine, figure with very frizzy hair – the then fashion – holding forth on a harpsichord, rather like a Georgian Les Dawson. He was clearly a great comic, but it was a waste of his talents. He often fell into debt; he spent time in a debtor's prison at one point, and he once avoided jail only by fleeing to France.

In all, Charles Dibdin wrote more than seventy dramatic pieces, and composed music for many other works, but he probably made the greatest public impact with his songs, of which the best-known is 'Tom Bowling'. He claimed to have written more than 900 – ninety of which were sea-songs – and a published collection of his lyrics ran to 306 pages, double-columned and closely printed. Some years after his death, the *Gentleman's Magazine* described him as 'our National Bard'.[12]

'My songs,' Dibdin once wrote, 'have been the solace of sailors in long voyages, in storms, in battle; and they have been quoted in mutinies, to the restoration of order and discipline.'[13] During the Napoleonic Wars, it was said, his patriotic sea-songs had recruited more men into the Navy than the press-gangs ever could. In 1805, with his talents in decline, the government awarded him a pension of £200 a year in recognition of the 'War Songs' he had written and performed by government decree. A year later, however, the pension was suddenly withdrawn when William Pitt lost office, and Dibdin fell victim to Whig cuts. Fellow musicians then clubbed together, despite their many quarrels with Dibdin over the years, and raised a substantial sum to fund the final years of his life.

'It is tragic,' concludes the *New Grove Dictionary of Music*, 'that so able and energetic a man should have squandered his inheritance as Dibdin did.'[14] In 1829, however – fifteen years after his death – Dibdin's work for sailors was given permanent recognition when a statue was erected at the Royal Naval Hospital at Greenwich, paid for by public subscription. The memorial was re-dedicated in 1985, which, by coincidence, was during Michael Heseltine's spell as Defence Secretary.

Charles Dibdin passed on his performing talents, and his energy and imagination as a writer, down the family line. He had two sons – Charles and Thomas – through his mistress, Harriet Pitt, the daughter of Ann Pitt, a celebrated comic actress who appeared at Covent Garden and Drury Lane throughout the second half of the eighteenth century. If Michael Heseltine cares to look when he visits the Garrick Club, he will find the portrait of Ann Pitt, his five times great-grandmother, hanging there. Harriet was also an actress, though less successful than her mother, and her second illegitimate son, Thomas John Dibdin, born in 1771 – Michael Heseltine's great-great-great-grandfather – would continue the family's theatrical tradition.

Thomas began life as an apprentice to a City 'furniture maker', but he had 'little taste for the elegant deceptions' of the trade and ran away to become an actor.[15] He soon developed a similar repertoire of talents to his father – as an actor, singer, song-writer, composer and playwright, specializing in farce and pantomime. He too had a prolific career, producing more than 2,000 songs and 200 plays and operas, but he also shared his father's obstinacy and his habit of acquiring debt. In later life he went into theatre management: among several of the London venues he looked after – though mostly unsuccessfully – was the Haymarket.

Thomas Dibdin's son, Thomas Colman Dibdin – great-great-grandfather to Michael Heseltine – was born in 1810 and shone in a rather different field. He began as a teenage clerk in the Post Office, but also had talent as a painter, with his first watercolours on show at the Royal Academy at the age of twenty-one. He took up painting professionally, and his gradual moves to larger and larger houses over the years suggest he was rather more prudent financially than his immediate forebears. Dibdin concentrated on landscapes and architectural views, and his works are in the collections of the British Museum, the Victoria & Albert Museum and the Ashmolean in Oxford, and are well-known in the West End salerooms. In May 1995, for example, a Dibdin watercolour sold at Christie's for £3,000. Among the keen collectors of Dibdin's work is Michael Heseltine.

Towards the end of the 1890s Michael's grandfather, John Heseltine, moved from Huntingdon to South Wales. It was a more logical move than one might think, for Heseltine, still in his twenties, had followed his father's footsteps and become a tea salesman, and Swansea docks were a major arrival point for tea shipments from India and China.

Michael Heseltine's cousin, Tony Heseltine, who lives in the Forest of Dean, recalls as a small boy visiting their common grandfather in Swansea just after the Second World War. After a lifetime in the trade, John Heseltine had developed a connoisseur's palate for tea. 'He would be phoned up every morning,' says Tony Heseltine, 'to give a report on the various teas he'd tasted that had recently arrived in the port of Swansea . . . He was a very learned man. He would quote great reams of Shakespeare to me, and seemed the perfect gentleman. He was very educated, and very, very good at French.'[16]

There was a good reason for his skill at French. In 1898 John Heseltine had married Marie Berthe Lefauve, the daughter of a French ship-owner, Julien Lefauve, who had sailed to Swansea, liked what he saw, and eventually decided to settle in South Wales. The Lefauves came from the village of Grimouville in Normandy. Those seeking signs of European roots and sentiment will note that Michael Heseltine's grandmother (who died of cancer when he was only a year old) makes him a quarter French, of course; close observers of the future Tarzan will also note that '*fauve*' is the French for 'wild beast'. In 1990, not long before Heseltine challenged Margaret Thatcher and was making a big issue out of Europe, he began taking an interest in his French ancestors. His sister made several inquiries on his behalf.

Marie Berthe's daughter Claude recalled in 1990, shortly before her death, that

because she came here as a teenager, my mother spoke perfect English . . . She was obviously well-educated, but she never had a career of her own. In those days women mostly spent their time bringing up the family, and that is what she did. Although we were not incredibly wealthy we did have a maid and a cleaner, and Marie Berthe spent a lot of time doing needlework and making clothes for the children.[17]

Marie Berthe's two sisters also married locally – one of them, Adèle, to one of the best-known jewellers in Wales.

John Heseltine's marriage to Marie Berthe seems also to have had a religious significance, for until then the Heseltines appear to have been Anglicans, but John now converted. 'Grandfather was a very staunch Roman Catholic, and all his children were brought up as Roman Catholics,' says Tony Heseltine.[18] So strong were his beliefs that John Heseltine was later very upset when some of his children married Protestants. Among them was Rupert Heseltine, Michael's father, who was born in 1901.

John Heseltine, his wife and four children (three others died in early childhood) lived in a large house, 'Brynteg', in Terrace Road on Swansea's Mount Pleasant. It was just ten minutes walk from the centre, but not a walk one would make readily: the streets climbing up from the town are extremely steep. The top floor of Brynteg had a panoramic view, looking down on the old town and out over Swansea Bay and the docks ranged around the mouth of the river Tawe.

Swansea's economy was largely based on the port. Initially the docks had exported coal from the South Wales mines, but during the nineteenth century the area saw the growth of copper smelting in the Tawe valley. It was a dirty, heaving, toiling town, but vibrant and bustling. 'In speaking of Swansea,' the *Daily Telegraph* said in 1882, 'one must not think of the beautiful but of the Useful with a capital U. Nobody talks of sea views and mountains here, but of how many ships were cleared last week, and what the export and import returns were, and the like . . . The soul of the town is in her docks.'[19]

An early photograph shows Rupert Heseltine with distinctive blond hair and very similar features to his son. He grew up to be tall and slim, and on leaving the local grammar school he joined the Army and qualified as a structural engineer. In his late twenties he served for five years in the Royal Engineers, with the Bengal Sappers in India, and became an expert in bridge-building. It would have been an especially challenging role in the subcontinent, where rivers can often be very shallow and several miles wide, or pass through deep ravines, turning into raging torrents during the rainy season. Many of the construction sites were miles from the nearest town, and badly served by roads. 'Bridges in India' was a subject on which Rupert Heseltine later gave talks and wrote occasional articles.[20]

On returning to Swansea in 1930, Rupert took a job with Dawnays, a medium-sized national firm which was based on the eastern shore of the bay, on the site of the modern Ford plant. There it manufactured steel girders and skeleton frames for buildings – a kind of giant Meccano. Heseltine visited architects as a company rep and engineering expert, but in 1938 he became manager of the Swansea plant, responsible for some 200 people. 'He was a formidable chap,' says Mansel Thomas, a former employee. 'His hair was the same as Michael's, exactly, and he had penetrating blue eyes – piercing eyes.'[21]

Although he'd left the regular Army, Rupert Heseltine retained his military-style moustache, and took up activity in the Swansea unit of the Territorial Army. 'A wonderful old chap he was – the real old-type soldier,' says Reg Pike, who served with him. 'You had a nice man in Rupert Heseltine. A very strict disciplinarian, mind. I dropped my stick once, and I had half an hour's stick drill with the adjutant. Not a chap to suffer fools gladly.'[22]

In 1932 Rupert married Eileen Pridmore, a twenty-four-year-old local woman. Eileen had been educated at a private school, but past generations of Pridmores came from a poor social background. Her father, James, was the son of an illiterate labourer, but had achieved considerable business success as a coal merchant in Swansea, where locals dubbed him 'Pridmore-the-Coal' from the days when he delivered sacks on his back. Around the period of the First World War, when the South Wales coalfield was at its peak, he made a fortune from coal exports, and in 1932 he was even described as a 'colliery proprietor'.[23]

Since the interwar years the business has gradually declined, though

Pridmore & Co. still operate as coal merchants in Swansea. Indeed a small shareholding Michael Heseltine inherited in the firm is one of the items he regularly declares in the House of Commons *Register of Members' Interests*.[24]

2. *Swansea Boy*

Michael Ray Dibdin Heseltine was born on 21 March 1933, a Tuesday's child. It was a time of historic and sometimes frightening changes: in the United States, President Roosevelt had just taken office and inaugurated the economic-recovery programme of the New Deal; in Germany, Adolf Hitler was about to proclaim the Third Reich and open the first concentration camp at Dachau.

For the time being, the Heseltines' baby was well insulated from both the impending world conflict and the widespread economic hardship of the times. 'We obviously enjoyed a very considerable degree of comfort,' he would later admit. 'It wasn't a background where in any way we felt the harshness of the 1930s in South Wales.'[1] Michael's parents were sufficiently well-off to employ two servants – a nurse and a cook – each of whom was paid ten shillings a week. Two years after Michael was born they had a baby girl, Yvonne, who was quickly nicknamed 'Bubbles' by her father, because of her habit, as a baby, of blowing bubbles. The name has stuck: family and friends rarely call her Yvonne.

At the time, the family lived in a three-storey terraced house in Eaton Crescent in Uplands, less than ten minutes' walk from the sea and about a mile from the centre of Swansea. Within a few years the Heseltines had moved just up the street to 1 Uplands Crescent, a larger detached house, on a slight bend in the Gower Road. Often their nanny, Betty Martin, would take Michael and Bubbles for walks in the local Cwmdonkin Park, a quiet haven with steep pathways and a wonderful variety of trees. It was the location for Dylan Thomas's poem 'The Hunchback in the Park'; the poet's semi-detached house in Cwmdonkin Drive was only a few hundred yards from the Heseltine home.

Whatever his future reputation, Michael was not the sort of child to have tantrums, Betty Martin recalled years later. He was 'quite shy' and 'mischievous sometimes'.[2] An aunt would later expose the young boy's habit of chasing cats. 'He didn't want to be cruel to them, he just wanted to impose his will on them.'[3] To magpies he was rather more respectful: whenever Michael saw one, he would salute it – a habit he had learnt from his father.

Betty Martin remembers the occasion when she asked Michael what he was giving up for Lent. ' "Salt," he said. "You can't give up salt, there's salt in everything." "Well, I won't add any." ' Another abiding memory is the difficulty of keeping his hair tidy, since it was fine and blew about with the slightest breeze. It was 'a very happy house altogether', she says.[4] At home he was always 'Michael'; friends usually called him 'Mike'.

'I am a Swansea boy. I come from the commercial middle classes of South Wales,' Michael Heseltine once declared. 'They didn't read. They didn't have great academic discussion. They didn't expect to produce intellectuals.'[5] But, as the name suggests, middle-class Uplands tended to look down on the rest of Swansea – the rougher docks and factory districts gathered around the eastern end of town and up the Tawe valley. Uplands and Sketty, which was further up the Gower Road, were communities that didn't mix with other parts. Their inhabitants were what local Welsh-speakers call 'crachach' – snobbish foreign imports – the Anglo-Welsh élite. They tended to be professionals – doctors, accountants and lawyers, managers of local works, and the occasional academic from the newly established University College nearby. They were well-off, and never spoke Welsh.

The television drama producer James Cellan Jones, who grew up in the same area with Michael Heseltine, says it was a 'very dug-in middle-class' community, full of 'frightful snobs'. Most boys from the area were sent to public schools, usually across the border in England. 'You would rather die than send your children to a state primary school.'[6]

At first Michael went to Parc Wern, a private kindergarten, and then to Oakleigh House, a small fee-paying school for four-to-eight-year-olds, which occupied a large semi-detached house right opposite the Heseltines' home. But Michael was not quick to learn to read – it took 'a lot of perseverance'. 'When I was a child,' Heseltine himself says, 'all I was conscious of was that I read slowly and found it difficult to absorb from the written word.'[7] Nobody realized it at the time, but Michael was probably suffering a mild form of dyslexia: he says he only 'learnt to read at about age seven or eight'.[8]

At the age of five, Michael very nearly died. He got meningitis, an illness which had killed three of his grandparents' children. 'He was desperately ill,' Betty Martin explains. 'It was touch and go. He was unconscious for twenty-four hours. He had been a very healthy, robust child, and never had an illness before that meningitis.'[9]

Betty Martin recalls how she sat up with the unconscious boy for two whole nights, until eventually he was given a lumbar puncture by a local specialist. 'I was in the bedroom when Dr Sladden said, "Give him an adult dose – kill or cure." ' She was greatly relieved when Michael woke in the early hours of the morning. 'About three o'clock he asked for a drink – I knew then he would be all right.'[10] Afterwards the family went to Newton, near Porthcawl, so that Michael could recuperate.

When the Second World War broke out, Rupert Heseltine left his job with Dawnays to return to the Royal Engineers, where he now held the rank of major. He and his family were initially posted to Narberth in Pembrokeshire, about fifty miles from Swansea. Then, around January 1940, the Heseltines moved to Northern Ireland, together with the nanny, Betty, and her sister Gwen, who worked as the family cook. They spent about fifteen months in Dundrum on the coast of County Down, south of Belfast. As a company commander at the local Ballykinder camp, in charge of about 200 men, Major Heseltine was an important local figure. He was assigned his own batman, and the family moved to the village's eighteenth-century Manor House.

Initially, the young Michael attended the local primary school – Dundrum Public Elementary – though its teaching seems to have been less than satisfactory. The school's strongest subject, concluded a visiting inspector, was needlework, while the weakest was writing.[11]

Perhaps because of the poor tuition at Dundrum, the Heseltines soon sent Michael off to board at Mourne Grange, a small fee-paying school in the shadow of the Mourne mountains. Almost twenty miles down the coast from Dundrum, not far from the fishing port of Kilkeel, Mourne Grange claimed to be the first preparatory school in

Ireland, and many pupils went on to English public schools. In 1941 Michael Heseltine's background would not have been out of place: several of the thirty or so boys had been sent there from England to escape the war.

One Dundrum resident, Tom McShane, remembers Michael as a 'very boisterous lad and well-liked in the village'. Rupert Heseltine, he says, came over to Ulster with his son a week or two earlier than Eileen. 'They attended the local Catholic church, but when the wife came that didn't continue.'[12] Rupert Heseltine, it seems, was not a particularly devout Catholic; indeed the family were not very regular church-goers either in Wales or in Ireland.

Nevertheless, the Heseltines made a lasting impression on the local Irish community. Gertie Barnes says she enjoyed many picnics with them, mostly at a local beach called Murlough Sands. 'It was a very sad day,' she says, when Rupert Heseltine's company left Northern Ireland in the spring of 1941. 'Village inhabitants turned up at the railway station to wish the Heseltines farewell. There were few dry eyes present as the band stopped playing and the train disappeared into the distance.'[13]

The family followed Rupert – now a lieutenant colonel – to postings in Clitheroe in Lancashire and then near Oxford. During term-time, however, Michael was again away at prep school, but now in the tiny Victorian spa town of Llanwrtyd Wells at the foot of the Cambrian mountains in mid-Wales. Officially he was attending the preparatory department of Bromsgrove School, which had been evacuated to Llanwrtyd in 1939 when its buildings in Worcestershire were suddenly requisitioned by the Ministry of Works.[14] Amid the tranquil Welsh hills, disturbed only by the rippling river Irfon, the bleating of the sheep and the chugging of an occasional steam train, the prep school occupied a large farmhouse on the outskirts of the community. A meadow in front served as a playing-field for cricket and football; an old barn at the back was used for assemblies. The conditions were primitive says Mike Rees, a former pupil: 'There was only one outside toilet, and you had to fight the cockerel off, which used to peck holes in our knees when we went out there.'[15]

Mike Rees also recalls the 'mad major' who taught the boys English. 'If we didn't behave, he had a habit of throwing an open pair of dividers across the room, and he would put chalk on your head and swipe it off with a ruler.'[16]

Like Michael Heseltine, many of the forty or so boys came from South Wales, though there were also some refugees from Europe, including two or three Jews. Some parents even sought temporary homes in Llanwrtyd to be with their sons in what was considered a safe area – though it seemed less secure when an RAF plane crashed nearby. Young boys on their own were often homesick. One day, the eight-year-old Michael Heseltine and two others gathered together what little food they could find, wrapped it up, and ran away. 'They hiked across country,' says the Bromsgrove archivist, Peter Fielden, 'came down on the road about two miles away, and thumbed the first car that came along.'[17] The driver who stopped was the headmaster, out searching for them. 'Mike wasn't disciplined for running away. Life went on as normal,' says Mike Rees, who's kept in touch with him ever since. 'He regards it as one of those humorous incidents, and says he'll learn to do his homework better!'[18]

When Rupert joined the Normandy landings in 1944, the Heseltines finally went back to South Wales. The Swansea they returned to was shockingly different from the one they'd left. Most of the town centre lay in ruins, with clocks fixed at the time at which they'd been hit during the dreadful 'Three Nights Blitz' of February 1941, when 240 people were killed and almost as many seriously injured. Although the worst of the bombing was over, and Uplands was largely unscathed, the family had beds in the cellar for protection against further raids.

Perhaps because Michael was unhappy at Bromsgrove, his parents soon moved him to another prep school, Broughton Hall, near Eccleshall in Staffordshire. It was his seventh school in six years. Located in a large, timbered, Elizabethan country house, complete with minstrels' gallery, panelled rooms and extensive grounds, it should have been idyllic. Boys could swim in the lake, explore the gardens, orchards and surrounding woods, or climb a huge monkey-puzzle tree. Yet, initially, Michael Heseltine seems to have been almost as unhappy at Broughton Hall as he was in Llanwrtyd – especially when his headmaster got embroiled in a quite extraordinary dispute which ended in violence.

The 'Invasion of Broughton Hall', as it was called, made the national press, and supposedly inspired the 1950 comedy film *The Happiest Days of Your Life*, starring Margaret Rutherford and Alastair Sim. It also led to Michael Heseltine's first appearance in the public spotlight, as a thirteen-year-old witness in court.

The argument involved two headmasters. In 1940 Broughton Hall had been rented by Kenneth Thompson for his prep school, but wartime conditions obliged him to share the premises with another school, Brockhurst, from Shropshire. The head of Brockhurst, John Park, moved in with about thirty 'Brocks' as they called themselves. Boys from the two schools shared classes, but they slept in separate dormitories, each head taking responsibility for the pupils from his own school. Such arrangements were quite common during the war, but it was far from satisfactory, and the two tenants of Broughton Hall soon became acrimonious rivals.

The two heads began to contradict each other in front of the boys. It was largely a personality clash, but there were also real issues at stake. Thompson, the Broughton Hall headmaster, tried to go back on an agreement to allow Park's two daughters to be taught at the school. More important, the heads disagreed about corporal punishment. While Thompson would sometimes beat his boys, Park believed the cane should be used only in exceptional circumstances. And Park was particularly angered by one incident in which Thompson thrashed several of his Brockhurst pupils when he was away. If Thompson did this again, Park reportedly threatened, 'he must expect to be knocked about himself'.[19]

As Lord Justice Goddard later declared in the Court of Appeal:

It is rather like having two captains, two crews and two sets of passengers on one ship with no provision as to who is to have command of it . . . Obviously nothing could be worse for the proper running of either school. The rivalry of the headmasters, or the differences of the headmasters, would naturally be reflected in the boys.[20]

One can imagine the disciplinary problems that must have arisen from having two sets of rules and two sets of sanctions operating side-by-side. Nor can it have helped that John Park would freely discuss with his older pupils disputes he'd had with Thompson, and accuse the other head of injustice and breaking agreements. Boys being boys, the gossip would instantly be relayed to Thompson's own pupils.

After a year of strife, Thompson asked Park to leave Broughton and take his boys with him. Park, who felt that he'd been shabbily treated throughout, refused to comply. He insisted he was legally entitled to stay at Broughton under their contract. So, during the Christmas holidays of 1943, Thompson removed his rival's belongings and furniture from the main house and put them into a damp outbuilding. On returning to school after the break, Park found himself locked out. He recruited a gang of ten to twelve villagers and, that evening, Park's men smashed down the front door, forced the internal room locks with crowbars, and reoccupied the building with the Brockhurst boys.

'A riot took place . . . a riot at common law,' said Lord Justice Goddard, adding that the invaders had 'behaved in a way which can only be described as absolutely outrageous'. Thompson applied for a court order to remove the Brockhurst forces, but won only on appeal with a judgement that set a legal precedent. The blame lay firmly with John Park, Goddard concluded: 'It seems to me that on his own showing he has been guilty at least of riot, affray, wilful damage, forcible entry and, perhaps, conspiracy.'[21]

This episode has also been described, in colourful terms, by the Tory MP Julian Critchley, in his memoirs. Critchley was a senior pupil at Brockhurst, and therefore knew Michael Heseltine a little (and years later became his best friend). He describes how the 'Brocks' returned to Broughton Hall at the start of term to find the driveway littered with what looked like 'detritus of a retreating army' – the Brockhurst equipment and furniture thrown out by Thompson:

Desks were piled on desks, blackboards sat on easels, books were scattered everywhere, saucepans, pots, pans and brushes lay on the ground in no good order, beds and bed-linen were strewn over the grass verges . . . We got out of the bus to find the windows of the Hall lined with [Broughton boys] their thumbs to their noses. The young Heseltine, his eyes pink with triumph, opened a bedroom window and yelled some imprecation. We were out on the street, lock, stock and barrel.[22]

Critchley then details how Park and his men stormed the house.

While it's rip-roaring stuff, it's not quite how others remember it.

Contemporaries insist that neither Heseltine nor any of the Broughton boys would actually have seen the returning 'Brocks' or witnessed the 'riot', as Thompson had ensured his pupils were not yet back at school. Nevertheless, Heseltine's education was obviously disrupted: for most of that term the Broughton boys either remained at home or were looked after in neighbouring houses.

Afterwards John Park would be accused by the Appeal Court judges of deliberately inciting his own pupils, so as to put pressure on Thompson. Given the slightest cue from their headmaster, the boys were naturally delighted to taunt and jeer the rival faction. Before the 'riot', when Park announced to his 'Brocks' that Thompson was going to sell Broughton to him, the boys triumphantly conveyed the news to the enemy camp with cries of 'Victory!' and 'Down with Broughton!'

In fact it wasn't true that Thompson was selling up, but Michael Heseltine was deeply upset by the rumour. 'Mr Park has bought Broughton Hall,' he wrote home to his parents. 'Isn't it awful? Please come and take me away.'[23]

Heseltine's letter was later used as evidence when conflicting claims for damages were finally thrashed out at Stafford Assizes in March 1947. Michael himself was one of four Broughton pupils who testified in court about the appalling effect the quarrel had on their schooling. By then Heseltine had actually moved on, to Shrewsbury public school, and had to be given a few days off to attend court. The hearing took place in Arctic conditions, and for a while the boy witnesses were snowed up in a Stafford hotel.

The first three boys gave evidence about the disagreements between the headmasters over accommodation and caning. Then it was Heseltine's turn, standing in the witness-box in a smart suit. The judge later summarized his evidence:

He remembered the Brockhurst boys coming down from the stables, rushing down, and shouting: 'We are Brockhurst now, not Broughton. Down with Broughton!' and things like that. 'Later,' he said, 'I heard that Mr Park had bought Broughton. I was unhappy and I wrote to my parents.'[24]

Heseltine and his teenage colleagues were 'a very impressive lot of witnesses', the judge said. 'They spoke with moderation . . . it was quite obvious that they were telling the truth.'[25] 'This boy should go far,' another witness recalls him saying of Heseltine.[26] Rosemary Fleming, John Park's daughter, was herself in court. She says her father thought it was wrong on principle for either side to call children as witnesses, but he conceded that Heseltine had been effective: 'My father thought Heseltine had done very well in giving evidence; he was impressed with his bearing.'[27] Park, in failing health, and conducting his own case, lost the action. He had to pay more than £2,000 in damages.

The judge was deeply concerned about the effect the dispute must have had on the boys' education: 'It is quite clear that it would have led to those boys going to their public schools having been miserably mismanaged.'[28] Though it did disrupt their schooling, the affair doesn't appear to have done that much harm – at least not to the young witnesses who spoke in court. They became respectively a vicar, an Army officer, a judge, and a Deputy Prime Minister.

In contrast to the astonishing troubles of his first twelve months, the rest of Michael's three years at Broughton Hall appear to have been delightful – probably the happiest days of his school career. 'I loved that place,' Heseltine told one of the other trial witnesses several decades later.[29]

Another Broughton pupil, Robert Gilchrist, recollects Heseltine as 'a fairly forceful sort of character, but he wasn't a bully. He used to lead things.' He seems to have been average academically, and showed no ability at sport. But Broughton was an ideal spot for Michael to pursue a growing passion for plants and birdlife, as it contained plenty of both. He and Gilchrist would prowl round the school grounds identifying birds with their binoculars.[30]

Michael was 'such an easy boy' his mother recently explained, and 'never ever any trouble' to bring up, though it seems he was not averse to asserting himself over younger boys:

The only trouble we had was when we were going back to prep school once and there was a new boy and his mother who were both crying. She was trying to get him on board the bus. I said I'd look after him but when they got on the bus Michael said: 'Hop it, that's my seat.' I was so embarrassed.[31]

Michael only lived in Swansea in the school holidays, but he still made a lasting impression there. He was clearly an inquisitive child.

Sheilagh Mundle remembers visiting her aunt and uncle whose garden backed on to the Heseltines':

Michael used to climb up the trellis at his side, and sit on top listening to our conversation. My aunt used to get absolutely livid and say, 'Michael, will you get off there and stop listening to us?' She found it a great nuisance. I thought it was extraordinary for a boy of eleven or twelve to be so interested in adult conversation.[32]

The Heseltines would sometimes travel on the electric tramway three miles round the bay to the seaside resort of Mumbles. It was regarded as something of a status symbol that the family should own their own beach-hut in Langland Bay, a more secluded up-market resort with palm-trees, just round the headland from Mumbles. Michael would spend hours combing the beach for shells, playing in the rock-pools, or exploring the cliff-tops, spotting birds. The area is a popular stopping-point for migratory species flying across the Bristol Channel.

The late political journalist Peter Jenkins, who also grew up in the vicinity, recalled Heseltine 'cutting a great dash' at Langland Bay 'in electric-blue swimming-trunks. He was also the only boy we knew with his own canoe.'[33] Michael had made the boat – a huge fourteen-foot craft – with his father one holiday, and used it for surfing in the bay.

After the war Rupert Heseltine returned to Dawnays, and became the firm's South Wales manager. He resumed his career in the Territorial Army and became honorary colonel of the 108 Welsh Field Engineer Regiment. In 1951 Colonel Heseltine was also appointed a deputy lieutenant for the County of Glamorgan – an unpaid ceremonial post which involved representing the King or Queen on official occasions. Rupert Heseltine was a natural Conservative, and Michael even remembers his father chairing a party meeting during one election campaign. But this was more a reflection of his local status than an indication of great political involvement. 'He was very impressive to meet,' say Geoff Hayes, who was perhaps Michael's closest teenage friend – 'a very jocular friendly sort of chap, with a rather commanding presence.'[34]

The Heseltines were moving up in the world – literally, as they bought a large white house, coincidentally called 'Broughton', up the Gower Road in Sketty. Their home was immaculate, with fine furnishings and antiques. But visitors say they never noticed many books around, though there were plenty of magazines. Rupert Heseltine's pride and joy was a collection of matchbox labels, which he pinned to the doors and walls of his wine store under the stairs. And the family had a passion for Alsatian dogs. One of them grew 'very large and very healthy', says Geoff Hayes, 'and I remember being pinned against the gate when I went there one day. It terrified me.'[35]

With a maid to do the housework, Eileen Heseltine spent much of her time entertaining friends, inviting them round for coffee-mornings or afternoon tea. Julian Critchley relates an occasion when he and Michael were invited to join the ladies. 'Over sandwiches and three kinds of cake I asked, innocently enough, whether anyone knew Dylan Thomas. A deathly silence fell. At last Mrs Heseltine said chillingly, "We don't talk about Dylan Thomas in Swansea." '[36]

'His mother was a dominant person – very talkative, very opinionated, very critical,' says Geoff Hayes. 'I think I was a little bit scared of her, actually, because she always used to ask very searching questions – "And what are you going to do today?" '[37] Another of Michael's friends, Patricia Mort, says, 'They were a very unlikely couple. She was very nice, but they didn't look at all suited.'[38]

Michael was fond of both parents, but his father especially. 'I hero-worshipped him,' he says. 'He was a profound rock in my life.'[39] Interestingly, Heseltine mentions his father in *Who's Who* but not his mother – an omission made by fewer than one in twenty of the directory's entrants (another, predictably, is Margaret Thatcher). Eileen Heseltine's absence is all the more strange since, unlike her husband, she is still alive, and celebrated her eighty-ninth birthday in 1996.[40]

The Heseltines' larger home, Broughton, allowed Michael to pursue an interest first sparked when he was given a small plot of ground – roughly three foot square – at one of his wartime prep schools. 'Into the patch went nasturtiums, Virginia stocks, the odd pansy, to create massive and instant colour. Then one thing led to another.'[41] At home, Michael would help the family gardener, and in time he found an enjoyable – and lucrative – source of income, tending the family and neighbours' gardens for five shillings an hour. 'That, I suppose, combined gardening with my other obsession . . .' he later joked.[42]

There was also an early interest in fishing. 'With my grandfather,' Heseltine has written, 'I watched the elvers – frenetic wriggling hyphen marks – chase each other up the streams of Clyne Valley.' Around the age of nine he had distinguished himself as junior angling champion of the local Brynmill Park. 'It is no mean feat to hook and land thirty-nine fish in two hours, even if the triumph fades away when it is revealed that the whole lot of them only weighed 11¾ ounces.'[43]

In his late teens Michael went fishing with Geoff Hayes on almost every river in the area. Hayes says he was impressed at how Heseltine 'would move heaven and earth' to get fishing licences, though if he failed they fished anyway. When Hayes invited his old friend to address a local meeting some years ago, he says Heseltine boasted how 'We poached almost every river in South Wales together.'[44]

Then there were birds, of the feathered kind. 'Jackdaws and magpies put themselves – well, found themselves – under my protection, hopping on and off my fingers.'[45] As a teenager Heseltine built a large aviary 'which he used to show off to all our friends', says Roger Lidstone, one of several local boys Michael met up with during the holidays.[46] They would play tennis twice a week on the courts of the Lidstones' home, or go out cycling all round the surrounding Gower peninsula. It was, Heseltine says, 'the model, happy childhood that one would provide for oneself if one could'.[47]

Later, of course, came a growing interest in girls. Another friend, Mike Evans, recalls how he and Heseltine were part of a large crowd from neighbouring communities who used to meet up for Saturday-night dances at the Langland Bay Hotel, or the Pier Hotel in Mumbles.[48] The events seemed to occur almost spontaneously: somebody booked a room and the band, and then word was quickly passed round by telephone.

Patricia Mort, one of Michael's first girlfriends, says he was a great organizer even then. He would arrange the dance, order buses to get people there, make a profit at the end of the evening, and carry off a few dancing prizes. 'He was very competitive, and we always had to win at the various dances we went to – ballroom dancing, waltzes, foxtrot. He was a very good dancer.' When Patricia Mort applied for a drama course at RADA, she says, Heseltine typed up her audition material, while she in turn advised him about his speaking style. 'He spoke with a soft "R",' she says. 'I said, "If you're going to be a public speaker you've got to get rid of that." And he did. He went and had speaking lessons.'[49]

With few pressures or threats, a happy, comfortable home background, plenty of interests and friends, Michael Heseltine's teenage years around Swansea and the Gower in the late 1940s and early 1950s must have come close to perfection. That could not be said, however, of his time spent away from home, at public school.

3. *Learning to Come Second*

In ancient Britain, when the river Severn marked the natural boundary between England and Wales, the settlement known today as Shrewsbury was an obvious fort and haven amid the constant border skirmishes. Seen best from the air, the river Severn snakes tightly around the old town in a horseshoe until it almost meets up with itself. A small neck of land, less than 300 yards wide, is all that separates one section of the Severn from the other and prevents the centre of Shrewsbury from being an island.

Shrewsbury School was granted its charter in 1552 by Edward VI, and it was first established near the town's Norman castle. In 1882 the school moved outside the medieval walls to the much larger property it occupies today – the 'site', as it's called – on a plateau high above the spot where the Severn bends most sharply. The school boasts a spectacular vantage point, looking out over the river and the church spires of the old town. Behind is the great expanse of the school playing-fields.

It is doubtful, however, whether the thirteen-year-old Michael Heseltine regarded the school as particularly attractive when he arrived there in January 1947. It was the middle of the 'great freeze', one of Britain's most bitter winters this century, when the school almost ran out of coke, and boys slept in their overcoats and played ice-hockey on a tennis-court. Postwar rationing was still in full force; it was a time of hardship and austerity, of shortages, quotas and permits, and the school had a rather dilapidated appearance. The premises hadn't seen fresh paint since 1939.

Shrewsbury has long been a popular school for the middle-class Welsh. Several times a year the teenage Michael would make the slow, four-hour train journey along the whole length of the mid-Wales line, the picturesque single track which winds from Swansea via Carmarthen and Llandrindod Wells to Shropshire, and which somehow has always survived successive rounds of BR cuts.

In 1947 Rupert Heseltine had to pay annual fees of £216 for his son's education; these had risen to £251 by the time Michael left, four and a half years later. But public-school fees in those days were comparatively cheap – the rough equivalent of about £4,000 today, compared with almost £13,000 a year in 1996.

Michael had done well to secure admission. Traditionally Shrewsbury was ranked as one of the seven so-called Clarendon public schools – alongside Eton, Harrow, Winchester, Westminster, Charterhouse and Rugby – although academically its reputation was principally for its classics teaching. The school magazine, *The Salopian*, was littered with snippets of Greek, and many of the school's institutions had Latin or Greek names. If anything, Shrewsbury's standards then were slightly higher than they are today, and Heseltine was almost certainly admitted on his maths. He reckons he got 98 or 100 per cent on one of his Common Entrance maths papers.[1]

His new headmaster was John Wolfenden, who had become head of Uppingham at the early age of twenty-seven and moved to Shrewsbury ten years later. Subsequently, Wolfenden achieved distinction for his ground-breaking 1957 report which recommended radical changes to the laws on prostitution and homosexuality – toughening the former and liberalizing the latter. In fact Wolfenden never gave the school his undivided attention, as is illustrated by his memoirs, where much of the chapter about Shrewsbury actually describes various high-powered national committees which required regular travel to London. 'I felt that somehow I had never made much impact on Shrewsbury,' he later admitted – adding that it was the kind of school which could 'have got on quite cheerfully without any headmaster at all'.[2] 'They'll miss him on the London train,' someone jibed at Wolfenden's farewell concert, to a burst of laughter.[3]

A far greater influence on the young Heseltine would have been his housemaster, Alan Phillips, a chemist who had played football for the outstanding amateur side Corinthians. More so than today, most of school life then revolved around one's house. Heseltine's house, Moser's Hall, is the only house outside the grounds – it is a red-brick building situated opposite the school gates. Heseltine ate his meals in the Moser's dining-hall; every evening he retreated to do his 'prep' in a small study he shared with three others; his house bedroom accommodated seven or eight boys aged between thirteen and eighteen.

Shrewsbury was a highly regimented place: at every moment house-masters were expected to know what each of their boys was doing. Six days a week the timetable began early, with a lesson at 7.45 a.m. before breakfast at 8.30. On every day except Monday the school assembled in the chapel at 9.30. There would be three more lessons before lunch, and another two afterwards – except for Wednesdays and Saturdays, when the afternoons were devoted to games. Sundays entailed two compulsory services in chapel – an hour in the morning and another at night. And, for a man who would go down as one of the great liberal influences of the twentieth century, Wolfenden was notoriously strict. 'If you coughed in chapel while he was reading the lesson,' says one Old Salopian, 'he would stop and freeze you to a pillar of salt.'[4]

Shrewsbury had only about 460 to 500 boys in Heseltine's day, so most of them knew each other. Although the school still had plenty of petty rules – about who was entitled to walk across the grass, for instance – it also prided itself on encouraging individual spontaneity and independence. The boys may not have thought so, but it had probably a more liberal regime than most public schools at that time, which helps explain the emergence, four or five years below Heseltine, of the *Private Eye* generation – Richard Ingrams, Willie Rushton, Paul Foot and Christopher Booker – all of whom were allowed to develop their satirical talents on *The Salopian*. However, Wolfenden's claim that 'everybody did pretty much as he liked until somebody for some reason or other told him to stop' was probably an exaggeration.[5]

Boys would still regularly be beaten for misdemeanours, by both masters and senior pupils. The school retained the practice of fagging, whereby younger boys performed menial tasks for their elders, though at Shrewsbury fags were known as 'douls' (from the Greek word for slave) and the practice was known as 'douling'. When a house monitor cried 'Doul!' (to rhyme with 'foul'), all the boys in the first two years were expected to come running as quickly as possible. The last to arrive had to perform the chore – making toast, carrying messages, or whatever. It was on one such occasion, during his first year, that Michael Heseltine first made a name for himself – though not as he would have wished. One contemporary, Roger Shakeshaft, remembers that Heseltine had been asked to clean a house monitor's shoes which were badly stained. He thought he had an ingenious solution, applying a chemical he'd found in the school laboratory. 'It resulted in the uppers separating themselves from the sole,' Shakeshaft says. 'The news spread around the school like wildfire.'[6]

Heseltine did not shine at all, in fact – at least not according to his superiors. A Shrewsbury tradition was for the monitor of each house study to write what were known as '*fasti*', internal reports on the younger boys. The *fasti* on Heseltine, discovered some years later and passed to the press, were blunt: 'He is rebellious, objectionable, idle, imbecilic, inefficient, antagonizing, untidy, lunatic, albino, conceited, inflated, impertinent, underhand, lazy and smug.' But then, thinking perhaps he'd gone too far, the monitor added in mitigation that Heseltine was also 'cheerful and probably rudimentally good-natured'. Twelve months later the verdict had hardly improved: 'has a certain spirit but incorrigibly idle and very reluctant to do anything when told'.[7]

In his early years at the school, Michael Heseltine's official class reports were almost as bad. In his first term he came twentieth out of twenty-six boys in his form, and thereafter he did worse: he finished third from last in both the Lent and summer terms of 1948. His best subjects, if any, were Latin and French, but even here he rarely made the top half of the class.[8]

Though he was undistinguished, Heseltine was certainly distinctive. People recall him as a bit of a loner, and say that he always stood out, especially with his shock of bright blond hair which made him look almost albino. 'Everyone was conscious who Heseltine was,' says Michael Charlesworth, one of his masters. 'His clothing and his hair were always a little different from anybody else.'[9] He is immediately noticeable on house photographs, for instance. The boys had to wear dark suits; several had pinstripes, but Heseltine's pinstripe stood out, just on the right side of the rules.

Michael Heseltine was sometimes treated as a bit of a school joke. Roger Shakeshaft recalls an occasion when a party of Liverpool boys visited Shrewsbury from the school's inner-city mission in the city, and took part in a concert of community singing in the hall. 'A rendering of "Clementine" was *de rigueur* for these sing-songs,'

Shakeshaft says, 'and in no time the chorus was ringing to the refrain of "my darling Heseltine" with more enthusiasm than could be reasonably expected. This in-joke would mean nothing to the mission boys.'[10]

'A maverick' is the most common memory of Heseltine among Old Salopians – a description which has applied ever since. 'He was always the odd man out,' says a former member of his house. 'He didn't fit into any slots. People were daunted by him. He wasn't an approachable figure in any way.' He was also 'deeply disliked' says the same witness. 'He was thought to be arrogant. He was thought to have a venomous tongue, and in my view was a bully. He was bigger than most people, and he was frankly a lot more intelligent than most people. There was very real hostility towards him.' Heseltine doesn't seem to have many life-long friends from his schooldays; in fact he doesn't seem to have had many close school chums at the time.

An exception was Robert Wild, also in Moser's, who shared his interest in bird-watching; he was later an usher at Heseltine's wedding. 'We were great ones for the bird bit,' says Wild, who recalls the pair spending their free time on Sunday afternoons watching birds in people's gardens or around the Shropshire countryside. 'You'd go up a cliff and bring back a young jackdaw and you'd think, "Christ, where are we going to keep this?" And we'd keep it in someone's garage and feed it.'[11] Heseltine has told how a bewildered John Wolfenden once 'caught me wheeling some Heath Robinson contraption full of greenfinches across the school site'.[12]

Robert Wild says that Heseltine 'wasn't a warm fellow'. And when he first displayed an entrepreneurial streak – 'very much the budding businessman,' wrote his study monitor – it didn't help his popularity.[13] One scheme involved buying crates of lemonade from the local post office and, when the tuck shop was closed, selling it by the glass 'to the heavy lads coming off the rugger field', at twice the price, as he later admitted.[14] One can imagine how the rugby players felt about Heseltine's exploiting them at a moment of need, when there was no alternative. He was also on constant lookout for discarded bottles, to claim back the deposits, but in winter he kept them for another commercial use. Just before bedtime Heseltine would fill several vessels from the hot tap and rent them out, at a penny a time, as hot-water bottles. Such initiative and enterprise caused suspicion. 'People were a bit sniffy about it,' recalls Robert Wild. 'While people used his services, there was always that feeling he was making a profit, and that didn't endear him.'[15]

Academically, too, he was getting into hot water. When he entered the sixth form, in 1948, Heseltine concentrated on science. His school report records that he had ambitions to be a 'surgeon'; several of his contemporaries in Swansea were the sons and daughters of doctors, and his interest in wildlife led naturally to biology. It was a disastrous decision. During 1948–9 he came bottom in a class of thirteen for three terms running.[16]

His former history master, Michael Charlesworth, has become something of a Shrewsbury institution, having been there for most of his life. He believes Heseltine was 'very ambitious and the school did not offer him scope for his undoubted talents – there was no particular ladder whose top he could reach'.[17] Broughton Hall had already warned Shrewsbury that Heseltine was poor at sport: he had no eye for the ball, and his highest team achievement was to captain the house football second XI. The problem was that promotion to positions of authority at Shrewsbury – whether in house or in school – required either academic or sporting achievement. Heseltine had neither.

There was no question of Heseltine becoming head boy, or one of the fifteen or so school prefects (given the Latin name *praepostors*, shortened to 'postors'), but then successful politicians rarely achieve such heights at school. Heseltine, though, was not even elevated within his own house. In his final year, 1950–51, six of the ten boys in the top year of Moser's Hall were made house monitors, and he was not one of them. This would have been the decision of his housemaster, Alan Phillips, who never thought highly of the future Deputy Prime Minister. One contemporary says that:

[Phillips] was very much the wrong kind of person for Heseltine, a total conformist – and that was the opposite to what Michael was – very straight along the line in terms of discipline, of team spirit – two things which Heseltine would have disliked a great deal – and above all playing the game, being one of a team, being sort of structurally minded, and that's what Michael wasn't.

Even when it came to public speaking, where one might have expected him to excel, Heseltine was never an officer of the debating society. Reports in *The Salopian* suggest he was never one of the main speakers either, though he made occasional contributions from the floor and revealed odd glimpses of the future politician. During a debate on the UN's attitude to Russia, for example, the magazine relates how Heseltine, 'with quiet confidence, pointed out that the only way to get things done was to take firm action'.[18]

Michael Charlesworth often relates the poignant story of how, in the spring of 1951, Heseltine finally found 'something he could do, and he really was quite good at it'.[19] The future Tarzan first learnt to swing through the air while performing the high-jump. Heseltine's height helped, of course – he grew to be 6 feet 2½ inches – but he also developed his own particular technique and practised so hard, with Charlesworth's coaching, that he made the school athletics team. By sports day he was favourite. But then Brian Smallwood, the school's leading all-round athlete, made a last-minute decision to enter the high-jump as well. Smallwood had won the contest the previous year, but hadn't practised since. 'The event was almost over when Brian appeared,' says Robert Wild. 'The chalice was in his grasp, which made it all the worse.'[20] Not for the last time Michael Heseltine had to grit his teeth, congratulate the winner, and contain his 'humiliation' at coming only second. It 'said it all about my contribution to Shrewsbury,' Heseltine says.[21]

Elsewhere in school life, Heseltine's family background perhaps helped his progress in the Combined Cadet Force. He was eventually promoted to sergeant – a rank attained by perhaps fifteen or so boys in any year. 'He has a fine figure for regimentals,' his headmaster wrote on one report.[22]

And one activity may have shaped Heseltine's response as a Cabinet minister thirty years later, when Liverpool was riven by rioting. Shrewsbury boys regularly travelled by train to the school's mission building in the Everton district of the city – a youth club and community centre known as Shrewsbury House, or 'The Shrewsy' as Scousers called it. It gave the future Minister for Merseyside an early insight into life in the inner-city slums, and seems to have been a memorable experience – so much so that Heseltine even mentioned it to a constituency newspaper when first picked for a safe seat fifteen years later.[23]

At the end of Michael Heseltine's fourth term in the sixth form his results began to improve, and John Wolfenden wrote that his report 'was a very encouraging document'.[24] Nevertheless, Heseltine evidently decided he was never going to make it as a surgeon, and abandoned science. Instead, he joined a division of the sixth form which had been established only recently, known as the General Side. He now took up history and politics, and a subject which had just been introduced to the Shrewsbury syllabus – economics. At a time when economics and politics were still not considered serious subjects, the General Side was a radical departure for a public school – especially one with Shrewsbury's classical reputation. It proved to be Heseltine's salvation. 'The work of this form has clearly been congenial,' Wolfenden wrote after his first term in the new class. 'He is *alive . . .* he is also far more organized.'[25]

After a long adolescent phase in which Heseltine seems to have been unenthusiastic about school work, he was suddenly thriving. His saviour seems to have been Shrewsbury's first economics teacher, a young New Zealander, Russell Wood – known to all as 'Rusty' – who arrived in 1949. He was an inspiration to Heseltine not just in economics but also at a wider level.

Studying these subjects seems to have encouraged Heseltine's political ambitions. Brian Jenkins, who shared a study with Michael in Moser's Hall, recalls him around the age of seventeen mapping out his targets for the future: 'He said he was going to seek a commission in the Grenadier Guards; then he said he was going to go to Oxford and he hoped to be president of the Union, go into the City, become an accountant and then go into politics.' Jenkins and his contemporaries didn't take him seriously, as Heseltine was often inclined to make 'outlandish remarks'; moreover, his school career had not been remarkable for its glittering achievements.[26]

Robert Wild, too, recollects Heseltine planning his future career in great detail. In later years, when Heseltine expressed surprise at whether he really had been so openly ambitious, Wild had to confirm to him that it was true. A seminal event seems to have been the general election of February 1950, not long after Heseltine had switched to a more political curriculum. The two boys would cycle to evening election meetings around the Shrewsbury area. 'We went to village halls,' says Wild, 'and then Michael would have his say and argue the toss and we'd ride back again.'[27]

Despite taking more congenial subjects, Heseltine still resented the way he was regarded by Shrewsbury's scholastic élite. Only once did he ever have anything published in *The Salopian* – a letter in which he lambasted the editor for rejecting, with what he calls a 'veritable volley of abuse', his suggestions for improving the journal. The letter is fascinating not for what the future publisher advocates – reducing the frequency at which the magazine appeared, so as to improve the quality – but for betraying a chip on the Heseltine shoulder about his more academic colleagues, especially those in the classical division studying Latin and Greek. 'I should have thought that this would have been obvious to so eminent a member of the School's intelligentsia,' he says at one point, and then adds, after outlining his own proposal, 'That is my answer, Mr Classical Side.'[28]

On the General Side the competition may not have been so fierce, but Heseltine was now doing well in history, politics and economics, thanks partly to extra individual (and paid) tuition from Rusty Wood. Throughout his final year, 1950–51, he was always top or second in each of his main subjects, and he shared the form prize each term – a transformation from his years as a budding medic. He gathered a string of impressive half-term marks from his new headmaster, Jack Peterson – B++ and B++ in the 1950 Christmas term, B++ and A–– in Lent 1951, followed by B+ and A–– in his last term, the summer of 1951. As Heseltine left Shrewsbury, Peterson delivered his final, perceptive, verdict: 'An interesting boy. I hope that his academic success, which has not been inconsiderable, will have led him to realize what a lot most of us do not know. He has considerable potentialities still, I feel.'[29]

'If you look at my record at Shrewsbury, it doesn't add up to much,' Heseltine admits. 'I don't look back on it as one of the most satisfactory parts of my life.'[30] He has subsequently shown little affection for the school, though he returns to give the occasional talk and puts his name to financial appeals. His own son, Rupert, was put down for Eton rather than Shrewsbury, though he ended up at Harrow.

Perhaps the greatest impact Michael Heseltine made on his old school came not while he was there, but sixteen months after he had left. As the years have passed, and Heseltine's fame has grown, the occasion has acquired a certain mythology.

In November 1952, in his second year at Oxford, Heseltine was invited back to the school with another old boy, Julian Critchley, to take part in a debate. It was surprising, perhaps, that Heseltine and Critchley should have been asked, for neither had done much speaking at school, and neither had yet made his mark as a debater at university.

The motion was not, as has often been reported, 'This House Would Abolish the Public Schools,' but the milder 'This House Deplores the Public School System.' It attracted what *The Salopian* described as 'a record audience' – more than 200 boys; almost half the school – for what the magazine called 'the most good-humoured but also the most controversial debate for some years'.[31] It provided the perfect opportunity for Heseltine to unleash his frustrations about life at Shrewsbury, in front of an audience which was delighted to egg him on. It was a good example of how as a young man Michael Heseltine seemed to take delight in shocking people and upsetting the Establishment.

Speaking first, and wearing a fancy brocade waistcoat, Heseltine argued that, unless the public schools were reformed while there was still the opportunity, a left-wing government might come to power and abolish the system altogether. According to one witness, the subsequent report in *The Salopian* was a rather toned-down account. It related Heseltine's claim that compulsory religion did more harm than good, and that enforced religious observance was morally wrong. As for corporal punishment, Heseltine felt it 'should be used as a last resort', and then solely by housemasters. 'It was disgusting,' he said, 'that a boy of seventeen years of age should be able to beat one of sixteen.' Instead, there should be more constructive punishments.[32] There were also attacks on fagging and the prefect system; and the public-school emphasis on games, he argued, encouraged the 'muscular moron' rather than the cultured mind.

What *The Salopian* didn't report, but which members of the audience recall clearly, was that a substantial part of Heseltine's speech tackled homosexuality. Ian Josephs, who accompanied the Oxford pair, says Heseltine claimed that the hierarchical, authoritarian nature of public schools forced junior boys into homosexual relationships they didn't want.[33]

His onslaughts against beating and homosexuality were especially sensitive given that the opposition was led by Anthony Chenevix-Trench, then a young Shrewsbury housemaster, who later achieved notoriety at successive schools for the delight he seemed to take in beating boys' bare bottoms and fingering them before and afterwards. In defending public-school privileges and the use of corporal punishment, he appears badly to have misjudged his audience. 'Chenevix-Trench took it very badly, because we made all the boys laugh at him,' says Josephs. 'Michael said the worst thing about corporal punishment was the pleasure it gave the masters.'[34]

Nobody could complain about the calibre of the two masters defending the public schools, judging by their subsequent careers. Anthony Chenevix-Trench went on to become in turn headmaster of Bradfield College and then Eton. The other, Michael Hoban, succeeded Chenevix-Trench at Bradfield. Nevertheless, 'Quite rightly they won,' says Hoban, adding that he himself had never debated before. He had been persuaded to speak only at the last moment, against his better judgement, 'when a rather panting boy appeared at our house and said, "Please sir, please sir, please, you must come and debate, sir." '[35]

Clearly neither Hoban nor Chenevix-Trench put enough thought into the debate, but then it seems that Heseltine and Critchley didn't put any great effort into their speeches either. Ian Josephs, who drove the Oxford debaters to Shrewsbury in his red MG, says they were more concerned with navigating through the heavy fog, which was so bad they could hardly see the road ahead. Anyway, Heseltine and Critchley didn't really need to prepare, 'because it was an easy subject'.[36]

The Oxford team won by 105 votes to 95 – declared, according to *The Salopian*, 'amidst a genial uproar of cheering and other noises'.[37] Some of those present agree that many boys – particularly the younger ones – voted for Heseltine and Critchley simply to cock a snook at their Shrewsbury superiors. And all along the Oxford men had stressed the need for reform rather than abolition.

There were no immediate ill-feelings about the outcome, and the debate was followed by an enjoyable supper party. Ian Josephs remembers that over breakfast next morning, however, Heseltine upset the wife of his old housemaster, Alan Phillips, by expanding on his previous night's comments on homosexuality, and describing just how prevalent it was at Shrewsbury and other public schools. 'We weren't against homosexuality itself,' Josephs explains, 'but against it being forced on us and compulsory, which it effectively was.'[38]

The real trouble didn't erupt until the undergraduates had left, when Julian Critchley conveyed news of their triumph to the national press. Short reports appeared in both the *Daily Express* and the *News Chronicle*.[39] The headmaster, Jack Peterson, was furious at being phoned by the papers for his comments, and the debating-society chairman, Richard Sachs, says he was severely reprimanded for not seeking the head's permission for the debate – though this was rather disingenuous, since approval would almost certainly have been granted, and Sachs could hardly be blamed for the press coverage.[40] Critchley was accused of selling the story, though he denied making money from it, and both debaters were treated very coolly by the school thereafter.

The story of the Shrewsbury debate had an amusing sequel a quarter of a century later. By 1980 his views about public schools had clearly mellowed – or perhaps he felt the institutions had sufficiently reformed themselves – for Michael Heseltine, now a Cabinet minister, arranged to see the headmaster of Harrow with a view to his son, Rupert, going there.

The head explains, 'My secretary showed him into my study and I sat him down in front of me, and he said, "We've not met, have we?" And I said, "Oh yes we have!" "But where?" I told him. "Oh God, was it you?" ' But after twenty-eight years Michael Hoban could forgive Heseltine for what he considered 'typical undergraduate immaturity' and an attempt to make a name for himself back in Oxford.

Rupert Heseltine duly went to Harrow the following September. Michael Hoban took clever advantage of his father's embarrassment to book him to speak to the school's political society.

'It was a fair cop!' he says.[41]

4. *The Cellar of the Oxford Union*

The Michael Heseltine who returned to his school debating society in November 1952 was already a very different person from the boy who had left Shrewsbury only a year and a half before – more prosperous-looking, more confident, and more directed. He blossomed at Oxford, says a contemporary, Bryan Magee. 'It was the chrysalis turning into the butterfly.'[1] While Heseltine largely ignores his old school, Shrewsbury, he never hesitates to acknowledge his debt to his university: 'Oxford was the most wonderful, liberating experience. It's where I found myself, really. Suddenly I was among my peers, operating in an environment I loved.'[2]

Yet arguably his school *had* played a major role in forging the future man, though not in a way intended. As his friend Anthony Howard later explained in the Oxford University magazine *Isis*, the way Heseltine was treated by everyone at Shrewsbury left 'an indomitable determination to show that – whatever the record books and the school reports might indicate – he was every bit as good as they were. That determination, born of insults and adversity, has been the dynamo which has driven him throughout his Oxford career.'[3]

By the time Michael Heseltine left Oxford, at the end of 1954, he was probably the most recognized student of his generation, and one of the most successful presidents in the entire 130-year history of the university's prestigious debating society, the Oxford Union.

The story of Heseltine's university career really begins three weeks before he arrived in Oxford, in the middle of September 1951, when the Prime Minister, Clement Attlee, called another election. Heseltine has often told of how he was walking down Walter Road in Swansea and spotted an election banner adorning the offices of the local Conservative candidate, Captain Henry Kerby, on the other side. 'I crossed the road, went in and said, "Can I help?" That was when I joined the Conservative Party.'[4]

With a Labour majority of barely 3,600, Swansea West was a prime marginal, and Heseltine immediately started organizing the women who were addressing election envelopes. 'Michael was the first person I met when I presented myself at the Conservative offices to offer my help,' one volunteer, Jean Taverner, has recalled. 'He was in charge – literally in charge. He told us all what to do and how to do it. Extremely autocratic.'[5]

Heseltine was too young to vote himself, since the voting age was then twenty-one. In any case, by polling-day, when Winston Churchill brought the Tories back to office, he'd already left for Oxford.

He'd originally tried to do a degree in commerce at Bristol University, but had been turned down. Reading University, where John Wolfenden was now vice-chancellor, rejected him too, but he was accepted by both Oxford and Cambridge, and chose the former.

Pembroke College has never pretended to be one of the great Oxford colleges: it boasts neither size nor wealth; neither academic reputation nor great sporting honours. This was especially true in 1951, when 'Pemmy' was the smallest college in the university and admitted barely fifty undergraduates a year. Yet it was a relaxed, friendly place. More important for Michael Heseltine, it was one of the few Oxford colleges which didn't require one to pass the university entrance exam.

Heseltine was officially reading philosophy, politics and economics (PPE). He hadn't come to Oxford for a good degree, though, but to shine in student politics, and in particular to achieve the ambition already declared at school – to become president of the Oxford Union.

Within days of arriving, Heseltine struck up friendships with two Pembroke undergraduates who would remain his closest companions for his student days and early adult life. Julian Critchley, the son of an eminent neurologist, Macdonald Critchley, had come to Oxford after a year at the Sorbonne, and had the unusual habit of always wearing a suit and bow-tie. He first bumped into Heseltine on a staircase in college the day he arrived. The two had met before – first at Broughton Hall and later at Shrewsbury, albeit briefly, since Critchley was two years older, and had left the school early. He was also reading PPE.

In time, Critchley and Heseltine became so close, and were seen together so much, that they collectively became known as 'Critchel-tine'. There was even gossip amongst undergraduates who obviously did not know them that they were homosexual lovers, though there was not the slightest grain of truth in the rumour. Many Oxford contemporaries felt it was Critchley who would reach the top, with Heseltine the loyal adjutant. Critchley, says Tyrrell Burgess, 'was the able one of the two – funnier, more likeable, more intelligent'.[6] Indeed, in the race to Westminster, Critchley would beat his Oxford chum by almost seven years.

The other significant friendship was with Ian Josephs, a non-religious Jew from London whose father was a carpet manufacturer. Josephs, who had been at Charterhouse and was reading law, says he first noticed Heseltine in the Pembroke dining-hall:

I was sitting next to this blond fellow and he was banging his glass with a spoon and saying, 'Order, order, order.' And I said, 'What are you doing that for?' And he said, 'Practising.' And I said, 'Practising? What for?' And he said, 'For being president of the Oxford Union.' And I said, 'What's the Oxford Union?' 'That's the debating society.' I said, 'What do you want to be president of that for?' And he said, 'Because it's the first step to being Prime Minister.'[7]

Josephs quickly decided that Heseltine was an interesting chap; they went together to the next Union debate and both spoke.

But Heseltine's Oxford Union career didn't get off to as quick a start as he'd hoped for. Although he frequently contributed from the floor, generally taking a Conservative line, his early reviews were modest. 'Will be good when he learns to relax,' wrote Peter Blaker, the president in his second term, who recommended 'greater variety of tone'.[8]

'He's a slow starter,' says Ian Josephs, 'but a good finisher.'[9] It's been true throughout Heseltine's life. A successful career in the Oxford Union typically used to start with election to the society's Library Committee, then progressed to the Standing Committee before advancing to the senior offices: secretary, treasurer, librarian and president. Heseltine had trouble with even the first step. In his initial shot at Library Committee, at the end of his second term, he came eleventh. After a year he did better, pushed into runner-up position by just three votes. But things were still going too slowly to hold high hopes for the future.

Heseltine did at least have the advantage of being a Conservative. Votes in debates suggest the Union membership at that time roughly held a three-to-two Tory majority, though this wasn't always reflected in elections, where members often ignored party loyalties. (Recent years had seen socialists such as Tony Benn, or Liberals such as Robin Day and Jeremy Thorpe, all attain the presidency.) Heseltine's plan was to launch his Union ambitions from a firm base in the Oxford University Conservative Association, known as 'OUCA' (pronounced 'Owka'). The problem was that, while he felt sure that he was a Conservative, he felt deeply uncomfortable in OUCA.

At that time the association was dominated by what Anthony Howard used to call the 'right-wing, port-swilling, Carlton oligarchy'. The Carlton in question was not the St James's club but a lesser establishment in Oxford, situated above a bank on the corner of Cornmarket and Magdalen Street. Its members tended to be upper-class – often Old Etonians – and attending the more powerful traditional colleges such as Christ Church and Magdalen. Typically they were wealthy, and often indulged in lavish dinners and drinking sessions; weekends were spent in the country, shooting, hunting or beagling. Some were even reputed to keep spaniels in their college rooms. Today they might be called Hooray Henries.

In previous years the OUCA presidency had been held by Edward Heath and Margaret Thatcher, both of whom were several notches below Michael Heseltine on the British social scale. But by the early 1950s the nobs and snobs were in charge, and they quickly came to view 'That Man Heseltine' with considerable distaste – as a middle-class arriviste, a vulgar johnny-come-lately who was so obviously out for what he could get. And how could one ever respect a man who came from a proletarian place like Swansea?

At that time the relationship between social background and politics within the Conservative Party was almost the reverse of today, both at Oxford and nationally. In recent years the aristocrats have generally been on the left of the party – socially concerned paternalists – while Thatcherism most strongly found favour with upwardly mobile Essex man. But in the early 1950s Heseltine found not only the attitudes and lifestyles of the Oxford Carlton group deeply repugnant but also their politics. Many of them regarded the 1950s Conservative government as decidedly pink – almost socialist. On the other hand, the Shrewsbury debate showed Heseltine's leftward leanings, and the people he met in OUCA probably drove him further that way.

College rivalries reinforced this. Pembroke lived in the shadow – almost literally – of mighty, upper-class Christ Church on the other side of St Aldates. Looking down on their neighbours, men from 'The House' would deride Pembroke as the 'Christ Church lats' (latrines).

Nevertheless, Heseltine tried hard in OUCA. He went to the meetings, asked intelligent questions of speakers, and made a promising start, winning election to the OUCA committee in his first term. But then he ran up against the association's anachronistic constitution. This ensured that the key officer posts were selected by the whole committee, but also that a large number of committee places were reserved for former officers. It meant the Carlton right-wingers kept a firm grip – acting, in effect, as a self-perpetuating oligarchy. As things stood, Heseltine soon realized, it would be very difficult for him to achieve high office in OUCA.

During the summer of 1952, Heseltine, Critchley and several other like-minded friends from OUCA – generally middle-class and on the left of the party, and from less prestigious colleges – planned a new Conservative ginger-group. Called the Blue Ribbon Club, it was launched in October 1952. Its founders had a variety of motives. To some, the Blue Ribbon was for organizing left-leaning slates in OUCA elections – people who saw themselves as progressive Tories in the style of Butler, Macleod and Macmillan. Another purpose, say former members, was to create a serious-minded, intellectual discussion group. They hoped to invite a broader range of speakers than OUCA, which they regarded as too much of a drinking and dining club.

But, while some members harboured high-minded intentions, most outsiders, and some insiders, cynically regarded the Blue Ribbon as, in Julian Critchley's phrase, 'Heseltine's Private Army'.[10] Ian Josephs, himself a Liberal, is convinced that Heseltine planned the club simply to further his Oxford career. 'His idea was a Conservative club that was going to deliver his vote in the Union.'[11] Surprisingly, though,

Heseltine himself didn't become president of the Blue Ribbon until its third term.

The Blue Ribbon was not a complete breakaway from OUCA, as has sometimes been suggested, though Conservative Central Office was so alarmed by developments that it sent an official to Oxford to bang heads together – without success. At times the factionalism was more bitter than the struggle against Labour. Heseltine's two fiercest opponents, both in OUCA and in the Union, were both Robins from Christ Church – Robin Maxwell-Hyslop and Robin Cooke (not to be confused with the Labour politician). Cooke was the first of many over the years to describe Heseltine as an 'opportunist who did not believe in the basic principles of Conservatism'.[12] And when Heseltine himself was prone to say things like 'We're all here for what we can get out of it' it is hard to blame Cooke, though friends say Heseltine never really meant such comments and was just being typically provocative.[13]

If securing a Conservative base was one part of Heseltine's strategy for winning in the Union, another was to improve his abilities as a debater. He might not have liked the people running OUCA, but Heseltine took full advantage of the association's speaking classes. These were held at teatime twice a week at the Conservative Party offices in Queen Street, under the firm direction of the renowned Stella Gatehouse, a woman of about fifty who had a distinctive large nose, smoked incessantly, and had the dubious honour of also having taught Margaret Thatcher, who says 'her emphasis was on simplicity and clarity of expression and as little jargon as possible'.[14]

Stella Gatehouse was the wife of the vicar of Piddington, a parish twelve miles from Oxford, and at weekends her pupils would be invited over for beer and sandwiches, or for afternoon tea. By all accounts she didn't like Michael Heseltine, but she tolerated him, and on one famous occasion her husband even invited him to give a Sunday-evening sermon in Piddington church. Heseltine adapted one of his Union speeches, and God barely got a mention. But then Heseltine has never been a great believer; he is probably best described as agnostic.

In time, Stella Gatehouse's training paid off, and Heseltine even won a student debating contest for the Conservative Party's local

Wessex region. Ian Josephs, who shared rooms with him for several terms, remembers how before any big speech Heseltine would spend hours rehearsing. 'He'd pose in front of the mirror, ask if his hand gestures were right, whether this phrase was right, whether his hair was too long.'[15] Another friend recalls bursting in on Heseltine and finding him with a tape recorder, scrutinizing his words and delivery.

Heseltine didn't record just his own speeches. Guy Arnold, a friend from the Blue Ribbon Club, recollects the week which several members spent campaigning for the party in Nottinghamshire. The climax was an evening rally with Charles Hill, a Tory minister who had become famous as the BBC's 'radio doctor'. Arnold was surprised not to see Heseltine in the front row with the rest of his Oxford friends. Afterwards he discovered why. Heseltine had been at the back, tape-recording Hill's speech with a view to improving his own style. Up to that point, Arnold reckons, Heseltine had always modelled his mannerisms on his great Welsh hero, Lloyd George. But by the next term at Oxford the style had changed radically. 'His speeches were Charles Hill! He was a great copyist. He learnt the tricks of the trade of other people.'[16]

'He's a very self-created person,' says Bryan Magee, a Union president in Heseltine's second year. 'When he started speaking at the Oxford Union he was a very poor speaker, but he made himself into a good speaker . . . He decided what sort of a human being he wanted to be and then made himself into it.'[17]

It wasn't until the end of Heseltine's fourth term, however, that he got his first 'paper' speech in the Union – as one of the main debaters whose name appears on the order paper, and who is required to dress in a dinner-jacket and black bow-tie. 'A great improvement on past form,' concluded the president, the future Tory minister Patrick Mayhew. 'With a bit more warmth he will be very good.'[18]

The following day Heseltine finally secured election to the Library Committee, and from then on he could count on giving a 'paper' speech once a term. The critics weren't always consistent, but the reviews never ignored him:

Mr Heseltine should guard against artificial mannerisms of voice and calculated flashes of self-conscious histrionics, for these give a sudden impression of immaturity and induce uneasiness in the House. This is only worth saying because he has the makings of a first-class speaker, and it would be a great loss to both himself and the Union if he were to develop in the wrong direction. (Bryan Magee)[19]

Mr Heseltine has many of the characteristics of a regular Hyde Park orator. He can answer interruptions very effectively, look breezily confident at times, and at others quiet and confidential . . . He will have to learn to make some of his tricks of oratory less obvious. (Sir Andrew Cuninghame)[20]

'Solemnly trite and boring' was the verdict on another speech, 'a respectful jog-trot through the pages of political cliché'.[21] 'He spoke in a monotone and far too quickly,' wrote 'Rufus' of *Isis*.[22]

May 1953 saw Heseltine and his friend Peter Tapsell – a future Tory MP, but then a Labour man – on opposite sides of an issue that would divide them again forty years later – European union – only in 1953 their positions were the reverse of today. While Tapsell 'was all-out for a Federal Union', Heseltine was against, 'in the interests of defence, the sterling area, and our Empire and Commonwealth ties'.[23] He wanted to see the original six European partners gain confidence amongst themselves before Britain considered joining them, though *Isis* also detected anti-American sentiment.[24]

Cherwell, the university newspaper, was often more generous. 'Probably the most able politician in the Union' it declared after Heseltine's second 'paper' speech. 'He was involved in some quick-firing repartee (the best for many terms) with the mover and came out on top.'[25] A year later Heseltine 'ran into a formidable barrage of interruptions from which he extricated himself with wit and aplomb. Indeed, it was just as well he did, for the rest of his speech was threadbare and theatrical, and . . . vigorously overacted.'[26]

Union colleagues remember Heseltine as a good but not outstanding speaker, and nothing like the star performer he would become. Several Oxford contemporaries – notably Anthony Howard and Jeremy Isaacs – were far superior. Heseltine's speeches often showed signs of being forced and overprepared; jerky arm movements would suddenly occur half a second too late. He was guilty of shouting and haranguing, and, above all, he was never really a debater, someone who would engage his opponents in argument; rather, his speeches were attempts at oratory, based on carefully prepared notes. As he has admitted:

They were immensely detailed notes. It was probably a pity, probably a mistake, but I was not all that confident. I never did get confidence in the Oxford Union. It was not until some time later that I felt properly at ease on a platform ... At the Oxford Union, I never remember feeling in command of an audience.[27]

Heseltine was particularly affected by an incident when one undergraduate suddenly forgot what he was going to say and had to apologize and sit down. 'I vowed that would never happen to me.'[28] Thereafter, he always prepared his words on paper, though he was often criticized for this. Even today, as a minister, though Heseltine may speak off the cuff, he usually has notes to fall back on.

A debate with Harold Macmillan at the Cambridge Union also influenced his style. Heseltine had not had enough time to prepare the end of his speech, so he bluffed his way through. Afterwards Macmillan touched his arm. 'He said to me, "That was a very good speech. A very good speech. But take my advice. Always prepare the end first." He had spotted exactly what I had done.'[29]

By Easter 1953, towards the end of his second year, the speaking practice paid off and Heseltine finally secured election to the Standing Committee, along with two future Commons colleagues, Peter Tapsell and Gerald Kaufman.

Nowadays the university might never have allowed Michael Heseltine to get that far. At that time, people studying PPE sat preliminary exams – 'prelims' – at the end of their second term, but it took Heseltine another twelve months to jump this hurdle. First time round, he failed all three papers he chose – constitutional history, economics and French. This was an especially poor result considering he had already studied two of the subjects at school. He passed the retakes in history and economics that summer, but, despite his French ancestry, he couldn't pass the language paper until his third go, in March 1953. Today Oxford colleges are much stricter, and usually send students down for failing prelims more than once.

Life was not all politics and PPE, however, and Heseltine pursued an active social life; people remember that his parents always supplied enough funds to do so. He and Julian Critchley regularly dined at a new restaurant called Long John's, where they became good friends of the flamboyant owner, George Silver, a bald man of more than twenty stone who had known Rupert Heseltine in the Army during the war. Silver later let the two undergraduates eat for half-price in the naïve belief that having well-known student figures might encourage custom.

Heseltine was certainly no 'Union Bore', according to Anthony Howard in his '*Isis* Idol', a profile in the university magazine. 'The diversity of his friends is enough to disprove it. Smart boys, sophisticated girls, theatre juveniles, Joan Hunter Dunns, or just plain poker players – Michael knows them all.'[30] He sometimes joined late-night poker schools, though not in a serious way.

Though Heseltine was a good friend of Patrick Dromgoole, the theatre director, and of the future novelist David Hughes, he never took much interest in the arts himself. 'Michael Philistine' quickly became one of several nicknames (two others were 'Steiners' and 'Von Heseltine', on account of his Germanic looks). 'He's not got much of a sense of culture,' says Ian Josephs. 'He never read a book. The only films he liked were Westerns. He didn't like music, paintings or anything.'[31] His favourite Western, apparently, was *High Noon*, which Julian Critchley says they saw 'at least half a dozen times'.[32]

Heseltine occasionally held vast Oxford parties to which anybody who was anybody was invited, and he became known for his very own concoction of punch – a recipe one friend still swears by 'since everyone gets drunk very quickly'.[33] 'He gave marvellous parties,' says Michael Pike, a friend who recalls an occasion when his host ferried thirty daughters of South American diplomats up from London. 'You can imagine the impact they had when they arrived in a room in Oxford. There was a coachload of extremely well-dressed, beautiful, Latin American girls. It really made the party go.'[34]

At a time when female students were confined to the five women's colleges, girls were always scarce. Initially Heseltine had continued seeing a childhood sweetheart, Diana Solomon, and Ian Josephs claims a helping hand in the missives he sent back to Swansea – 'more amusing than love letters, to make her think how clever he was'. Later Heseltine and Critchley assigned Josephs the job of finding girlfriends in Oxford: 'Julian was incredibly good-looking and Michael was very striking,' he says, 'and neither of them would ask a girl out, so I did it for them.'[35] Julian Critchley claims that for one event Heseltine even advertised in the student press for an escort, and took his pick of the respondents.[36]

Then there was the daughter of the Portuguese countess. Michael was 'potty' about her, says Josephs. 'She begged him to write to her and they had this sort of romance – I don't think it went further than a kiss and a cuddle in the end, and I remember how upset he was. So he wrote to her about five times and never got any answer, which was a blow to his pride.'[37]

But Westerns, girls, parties and poker were distractions from the principal goal – the presidency of the Union. Ian Josephs claims Heseltine was forever 'scheming' for the job – to the extent, he says, that he would 'advise people whom he saw as rivals to stand for offices where they were bound to be defeated . . . He would calculate and scheme endlessly to get what he wanted in a quite cold-hearted and even ruthless manner. But he would never lie or do anything dishonest.'[38] Within days of first being elected to the Standing Committee, Heseltine declared his intention to go for the presidency the following term, standing against the society's librarian, the baronet Sir Andrew Cuninghame. He was not considered a serious candidate, but seemed to think of it as a dry run. 'Michael Heseltine has his eye on the future,' *Isis* commented. 'Not for nothing is he known as the calculating machine on two legs.'[39]

Although he lost to Cuninghame, the result was respectable. His campaign ensured that he topped the next poll for Standing Committee, and established him as a serious Union contender.

The following Christmas, Heseltine organized a highly successful Union ball, with Ned Sherrin running the cabaret. He also persuaded members to let the BBC televise a debate for the first time, though he himself didn't appear on the nation's screens. In December 1953 he was also easily elected Union secretary, and must have gained some satisfaction from beating his old OUCA adversary, Robin Maxwell-Hyslop.

The winter of 1954 saw one of the Union's recurrent financial crises, and a bitter argument over the whole future of the society, in which Heseltine played a leading role. The trouble was that only a minority of Oxford undergraduates were joining the Union (women were still barred altogether), and subscription income was insufficient to keep the society solvent.

A majority of the Standing Committee said they should raise membership fees; this group included the senior treasurer, George Richardson, a young economics don from St John's who had tutored Heseltine for his prelims retakes. The proposed rises were fairly modest – to increase the £11 life subscription, which had been unchanged for decades, to £12, and the termly rate from thirty shillings to thirty-five or forty.

Normally the senior treasurer's opinion would have carried the day, but Heseltine argued vociferously against him. Increasing the subscriptions, Heseltine countered, would make the Union even more of a rich man's club. His unstated fear, no doubt, was that the society would become the preserve of the Carlton Club snobs he despised so much. The alternative, he said, was 'an expansionist policy – to get more people to pay less, rather than the other way round'.[40]

The dispute raged for several weeks, until Heseltine persuaded his opponents to back what became known as the 'Brighter Union' policy. The defeated George Richardson felt obliged to resign, though with hindsight he now feels Heseltine 'was right and I was wrong'.[41] Nor had the debate divided along traditional party lines. Two of Heseltine's strongest allies were Anthony Howard and Jeremy Isaacs, both committed Labour men, who have been good friends of his ever since Oxford.

Howard, the son of an Anglican clergyman, was reading law at Christ Church. While at Oxford, he achieved both the editorship of *Isis* and the presidency of the Union, and in the university magazine he became a keen supporter of Heseltine and a close commentator on his progress. Though Howard was 'squeamish' about his friend's contention that the Union was a 'commercial undertaking', he believed that Heseltine's 'energy of nuclear fission' could only benefit the society.[42] 'When Michael has been seriously opposed in Union elections,' he later wrote, 'he has fought as though for his life; and it has, in fact, quite literally been his life for which he was fighting.'[43] Howard knew what he was talking about, for he had been the main opponent when Heseltine won the Union treasurership in March 1954.

Even without this new responsibility, the Trinity (summer) term of 1954 should have been busy enough for Heseltine: he was about to sit his final exams, having done little academic work. But now he was also mounting a serious challenge for the Union presidency, and had the chance to use the office of treasurer to show how the society could be run in a more businesslike way.

The main plank was what he drily called 'the economics of feeding' – a programme to beef up the society's dining-room, which often languished half-empty, running up a heavy deficit. One term the restaurant had lost more than £1,000 – the equivalent of almost a hundred life subscriptions. Now, Heseltine sacked the Union chef, no longer closed the restaurant on Mondays, and introduced better-value meals. 'Four course lunches – two and six; five course dinners – three and six' soon became the sales pitch, as a *Cherwell* cartoon depicted Heseltine with a placard saying 'Frying Tonight'.[44]

The new menu satisfied a real appetite. Postwar rationing had not quite ended, and there were still relatively few places outside college where Oxford students could eat cheaply. One freshman wrote home to his parents, 'We had the new Heseltine five-course dinner for 3s. 6d., which was excellent. The new meals . . . are packing the dining-room . . . a new waitress has already had to be engaged, and still the service is bad.'[45] Soon the kitchens were serving 2,000 meals a week, and local Oxford restaurateurs seemed worried. 'If only I had a Heseltine working for me,' remarked George Silver, as he cut prices at one of his premises.[46]

Using the improved catering to attract new members, Heseltine began a vigorous Union recruitment drive. With a temporary cut in the application fee, he signed up another 200 members that term; it compared with just thirty new recruits the previous summer.

Another initiative would ultimately have a much greater benefit for Heseltine personally than it ever did for the Union. He let the university newspaper, *Cherwell*, rent a small brick hut in the society's garden for £5 a term – hardly a sum to make a dent in the Union deficit.

The undergraduate proprietor of *Cherwell*, Clive Labovitch, was already a regular guest at Heseltine's parties, but renting the Union office would lead to a vital business partnership. Though they were never particularly close at Oxford, both undergraduates were seen as up-and-coming entrepreneurs, and their obvious ambition prompted an irreverent satirical ditty, 'Labovitch and Heseltine'. It was based on a famous calypso of the period about the two West Indies bowlers, Ramadhin and Valentine, who had wreaked havoc on England's batsmen in the 1950 Test series. Of the Oxford version, alas, only a fragment remains in people's memories:

> Walking naked down dee High,
> Anything for pub-li-ci-tie

'Even then, Michael was a good self-publicist,' says a former *Cherwell* editor, Fred Newman. 'He must have felt that being our landlord he was ensured fairly good coverage.'[47] Certainly *Cherwell* mentioned Heseltine a lot, and mostly favourably. Good coverage in the student press was invaluable to a Union politician, since canvassing and campaigning in the society's elections were forbidden. Voters had to judge candidates largely on public performances.

As the term progressed, Heseltine seemed to go out of his way to court the left. First, in debate, he delivered an outspoken attack on the Churchill government's foreign policy, calling for cuts in arms spending, and urging economic expansion in the Third World at the expense of living standards in the West. But Michael Heseltine has never been a convincing trimmer, and that evening he provoked only loud jeers. The speech 'might have evoked more respect,' one critic suggested, 'if the House had been prepared to forget the mover's political past. As it was, it unhappily proved to be a damp squib.'[48]

The same week, Heseltine also got involved with the Oxford H-Bomb Committee – a decision which would return to haunt him thirty years later. The committee sprang from efforts to organize a nationwide petition against the bomb, and many of those involved later formed CND – the Campaign for Nuclear Disarmament. Indeed, one could say that Heseltine played a role – a very small one – in the early days of the British peace movement. When this episode from Heseltine's student past emerged in the press in the mid-1980s, and accounts suggested that he had been a Ban-the-Bomber, Heseltine frantically began ringing Oxford friends to get them to confirm he had done nothing embarrassing. 'I was pursued by telephone calls from his office,' says Jeremy Isaacs, who had himself served on the H-Bomb Committee. ' "The Secretary of State would like to talk to you." Michael asked, "Was it true? Jeremy, can you help me?" I thought it was quite amusing.'[49] In fact Heseltine's *views* about the bomb in 1954 seem consistent with his later position as Defence Secretary. What were very different were his tactics.

More than once Michael Heseltine attended meetings which brought together students from across the political spectrum who were worried about the bomb, to try to achieve a common position. A few of those he was working with were Communists and sympathized with the Soviet Union. Indeed, Heseltine was making precisely the kind of political associations for which he himself would regularly condemn CND in the 1980s.

Initially, discussion revolved around a local petition calling for the H-bomb to be banned 'because it is morally wrong'.[50] Heseltine argued that if the petition was to be anything more than a 'political smear' it must 'achieve unanimity in the political clubs'. He successfully proposed a new wording which called on the government to make 'vigorous efforts' to secure 'universal disarmament'. The earlier phrase about the H-bomb being 'morally wrong' was dropped.[51] In essence, Heseltine had managed to press the multilateral case against those who wanted Britain to take a unilateral lead, though these terms were not generally used at the time. He duly signed the revised petition along with several other members of the Blue Ribbon Club, though he never served on the twelve-strong Oxford H-Bomb Committee itself. Many on the right of OUCA boycotted the petition, however, arguing that the motion was Communist-inspired.

Much more frivolous was Heseltine's performance in the Union's Eights Week debate at the end of May – an event for which the officers traditionally wear fancy dress. Heseltine donned Indian costume, squatted on the floor, and began playing on a tin whistle. Slowly a rope uncoiled and gently rose into the air, assisted by a helper tugging a fishing-line from the gallery above.

Heseltine's own rise required no such tricks. By the middle of term it was obvious that his Brighter Union policy would deliver him the Union presidency, although it helped that none of his three opponents was particularly formidable. Two of them, the librarian, Roger Booth, and the secretary, Bruce Burton, were Liberals, while the fourth contender, Jonathan Boswell, had been chairman of the Labour Club. Politically, Conservatives had no option but to choose Heseltine, though some Tories probably despised him enough to vote for his opponents or abstain. More important, he gained the backing of socialists like Anthony Howard and Jeremy Isaacs whose party loyalties might have told them to support Boswell. Both felt Heseltine was simply the best man to secure the Union's future.

Howard and Isaacs even supplied material and jokes for Heseltine's speech in the debate against the other presidential contenders. Bryan Magee and Peter Tapsell were also consulted. In drafting what was then the most important speech of his life, it is amusing to note that he should have been assisted by four socialists.

'Hes is Pres,' proclaimed *Cherwell*, as he won decisively on the second round, after Bruce Burton's votes had been redistributed among the remaining three candidates.[52] 'Never perhaps had anyone wanted anything quite so much as Michael wanted this,' Anthony Howard wrote afterwards.[53] 'It's a wonderful feeling,' Heseltine told his Swansea friend Geoff Hayes.[54]

Almost forgotten amid the triumph of winning the presidency, Heseltine also passed his PPE finals. At that time Oxford was still awarding fourth-class degrees – one recipient was Julian Critchley – so Heseltine's second was highly commendable, though his tutor called it 'a great and undeserved triumph'.[55] Swotting during the final weeks, Heseltine had borrowed model essays from several of his more scholarly friends: he always credits a former Union treasurer, John Stewart, with getting him through. Stewart, who is also a socialist, remembers merely a 'half-hour over lunch' explaining how contemporary philosophy was 'mainly linguistic – about words – and that it was fairly easy to write answers to papers on that basis'.[56]

Serving as president, of course, meant staying on in Oxford a further six months beyond his degree course; this was entirely within the Union rules and is quite common for Michaelmas term (autumn) presidents. Rupert and Eileen Heseltine seem to have paid their son's way – the Union certainly wouldn't have done – and they proudly came to watch Michael preside over the house.

One of the new president's first acts was to secure the expenditure of £600 on his *pièce de résistance* – the conversion of the Union's old coal cellars into a nightclub. The plan was to hold dinner-dances, jazz concerts and late-night dancing on Saturdays, and to provide a regular bar – a far more audacious scheme in the 1950s than it sounds today – so as to attract into the Union people who weren't interested in debates.[57] It was the project for which Heseltine's presidency has always been remembered, but the idea was not entirely his. One account suggests it actually arose from a light-hearted remark by his presidential opponent, Jonathan Boswell, as he speculated about what Heseltine might think of next.[58]

An architecture student was roped in to draw up the plans, and Heseltine himself spent part of the summer helping with the rebuilding work, as two rooms were knocked into one, the floor was levelled, and lino was laid. One Union employee recalls his surprise on seeing his president stripped to the waist down in the basement, drenched in sweat, wielding a pickaxe and clearing out rubble.

The nightclub – complete with multicoloured walls, cave designs and low-level lighting – was opened three weeks into the Michaelmas term. The first-night guests of honour were two 1950s celebrities, Sir Bernard Docker and his wife, Norah, who were well-known for flaunting their wealth and driving a gold-plated Daimler (although that evening they came to Oxford in their pale-green model). Michael Heseltine apologized for the delay in opening the new premises: 'As you know, the dockers have been on strike.'[59]

The evening has gone down in Union legend. Norah Docker was clearly much taken by the tall, handsome host dressed in his white tie and tails, and together they took to the dance floor. When she learnt from the designer that the refurbishment had cost £600, Lady Docker turned to her husband and made him write out a cheque for the whole amount.

Indeed, the Dockers were so impressed by the Union president that shortly afterwards they even let him borrow one of their famous Daimlers for an evening out. The chauffeur drove to Oxford and took Heseltine and his then girlfriend, Sarah Rothschild, up to London. 'We behaved like animals,' he later told a friend, referring to the return journey.

Several people recall his affair with Sarah Rothschild, daughter of

Lord Victor Rothschild, though she herself now denies even knowing Heseltine at Oxford. Her memory seems at fault. It was an 'uneven relationship', says Michael Pike. 'I think he wanted, so to speak, to show her off, and she refused to be shown off.'[60] For one Union dinner she turned up in the shabbiest of dresses, as if deliberately to embarrass him. But in her regular column in *Cherwell* Rothschild could not stop writing about the man:

He is rather rude, does not pander to women's femininity, is unaristocratically unromantic about money, and he is Welsh. But he is the sort of person who could cause a revolution in the meaning of the word 'eligible'. Mr Heseltine is 6 ft 2 inches tall with peroxide white hair and ultra pale blue eyes. A physical combination which apparently prophesies a brilliant future as either a statesman or a murderer.[61]

Michael Heseltine's programme of debates looked fairly unexciting. His old headmaster John Wolfenden came to explain the limitations of humanism, and Heseltine admitted choosing a debate on Ireland 'in the hope that some sparks would fly', though they didn't.[62] But an end-of-term verdict was that the debates had been 'consistently full, have been of a consistently high standard, and have aroused continual interest. As a Club it has flourished: when Michael Heseltine goes down the Society will lose one of its greatest benefactors.'[63]

He had been a respected president, rather than popular. 'He has never, as he is the first to own, been considered "a nice chap" by those who know him only from afar,' Anthony Howard wrote in his '*Isis* Idol'.[64] At times, he could be high-handed. Philip Swindells, now a vicar, says the experience of Michael Heseltine chairing a religious debate 'is seared in my memory'. 'There was a rule you could only speak if you had put your name down in advance,' Swindells explains.

As the debate progressed I thought of some things I would like to contribute, so I wrote a note on a scrap of paper requesting a dispensation which was duly passed from hand to hand up to Michael in the Chair. He looked at it, then slowly scanned those present . . . until, I imagine, from my hopeful expression he established who had dared to send the note. He then very slowly and deliberately crushed the note into a ball of paper. Of course I was never called.[65]

Nevertheless, over 1,000 people joined the Union that term, which was about a third more than usual. The Brighter Union strategy seemed to have worked, though Heseltine's period still incurred a trading loss of £270.[66] But there had been a new buzz about the society; in subsequent terms the Oxford student press would complain that the Union wasn't as exciting as it had been in Heseltine's day.

The cellars thrived for several years – and even provided a venue for the undergraduate pianist Dudley Moore at one point – before they slowly went into decline. And the Union has continued to face recurring financial crises, the latest in 1996.

Michael Heseltine had made no secret that the Oxford Union was merely the very first stage in his assault on the political summit. Julian Critchley often relates a famous story of his friend mapping out his future plans on the back of an envelope. The incident occurred one evening in Long John's, when Heseltine pulled out an envelope and drew lines across it for each of the remaining decades of the twentieth century. Against the 1950s he wrote 'millionaire'; the 1960s, 'MP'; the 1970s, 'minister'; the 1980s, 'Cabinet'; and finally, for the 1990s, 'Downing Street'. Heseltine himself always denies the story, but Ian Josephs claims he was present too, and confirms Critchley's account.

Even if details of the Long John's conversation are not completely true, the gist of it certainly is. Bryan Magee remembers Heseltine outlining very similar plans on a trip to a debate in Ireland. 'Either he did it more than once,' Magee says of Critchley's 'envelope' story, 'or it's a very slight modification of an incident that did, in fact, happen to me.'[67] Tyrrell Burgess recalls Heseltine going even further, and announcing 'when he was going to get married'.[68]

Another Oxford contemporary, Paul Winner, tells of the time he approached Heseltine to hire the Union debating hall for a big public meeting with the London chargé d'affaires for Chairman Mao's new régime in China. 'His reaction was, "I'm not going to have these Communists here. I've got to watch my reputation. I'm going to be Prime Minister by the time I'm fifty, and I've got to be careful about who I keep company with." '[69] Michael Heseltine not only knew his goals, but would always be determined not to do anything that might jeopardize them.

Ian Josephs remembers another occasion involving the three

Pembroke friends, in which Heseltine declared his aims more starkly still. 'We said, "Let's write down what each of us wants out of life in one word." Julian wrote "Fame", I wrote "Pleasure" and Michael wrote "Power".'[70]

5. *Opportunities for Graduates*

Serving as president of the Oxford Union 'puts you on a pedestal,' Michael Heseltine once explained, 'and, before you know where you are, you're – as I discovered to my amazement – an articled clerk working at a slaughterhouse in the Angel Islington in the snow.'[1] By day he was in a back office checking rows and rows of figures and adding them up. By night he was studying for his accountancy exams through a correspondence course, and working harder than he ever had at Oxford.

Originally Rupert Heseltine had planned for his son to go into accountancy straight from Shrewsbury, and had even fixed him up with articles in a local firm in Swansea. But now, after coming down from Oxford, Heseltine was able to join the far more prestigious City accountants Peat Marwick Mitchell. As a graduate articled clerk it would be three years before he was fully qualified as a chartered accountant. In the meantime he was expected to spend about three-quarters of his time out of the office, working on audits for Peat's clients. In theory, his accountancy studies – including the occasional lecture – came on top of a full day's work. Derek Budden, a more senior articled clerk who worked closely with him for a period, remembers Heseltine bringing his tuition papers one day and asking for assistance:

He said, 'Derek, I've got to get this off today. Please help me!' And we sat down and I helped him with part of the paper. When we finished I said, 'Mike, why are you doing this? Why are you trying to become a chartered accountant?' And he said, 'Derek, one day I'm going to be Prime Minister of this country, and when I am Prime Minister I want the Civil Service to respect me for being a chartered accountant, not for being a politician.'[2]

If this was the route to Downing Street, it was likely to be a slow, tedious one. He clearly had neither the aptitude nor the interest.

Before long he was being diverted by outside business commitments, and his accountancy work suffered.

Michael Heseltine was determined that before entering politics he was going to make money, and do so as quickly as possible. His initial stroke of fortune was to acquire £1,000 in National Savings certificates, which his Pridmore grandparents had been saving up for him over the years. In fact Heseltine very nearly frittered the money away. His initial thought was simply to use the funds to supplement his modest £7 a week wages as a clerk. A thousand pounds spread over the three years of his articles, he calculated, would provide another £6 a week. That would bring his income into line with the £12 or £13 most of his fellow graduates were getting. 'But then I thought, "That's mad. At the end of three years my £1,000 will be gone." '[3]

Instead Heseltine decided to invest the money, and he teamed up with his Oxford friend Ian Josephs, who was also doing articles with Peat Marwick. Josephs supplied a further £1,000 and they registered themselves as a company, Michian Ltd – a combination, of course, of their first names. Josephs's father, who dabbled a little in property, found them their first investment, a large, run-down house in Bayswater.

Clanricarde Gardens runs north from the point where Bayswater Road becomes Notting Hill Gate. It's a narrow, cavernous cul-de-sac of early Victorian terraces, and Michian's property, number 39, was towards the end. Combining their two £1,000 stakes and borrowing a further £1,750, the partners paid £3,750 for a lease which had about fifteen years still to run.

Today a small sign by the door of number 39 still reads 'Thurston Court Hotel', the name it carried when Heseltine and Josephs bought the property in 1955, though the building bore little resemblance to most people's notion of a hotel. Certainly one couldn't turn up and expect a bed for the night; all the rooms were rented by full-time tenants.

The property occupied five floors and was divided into sixteen bedsits. By all accounts, it was an appalling fire-trap. Each room had a metered gas-fire, a gas-ring for cooking, and a washbasin with a hot tap. There were just two shared bathrooms for the whole house, equipped with old-fashioned geyser heaters. And there was one coin-box telephone, on the ground floor.

For Heseltine and Josephs, Clanricarde Gardens wasn't just a business investment; it also solved the difficult problem of finding somewhere to live themselves, since both begrudged paying extortionate rents. Heseltine now occupied two rooms on the top floor, while Josephs had a room lower down, equipped with a TV set, which was something of a rarity in those days.

Another Oxford friend, Jeremy Isaacs, recalls visiting the house and being surprised at the conditions tenants would tolerate. When Heseltine took him down to the boiler room, Isaacs noticed there was even a bed on the floor there; he then pulled back the blanket to reveal stained sheets. 'It was a sign of how difficult it was to get accommodation that Michael was even able to rent out a boiler room.'[4]

The building was officially looked after by a Mrs Taylor – nobody knew her first name – who had her own quarters in the basement. Her job was to clean the rooms, change linen once a week, and collect the rent. Mrs Taylor's husband was an Irishman who worked as a chauffeur; often his drunken return home was the prelude to screams from the basement as he and his wife rowed. Heseltine didn't really know how to handle this. 'He was always threatening to throw them out because of the beatings and disturbance,' says one tenant, 'but she always talked him round.'[5]

Sixteen rooms, each worth two or three guineas, depending on size, should have raised a weekly income of about £40 or £50; but it wasn't always so simple. One room on the top floor was occupied by Julian Critchley, and subsequently by Anthony Howard when he came down from Oxford in the summer of 1955. Howard found that rain came in through the skylight above his bed, so he refused to pay Heseltine any rent until it was repaired. It wasn't fixed, so Heseltine got no money.

The landlords were less lenient with other tenants, however. Rent day was Friday, and anyone who hadn't paid would find a hasp and padlock on their door on their return. They weren't being thrown out, Ian Josephs insists: this measure was to prevent tenants from hiding, and forced them either to pay or to explain why they couldn't. 'We never evicted anybody,' he says.[6]

As far as one can gauge from the annual electoral registers, none of the tenants Heseltine and Josephs inherited in 1955 was still there a year later. Josephs admits that their aim was to get rid of the people they didn't like and acquire a higher class of tenant – young professionals who were willing to pay a bit more. As the quality of tenant went up, so too did the value of the property. 'We gave notice on the grounds that people were unpleasant, and then put the rents up a bit. We gave people a week's notice.' Some didn't need any persuasion to leave. 'The older people went because there were always parties and lots of noise.'[7]

The atmosphere at Clanricarde Gardens seems to have been riotous, and Heseltine appears to have been overwhelmed by it at times. Josephs recalls one night when his colleague came down in his pyjamas to complain about the noise, only for a girl to fling her arms round him. Whereupon a drunken American thought Heseltine was trying to steal his girlfriend and poured beer all over him. Never one for a punch-up, Heseltine fled back upstairs.

The building attracted interesting tenants, including two Canadians, Gerry Loughlin and Cindy Riddell, whom Heseltine had met on holiday in Paris; Loughlin belonged to a Canadian band called The Grads. Cindy became Ian Josephs's girlfriend, though he says Michael Heseltine had his eye on her too. Other Clanricarde tenants were Mike Davies, then one of Britain's leading tennis players, and his brother Leigh, who coincidentally came from Swansea. Mike Davies, in turn, introduced Jean Taverner, who had already met Heseltine during the 1951 election campaign in Swansea West.

There were also two female tenants apparently working as prostitutes, although Heseltine didn't spot this. He couldn't understand why Mrs Taylor was constantly calling them to the phone. 'Michael used to say, "My God, they're popular, those girls!" The phone was always ringing,' recalls one tenant. Ian Josephs denies that any call-girls used the house to entertain clients; the girls concerned were just 'enthusiastic amateurs', he says.[8]

For the time being, Heseltine put his political ambitions to one side. While at Oxford he had persuaded Edward Heath, then the

Conservative Party's Deputy Chief Whip, to put him on the list of suitable Tory candidates. Indeed, on the former Prime Minister's eightieth birthday, in 1996, Heseltine thanked him for this. But he seems to have made no great effort to find a seat for the 1955 general election. True, he would have been only twenty-two, but MPs were at that time quite often elected in their twenties. Heseltine's sole contribution to the 1955 campaign appears to have been a series of Wednesday- and Saturday-afternoon street meetings outside Notting Hill tube station.

In fact Heseltine was going through a spell of introspection, with strong doubts about whether he'd joined the right party. 'There was probably some uncertainty for about six months,' he recently confessed. 'I think a psychiatrist would have described it as a period of adjustment.'[9] The snobbery of many people in OUCA, which still rankled, was one factor; another was the 'scale and remoteness' of what he found in the City of London.[10] 'I saw many admirable things when I was there, but it is such a concentration of activity and wealth that it confronts you with a range of questions about the nature of the capitalist system.'[11]

His experiences at university had certainly pushed him to the left, and Anthony Howard believes his friend even contemplated joining the Labour Party. 'I thought at one time at Oxford that he might have been a socialist.'[12] Heseltine admits to toying with defection, but not seriously. 'Finally I think it was the sheer awfulness of the Labour Party, even in those days, that made me stay where I was.'[13]

Michael Heseltine still made it clear that he intended to be Prime Minister. There was the odd Conservative speaking engagement, and if he and Josephs had nothing better to do on Sunday afternoons they might amble down to Speakers' Corner in nearby Hyde Park, to listen and to heckle. Heseltine – like the young John Major a decade later – attempted the odd bit of pavement oratory himself. Ian Josephs recalls, 'People would say, "Well, if you're so clever, why don't you come up here and speak?" ' So Heseltine did. 'He speaks better with a hostile audience than with a friendly one, and once they'd invited us up they couldn't get us off.'[14]

Early in 1956 Heseltine and Josephs sold Clanricarde Gardens for £5,750 – a £2,000 profit on their investment of a year earlier. After paying off the mortgage, they were left with £4,000. Josephs, meanwhile, had found another property for them a few streets away – the New Court Hotel in Inverness Terrace. The twenty-year lease cost £14,000, and required a new mortgage of £10,000.

The New Court Hotel was a much more substantial venture; it was a genuine hotel, with more than forty rooms. About half the residents were elderly people who lived there permanently in bedsits with cookers – using it as a kind of retirement home – but the premises also welcomed traditional bed-and-breakfast customers. This meant employing several staff, and Jean Taverner agreed to act as manageress-cum-bookkeeper-cum-barmaid. There were also various Irish maids, including Bernie, a humpback with 'a foul mouth', says Jean Taverner. 'She would harangue the guests and scream up the passageway in four-letter words, and Michael would go down to try to sort it out. But he didn't know how to handle it.'[15] Another character, employed as night porter, was later found in the Portobello Road selling the hotel's sheets.

The hotel inevitably involved a far greater commitment from Heseltine himself. After a long day in the City, or working on some client firm's books, he would return to Bayswater, exchange his pinstripes and bowler for overalls, and spend the evening in physical toil. When guests arrived, Heseltine carried their bags up to their rooms and 'would pocket the threepence they gave him,' says Jean Taverner, 'and he would be very happy to do so'.[16]

Newcomers quickly learnt that the hotel stood directly above the Circle Line, and vibrated whenever a train passed underneath. Room 9 was the worst; anybody there got a short night's sleep.

When they bought the hotel 'it was a dump', says Heseltine, who explains how he did much of the redecoration himself:

I would get in there and paint the walls and ceilings, and as soon as I had painted them we would let the rooms . . . The work – the physical effort of working in the City as an accountant with a certain amount of study and the physical effort of being one's own building firm – was, of course, terrific.[17]

One weekend, however, Heseltine persuaded his old Swansea friend Geoff Hayes to recruit some fellow medical students into decorating. For two days' work they were paid £5 and, Ian Josephs says, all the food and alcohol they could consume.[18] 'It was an absolute riot,' says Hayes. 'There we were, painting and hammering and dividing rooms into two, and this sort of thing, and people were coming out of the rooms and putting their feet into paint-pots.'[19]

Sometimes Heseltine would work behind the hotel bar, and occasionally he rose early to prepare breakfasts. The journalist Alan Watkins tells a story from this period which nicely illustrates Heseltine's roguish frankness. At a party one evening the hotel-keeper was defending himself against accusations from a socialist woman that he must be exploiting people. 'He said that he worked very hard and had, in fact, been up at six that morning. What, she asked, was he doing at that hour? He replied: "I was mixing the butter with the marge." '[20]

On one occasion the New Court was host to Seretse Khama, the future President of Botswana; on another there was a hard-drinking Australian cricket team. And one weekend hordes of rugby-league fans came up to London for the cup final on a special deal Heseltine had dreamt up.

Heseltine has also told how his days running the New Court were the first time he really came across 'flagrant prejudice and discrimination' against black people. If the hotel was full and somebody turned up for a room, Heseltine says he would ring round to try to find a vacancy nearby. But black people often found that when they showed their faces at the alternative venue the vacant room was no longer available:

After two or three such failures, I took a black guest round myself to see him register, but again the neighbouring hotel had suddenly filled up. It was explained to me that the other guests might be upset. The hotel did not wish to give offence, I was told, but they could not afford to lose business.[21]

Ian Josephs, however, finds this account out-of-character. 'I don't believe Michael would put himself out for a black fellow looking for a room – or for a white fellow for that matter. He wouldn't put himself out to help anybody about anything. He wasn't the sort of person who'd put himself out unless it furthered his career.'[22] Perhaps Heseltine thought it would be good for business.

Life at the hotel seems to have been even more uproarious than at Clanricarde Gardens. The New Court was a favourite haunt of American servicemen, and Bayswater was a popular spot for prostitutes, who at that time paraded every night quite openly along the edge of Hyde Park. Anthony Howard used to tease Heseltine by asking, 'How's the brothel?', though in truth the New Court was more respectable than many establishments in the area. Despite his own active sex life, there was always a prudish streak about Heseltine, a belief that the proprieties should be observed. He had a regular struggle to stop US soldiers bringing call-girls back to their rooms.

At times the building appears to have descended into drunken chaos. One evening saw condoms hung from the candelabra. On another occasion, when Heseltine organized a party for his sister, Bubbles, an American sergeant put his shoes and socks in the punch-bowl.

There was also the woman who conducted her own abortion in her bedroom; Heseltine 'went potty' and insisted her boyfriend pay for a new mattress. But perhaps the most bizarre episode was when Jean Taverner found a party of ten drunken American soldiers in one of the rooms. She was horrified to see that one man had been tied to a chair, while the others were cutting him with a knife. On the floor outside lay a naked woman. Heseltine, she says, had taken flight and barricaded himself into his room.[23]

Whatever his tenants and guests were up to, Michael Heseltine found time to lead a relatively discreet love-life himself. For one party in Clanricarde Gardens, Julian Critchley's wife, Paula, brought a friend she hoped might interest Ian Josephs. 'She wasn't my type,' Josephs says, recalling how Heseltine certainly *was* interested. 'Within three-quarters of an hour he was in bed with her, and he never got in touch with her again after that.'[24]

The Bayswater days also saw Heseltine's first serious affair, with a girl called 'Rusty' Rouane. Originally she shared Jean Taverner's room in Clanricarde Gardens, and then went with her to become the receptionist at the New Court Hotel.

Rusty Rouane was a nurse who had returned to England after spending much of her childhood in Canada. Although she came from a working-class background, she had acquired an educated voice with a Canadian accent. A redhead – as her name suggests – she was the sort of woman men couldn't resist. 'She was a very outgoing type,' says Leigh Davies. 'The English girls were rather prim and proper, so she was rather refreshing. She was always laughing, and fun to be around.'[25]

Rusty was already engaged to an RAF officer when she met Heseltine – but the engagement was soon broken, and the pair effectively began living together, though formally they occupied separate rooms. It was far from an ideal match. Rusty may have spoken in a soft voice, but she liked to get her way. Nor did she hesitate to say exactly what she thought about anything, or anybody.

At one point, when the relationship was getting serious, Jean Taverner went home to Swansea with Rusty, and the pair dropped in on Heseltine's parents. 'His mother didn't want to know Rusty. Let's say we weren't welcome. But his father was very charming,' she says.

There was no way Rusty would ever have become a Conservative wife. He tried to make her something she wasn't. She was a very outgoing person – vivacious. She played practical jokes. She wasn't a bit stuffy – quite the opposite. He bought her a poodle and bought her clothes. He opened a savings account for her, to try to get her to save her wages. It just didn't work.[26]

Often Rusty would go out with other men just to make Heseltine jealous. He would get upset about her pinching his monogrammed handkerchiefs – ' "M" for mine,' she joked. There were frequent screaming rows, and Rusty regularly embarrassed Heseltine in front of friends or staff. On one occasion Jean Taverner returned to the hotel to see 'Michael running towards us from the kitchen and all these grapefruit coming through after him, and Rusty screaming at the top of her voice'.[27] 'He put up with hell from her,' says Ian Josephs. 'I think she was one of the few people who ever humiliated Michael. She treated him like a load of shit.'[28]

Nor was the hotel proving a great investment for Heseltine and Josephs. It was difficult to keep up with the mortgage and staff wages, even though they tried everything they could to make a profit. So keen were they to fill all the rooms that in summer, when hotel beds were scarce in London, they'd let out their own bedrooms and sleep in the corridor or stay up all night. On one occasion they even let some guests pitch a tent in the backyard.

And the partners delayed paying bills for as long as they could, says Ian Josephs. They used all the well-known tricks:

There was the practice of sending out cheques which needed two signatures and signing only once. The cheque would come back and we could say we had forgotten the signature. That would delay things a week. There was nothing dishonest about it . . . We would keep people waiting simply because we couldn't pay. The other way is to ensure words and figures on the cheque do not match. You write £330 on the cheque and write £320 in words.[29]

His former partner argues that Heseltine would never have done anything that was actually illegal or dishonest, simply because he had his future political career in mind. Jean Taverner agrees he was 'totally honest and straight', and that there was 'no way Michael would do anything untoward or illegal'.[30]

By the spring of 1957, it was clear the partnership wasn't working, so they sold the New Court Hotel for £19,000. The sale is interesting not because of the profit – about £5,000 – but for who bought the hotel. The official purchaser was a man called Colonel George Sinclair, but within months, if not weeks, the building had passed into the hands of Peter Rachman, the notorious slum landlord of the late 1950s and early 1960s.

The period when Michael Heseltine became involved in property coincided with Peter Rachman's emergence as a powerful landlord in the Bayswater area. Rachman, of course, achieved notoriety – and his name a place in the dictionary – for the way in which he exploited poor tenants crammed into slum properties. He regularly used George Sinclair as a front-man: indeed it was Sinclair who turned Rachman into a landlord originally, and fixed up many of the mortgages on his properties.

A dapper man who wore a camel-hair coat, Sinclair exuded respectability. Frequently he would simply buy up leases and then hand them to Rachman – which is what seems to have happened with the New Court Hotel. Heseltine may not have realized the property would end up in Rachman's hands, but Ian Josephs says that when they sold to Sinclair they 'knew he was well associated with Rachman'.[31]

In 1957 Peter Rachman did not have the reputation he subsequently acquired, yet Michael Heseltine already knew that he was an unsavoury character. By Heseltine's own account their one brief encounter left him 'absolutely horrified':

He turned up outside the New Court Hotel one day and I was standing talking to someone . . . The chap I was talking to turned to him and said, 'We've had an accident – a little baby girl has fallen from the balcony of a property.' And Rachman, without flickering an eyelid, just said, 'Were we insured?' I'll never forget that. It was the only time I ever saw him. Awful.[32]

Heseltine's former hotel soon became one of Rachman's favourite haunts, especially after he set up a gambling joint – the New Court Club – in the basement. Rachman would visit the New Court several evenings a week, sometimes for supper and occasionally with his mistresses, Christine Keeler and Mandy Rice-Davies, the two women who were later at the heart of the Profumo scandal.

Jean Taverner believes that Heseltine knew that once the hotel changed hands the elderly permanent residents were likely to be evicted. Shortly after the property was sold, she recalls returning to the New Court to retrieve some of his possessions which had been left in the hotel safe:

They wouldn't allow Michael on the premises. We had to go in with this Mafioso type to open the safe and take out his personal belongings. There were all these old people crying to me, 'What's going on?' and 'Can't you help us?' It was horrible . . . Then, apparently, all these heavies came in and all the old ladies we had there, who were the bread and butter, were frightened off and had to leave – thrown out really. He knew who Peter Rachman was – that he would no way keep old people there paying £5 a week for a room when they could be making a fortune out of it.[33]

Ian Josephs confirms that their elderly residents were thrown out when they sold the hotel, but considers that neither he nor Heseltine bears any responsibility for this. Nor did the new purchasers warn them what they were going to do. 'But it wouldn't have worried me if they had. It wouldn't have stopped me selling it, and it wouldn't have stopped him.'[34]

How Rachman and Sinclair came to buy the New Court Hotel from the two partners is also interesting. According to Ian Josephs, the original link was through Raymond Nash, a Lebanese-born businessman who was also known as Raymond Naccachian. Nash and Rachman jointly owned the El Condor club in Wardour Street – one of the most fashionable night-spots in London. Later, Nash achieved his own infamy when the Japanese gave him a suspended eighteen-month jail term for gold-smuggling offences; the British authorities refused to let him return to the UK.

Josephs visited the El Condor several times and says he met both Nash and Rachman. At one stage, he adds, Heseltine even agreed to do some bookkeeping for Raymond Nash. 'We both knew he was a dodgy character. If Michael didn't know it at first, he certainly did when he started to do the books at the club.'[35] Heseltine soon abandoned the work, says Josephs, because he refused to fiddle the accounts in the way Nash wanted. When he was asked about Raymond Nash in 1990, however, Heseltine said he had no recollection of him or the incident.[36] Nor does Nash recall employing Heseltine.[37]

The sale of the New Court Hotel marked the end of the Heseltine–Josephs partnership, though they remained friends. There had been disagreements over how the property should be run: Josephs wanted it to be more of a boarding-house with permanent residents, while Heseltine envisaged more of a hotel. The underlying problem, however, was financial. Heseltine might now have acquired his favourite car – a Jaguar – but he still felt he wasn't making money fast enough.

Moreover, in the spring of 1956 Heseltine had found himself a more promising business partner. Clive Labovitch, also an articled clerk, said they bumped into each other one day while going to an accountancy lecture in the City. Heseltine's own recollection is that a phone call brought them together. Each naturally inquired what the other was up to. Labovitch mentioned a new publishing venture of his called the *Directory of Opportunities for Graduates*, or *DOG*, a careers guide for undergraduates at Oxford and Cambridge. Heseltine suggested that it ought to go out to students at every university, and then it could charge better advertising rates. 'It was that single sentence,' Heseltine once claimed, 'that turned me into a publisher.'[38]

'I made an instant decision to ask him to join me,' Labovitch explained years later. 'I was so struck by Michael Heseltine's instant grasp of the problems of an activity he had never previously thought about, and by the way he went straight to a central problem, analysed it, and solved it.'[39]

Clive Labovitch's family worked in the West Yorkshire tailoring industry, which by coincidence was the same background as some of Heseltine's ancestors, of course. The Labovitches, however, had come to Britain from Byelorussia early this century. Clive's father, Mark, had begun as a tailor's apprentice in Leeds, and then made millions between the wars building a clothing company called Darley Mills. The firm manufactured off-the-peg garments for the growing middle market which had enough money to buy new clothes but could not afford traditional tailoring. Mark Labovitch had become a well-known patriarchal figure in Leeds – a charismatic man who was known to his employees as 'Mr Mark', and who was the 'lay leader of the local Jewish community'.[40] In time, he expected his three sons to take over the family business.

But Clive Labovitch, his youngest boy, had ideas of branching out on his own. Although he was a quiet, gentle, rather shy character, he'd entertained ideas of becoming a successful publisher from his schooldays at Clifton College, when he'd started a magazine and learnt calligraphy. At Oxford he'd spent £2,000 buying *Cherwell*, then a run-down student magazine, and turned it into the weekly university newspaper. Apart from negotiating to hire an office from the Union, he and Heseltine had then also discussed the idea of the debating society buying the paper from Labovitch. Fortunately the plan was dropped – it would have been disastrous both for the Union's finances and for *Cherwell*'s editorial independence.

Clive Labovitch's long-term aim was to start a national glossy magazine – a version of the American magazine *Esquire*. In the meantime, *DOG* looked like a money-spinner which could establish a financial base from which Labovitch could launch his British *Esquire*.

In time, *DOG* would become the 'underlying strength', in Heseltine's words, on which his early business was based.[41] 'Forty pages at £40 a page,' he would recall years later, 'which was about £1,500 revenue per issue.'[42] Yet the careers directory landed in his lap thanks only to some business dealings which left Labovitch's initial associates feeling decidedly bruised.

The first problem was that, though Clive Labovitch is often credited with inventing *DOG*, it wasn't his idea. It had originally been suggested to him by a Cambridge graduate, Robert Myers, who worked in the same accountancy firm. Labovitch, who still owned *Cherwell*, was explaining to Myers the difficulty of selling advertising space in an annual handbook *Cherwell* also published, called *Oxford University What's What*. Myers suggested including a supplement about graduate recruitment, and offered to sell the advertising space, provided Labovitch paid him 12½ per cent commission plus 30 per cent of the ultimate profit. The resulting first edition of the *Directory of Opportunities for Graduates* appeared in October 1955, inserted into that autumn's edition of *What's What*. The booklet was then reprinted and sent to Cambridge students too.

DOG was a brilliantly simple concept. From today's standpoint, when companies spend millions on recruiting graduates, it also looks blindingly obvious. But in 1955 there were no directories with lists of companies interested in hiring people with degrees, or details of what the jobs entailed. Myers had got the idea of an employment directory partly from watching the problems his friends had in choosing suitable employers after university. Selling the advertising took remarkably little effort. 'I just wrote to them,' recalls Myers; 'I didn't have to telephone.' His girlfriend typed out circular letters and sent them to personnel managers suggested by the Oxford Appointments Committee, and the orders came flooding in. Once the top graduate recruiters – such as ICI and Shell – were signed up, other firms felt they too had to buy space. 'This was money for old rope, really,' Myers confesses. Nearly every page was paid for, with hardly any space devoted to unpaid editorial content. He soon envisaged other directories for school-leavers and qualified men.[43]

Today, Robert Myers confesses to naïvety in his dealings with Labovitch, though he attaches no blame to Heseltine, whom he never met. Myers had assumed the deal for 12½ per cent commission plus 30 per cent of profits would stand for all subsequent editions, but Labovitch had other plans. In the end Myers parted with his idea for just £450, even though he realized it could have made him a fortune.[44]

In fact this prospect had made him uncomfortable: 'I knew I need never have worked again. I thought it was immoral.'[45]

When Labovitch suddenly decided to bring Heseltine on board, he faced another problem: he had already recruited a partner to help in publishing *DOG*. Michael Kavanagh, who'd been at New College with Labovitch, didn't like what he'd seen of Michael Heseltine at Oxford and was not prepared to work with him. Somehow, though it is not quite clear how, Kavanagh was eased out. For ever after Michael Kavanagh, too, would be aggrieved at the way he was pushed aside in favour of Heseltine and thus denied a share of the huge profits which *DOG* later generated.

For Heseltine, Clive Labovitch didn't just supply a brilliant idea in *DOG*: there was also an added financial advantage. In February 1956 Mark Labovitch had died, passing his fortune to his sons. Although most of it was tied up in Darley Mills and Labovitch could not easily release it, the family wealth would underpin the new partners' future ventures. 'Of course,' Labovitch himself once admitted, 'I knew I wouldn't starve if the thing went wrong and I lost my money. If you've got . . . no family to fall back on perhaps it is less easy to take a risk.'[46]

Although their publishing business was called Cornmarket Press – after the street in Oxford – the two partners actually worked from the London offices of Darley Mills in Lower James Street in Soho. They had only limited space, but when they needed to impress visitors they could also use the Darley Mills boardroom, complete with its textile displays.

In 1957 the second edition of *DOG* came out as a hardback book – increased from 44 pages to 160 – and was distributed to students nationwide, as Heseltine had suggested. It was soon obvious that gathering the recruitment advertising took only about four months each year, so Labovitch and Heseltine quickly took up Robert Myers's other ideas of a *Directory of Opportunities for School Leavers* (*DOSL*) and a *Directory of Opportunities for Qualified Men* (*DOQM*) to fill the remaining eight months. Publishing the three volumes at four-monthly intervals meant the workload was spread throughout the year. By 1959 they were planning the first overseas editions – for Canada and then the United States.

Heseltine and Labovitch soon took on a secretary, and also employed Michael's sister, Bubbles. They set up a string of limited companies, and Heseltine made full use of his accountancy connections to enhance the boards of directors. Until 1958 he was still an articled clerk, though when he passed his intermediate exams he moved from Peat Marwick to a smaller firm – Shipley, Blackburn. From his new employers Heseltine recruited Cyril Solly, a distinguished elderly accountant who dealt with Charles Forte's financial affairs, and Thomas Ackland, who agreed to look after the two partners' books. 'He and Clive Labovitch ran it by the seat of their pants,' says Ackland. 'It was very much a hands-on operation, and they worked all the hours that God sent.'[47]

Far more significant, especially in the long term, was Heseltine's decision in May 1958 to appoint a new advertising manager for the directory series. Lindsay Masters, who was paid an initial salary of £850 a year, proved to be a brilliant choice. Over the years Masters has probably done more than anybody else to make Michael Heseltine's fortune – certainly more than Clive Labovitch ever did, and arguably more than Heseltine himself.

Yet, at the time, few would have predicted great things for Masters. Though he was the son of a rich businessman, he'd had a troubled childhood and led a drunken, dissipated, bohemian life through his late teens and early twenties. He had actually been at Oxford at the same time as Labovitch and Heseltine, but they knew him only slightly, and then he was sent down for forging his landlady's signature on a library form. After Oxford, his wealthy mother refused to support him any longer and he took a string of odd jobs, generally selling things. He traded blankets to American GIs in Germany, then trudged door-to-door with the writer V. S. Naipaul, trying to persuade people to buy encyclopaedias. He'd sold dresses in Mary Quant's shop, and most recently had spent time as advertising salesman-cum-journalist on the magazine *The Baker*.

Heseltine was content to let Masters and Labovitch concentrate on the publishing side of the business, while he continued trying to make money from property. In the 1950s everyone assumed there was a killing to be made in property; and here he now got more family funding.

In April 1957 Rupert Heseltine had died suddenly of a heart attack. It was a great shock to the family, since he was only fifty-five. His son would always miss his support, and regret that his father never saw his career unfold. Michael's mother, Eileen, was prompted by her husband's death to embark on various ventures of her own with the £6,000 she inherited from her husband. In Swansea she started a small shop which ran an interior-design business. She also invested with her son and Clive Labovitch in their first property purchase together.

With a £10,000 mortgage they bought two neighbouring houses in South Kensington. Numbers 29 and 31 Tregunter Road were far smarter addresses than either of Heseltine's previous premises, being barely a hundred yards from The Boltons, a street which today supposedly has more Rolls-Royces per parking-meter than almost any in London. Later they bought two more houses in the next street, whose gardens backed on to the Tregunter properties – numbers 30 and 32 Cathcart Road. Here the two partners developed what they liked to call, rather pretentiously, 'executive suites' – fairly large rooms for which young professionals, generally living two to a room, paid £5 a week. For that, the tenants also got breakfast and dinner, and lunches at weekends, all served in the dining-room. There was a communal sitting-room too.

Originally the 'Mrs Taylor' role was assigned to a retired Army officer, Major Denny, until an auditor reported that he'd embezzled nearly £1,000 from rents. 'I remember Michael dealing with him rather summarily,' says Thomas Ackland. 'Heseltine hauled him in and confronted him, and said, "Out!" Dismissed him on the spot.'[48] He didn't bother to prosecute. Denny's place was taken by a young architecture student, and later by a middle-aged American couple called West.

Initially Heseltine himself lived in the basement of Tregunter Road, which was cut off from the rest of the building. His flat seems to have had considerably more style than either of his previous dwellings. People recall a large drawing-room dominated by a magnificent chandelier, with lush carpets. There was even a form of underfloor central heating. 'The most remarkable and amazing thing,' says Anthony Howard, 'is he had a chauffeur with a uniform and a peaked cap. I used to say to Michael, "Michael, why? What on earth do you want that for? Why don't you take the tube or the bus, like me?" And he said, "No. People take you at the evaluation you give yourself." '[49]

Suddenly, without having yet made much money, Heseltine had acquired the trappings of wealth; yet officially he was still an articled clerk. One reason for his new lifestyle was his relationship with Clive Labovitch. But the tenants of Tregunter and Cathcart Roads never saw much of their young landlord. They thought of him as a remote, patrician figure who had acquired a rather dandified air; they might occasionally get a glimpse of him dashing in late at night with his overcoat draped over his shoulders like a cape.

Heseltine, the Wests and the whole set-up in South Kensington later achieved the distinction of being portrayed in fiction. The American writer Gail Godwin lived there as a tenant, and her story 'Mr Bedford' disguises the ménage very thinly. 'Tregunter', as Godwin calls the house, appears almost unaltered; the Wests become the Eastons, while the landlord she never meets is Martin Eglantine:

'Eglantine's a real entrepreneur,' said Mr Easton. 'He owns dozens of houses like this, all over London. Buys 'em up quick as I can snap my fingers.'[50]

Another future writer lodging in 'Tregunter' was a teenaged and impoverished Nigel Dempster. The future *Daily Mail* gossip-columnist lived there 'illegally', sleeping on a friend's sofa, and availed himself of daily breakfasts, though not, he insists, the Heseltine suppers. Dempster remembers the property as being 'rather like a country school'; the tenants tended to be 'lads and lassies up from Lancashire and Yorkshire' rather than public-school types, and they were generally in their twenties. There was much 'fraternizing' between them, and one girl living on the Cathcart Road side was known for being especially generous to the male residents. 'She loved bonking,' says Dempster. 'She had a single room to herself. She came from up north, and she was an easy bonk. And when we got unhappy we used to wander down the garden and knock on her door.'[51]

A hard-nosed landlord Michael Heseltine certainly was not. The only rule he imposed was that tenants could not come down to Sunday breakfast in their dressing-gowns. Heseltine was rarely around, and left the Wests to run things. They allowed one tenant, Andrew Baker, to stay there even though he could no longer afford any rent because of heavy fines from a car accident. Baker was allowed to live in a small space at the end of the passage, which he cordoned off with a velvet curtain and filled with a bed and a potted palm. The architecture student who'd once managed the property stayed on secretly for several months after being sacked – he simply retired to a tiny room he'd built in the loft-space, which he'd carpeted and hooked up to the electricity.

If Heseltine was being inattentive, then one should bear in mind that by 1959 the Tregunter/Cathcart Road site was only a small part of his growing property empire. Another house was acquired in Clanricarde Gardens and then let as four flats. The most ambitious project, though, involved an investment of more than £11,000 on the freehold of a row of seven houses in Stafford Terrace, just off High Street, Kensington. The scheme was gradually to convert the block into self-contained flats and maisonettes, and then sell them one by one. To do this Heseltine and Labovitch set up their own building operation; it was run first by Major Denny and then by Ron Rumble, an old acquaintance from Swansea whose family was in the building trade.

Their very first buyer in Stafford Terrace later served as a Tory MP with Heseltine. Thomas Stuttaford can still picture the way Heseltine, Labovitch and Denny would 'walk up and down the street full of clipboards and looking important'. Stuttaford had 'no grumbles' with the conversion work, but his was the show-flat.[52] Much of the development ended up accommodating family and colleagues. Michael's sister, Bubbles, took a flat; then both Clive Labovitch and Lindsay Masters moved there; and later so did Heseltine himself.

One of the leaseholders – a film producer called John Box – recalls the time they formed a tenants' association to negotiate with the landlord. 'We talked to Michael about it, and he may have had his tongue in his cheek but he said, "Fine, as long as there's no women on it!" '[53] Years later Box would relate the story to Denis Thatcher, for potential use as ammunition.

By the end of 1958 Heseltine was on his way, making good progress after the first two stumbling years with Ian Josephs. At the beginning of 1959 the rising publisher and property developer was tipped in the

Daily Express as one of the seven 'daring young men' most likely to succeed over the coming twelve months. Under the heading 'My Kind of Men', the writer listed the 'unstodgy' Heseltine alongside the fashion designer Alexander Plunket-Greene, the guitarist Julian Bream and the comedian Joe Melia.[54]

To those in the know, the feature must have raised a smile – not least because it had been written by Heseltine's old flame from Oxford, Sarah Rothschild. Heseltine was indeed 'likely to go places', but not in 1959.

6. *Sixty-One Days in the Guards*

Tuesday 6 January 1959 was the day Michael Heseltine had been trying to avoid for the last seven and a half years. Along with twenty-two other recruits, he was ordered to report to the Guards depot at Caterham in Surrey – the centre where all guardsmen did their basic training. His National Service had begun.

'Life became hell for eight weeks,' says Johnny Rickett, who arrived at Caterham on the same day and ended up as a brigadier. 'It was one of the blackest days of my life . . . It seemed a ghastly place – more like a prison than a training establishment.'[1]

National Service had been introduced in peacetime in 1947. All men above the age of eighteen were liable to spend twelve months – later increased to two years – in either the Army, the Navy or the Air Force, unless they were medically unfit. But, along the way, there were accepted reasons for people to defer the start of their conscription.

There had already been two occasions when Michael Heseltine might naturally have been expected to begin his National Service. The first was when he left Shrewsbury in 1951 – it was quite common for men to go straight into National Service after school. However, the Korean War had already started, and thousands of conscripts were being sent out to fight in the Far East; there was therefore a serious possibility of being shot at or even killed. Oxford, in contrast, was a safe option, and a way of deferring matters. Indeed, one of the great advantages of Pembroke had been that the master of the college, Frederick Homes Dudden, believed strongly that students should go straight from school to university, and leave any military duties until afterwards.

The second occasion was when Heseltine left Oxford at the end of 1954. 'They seem eager to have me,' Heseltine told *Cherwell* the following March, 'and send me lots of correspondence.'[2] He himself was somewhat less eager. Fortunately his accountancy training in London provided at least three more years' grace, since any professional studies were considered good reason to postpone the call-up. As time passed, Heseltine must have been confident of avoiding conscription altogether, as it was becoming increasingly clear that it would soon be abolished.

There had been big cuts in defence spending following the Korean War, and National Service was an obvious candidate for savings. In 1957 the Defence Secretary, Duncan Sandys, published a White Paper announcing that conscription would soon be phased out. In the years that followed, however, there was considerable confusion over how long abolition would take, and over who was still liable to be conscripted. Initially the government spoke of the final recruits being called up by December 1958, but this deadline was soon put back. Then there was the question over what happened to those men, like Heseltine, who had so far managed to defer National Service. At first the government decided that, as from April 1958, men on deferment would not be called up. But then, suddenly, this policy was reversed. Instead of exempting deferees altogether, ministers decided that it was much fairer to concentrate the final National Service intakes on the very men who had so far avoided it.

Having failed his accountancy finals in 1958, Heseltine could no longer defer his conscription on the grounds that he was completing his professional training. Yet, even while he'd been postponing his National Service, Heseltine had been making preparations in case the awful day did arrive. If he had to join the forces, he would apply for a distinguished regiment and try to secure a commission as an officer. In late 1955, eighteen months before he died, Colonel Heseltine had begun pulling strings among his South Wales establishment friends – notably through Brigadier Sir Michael Llewelyn, a Territorial Army officer who was also lord lieutenant of Radnorshire. He wanted Michael to secure a commission with the Welsh Guards, one of the most popular regiments. The interview went well, and Heseltine was eventually given the choice of beginning National Service in either September 1958 or the following January. He chose the latter.

In a way, Heseltine was rather unlucky, for he was called up at almost the last possible moment. In July 1958 the War Office introduced a rule that 'With a few exceptions, men remain liable to call-up only until they reach the age of 26.'[3] Michael Heseltine would reach the age of twenty-six in March 1959, and when he arrived at Caterham that January he must have been one of the oldest National Service recruits in the whole of the armed forces.

But, if military training could no longer be avoided, Heseltine had a new plan which would ensure that his stint was cut short – but in a way that appeared reasonable, and even respectable. Harold Macmillan was bound to call a general election by June 1960, and in all likelihood polling would take place well before then. Heseltine had discovered that under Queen's Regulations any serviceman who became a parliamentary candidate automatically had to leave the forces once the election was called, and he would not necessarily be made to return afterwards.[4] The election, then, offered an opportunity to revive his dormant political career, and to get out of the Army.

His former business partner, Ian Josephs, confirms that Heseltine had carefully organized things this way. 'His whole idea was that he would stand for Parliament so that he could be discharged from the Army. That was always the plan from the word go.'[5] The scheme might not have worked had he started his military service even a year earlier, but Josephs says that Heseltine timed matters so that his two years' training was bound to be interrupted, if not curtailed, by a general election.

In fact only a month after arriving at Caterham, Heseltine was chosen as the Conservative candidate for Gower, close to his home town of Swansea. There was no competition for the Tory nomination; indeed, the local party was probably delighted to find such a young, enthusiastic and glamorous candidate to fight what was a solid Labour seat. But Queen's Regulations formally prevented Heseltine from campaigning in public before the election was called, and in practice it would have been hard for him to get away from the barracks.

The brigade squad Michael Heseltine had joined at Caterham seems to have been a fairly select group, with a number hoping to secure Army commissions. Most were still teenagers, only months out of school, and in many cases this meant public school. All were there to be transformed from civilians into soldiers.

Although many had experienced the Officers' Training Corps at school, Caterham was the real thing, and none of them found the change easy. 'It was non-stop drill, physical training, weapons training, cleaning kit,' Johnny Rickett remembers. 'I used to be cleaning my boots in the bog at midnight, and Michael did too. He loathed it.'[6]

'It was very tough indeed,' remembers John Skeffington, who later succeeded as the seventh Viscount of Massereene and Ferrard – 'mostly drilling from seven in the morning until dark.' To the much older Heseltine, he feels, the rest of them 'must have seemed like a lot of stupid little schoolboys. Five years makes a lot of difference at that age.'[7]

Although Caterham was considered quite a good posting for officers, and the site boasted fine sports facilities, the depot was hardly an attractive prospect for fresh recruits, especially in the middle of winter. They lived in two wooden huts, each accommodating about ten men, ten beds and ten lockers, and heated by a tortoise stove which had to be kept going all night. Their latrines and showers were in a separate building; in the harsh winter of 1959 the fifty-yard walk often had to be made in the rain or freezing cold.

Sergeant Peter Horsfall, the Yorkshireman in charge of the brigade squad's every move for the next nine weeks, had a reputation for toughness. 'Horsfall was very fierce,' says George Rees, who later joined the Welsh Guards with Heseltine. 'He had a waxed moustache, and when he was drilling us on the parade ground, marching us up and down in double quick time, he would shout so loudly and constantly that foam would drip off his moustache. It was quite terrifying! We were scared of him, but we knew it wasn't going to go on for ever.'[8] 'He chased us from morning till night,' remembers another recruit.

'It was a high-pressure course – physically and mentally,' Horsfall himself explains. 'It was quite a struggle for them to get through.' The day began with reveille at 6.15 a.m., then breakfast at seven before the first parade at eight. There followed nine periods of forty-five minutes – five in the morning and four in the afternoon – concentrating on drill, weapon training and PT. At about six in the evening recruits would clean their kits, or study, or prepare lectures. 'They were very lucky if they got to the NAAFI [the canteen] for half an hour,' says Horsfall.[9] 'Lights out' was at 10.15 p.m.

On day two they were marched to the barber's for the traditional short back and sides. Heseltine was particularly upset about losing

1. Michael Heseltine's ancestor Charles Dibdin, the eighteenth-century composer, actor, dramatist and song-writer.

2. Heseltine's great-grandfather William made money in the tea trade and was a pioneer of grocery chains. In 1890, when he discovered his fortune was lost, he shot himself.

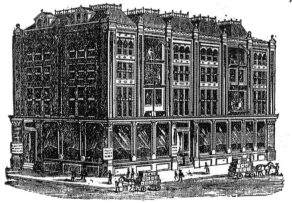

W. HESELTINE & SON,

Wholesale Tea Dealers and Blenders to the Trade,

WILSON STREET and EARL STREET, FINSBURY, E.C.

Blended Tea Department.

Terms: Two Months Nett.

Discount: ½d. per lb. from 1/3 to 1/7, and 1d. per lb. from 1/9 to 2/6 for cash in 14 days.

Carriage is allowed upon Chests (100 lbs.) and Half-Chests (60 lbs. and 40 lbs.) and may be deducted from Invoice.

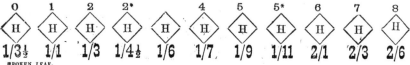

0	1	2	2*	4	5	5*	6	7	8
⟨H⟩	⟨H⟩	⟨H⟩	⟨H⟩	⟨H⟩	⟨H⟩	⟨H⟩	⟨H⟩	⟨H⟩	⟨H⟩
1/3½	1/1	1/3	1/4½	1/6	1/7	1/9	1/11	2/1	2/3	2/6

BROKEN LEAF.

3. Six days old, with his nurse, Elizabeth Davies.

4. Michael and his father, Rupert Heseltine, a Territorial Army officer.

5. Michael (centre) at Langland Bay near Swansea, where the Heseltines had a beach-hut.

6. In the back row of the Moser's Hall photograph at Shrewsbury. With his blond hair and pinstripe suit he always stood out.

7. A fishing expedition on the river Tawe. Later he would light-heartedly claim to have poached every river in South Wales.

FRYING TONIGHT

GEORGE BENNETT

8. How the university newspaper *Cherwell* portrayed Heseltine's promotion of cheap meals in the Oxford Union restaurant.

9. From his days as secretary of the Oxford Union in 1954, Heseltine's distinctive appearance has always attracted cartoonists.

10. The 1950s celebrities Sir Bernard and Lady Docker opened Heseltine's new nightclub in the Oxford Union cellars, and then offered to pay the £600 cost of development.

11. Hosting an Oxford Union debate dinner. Heseltine loved the glamour and ceremony of being Union president.

12. Presiding over a Union debate.

13. Heseltine, in the middle row, put off National Service for eight years before joining the brigade squad at Caterham Guards Depot in 1959.

14. Heseltine's military training was ended after only eight months when he fought Gower in the 1959 election.

15. The young entrepreneur with his several lines of business.

16. The glossy magazine *About Town* was revolutionary for its day, and great fun, but proved a financial disaster.

17. Outside Stafford Terrace, Kensington, which he turned into flats. In 1962 Heseltine's property ventures brought his business close to bankruptcy.

18. Although Clive Labovitch split from the partnership in 1966, Heseltine had begged him to stay and they remained friends.

his flowing mane. 'He was cropped like a convict,' says a friend. 'To Michael, it was like shearing Samson of his locks.'

In the first week three recruits dropped out, and Heseltine was one of several men to be injured, in his case on the right ankle. 'That year,' says Horsfall, 'the ground was so frozen that the first time they went over the obstacle course they got ankle injuries. Many of them hadn't worn boots before, and some of the obstacles were eight-foot high. I just let the PT instructor go ahead as normal, not realizing the ground was so hard. I got a bit of flak over that. They were hobbling around for several weeks, but it proved their merit because they still managed to complete the course.'[10]

The squad didn't know it, but Peter Horsfall felt they were an unusually promising bunch. His judgement proved to be right, for the group eventually produced a brigadier who commanded the Welsh Guards in the Falklands, several successful businessmen, two members of the House of Lords and, of course, a Deputy Prime Minister.

Michael Heseltine stood out not just as much older than most of the squad, says Horsfall, but also for his skill at one particular exercise. 'Captain Trevor Dawson, the commander, used to get me to set them lecturettes – talks lasting about five minutes – during the period they were cleaning their kit in the evening. They had to stand up in front of the boys and talk on any subject. Some of them would struggle, but it was Michael Heseltine's forte. Sometimes his lectures were more than five minutes, but it didn't matter. The only principle we applied was it had to have a beginning, middle and end.'[11] Later on, Dawson chose the subjects himself; the recruits researched them in their spare moments, and then they spoke for fifteen minutes at a time.

It was to be expected, of course, that Michael Heseltine should quickly and quite naturally assume the role of unofficial squad leader. Generally the others respected his experience, though there was also some envy. According to George Rees, 'He had a good team spirit, which you need in an environment like that. He mucked in very well and was helpful towards others.'[12] Johnny Rickett agrees: 'It was clear to us he was the most mature, and had lots of drive and responsibility. He was a very dynamic person.'[13] Tom Wills, who was in the same block as Heseltine, thought he was a bit of a barrack-room lawyer. 'I wouldn't say he was arrogant, but he made it known he was top dog, as it were. I think we all liked him.'[14] And certainly Heseltine never disguised his long-term ambitions. Nobody recalls his discussing politics much, but several colleagues recollect his openly expressing determination to reach the top in Civvy Street, or more particularly Downing Street.

Unusually, the would-be premier and soon-to-be tycoon was permitted to pursue his business life in the few spare hours recruits were granted. Johnny Rickett says that, quite apart from the lack of time, 'it was difficult to make phone calls; you had to queue up. We weren't allowed out, and the only leave was one weekend after four weeks.'[15] Heseltine's former Army colleagues recall him explaining how a manager was running his business while he was away – by this, presumably, he meant his partner, Clive Labovitch.

Heseltine was given special permission to meet Labovitch on Saturday afternoons. Labovitch would drive down to Caterham in the company car. 'This fellow used to turn up in the Jag, and Michael would sit alongside him,' recalls Peter Horsfall:

They weren't allowed to come into the barrack room to discuss business. Captain Dawson had instructions from above to say we mustn't stop this young chap who was doing exceptionally well. There was grumbling about it, and Captain Dawson was a bit put out about it himself. But they had a point. When you get a chap who's making his mark in Civvy Street, it would be unfair not to let him have his head. It never interfered with his duties.[16]

After a month recruits were given their first weekend pass, but getting past the sergeant on the front gate, to leave the barracks, could take hours. 'We were always sent back,' says Tom Wills, 'either with a loose thread or a dusty eyehole or something. We had to look immaculate.'[17] Heseltine apparently had no such difficulties: his chauffeur came to collect him in the Jaguar and whisked him out through the back gate unchallenged.

After nine weeks of basic training Heseltine had done so well on the assault course that Peter Horsfall made him and a colleague, Christopher Madden, 'first among equals' recruit leaders, which entitled them to wear a little white strip on their sleeve at the passing-out parade. This was held in mid-March before the Caterham commandant, Colonel Vernon Erskine-Crum of the Scots Guards. 'I was really proud of them at the end,' says Horsfall. 'They were an amazing squad. Colonel Erskine-Crum said, "I've got to tell you, and the regimental sergeant-major would agree, that it's the best turned out squad I've ever seen." '[18]

Michael Heseltine was particularly commended for his 'turnout', but in other respects his superiors found him a disappointment. Trevor Dawson felt Heseltine was too self-opinionated and complacent, but recognized he was also intelligent and would do well if he put his mind to it. Heseltine's weapon training had shown promise; his arms drill had been average, but his foot drill had been less than satisfactory, partly because he had been injured for much of the two-month course.

His weight had fallen sharply, from 195 down to 171 pounds. Friends recall being shocked by Heseltine's gaunt appearance when he returned home on leave and dropped by, hoping for a good meal.

In March 1959 Heseltine moved to a rather more civilized regime, the Mons Officer Cadet School at Aldershot. He lived in what was known as 'spider accommodation' (because it looked like a spider from the air) and had the luxury of a lavatory and washbasin in the same block. Mons provided a sixteen-week course to teach potential officers how to lead infantry platoons. By then, about a third of the original twenty-three-strong brigade squad had left. Six had failed the War Office Selection Board's exams, known as the WOSB – a series of intelligence tests together with practical exercises to establish leadership qualities, teamwork and initiative (such as leading a platoon across an imaginary river infested with crocodiles).

Mons involved yet more drill, this time under RSM Desmond Lynch, the senior non-commissioned officer, who was described by one of his superiors as a 'tyrant'. 'Lynch was a huge man,' says Christopher Madden. 'He gave us a speech and told us, "You call me 'Sir', and I call you 'Sir'. The difference is that you mean it and I don't." '[19] Lynch himself remembers Heseltine as an exceptionally good recruit. 'He was always very smart and well turned out. His boots were always well-polished and his belt properly blancoed.'[20]

'We had lectures and a lot of physical exercise,' Johnny Rickett explains, and there were a couple of exams on military tactics. 'We spent three months there, and our final exercise was at Sennybridge near Brecon. It was a tough experience – out for several days in the Welsh rain – but it went OK. We learnt how to live in the field.'[21]

Another cadet at Mons was Hugh Myddelton, also an older entrant, who became friendly with Heseltine and later worked for him. 'There wasn't much time for socializing,' he remembers, 'but we were occasionally given evenings off. On our rare excursions out, four or five of us would go together to the same place. We were mostly frightfully hungry, so we tried to find the best restaurant in the vicinity and eat as much as we could.'[22]

At Mons, four cadets were traditionally picked to be junior under officers – or JUOs. Heseltine, Madden and Myddelton were among those chosen, and the practice then was that one of the four JUOs would later be appointed as the senior under officer, or SUO, whose job it was to command part of the passing-out parade in front of some distinguished inspecting officer. The choice would be made by the company commander at Mons, Major Harold Gatehouse, who coincidentally – and neither man knew it at the time – was a distant relation of Stella Gatehouse, the woman who had taught Heseltine public speaking at Oxford.

The Mons cadets reckoned there was only one contender for the job of senior under officer. Michael Heseltine was older and more mature than most of the others, and he himself seemed confident of getting the post. Christopher Madden vividly remembers how things turned out: 'I was in a lecture and was called out to go and see the company commander. As I marched down, I saw Michael Heseltine coming back from seeing him, looking like thunder. Then I was told it was me who was going to take on the SUO rank.'[23]

To this day, Madden is still baffled that he got the job, rather than Heseltine. Major Gatehouse undoubtedly held a high opinion of Heseltine, and one of the platoon instructors, Captain Peter Mitchell, recommended him as an outstanding candidate, with charismatic leadership qualities. But the other instructors had reservations about his character.

A critical issue was almost certainly what one might call Heseltine's overconfidence, or, more bluntly, his arrogance. 'He made everyone assume he was top dog,' says Madden. 'He may have rather overdone it with the company commander – making him feel he reported to

Mike and not the other way round!'[24] More telling, perhaps, was that Heseltine was frank about his intention of staying in the Army no longer than National Service required. Indeed, Peter Mitchell remembers Heseltine explaining at his initial interview that he'd hoped to avoid National Service altogether by going to Oxford first.[25]

Initially, says Christopher Madden, Heseltine found it difficult to accept that he was not in charge, and was not very supportive. 'I think Michael had made the assumption, as had all of us, that he was going to be it almost by right, and that caused the difficulty.'[26] Having overcome much stiffer opposition to reach the prize he coveted at Oxford, Heseltine must have regarded it as a formality to achieve the senior position available at Mons, especially when so many of his colleagues were much younger and less experienced.

'We had the proverbial drink, at my invitation,' says Madden, 'and I said to him, "If this is going to work, we have to work together, otherwise it's going to be rough on both of us. It wasn't my fault, but there it is – that's how the cards have fallen." And I have to say, to his eternal credit, he actually helped me tremendously from thereon in, with advice and support and guidance. That couldn't have been easy for him, but he did. And, goodness me, it was a tremendous help.'[27]

In a way, this was a salutary experience for later life. It would not, of course, be the last time that Michael Heseltine was denied the top job. Three decades later, he would again be forced to overcome intense disappointment and assume the role of loyal second-in-command to a younger, less experienced rival who had emerged only at the final moment.

One way Heseltine swallowed his pride was to help Madden in an area where he had some expertise. At the July 1959 passing-out dinner, the senior under officer was required to make a speech on behalf of the company in front of all the Mons top brass. The occasion, held on the night before the passing-out parade itself, was regarded as a chance to let off steam, and the SUO's speech was traditionally an opportunity for the cadets to get their own back on the instructors who had given them such a hard time for the previous four months. Christopher Madden was extremely nervous about the whole prospect. 'I'd never made a speech in my life. I turned to Mike, with his experience of the Oxford Union, and he coached me and helped me with the contents of the speech, and suggested how I should deliver it.'[28]

Heseltine was now formally commissioned as a National Service officer, with the rank of second lieutenant – or a 'one-pipper' as it is known. With Johnny Rickett and George Rees, he reported to the 1st Battalion Welsh Guards at Pirbright in Surrey, where he was posted to the Prince of Wales Company and expected to take command of a platoon of about thirty men. After the rigours of training, his new routine was not arduous. It left some time to look after his business affairs and for the political commitment which was to ensure that his time with the Welsh Guards was brief.

Even before leaving the Mons Cadet School in July 1959, Heseltine had sought permission to stand in the forthcoming general election, which was now expected in the autumn. Peter Mitchell says he had been warned long in advance about Heseltine's political commitments. 'I remember he said with some glee that if an election were to be called he would have to leave the course.'[29]

Heseltine seems to have made a less favourable impression on his fellow Welsh Guards than he did at either of the training schools. 'He wasn't really interested,' says Major Ivor Ramsden. 'It was just something to be done.'[30] 'His Army service was a disaster,' another argues. 'He gave a bad impression. He was arrogant, very self-assured and, generally speaking, not interested in soldiering, and it showed. His time with the regiment was undistinguished to say the least.' But then Michael Heseltine hardly had much time to distinguish himself: he was with the Welsh Guards for just two months.

Among his fellow second lieutenants in the regiment at that time was Charles Guthrie, who is now Sir Charles and in 1996 was appointed Chief of the Defence Staff, the top British military officer. 'I have no doubt that he was a somewhat reluctant soldier,' Guthrie says of the future Defence Secretary:

There were many officers and soldiers in the Welsh Guards who would prefer not to have been conscripted and felt they could have been doing something more useful. His contemporaries liked him and enjoyed his company but I do think some of the more senior officers of the Battalion were irritated by the fact that he made it fairly plain that he would prefer to be doing something other than soldiering. He became something of a spokesman for the young officers and I remember him advocating our case with the Adjutant when our collective performance was criticized.[31]

Like his father during the war, Heseltine did a brief stint in Northern Ireland – the ten-day Exercise Red Onion over rugged, mountainous terrain near Limavady in County Londonderry. But his days in the Welsh Guards are remembered for one particular blunder at the Pirbright camp.

During his first rifle inspection in charge of his platoon, Heseltine tried to assert his new authority by examining not only the weapons of the lower ranks but also the rifle belonging to his platoon sergeant, David 'Smokey' Lloyd. This was a terrible *faux pas*, contrary to all Army procedures and traditions, and likely to ruin the relationship with his second-in-command. 'You trust your sergeant,' says Johnny Rickett, 'as he is your right hand man.'[32]

'Smokey' Lloyd himself still fumes about it:

My very first encounter with him was when he walked into my room, which was strictly prohibited according to the CO [commanding officer]'s orders, and he was inspecting my rifle when I walked into the room. I reminded him that only the CO could inspect my weapon and I would be given notice. It didn't seem to make any difference, because that's the type of person Heseltine is. He just shrugged it off. I was absolutely furious. I reported him – that he'd gone into my room without notifying me. I don't know if anything was done.[33]

Lloyd believes that Heseltine wasn't a very good platoon commander, because he lacked man-management skills. But he did not have to tolerate his new boss for long. Some of Heseltine's time as a Guards officer was taken up by ordinary leave, and he was also given several weeks' compassionate leave to help him sort out his family's complicated financial affairs following his father's death. This was generous, perhaps, given that it was now more than two years since Rupert Heseltine had died.

On 8 September 1959 Harold Macmillan called a general election, with polling due exactly a month later. The following day Michael

Heseltine applied to resign from the Army; his request was granted immediately and posted in the *London Gazette*.[34] Having been commissioned only on 11 July, his spell with the Welsh Guards had lasted just sixty-one days, and his days of active duty were far fewer than that. He had completed a mere eight months of National Service – only a third of the expected period.

A colleague recalls the moment Heseltine turned up to tell the commanding officer at Pirbright, Lieutenant Colonel John Miller, that he was going. 'Heseltine came marching in and explained at great length why he was cutting short on the grounds the law allowed him to, because you can't be a parliamentary candidate and servant of the Crown. On the face of it, it was cheeky . . . I think he was expecting an explosion from the CO, but all he said was, "OK, yes, go."'

Miller – now Sir John, and one of Heseltine's constituents in Oxfordshire – had known him as a teenager during the war. Michael used to visit his father at Shotover Park, the Miller family home near Oxford, which had been requisitioned for the Army. 'I knew perfectly well about his political ambitions,' Sir John says:

I knew he was entitled to stand for Parliament, and I had no authority to stop him . . . so I didn't try. I think I said, 'I wish you luck but I'm afraid I don't think you'll succeed.' I told him he wouldn't get in [at Gower] but it was sensible to try himself out there and not immediately seek a safe seat.[35]

Miller says the discharge was not resented, and he doesn't believe Heseltine made the move so as to get out of the Army. 'He would have made a very good soldier,' he adds. 'He would have gone a long way.'[36] Others are less charitable. 'We officers were all very pleased when he left,' says one. 'He was very unpopular.'

Three years later the election loophole which had enabled Heseltine to leave the Army was closed. It was being widely exploited by disenchanted regulars who could not afford to buy themselves out. The rules were such that, absurdly, a serviceman only had to *apply* for the papers necessary to stand for Parliament; once discharged, he could promptly abandon any political 'ambitions' without forfeiting an election deposit. The rules were eventually tightened when hundreds of servicemen applied for nomination papers to contest several forthcoming parliamentary by-elections.

Through a historical quirk, Heseltine officially fought his first election as a 'National Liberal and Conservative'. In 1931 Sir John Simon had led a group of twenty-three MPs who broke away from the official Liberals. His Liberal National Party had eventually united with the Conservatives, and Gower was one of a handful of seats where the two party organizations had amalgamated and fielded candidates under a joint banner.

To most outsiders the name 'Gower' immediately suggests the beautiful moorland, marshland, nature reserves and secluded beaches of the famous peninsula to the west of Swansea. It is an official Area of Outstanding Natural Beauty, and one of the most attractive parts of South Wales – a natural Conservative area, one might suppose. But in 1959, as today, the Gower peninsula formed only part of the parliamentary seat. Most of the voters were to be found in communities to the north-west of Swansea and on the eastern fringes of Llanelli, and in working-class towns at the foot of the valleys, such as Gorseinon and Pontardulais. This was natural Labour territory.

In 1955 Labour had won a majority of more than 18,000. The MP, Dai Grenfell, who was in his seventies, had represented Gower since 1922 and had eventually become the Father of the House, the longest-serving member. As the 1959 election approached, the local Labour Party persuaded Grenfell to retire and selected a younger candidate, Ifor Davies. But, no matter who stood for Labour, the party's position in Gower was virtually impregnable.

Heseltine had decided that if he wasn't going to win he could at least store up credit for the future by fighting a lively, high-profile campaign. All four Tory candidates in the area – contesting Gower, Neath and the two Swansea seats – were in their twenties or early thirties, and they decided to work together in challenging the long-standing and elderly local Labour MPs. Heseltine's driver for much of the campaign was Ron Rumble, the man who maintained his London properties. He recalls how Heseltine incessantly repeated at public meetings and from his loudspeakers, 'I'm a young man looking to the future, not an old man grumbling about the past.'[37]

Heseltine was adept at creating controversy. Indeed, he seems to have obtained more coverage in the local evening newspaper than any of the area's incumbent MPs or the Tory candidate for Swansea West, Hugh Rees, who stood a chance of winning his seat. 'It suited me,' he says, 'that you had this flamboyant character there to cause a rumpus, rows and everything. I said it keeps the "shout" going. It presented the Conservative Party as a young and up-and-coming party.'[38]

Various images have stuck in the minds of those involved with the 1959 campaign: Heseltine speaking from the back of his Land-Rover; campaigning with his Alsatian dog, Kim; getting involved in slanging matches with his Labour opponents. Heseltine had only a small team, consisting mostly of Young Conservatives, and he knew that resources would often be diverted to the two marginal seats in Swansea. To generate publicity, his strategy seems to have been one of direct confrontation: taking his campaign to the enemy.

One evening Heseltine went along to a Labour rally addressed by the Labour orator Nye Bevan, and 'took the traditional position of the would-be heckler at the back of the hall and waited my chance'. Bevan proceeded to introduce the local Labour contenders one by one, starting with the candidate for Gower, whereupon Heseltine says he cried out, 'We're both here,' or something similar:

The atmosphere was electric. A thousand pairs of eyes sought the irritant intruder. Nye hunched; a stubby finger stabbed the darkness. 'Ah,' he said, 'I think we hear the voice of an Englishman.'[39]

Michael Heseltine loved a good dose of heckling, especially when it was against him. He even arranged for his friend Geoff Hayes to hurl abuse from the back of his own meetings in Gower, pretending he was a Labour supporter. 'Seeing him at the dispatch-box,' says Hayes, 'I can see him again as he was – absolutely in his element – taking the abuse and catcalls across the floor and responding very quickly as he always used to.'[40]

The biggest controversy erupted when Heseltine challenged Ifor Davies to a public debate. Davies accepted at first, but then changed his mind. 'I even suggested a place,' Heseltine told the local paper. 'I said I would go to Ifor Davies's home town, to that place where they know him best . . . I offered to go into the lion's den. I expected a roaring lion, but all I find is a whimpering mouse.'[41] Such challenges are, of course, a typical ploy for no-hope candidates trying to grab attention, and it's common for the leading contender to turn them down.

Heseltine refused to let the matter drop. He turned up at one of Ifor Davies's public meetings, sat in the audience, and heckled the Labour man from the floor. There was uproar when Heseltine got up during questions and repeated his challenge to a debate. 'You are fighting for Labour. I am fighting for truth,' he declared. 'You first accepted my challenge, but since then you have refused. Name the date!'⁴² When Heseltine approached the platform, Labour stewards barred his way, not realizing at first that he wanted simply to shake Davies's hand, but then they moved aside to let him do so.

Heseltine's protests in 1959 look somewhat hypocritical considering the stance he has since taken when defending safe seats. In recent elections Labour and Liberal opponents in Henley have frequently challenged Heseltine to face them on a public platform, but the MP always avoids such confrontations. Indeed, outside the House of Commons he has always been surprisingly reluctant to engage with adversaries in situations where they might gain advantage or publicity.

Heseltine ended the Gower campaign with typical hyperbole, and a hint of the future Harold Macmillan. 'There is a breeze blowing through the valleys of Wales,' he told his final meeting, 'and this breeze will become a wind, and this wind will become a gale which will blow the word Socialism from the minds of men.' But it certainly didn't happen in 1959, and in the same speech he seemed to concede defeat – and insult potential voters – by claiming it was 'difficult to undo the prejudices of generations in a matter of weeks'.⁴³

Despite the increased Tory majority nationally, and despite giving the vote of thanks to Harold Macmillan when the Prime Minister spoke at Swansea's Brangwyn Hall, Heseltine barely dented the Labour majority. It fell from 18,169 to 17,604, with a swing of 2.12 per cent to the Tories – slightly better than the national average.

Having given up National Service to fight Gower, Heseltine never returned to the Army afterwards. During and after the Second World War servicemen who lost an election had been expected to return to the services, but by the late 1950s the situation had become unclear. Were the Welsh Guards expecting Heseltine back afterwards? a mischievous Fleet Street reporter inquired during the campaign. 'Oh, Lord, yes,' the adjutant replied, 'and we are looking forward to hearing all about it.'[44]

By polling-day, however, Heseltine had already ensured that he would not have to return to the regiment. Even in the middle of a busy campaign schedule, he had made intense efforts to get exemption from completing the remaining sixteen months of his military service. He assembled an elaborate case as to why returning to the Army would do immense damage to his business, while his accountants and advisers lobbied the War Office with evidence on his behalf. Heseltine's continued absence, they argued, would jeopardize several overseas publications he and Clive Labovitch were planning, as well as some important property developments in London.

The fact that one of his managers had recently been dismissed for embezzling several hundred pounds was evidence, Heseltine claimed, that he simply could not delegate his work to others. But his overall case was far from compelling, since Labovitch was still there to run the business. Heseltine also over-egged the pudding somewhat by arguing that his mother and sister depended upon his work financially. Yet his family was pretty well-off compared with most people.

Despite his exaggerated claims, the War Office and the Welsh Guards were sympathetic to Heseltine's position. The government had become increasingly concerned about the problems of National Servicemen who were required to neglect their businesses and the well-being of dependants. 'In 1959 and 1960,' Sir Charles Guthrie explains, 'when the ending of conscription had already been announced, the Army took a very helpful line with those who had good reason to terminate their National Service early.'[45] Michael Heseltine was allowed to go, though he later joined the officers' reserve list.

In the political life that followed, Michael Heseltine would be dogged by the question of his National Service, and how he had managed to leave early. He himself has only compounded the problem by trying to make political advantage from his military career. Even though he was an officer for a mere two months, he invariably mentions his commission in election literature. The affair certainly aroused resentment during his early days in the Commons, at a time when many older colleagues boasted distinguished war records, and the carping naturally revived during his three years as Defence Secretary in the mid-1980s. Others in Heseltine's position would have played it more carefully, letting a less than glorious episode be quietly forgotten.

And Michael Heseltine frequently wears the distinctive striped red and blue tie of the Brigade of Guards – particularly on significant occasions, such as his famous 1986 resignation over Westland. The tie seems such a favourite of Heseltine's that he certainly must have worn it on more days than he actually served in the Guards. 'It's ludicrous he wears it after so little time in the Army,' says one of his old Pirbright comrades.

In the eyes of some guardsmen, Heseltine commits a final insult by wearing the tie with red on top of the knot. 'The knot should be blue,' says a former senior officer. 'Harold Macmillan would never have worn his tie the wrong way!'

7. *Man About Town*

'The crunch came on December 21, 1962,' Michael Heseltine would explain twenty years later:

There wasn't anywhere left to go – except to my bank manager.

'Look, this is the position.'

He said: 'What have you got?'

I handed in my shares, the deeds on my house, the keys to my car, my gold watch. He gave me the money. He retired that day. That man and that decision saved my career. I wrote to him several times later, but I never saw him again.[1]

Just three years after returning to the businesses which in 1959 had such a pressing need of his services, Heseltine and his partner Clive Labovitch were on the verge of bankruptcy. They owed about £250,000 – the equivalent of £3 million today – although there were property assets to set against their debts.

Like many ambitious young businessmen, Heseltine and Labovitch had overextended themselves with a series of expensive, high-profile ventures which had seemed like good ideas at the time but which consumed the money generated by the profitable parts of the group. Two of the costly projects were on the publishing side; the third, and the most disastrous, was a property development.

The first investment, in the magazine *Man About Town*, was made three years to the day before Heseltine's fateful encounter with his bank manager. It was his and Labovitch's first move into the magazine market, and a bold step which would make their names as bright young publishers. But the publication would make a profit only once in the eight years they owned it.

Man About Town was a quarterly magazine which had been launched in 1953 by a firm called Tailor and Cutter. A product of its times, it was intended for the man who had the leisure to read it while at his tailor's, left out to be browsed through while he waited to be measured for a new suit. The magazine set out to inform affluent readers on 'clothes, food, wine, relaxation, and all the other aspects of the Good Life'.[2] It gave advice on hangovers, on evening dress, on how to propose, and even on how to kiss a girl under water; its pages were crammed with clothing ads and pictures of elegantly dressed males.

By the end of the 1950s the ultimate owners of *Man About Town*, United Trade Press, had decided that the consumer-oriented title did not fit with the rest of their range, which was mostly trade journals. It was a conclusion to which Clive Labovitch and Michael Heseltine should perhaps have paid more attention.

The two entrepreneurs presumably learnt that *Man About Town* was for sale via the Labovitch family clothing firm, Darley Mills, in whose offices they were still based. They were able to afford it only as a result of a highly fortuitous property deal. A few months earlier the partners had bought a site in Mackennal Street, just off the northern side of Regent's Park, planning to develop it. Suddenly they received an offer for the property from Jack Cotton, a close associate of the property tycoon Charles Clore. It brought them an immediate profit of about £10,000, which just happened to be what Tailor and Cutter wanted for *Man About Town*.

For Clive Labovitch the magazine offered a chance to fulfil his long-held dream of publishing a glossy British equivalent of *Esquire* or *Paris Match*. He installed himself as editor and Heseltine became 'executive director' as they announced plans to publish monthly, intending to widen the appeal well beyond tailors' shops.[3] As well as the foreign magazines they admired, there was also a British example worth emulating. *Queen* had been acquired by Jocelyn Stevens in 1957 and transformed into a modern women's 'glossy'. Labovitch – perhaps ahead of his time – believed that 'quality magazines have too long ignored the male reader'; the target audience for the refashioned *Man About Town* was to be 'a young man with a car and conscience'.[4] (Nowadays the target readership might be termed 'yuppies'; the nearest current equivalent to the magazine would be *GQ*.)

From the start, Labovitch and Heseltine introduced two notable features to *Man About Town*. There was a significant literary content, with short stories by both up-and-coming and established writers. Over the years these included Brian Moore, Malcolm Bradbury, John

Updike, Graham Greene, Len Deighton, William Trevor and J. P. Donleavy.

The second feature was more important, especially for Heseltine's long-term success. The art director, Tom Wolsey, who proved to be a brilliant appointment, devised a revolutionary new layout. The first edition under the new owners printed the title *man about town* in lower-case letters, photos filled whole pages right up to the edge, and headings were sometimes superimposed on pictures. Often a middle section was printed on brown paper. Such devices were unheard of then. Glancing through copies of the magazine from the early 1960s, it is surprising how undated the editorial pages look; what gives away the period are the advertisements, with old-fashioned line drawings of men in smart suits and hats. Wolsey was even accused of thinking the design was the *only* thing that mattered.

As a teenager, Clive Labovitch had always been fascinated by the former magazine *Picture Post*, and now he hoped to revive the art of photo-journalism. An early picture feature by Terence Donovan contrasted 'dirty and hopeless' Nelson in Lancashire, with 'clean and bright' Watford. The scenes look tired now – cobbled streets, TV aerials on terraced houses – but they were striking at the time. Other photographers included David Bailey and a twenty-five-year-old Don McCullin.

A list of *Man About Town*'s contributors read like a *Who's Who* of the 1960s. Kingsley Amis wrote about drink, Benny Green on jazz, and Lord Montagu of Beaulieu on motoring. Others included Christopher Booker, Shirley Conran, V. S. Pritchett, Ray Bradbury, George Melly, Kenneth Tynan, Adrian Mitchell, Malcolm Muggeridge, David Hockney, Clement Freud, Ted Hughes, David Frost, Bernard Levin, Tom Stoppard, Tom Wolfe and Mel Calman. Of Heseltine's friends, Anthony Howard wrote occasionally about politics; and for one issue Julian Critchley supplemented his meagre pay as a newly elected MP by modelling 'The Best of Savile Row' (much to the disgust of the Tory whips).[5] Lindsay Masters reviewed jazz under the name 'John Lindsay'.

Heseltine and Labovitch would experiment in every issue – and not just with contributors, it seems, but even with the name of the magazine. First the word *Man* was dispensed with, and the title became *About Town* – presumably to widen its appeal to women readers. Then *About* was reduced to very tiny letters, before that vanished too, leaving a solitary *Town*, which looked more of an obvious rival to *Queen*.

An early edition of *Private Eye* parodied the magazine as *about*, adding the words 'for pseuds'. The photo feature on Nelson became a profile of 'Slagville', while 'Clive Brilliantine' was chosen as one of the *Eye*'s 'Pacesetters of 1962'.[6] In the *Town* office they were sometimes dubbed Rosencrantz and Guildenstern – or, behind their backs, Grabovitch and Brilliantine.

Some of the features run by the magazine seemed to have been designed to bolster their proprietor's political ambitions. In March 1961 Michael Heseltine and Godfrey Smith conducted a survey of the Tory party based on interviews with leading players, from the Prime Minister, Harold Macmillan, downwards. But Heseltine's most revealing item – at least in hindsight – was a two-page feature run three months later, entitled 'Europe Means Business'. Knocking past 'dilatoriness' over Europe, he urged the Prime Minister to take Britain into the Common Market.

Today Europe is still waiting for Mr. Macmillan to make up this country's mind. It has waited long enough . . . If a peaceful evolution is possible it will come from a union of the major power blocs. First Britain must fuse with Europe; then an Atlantic federation. A dream yet, but how many dreams of fifty years ago are realities today?[7]

Only a few weeks afterwards, Harold Macmillan announced Britain's first application to join the Common Market – though not, history will probably judge, because of anything written in *About Town* by Heseltine.

Much of Heseltine's argument for European or north-Atlantic federation was based on notions of the East–West strategic balance, though his former Army colleagues might have been surprised to discover that the man who had spent years avoiding National Service now had the nerve to suggest that Duncan Sandys had been wrong to get rid of it:

Britain is the only NATO country to have abolished conscription – hardly an inspiring example to our allies. One day, someone is going to do some

fast talking when Sandys's 165,000 strong army is exposed for what it is –
a political and economic expedient in the one field where these criteria have
no relevance.[8]

European unity wasn't the only theme of Heseltine's later political
career to emerge first in *Town*. An item on 'London Renewal' dwelt
on several of his future interests as an environment minister – urban
regeneration, London, and planning. Strictly speaking the article was
only based on interviews by Heseltine: it was written by David Hughes,
his friend from Oxford, who had joined the magazine as features
editor. Hughes suspects it was more a case of him having to rewrite
what his boss had originally drafted. (Heseltine has never been a good
writer; the odd article he produced at Oxford was invariably ghosted
by journalistic friends such as Anthony Howard.) The same edition
attacked the new Shell building on the South Bank as 'taking neo-
Georgian to a blank, styleless extreme', and called for a Minister of
Planning.[9]

David Hughes eventually took over from Clive Labovitch as editor
of the magazine, on what he says was an 'extremely generous' £2,000
a year. He admits to a 'twinge of conscience' about Heseltine's Europe
article, mainly because it occupied the first two inside pages and thus
appeared 'to have the magazine's authority behind it'. That aside, he
remembers no proprietorial pressure or interference.[10]

Yet Brendan Lehane, who was briefly features editor, recalls Heseltine getting very upset about one proposal. Tom Wolsey wanted a
cover picture of a pretty girl which would show one of her nipples.
'This surreal argument took place, with Michael saying, "We cannot
have the nipple," and Tom getting sulky and angry. Michael, of
course, won. We all felt he had his eye on his political friends. It was
a lovely picture.'[11] The photo was cropped short, but battles over how
far *Town* could venture along the girlie route would recur throughout
its life.

Overall, *Town* was very much 'Clive's baby'; Labovitch was fascinated by the details of publishing – the design, the cover, the content,
the pictures, the finances. Heseltine, says David Hughes, was interested 'in the nature of its success, and the possibility of its success'.[12]

Town's journalists and photographers were crammed into the increasingly overcrowded Darley Mills offices in Soho. Heseltine and Labovitch occupied two tiny rooms of their own, while *Town*'s editor shared a desk sitting opposite Ron Rumble, who acted as a kind of clerk of works for the growing property business. It was an incongruous combination. On the one side sat David Hughes, the sophisticated, Oxford-educated intellectual whose ambition was to write a great literary novel, and who might be commissioning a story from some future Booker winner. Facing him was Rumble, arranging plasterers for the flats in Stafford Terrace, or arguing with workmen who'd dropped in for their weekly pay-packets.

'They were such small rooms,' says Jeanette Collins, one of the design team, 'and this tall figure with this blond hair was quite an impressive sight.' Heseltine's political ambitions were no secret, and Collins recalls him telling someone, albeit light-heartedly, 'You're speaking to a future Prime Minister.'[13]

Women staff, on the whole, seem to have less favourable memories of Heseltine than men. 'He was cold and detached and uninterested in the magazine,' says Prudence Fay. 'Clive was a little more approach-able. He invited me and my husband to dinner – it was unthinkable Michael would have done that.'[14] 'He was not the kind of person who came to the pub with you,' Corinna Adam recalls. 'We were his workers, and I don't think it would have occurred to him.'[15] Some say he would be particularly arrogant and dismissive towards his most junior employees. Felicity Solesbury, who worked for Heseltine a little later, says she and her colleagues found him 'terrifying'. 'I remember I went into his outer office once and he was absolutely screaming at his secretary.'[16]

Towards the end of 1961 the growing business moved to new offices, above a supermarket in the Edgware Road. By now Clive Labovitch was claiming that *Town* was more than breaking even: circulation, he said, had jumped from 20,000 to 60,000, though former staff say the figures were always exaggerated. David Hughes believes the magazine could have succeeded had it not been for the launch of the *Sunday Times* colour supplement that year. Why should the public *buy* a glossy magazine when they could now get one free with their Sunday paper?

Town went through an editor almost every year. David Hughes was soon replaced by Nicholas Tomalin, one of the brightest young journalists of his time, who was later killed in the 1973 Arab–Israeli war. Tomalin envisaged *Town* as a 'glossy *New Statesman*', though one can't imagine this had Heseltine's blessing.[17] It was also a constant drain on resources. Colour printing, top-class writers and photographers, and regular promotion didn't come cheap, though the magazine became notoriously slow at paying. (Anthony Howard, who rejected the editorship, was known for refusing to hand over his copy until he was given a cheque in exchange.) Nor was it easy to tell how well the magazine was selling. It might take weeks before the returns came back from some remote outlet in Wales. On one occasion staff from *DOG* were sent round the country to persuade tailors' shops to take bulk orders.

Despite the losses sustained by *Town*, in May 1962 the partners invested in another loss-making publication. *Topic* was a weekly news magazine which had been launched only the previous autumn by a group of right-wing businessmen, and was losing £2,000 every issue. Yet Heseltine and Labovitch agreed to pay a staggering £50,000 for the publication.

Clive Labovitch had been looking for a title he could turn into a current-affairs journal, for he was convinced that there was an opportunity to launch a British version of the highly successful American news weeklies *Time* and *Newsweek*. Initially they had tried to buy the magazine *Time and Tide* from the flamboyant young clergyman and publisher Tim Beaumont, who owned a number of journals. Then there was discussion of Beaumont buying *Topic* in partnership with Heseltine and Labovitch. At the last moment, however, Beaumont decided against a joint investment. Instead, he lent £50,000 to Heseltine, at commercial rates of interest. It was an unlikely arrangement, given that Beaumont was also treasurer of the Liberal Party at the time. 'I liked Michael,' he says. 'He was my kind of politician – thinking and caring.'[18]

Topic was a disastrous mistake. The magazine could afford only a handful of journalists, albeit talented ones. Michael Parkinson was moved from *Town*, where he'd briefly been features editor, and Nicholas Tomalin was seconded as editor for a while, until Heseltine and Labovitch recruited Clive Irving from the *Sunday Times* magazine.

Irving recalls the pair taking him to lunch at the Carlton Club – not the most sensible venue, he suggests, to impress an 'unreconstructed left-winger'.[19]

'Clive was interested in the journalism of it,' Irving says, 'and Michael in the status.' He believes that, in acquiring his magazines, Heseltine had been impressed by the example of Ian Gilmour, who had considerably improved his standing in Conservative circles by buying *The Spectator*. 'In a superficial way it was a statement of modernity: rather than owning a brewery, he owned a magazine.'[20]

However, neither Labovitch nor Heseltine seemed to have much idea about what to do with *Topic*, beyond the ambition of emulating American news magazines. But Irving certainly had ideas. He was particularly keen that *Topic* should break out of the 'twenty-four-hour news cycle' which afflicted Fleet Street. A weekly journal would have the opportunity to probe behind the news and understand precisely why things had happened, and how government – in the widest sense – worked. It was an era in which 'deferential journalism' was coming to an end. Irving was particularly influenced by the type of detailed analysis published by the *New Yorker*, and also by several features run by *The Observer* when he had worked there. One series, written and researched by the Labour MP Roy Jenkins, had described, in forensic detail, a takeover battle between ICI and Courtaulds. Given his urbane public image, it's interesting that Jenkins should have been a model for what later became known as 'investigative' reporting. 'He suggested a type of journalism to us about how life really works,' says Jeremy Wallington, another *Topic* reporter.[21]

During the six months when the magazine was owned by Heseltine and Labovitch, *Topic* couldn't boast any major scoops – the staff was simply too small. 'We were doing it all from cuttings,' says Corinna Adam. 'We didn't go out and interview people; we just sat there and made stories out of other people's stories – second-hand.'[22] Clive Irving did one notable feature himself on that autumn's Cuban Missile Crisis. Clive Labovitch had arranged a free air ticket for him, so the editor flew to America and, rather than do original research, spoke to all the Washington reporters he could find.

The only time Heseltine got nervous editorially, says Irving, was when *Topic* ran a series on major defence contracts that were going wrong. When the magazine was tipped off that ministers were about to cancel the Skybolt missile, the proprietor seemed concerned that the coverage might be politically motivated. Heseltine acknowledged it was an important story, but Irving remembers being told, 'I wouldn't want it to come out in a way that would embarrass the government.'[23]

Topic couldn't last. On Wednesday 19 December 1962, Heseltine gathered together the staff in the office. That week's edition would be the final one, he announced. Just before Christmas was not the best moment to break such news, and *Topic* journalists had mixed feelings about the way Heseltine handled it. 'He fired us in a dignified way,' says Ron Hall, 'paid us what he owed us and said he was very sorry . . . he was genuinely upset. There were tears in the corner of his eyes. We all felt he'd done a decent job trying to keep the magazine funded.'[24] Jeremy Wallington, too, felt Heseltine had been an 'extremely decent proprietor'.[25] But Clive Irving was angry. 'I felt betrayed. We were only just beginning to make it into the magazine we wanted.'[26]

Irving says Clive Labovitch argued vehemently with Heseltine to keep the magazine going. Some former staff think that, given more time, it might have survived. Circulation had already risen from 20,000 to 42,000 in six months – or so the magazine claimed.[27] And a rush of ads apparently came in just after the closure was announced. There was also the possibility of a new buyer. Heseltine had tried to interest the Carr family, the owners of the *News of the World*, and senior staff systematically approached other proprietors in Britain and America, but nothing resulted. There wasn't the demand for a British weekly news journal, as Sir James Goldsmith would find with *Now!* magazine nearly twenty years later. Americans buy *Newsweek* and *Time* because large areas of the US don't have good daily papers. It had been an expensive error.

The proprietors promised they would continue to pay staff until they found new jobs, although Alan Brien, who didn't have a contract, claims he had to force compensation out of Heseltine: 'I wrote to him and said one thing I'd learnt about politics was that Tory constituencies did not like MPs who were dodgy with money. And unless I got paid a month's notice I would see what I could do to alert his constituency to this man who was firing people and not giving them money.'[28]

Brien got paid, and it was perhaps a sign of the reputation *Topic* had achieved during its brief life that most staff got new jobs very quickly. Michael Parkinson, for instance, began his successful career in television. More significantly, the trio of Clive Irving, Ron Hall and Jeremy Wallington was quickly snapped up by the *Sunday Times*. There they founded the famous Insight team, and developed the kind of in-depth, forensic reporting which they'd wanted *Topic* to pursue. Over the next decade and a half Insight would prove to be the most successful team of journalists in Fleet Street, but Clive Irving believes that it would never have happened without *Topic* as a test-bed.

The closure of *Topic* was only the most public sign of a looming financial crisis. Michael Heseltine effectively threw himself on the mercy of his bank manager, and the bank lent the companies £60,000 to get through the worst. For a while, Heseltine explains, he himself 'authorized personally every petty cash voucher for fifty pence or more. There were not that many fifty pence pieces to go round.'[29]

Yet again Heseltine had been lucky, for these days it is unlikely that a bank manager would have the discretion to make a loan of that size (the equivalent of some three-quarters of a million pounds today) to a business which had overreached itself.

The manager also advised Heseltine to put 'several companies into liquidation'. Since different parts of the business were run as separate limited companies, Heseltine and Labovitch could have done this quite legally, simply continuing with the profitable parts such as the *Directory of Opportunities for Graduates*. Heseltine thought that this would be wrong, however. He also felt it would ruin his hopes of a political career.

I said: 'I'm sorry. I got those companies into that mess. I'll see it through.' I thought that people who had done business with me would never believe it was right for me to go into public life if I had let a company with which I was associated go under. 'All right,' said the bank, 'it's on your shoulders.'[30]

It was a traumatic period for Heseltine. But, by a stroke of fortune, an encounter with the Earl of Suffolk had resulted in the offer of a small gamekeeper's cottage on the earl's country estate for a pound a week. On Friday evenings Heseltine dashed down to Wiltshire and took to the local undergrowth with an axe. 'That cottage and the trees that I chopped down at weekends were the things that literally restored sanity at the end of the week.'[31] His debts could not be cut down so easily. They would take almost a decade to clear.

For a time there were three categories of creditors in this disastrous situation: those who sent solicitors' letters, those who had just issued writs, those whose writs were about to expire. You can guess which of the three we paid. If you do that every week – and survive – you remember the lessons.[32]

Tim Beaumont eventually got back the £50,000 he had loaned Heseltine to buy *Topic*. 'The repayments were on time,' he says, 'all interest was paid on time, and I never had a moment's worry from the time I lent him the money.'[33]

Whatever the drain of resources on the publishing side, it was a property venture which was more crippling. Heseltine and Labovitch were the victims both of their own stupidity and of an economic downturn: the Chancellor of the Exchequer, Selwyn Lloyd, had imposed a credit squeeze and, as a result, the property market had collapsed.

After setting out as landlords – letting rooms and bedsits – Heseltine and Labovitch had become property developers. First they'd done straightforward renovation, as with the row of houses in Stafford Terrace, but then they moved into new developments. One project involved a row of narrow bijou maisonettes in Queensborough Mews, Bayswater. Their most ambitious venture also proved to be the most disastrous: a new estate in Tenterden in Kent.

When *Topic* closed, Clive Irving accused Heseltine of making 'a choice between a housing estate and a magazine, and you chose the housing estate'.[34] *Topic* was being sacrificed for Tenterden, he argued. And he was right. But, really, Heseltine had no option: after all, you can't close houses.

Tenterden, a pretty town of timber-fronted buildings, a wide main street and antique shops, has the air more of Virginia or Maryland than of Kent. It's only about fifty miles from London but, even today, remote from both rail and motorways, the community is not easily accessible. In the early 1960s it had the distinction of being the biggest town in England without its own railway station. Early in 1961 Heseltine and Labovitch spotted an ad in one of the London evening papers for a twenty-acre piece of farmland on the edge of the town which already had outline permission for house building.

The pair went to Kent at once, accompanied by an architect. The site, known as Turners Fields, was owned by a local bricklayer-turned-builder, Albert Dollimore, who had just received an enormous stroke of luck. He'd bought the land a few months earlier, for £12,000, simply to obtain access to an adjoining site. But then Kent County Council, which was eager to see new homes in the area, unexpectedly granted planning permission for part of it, which meant it immediately soared in value. Dollimore says Heseltine and his two colleagues turned up at his home without warning; he showed them round the site and said he wanted £60,000. 'They were three young kids and they were trying to knock it down,' says Dollimore, a blunt-speaking man, who remembers Heseltine particularly as 'a cocky bastard'.[35]

They were reluctant to pay his price, Dollimore recalls. 'I said, "You boys have never done a deal like this, have you?" I had other people bidding. I said, "You three boys go home. Talk it over. Don't waste my time." '[36]

Dollimore claims he then had a separate bid, later that day, for £80,000. 'Sure enough, Heseltine phoned. He said, "Mr Dollimore, we've decided to have that land." I said, "Hold on a moment. You should have made up your mind this afternoon, because the ground's gone up another £20,000." I thought I heard an explosion. "Do you mean to tell me that that journey cost us £20,000?" "Yes, Mr Heseltine, and if you're rude to me it'll cost you another £20,000." '[37] So Heseltine and Labovitch had to pay £80,000.

No doubt Albert Dollimore's account has become embellished with time, but his memory should be good – it was the deal of a lifetime. Overnight he was as wealthy as a millionaire in today's money. He celebrated like a pools winner, with a holiday to Tangier and a new Jaguar. But, just as with *Topic*, Heseltine had paid far too much.

A curious aspect of the transaction was that Dollimore's bank manager, at the National Provincial in Ashford, was Cuthbert Heseltine, Michael's uncle. Dollimore believes the manager tipped off his nephew that the land was up for sale, but Cuthbert Heseltine's son,

Tony, denies this. Indeed, he says, his father strongly advised Michael Heseltine *against* buying the property.[38]

Within weeks, detailed plans had been approved, and Heseltine and Labovitch – through their company Bastion Construction – had appointed a respected Maidstone builder, Corbens, to build the first homes. In line with the spirit that guided *Town*, these were built to the most modern designs. The houses boasted central heating and fitted kitchens – then uncommon – and some had a pitched roof which was insulated to keep the interior warm in winter and cool in summer. It was the first private housing estate to be built in Tenterden, and the modernist architecture was extremely unpopular with locals. Today the properties simply look ugly and badly positioned. Ten Heseltine bungalows along what became Turners Avenue resemble a row of giant matchboxes, with roofs that look flat rather than gently sloping. On the other side of the street are four rows of houses built along pathways leading down from the road, and facing sideways to it. These homes are detached, but stand only two or three feet apart. Locals were so upset by the style of the buildings that when Bastion applied to build a second phase, in 1964, Tenterden Council insisted they should 'break away from the present style of development by erecting something more traditional'.[39]

The whole venture – especially the initial phase – was handled appallingly badly. Heseltine and Labovitch were simply amateurs. Perhaps their worst mistake was not to build the show-house near the entrance to the site. 'We, of course, built it as far from the main road as possible,' Heseltine explained years later. Then it rained heavily.

I'll never forget that lonely show-house in its sea of mud . . . Sitting there waiting for buyers was the worst nightmare of my life. Eventually a chap turned up, and, I'll always remember, just said 'You're in trouble, aren't you?'[40]

They sold him the show-house at a huge discount, in the hope that having one buyer living there would encourage more. It did, but the process was painfully slow, and Bastion had to offer further reductions – from £6,000 down to £4,500 in some cases. It was also a mistake to try to sell the houses on leases rather than freehold, though this policy was quickly abandoned. A further problem was that building societies didn't like giving mortgages on properties with pitched felt roofs.

Worse was to follow. For five years Heseltine would be dogged by complaints about building faults; he was still coping with these after his election as an MP. One resident, Alec Hutchison, recalls that during heavy rainstorms 'water just poured through, and we found there was no damp-proofing or anything at all in the house'.[41] And there was severe flooding. 'We came downstairs on the first morning,' says Val Hutchison, 'and I said to my husband, "There's a lovely shine on the floor." And it was water.'[42] Another time, Alec Hutchison's foot went straight through one of the wooden steps on his staircase.

Other buyers encountered similar defects. Plastering and brickwork had been badly done; damp-courses were incomplete, split or non-existent; there were electrical faults, and waste pipes weren't properly connected. A drainage system along the bottom of the field had become blocked up, causing overflows in properties lower down. Another resident, Bryan Collins, himself an architect, recalls, 'Every time it rained, patches of damp appeared which coincided with the pattern of wall-ties. They were so badly built – talk about cowboys! – the mortar droppings in the cavity were piled six inches high on each wall-tie, and the muck was so deep water just came straight through.'[43]

Alec Hutchison and his neighbours eventually threatened legal action. A surveyor compiled a dossier of faults, and a date was fixed for a court hearing. But then, says Hutchison, Heseltine chose to settle things personally. 'One sunny afternoon I looked out of the window and there was this fellow walking down the road, blond hair, and he actually knocked on the door and it turned out to be Michael Heseltine.'[44]

The Hutchisons both vividly recall how their visitor sat down in their living-room while they listed everything that had gone wrong with their home. Eventually Bastion agreed to spend several hundred pounds on rehousing the family for six weeks while scaffolding went up and the faults were corrected. But Alec Hutchison remains upset that Heseltine seemed to be aggrieved that their complaints might ruin his political reputation. 'Had he come down and said "I'm sorry" just once, it would have alleviated a lot of the agony that was caused by the disruption,' he says. 'His attitude wasn't good. It was a bully-ing sort of "I'm a public figure and you aren't, and you're going to damage me, and I wish you wouldn't," which didn't please me too much.'[45]

Other residents – including Alec Hutchison's wife, Val – feel Heseltine handled their complaints quite properly. 'Once he'd accepted the need,' Val Hutchison says, 'the work was done well, and no further problems arose.'[46] 'His attitude was he wanted it cleared up. It was no problem,' says a purchaser whom Heseltine placated over lunch at Simpson's-in-the-Strand. Bryan Collins's problems were eventually resolved when Heseltine drove down from London very early one Saturday morning, visited his house, and then signed a legal commitment to remedy forty or more defects.

In turn, Michael Heseltine was involved in protracted legal disputes with both the builders, Corbens, and his architects. There were also regular skirmishes with Tenterden Council over Bastion's failure to complete on time various services to the estate, such as street lights, footpaths and roads. 'I should be glad to know when the work outstanding on the estate road . . . will be put in hand,' the borough surveyor wrote in one of many similar letters. 'Many complaints' had been received, he added, and there were 'a number of defects requiring correction'.[47]

A major difficulty seems to have been that, while Corbens were meant to be Bastion's builders, they instead subcontracted much of the work. In turn, the subcontractors passed the jobs to other firms. The men actually doing the work, at the bottom of the chain, were badly paid, rushed and poorly skilled. 'I've never seen such workmanship in all my life,' says Rhys Morgan, who was later employed by Heseltine as site manager to sell the remaining homes.[48]

But Heseltine and Labovitch deserved much of the blame. Naïve and inexperienced, they assumed one could employ architects and builders and expect them to get on with the job. Every trip to Kent took up the best part of a day. With so many other commitments, neither of them had time to keep an eye on progress – especially Heseltine, who was most keen on the venture. He was already the publisher of several careers directories and magazines, and there were other property dealings too – and, of course, his continuing political ambitions. And, if all this wasn't enough, Heseltine found time during the early 1960s to pursue another high-pressure occupation.

Michael Heseltine's career as a television presenter is all but forgotten, though at one time he considered it important enough to mention in *Who's Who*. Between 1960 and 1964 Heseltine acted as a presenter or reporter with four different series for ITV.

Heseltine's first work was for Granada Television. The station broadcast a weekly fifteen-minute live programme called *Who Goes Next?* Three top politicians – one from each major party – would each be given two minutes to state their position on some issue, and then they questioned each other. Guests included Richard Crossman, Peter Thorneycroft and Jeremy Thorpe. The producer, Milton Shulman, invited Heseltine to stand in for the usual presenter on six programmes during the summer and autumn of 1960. Shulman thinks he first met Heseltine at a cocktail party. 'He was a good-looking young man, argumentative and fluent.'[49]

Heseltine must have performed quite well, for he was soon collared by Jeremy Isaacs, his Oxford friend, who was now a producer with Granada. Isaacs was keen to devise a new ITV current-affairs programme which would overcome the then very strict rules about impartiality. His answer was *Look Twice*, which involved two reporters of opposing views presenting short films on the same topic. In October 1960 Isaacs produced a pilot, for which he went no further than two old Union colleagues: Bryan Magee from the left and Heseltine from the right. They looked at housing – a subject in which the latter had a considerable business interest, of course.

The pilot was transmitted to the Granada boss, Sidney Bernstein, on a direct link from the Chelsea studio to his office in Soho. Isaacs recalls how Bernstein asked Heseltine to get up and walk around, so that he could see what the potential presenter looked like standing up. A recording was then shown to the Granada Programme Committee, but Isaacs knew that a series was unlikely ever to be commissioned, since there was neither the transmission slot nor the funds. 'It required the simultaneous use of two film units,' says Magee, 'and since both Michael and I were unknowns they came to the conclusion that this was risking too much money on too risky a venture.'[50]

Besides, the Programme Committee had other worries that day.

They had just viewed the first episode of a new drama series based on a working-class community in Lancashire, which was due to start in only a few weeks' time. The committee couldn't understand the accents, hated the drama, and were worried what to do. 'So my little effort, *Look Twice*, died the death,' says Isaacs, 'as the whole question was what to do about *Coronation Street*.'[51]

Pushed aside by Granada to accommodate the needs of soap opera, Heseltine then worked for the London and Midlands ITV company, Associated-Rediffusion, on two more programmes produced by Milton Shulman. *Questions in the House* was similar in style to *Who Goes Next?*, with leading politicians answering questions. Normally it was presented by Kenneth Harris, but Heseltine stood in for a few editions. More substantial was his work for *Decision*, a fortnightly current-affairs programme which ran for nine months in 1962 and 1963. Heseltine was employed as a roving reporter, interviewing people on topics such as racial discrimination, the arts, opinion polls and the House of Lords. After an item about universities, one TV critic wrote that 'in Michael Heseltine, they have a most attractive reporter, incisive, shrewd, and easy on the eye.'[52]

Heseltine's final spell of television work was in a short studio-based interview slot for ITN in the autumn of 1963. *People in London* had been inherited from Rediffusion, and was broadcast in the London area after ITN's short early-evening news. It usually went out live and lasted just seven minutes. The format was simple: a straight interview with someone in the news, who, as the title suggests, happened to be in London – a kind of mini-Wogan. Most of the guests were from the arts or show business: Heseltine's interviewees included Kingsley Amis, Spike Milligan, Dusty Springfield and, one evening, David Nixon and Denis the Rabbit. For one edition he had to handle an absurd double-act – combining the French singer Françoise Hardy, who spoke poor English, with a deserter from the French Foreign Legion who'd cycled to the studio from Watford. 'It wasn't one of the most successful programmes,' confesses the producer, Michael Weigall. 'Françoise Hardy glared at the legionnaire and he glared at Françoise Hardy, and Michael Heseltine glared at them both.'[53]

The only fragment of film that seems to survive from Heseltine's

television career is from a *People in London* interview with the Miss
World of 1963, Miss Jamaica. Heseltine, as ever, was intrigued at how
she'd achieved her success; but she wasn't the most articulate of
guests:

HESELTINE: When you actually were walking in front of the judges, you
were, first of all you had an unusual swimsuit on, but did you have any
other sort of tactics?
MISS WORLD: No.
HESELTINE: Did you smile at them or wink at them or anything like this?
MISS WORLD: No, I didn't.
HESELTINE: You just stood there.[54]

He had ignored one of the first rules of TV interviewing: don't ask
questions which can be answered 'Yes' or 'No'.

Heseltine was never really at ease interviewing celebrities, and
much preferred politicians, such as the Education Minister, Sir
Edward Boyle. His style was always too stiff, and he tended simply
to read out questions from a list on his lap. Diana Edwards-Jones, a
celebrated ITN studio director who had grown up with Heseltine in
Swansea, says he didn't think about what he was asking. 'He once
said to Lionel Bart, "What is the name of your new musical, *Maggie
May*?"'[55]

There were also recurring worries about whether Heseltine would
get to the studio on time, which for a live show was obviously vital.
People recall him tearing into the then ITN offices at the bottom of
Kingsway having raced across London. When he got there, he hadn't
always done enough preparation. Often, they reckoned, he had simply
skimmed the newspaper cuttings in his cab on the way. According to
the former editor of ITN, Sir Geoffrey Cox, 'It became a matter of
him arriving from some other meeting almost breathless, and it needed
somebody who would be in for a couple of hours in advance, and
getting himself fully prepared.'[56]

Cox sacked Heseltine after a few weeks, and replaced him with an
ITN reporter, Reggie Bosanquet. 'Years later, at drinks parties, he
would, with a broad smile, introduce me as the only person who had
ever fired him.'[57]

The puzzle is why Heseltine tried television at all. It wasn't well-paid, and he seems to have entertained no thought of broadcasting as a full-time career. The only explanation seems to be that he saw it as a way of becoming famous before reaching Parliament (as the MP Geoffrey Johnson Smith had done). An evening programme on ITV, of course, would have been watched by millions. 'I got very strongly the impression that this was a chap who enjoyed the work,' says Cox, 'but keeping himself in the public eye was the main object of the exercise.'[58]

It is also notable that ITV companies were willing to employ Heseltine as a presenter when he was actively seeking a political career. His first appearances for Granada, as an impartial moderator on a highly political programme, were less than a year after he had stood for Gower. By the time he was working for Rediffusion and ITN, Heseltine had been selected for a new seat and an election was due shortly.

In the immediate aftermath of his 1959 campaign in Gower, Heseltine's main political activity was with the Bow Group, the left-leaning, socially concerned Conservative research body founded by Geoffrey Howe in the early 1950s. In 1960 Heseltine became the managing director of Bow Publications, which really meant being business manager for the group's magazine, *Crossbow*. Both advertising and circulation improved during the twelve months Heseltine held the job, and he remained as a director until 1965 – though not a very active one. Heseltine does not appear to have done anything very political within the organization: he didn't write any pamphlets, for instance, or articles for *Crossbow*.

The news of his Bow Group appointment coincided with an item in the *Evening Standard* in which Heseltine revealed that taking over the tailoring-oriented *Man About Town* had caused a 'revolution in my attitude towards clothes'. He now boasted a suit of eight-ounce silk and worsted, post-boy waistcoats ('only in winter') and a shawl-collar mohair dinner-jacket.[59] This prompted a limerick in *The Observer*:

> There were some young Tories from Bow
> Who were serious, hard-working and slow
> Till some men about town
> Came hurrying down
> And decreed that the Bow should be Beau.[60]

This, combined with the observation that he was 'part of the new dandiacal trend in Young Britain', prompted Heseltine to think of suing *The Observer* on the grounds that it implied he was homosexual. Friends warned him that he was reading too much into the piece and advised him against taking legal action.

Heseltine's new sartorial image would not have impressed people in South Wales, but in 1961 Heseltine agreed to fight Gower again. This was surprising, since he was hardly going to overthrow the 17,000 majority from 1959; it appears to have been insurance, while he waited for a better seat. The Gower party allowed Heseltine to step down when one duly turned up later that year.

Coventry North was theoretically a marginal constituency, Labour's majority having been reduced from more than 11,000 in 1950 to just 1,241 in 1959, though Heseltine knew he could win only 'if the national swing were marginally in favour of the Conservatives'.[61] Its sitting MP was the novelist Maurice Edelman.

Heseltine was chosen from an original short list of twenty-nine, half of whom were interviewed. His main opponent was Doug Mann, a local aeronautical engineer, who says that the final selection went to two meetings. The first evening Mann appeared with his wife, while Heseltine was on his own. Mann's lasting memory is of Heseltine turning up clutching 'a pile of *Hansard*s with paper markers inserted, indicating quotes. He didn't use them as it happens.'[62] The result was a dead heat, and the contest was rerun two weeks later.

Having tossed a coin to decide the order in which they would speak at the next meeting, Doug Mann opted to go second, which is generally considered the better position. 'But then,' Mann explained, 'Michael rang up and said he had had a puncture on the M1 and asked whether I would go on first.' When Heseltine finally entered the hall, he was accompanied by an attractive young female whom he promptly introduced as the woman who had just consented to be his wife. 'That got a lot of applause,' Mann recalls. 'There were quite a lot of ladies in the audience, and they all obviously thought this was marvellous . . . There was no comeback on that one!'[63]

So it was that Michael Heseltine clinched the nomination, with a little help from his future wife, and a flat tyre. But had there really been a puncture *en route*? 'I think he was telling the truth,' says Mann. 'I wouldn't know.'⁶⁴

Since he parted from Rusty Rouane, there had been several other girls in Michael Heseltine's life. They included Lena Eddowes, a Danish model who was quite well-known at the time. Lindsay Masters's wife, Marisa, says Heseltine dropped Eddowes after he turned up one evening at her mews house and she shouted down, 'I'm washing my hair.'⁶⁵ Heseltine didn't like that kind of treatment, and before long he'd found a new partner.

He met Anne Edna Harding Williams at a party early in 1961. A languages graduate, she now worked in a Knightsbridge art gallery, having previously been a secretary for the left-wing publisher Victor Gollancz.

Anne would later relate how Michael Heseltine had proposed to her the day before the Coventry selection. ' "You'd better come up with me tomorrow night", was his comment. "They'll want to see who I'm marrying." '⁶⁶

It was not an easy engagement; after one row Michael called it off and Anne disappeared to the south of France. 'It was the classical thing the woman does,' says Marisa Masters. 'She was so clever. She went off with a girlfriend saying, "I'm gone," and that made him terribly worried. He bought her a very expensive emerald ring and went off to cajole her.'⁶⁷ Michael eventually discovered where Anne was staying, only to find she'd gone out for the evening. 'I returned to find him in my room,' Anne once related. 'He'd climbed the wall and there he was, trousers ripped, hair everywhere. And that was it.'⁶⁸

Michael and Anne Heseltine were married in August 1962 at Holy Trinity church, Brompton, in West London. The reception was held at the Savoy, where the best man, Julian Critchley, remarked on how well Anne's legs would look on any election platform. Whereupon, Critchley says, Geoffrey Howe's wife, Elspeth, was heard to remark of the two friends, 'What a couple of shits!'⁶⁹ Her words may not have been quite so inelegant, but she was certainly disgusted. So were others.

It was a big occasion, with hundreds of guests, including many of Michael's friends from Swansea, Oxford, publishing, the Bow Group and the Conservative Party. Yet there was one notable absentee – Ian

Josephs. The two had continued to meet regularly for meals in the five years since they had ended their business partnership, and just a few weeks earlier Josephs had suggested they might have lunch in September. Heseltine explained that he would be away on holiday then. 'It was only from Julian,' says Josephs, 'that I heard he was going on his honeymoon, and that he was getting married.'[70]

Josephs surmises that, amid the rising Tory stars, Heseltine regarded him as an embarrassment. Josephs had actually been elected a Conservative councillor in Kent the previous year, and was regularly being reported in the national papers for outrageous remarks about the Tories who ran Kent County Council. 'I was a wild card who did awful things,' he says.[71] (Josephs, who admits he was really a Liberal at heart, would later, in 1970, cause Heseltine even greater embarrassment by backing a man who changed his name to 'Edward Heath' and stood against the Tory leader.)

Yet Heseltine himself was not afraid to be outspoken on contentious issues. The Common Market was 'a chance at last to unite Europe', he said within days of his selection for Coventry. And on race he made it plain that in no circumstances would he 'accept any distinctions in colour', and he would ask the government to amend its proposed immigration bill 'to make it illegal to impose a colour bar in this country'. Coloured immigrants, he insisted, 'must be permitted the same rights as first-class citizens that would be extended to men, women and children born with paler skins'.[72] Here he was foreshadowing the new race-relations laws that Labour would introduce later in the 1960s.

For almost three years Michael Heseltine's Jaguar sped up and down the newly opened M1. The Tory activist Cynthia Hubbard recalls how she and her friends in Coventry used to call Heseltine 'Mr Goldilocks' – which may be the first use of this nickname. She particularly remembers his canvassing technique. Whenever Heseltine knocked on a door, he rarely discussed politics directly. Instead, with a car-worker, for instance, he would chat about the latest models coming off the Coventry production lines; if he saw a well-kept flower-bed he would congratulate the owner, name individual plants, and perhaps swap the odd gardening tip.[73]

He tended the Coventry constituency diligently. And by the time of the October 1964 election Heseltine had not just an attractive young wife to parade before the voters, but also a baby girl – Annabel, born in 1963. 'He was the most threatening candidate my father ever had against him,' says Maurice Edelman's daughter, Sonia. 'He appealed to the same sort of people.'[74] In fact the two camps got on surprisingly well – perhaps because both men came from Wales. Also, Sonia Edelman had been friendly with Anne Heseltine at secretarial college; and the MP's widow, Tilli, recalls that after a long day campaigning against each other the two candidates occasionally met for dinner.[75]

Despite the Tory slogan – 'This Time Heseltine' – Maurice Edelman need not have worried. As Harold Wilson took his party back into office after thirteen years, Labour secured a 2.6 per cent swing in Coventry North, though it was slightly weaker than the national trend:

Edelman, Maurice (Labour)	23,355	(52.7%)
Heseltine, Michael (Conservative)	19,825	(44.8%)
Robinson, Ronald (Independent)	1,112	(2.5%)
Labour majority	3,530	(7.9%)

It hadn't been 'This Time Heseltine'. Next time it had to be.

8. The Last Member for Tavistock

A regrettable aspect of the regular redrawing of parliamentary boundaries is that historic seats can suddenly be erased from the political map. The ancient Devonshire division of Tavistock survived 679 years from 1295 until its removal by the Boundary Commission in 1974. And during those seven centuries Tavistock sent more than its fair share of big names to Westminster, including John Pym, the leader of the parliamentary opposition to Charles I before the English Civil War.

Tavistock also has the rare distinction of having two former MPs who later went on to become Prime Minister. The Whig Earl Grey, whose premiership saw the passing of the 1832 Great Reform Act, spent four months as member for Tavistock in 1807, while another Whig, Lord John Russell, enjoyed two spells as the town's MP, before serving twice as Prime Minister in the mid nineteenth century.[1]

Before its demise, the seat was one of the largest in England, spreading across 329,000 acres. Tavistock, fifteen miles north of Plymouth, is an attractive town whose wealth was once derived from local tin-mining. But Tavistock itself was only a small part of the constituency, which by the 1960s stretched across the peninsula of south-west England, from the English Channel almost to the Irish Sea, like a garter round a plump calf.

The southern part of the seat, containing most of its population, included commuter suburbs to the east of Plymouth and the rapidly expanding towns of Plympton and Plymstock. To the south-east lay Wembury Bay, and the secluded sailing resorts of Newton Ferrers and Noss Mayo on the pretty river Yealm. The division also covered two-thirds of the Dartmoor National Park, including the high-security prison at Princetown. The river Tamar, the Devon–Cornwall border, provided a natural western frontier, although just north of Launceston part of the seat stuck out four miles – an aberration caused by ancient land ownership. To the north, across rich farming land beyond

Holsworthy, the constituency came within four miles of the seaside town of Clovelly on the north Devon coast. The geography made it a daunting seat for any MP – almost fifty miles north to south, and thirty east to west. The roads were poor, and most of the passenger rail services, including stations at Tavistock and Holsworthy, had been condemned to closure by Dr Beeching. If local travel was difficult, then so were the trips to and from Westminster. In the sixteenth century the journey had taken five to ten days on roads 'cumbersome and uneven, amongst rocks and stones, painful for horse and man'.[2] By the mid-1960s the trip was quicker but still inconvenient, taking four and a half hours at best, by car or train.

Such physical burdens would scarcely have worried Pym, Grey or Russell. In their day an MP might descend upon his distant constituency as often as modern members of the Commons might visit Portugal. Indeed, there is no evidence that Earl Grey ever did visit the seat he briefly professed to represent. But in modern times, when constituencies expect to see rather more of their MPs, it was hardly the place for a young man in a hurry, looking for a convenient stepping-stone on the way to the top.

Devon had preferred the traditional Tory knights of the shires in the postwar years, and there was none more knightly nor more shire-ish than Tavistock's Sir Henry Studholme, who had sat for Tavistock since taking it unopposed in a wartime by-election in 1942. A product of Eton, Magdalen College, Oxford, and the Scots Guards, Sir Henry had married well – to a member of the Whitbread brewing family – and lived at Wembury House on the southern coast. He had also held minor government office, as a whip for many years under Churchill and Eden. Indeed, it was perhaps as well Sir Henry was confined to whipping duties, for by all accounts he was an appalling speaker, and whips are not expected to utter anything in the Commons. In Tavistock, however, the baronet was considered a diligent constituency member and was widely liked, even by his opponents. People regarded him as the true English gentleman, a squirearchical figure who seemed to know his stuff about farming, which accounted for a large part of the local economy.

Jim Cobley, who was Studholme's agent in his final years, recalls how eating at Wembury was like a parody of the country-house dinner for two, with Sir Henry's butler quietly toing and froing along a polished table to serve the isolated figures at each end. Every now and then Sir Henry would turn up in his car outside the Conservative offices in Tavistock to collect his agent, whom he addressed as plain 'Cobley'. 'The chauffeur,' says Cobley, 'would come upstairs and say, "Sir Henry is ready for you." I'd come down and get in the back, and the chauffeur would drive us to Holsworthy or whatever, and then he would walk round.'[3]

Within weeks of the October 1964 general election there were rumours – stirred by keen local Liberals hoping for a by-election – that Sir Henry, having reached the age of sixty-five, might soon retire. Forced to reveal his plans earlier than intended, Sir Henry announced in January 1965 that he would indeed be leaving Parliament, but not until the next election. With Sir Alec Douglas-Home expected soon to resign as Tory leader – quite apart from the death of Sir Winston Churchill that month – Tavistock Conservatives must have felt they were witnessing the end of an era: the passing of the old patrician Tory grandee. Studholme and Home were both 'amateur' politicians in the old-fashioned, honourable, sense of the word – motivated not by ambition but by a sense of public duty.

The Tavistock Conservatives acted quickly to find a replacement; with a majority of just three, the Labour Prime Minister, Harold Wilson, might call another election at any moment. A small selection panel whittled the fifty-one applications to a more manageable list of fourteen names, including six locals. All fourteen men – there seem to have been only men – were invited for a preliminary interview. They included Toby Jessel, the future MP for Twickenham; Robert Hicks, chairman of the Tavistock Young Conservatives, who later became member for neighbouring Bodmin; and Major Archie Jack, a local farmer. Jack's credentials included being a former local chairman of the National Farmers' Union, secretary of the Devon Country Landowners' Association, and an Olympic sportsman (having competed in the pentathlon at the 1936 Berlin Games). Unlike some of the other contenders, Archie Jack certainly wasn't a career politician. Sir Henry Studholme – a close friend – had suggested he might go for it, Jack says, and he adds that 'I was asked the same week to stand by my bank manager, my vet and my doctor.'[4]

In the end all of these contenders were excluded from the final short list of three. The favourite was thought to be Tim Fortescue, who was forty-eight, blessed with a famous West Country name, and had been interned by the Japanese during the war. Fortescue knew his agriculture, and in particular was expert in dairy farming, which dominated the Tavistock division, having held a senior position with the Milk Marketing Board. James Taylor was a local-authority lawyer from Dorset who'd once fought a Bristol seat and had family experience of farming. And then there was the thirty-one-year-old Michael Heseltine.

For Heseltine it was a chance that might not easily recur, an opportunity to put his political career back on track. Several of his Oxford contemporaries had got to Westminster well ahead of him. Of his old OUCA sparring partners, Robert (Robin) Cooke had been an MP for almost a decade, while Robin Maxwell-Hyslop had won a by-election in Tiverton, on the other side of Devon, five years before. Two of his Oxford friends – Julian Critchley and Peter Tapsell – had become MPs as long ago as 1959, though both had lost their seats in 1964. Yet Heseltine was fortunate that the 1964 poll had been so inconclusive and a further election was looming, providing another chance to get into Parliament. On the other hand, very few Tory MPs were expected to announce their retirements soon, and it wasn't worth trying for another marginal seat like Coventry. Tavistock might not have been ideal in terms of geography, but the opportunity had to be taken.

James Taylor remembers little about the selection meeting in March 1965, except that it was a bitterly cold evening. Travelling on the same train as Heseltine, he quickly realized he faced a serious rival. 'Every single time the train stopped,' he says of Heseltine, 'he popped out and went to see that his publications were properly displayed and stocked on the stations . . . he was obviously a more able, industrious chap than I.'[5]

Michael Heseltine had prepared for the selection meeting just as industriously. Again he was ahead of his time. Today, budding MPs often put enormous effort into such contests; then, however, it was not uncommon for contenders just to turn up on the day and be chosen on their very first visit. Michael and Anne had spent several days driving round, talking to locals, and getting a feel for the area. With a publisher's instinct, perhaps, Heseltine also contacted Tavistock's two weekly newspapers and ordered every issue from the previous year. When it came to questions, Heseltine sounded rather more knowledgeable than local Tories expected. Such background work never occurred to James Taylor, and Tim Fortescue says he had neither the time nor the money for it.

Heseltine's approach quickly persuaded Jim Cobley that here was the man to preserve the seat against a challenge from the Liberals: 'When I first met him it was very obvious that this bloke had ability, and was going to go somewhere. I gave him all the assistance in terms of information about the constituency, what was happening in the constituency – all I could.' Cobley was, of course, ignoring the strict neutrality that party agents are expected to observe on such occasions, but he shrugs off any suggestion that helping Heseltine was improper. Did he offer similar assistance to the other contenders? 'Nobody else asked me,' he replies with a mischievous grin.[6]

Anne Heseltine's memory of the event was of the weather. 'Dartmoor was covered in snow,' she recalled shortly afterwards. 'Most of the trains were cancelled and the other hopeful candidates' wives wore fur coats. I felt a complete idiot in a light bouclé cream coat and dress, and emerald green Liberty print turban. I shivered throughout the meeting from cold as well as fright but anyway Michael was adopted and there were several favourable comments on my hat!'[7]

The Tavistock Finance and General Purposes Committee consisted of about 100 to 120 people. When it came to questions, members were impressed at how Heseltine skilfully used questioners' names in his answers. He came out on top 'at the first vote', it was reported, by 'a definite, clear majority'.[8] Fortescue, who was runner-up, later became MP for Liverpool Garston.

Dick Broad, a party official, says that Heseltine greeted the news of his selection by declaring what a pleasure it was to be chosen for a safe seat. 'A woman in the audience said, "There's no such thing as a safe seat." "There is now, madam!" he shot back.'[9] Another woman recalls telling him she was sure he was Cabinet material and would get to the top, and then she added, in an aside to her husband, 'on the faces of those that put you there!'

When news of their likely new MP appeared in the Tavistock press, the *Gazette* announced on its front page that he had a local family connection. It was a tenuous link, of the kind often dredged up by political candidates: Michael's uncle Cuthbert and his family had lived for a short spell in Tavistock during the war.

But all was not secure yet. The candidate was required to be adopted by a full meeting of the Conservative Association. This is normally a formality, but as the day approached there were murmurings that the party had picked someone unsuitable. Much of the dissent came from the farming community, who had been poorly represented in the selection process. Some would probably have preferred Archie Jack. What did this carpet-bagger from London know about agriculture? He was, they felt, an opportunist who would exploit Tavistock to further his ambitions. The way he spoke openly of making himself rich so as to pursue a political career also seemed distasteful. It was all too calculating.

A second strand of anxiety centred on *Town* magazine, though one can't imagine it was a best-seller in south-west Devon. Hilda Collinssplatt, a former party official, was unexpectedly approached by the wife of a retired soldier. 'One afternoon a friend of mine came into my room and flung this magazine at me and said, "Hilda, I will not vote for this man whose morals will corrupt my child!" ' On glancing through the offending journal Miss Collinssplatt couldn't see what the fuss was about, but, to make sure, she invited four prominent colleagues – all men – to come and examine the copy of *Town* in detail. 'They were four very sensible men, very high up in the constituency. The four came and read it and they said there's one smutty bit, but said, "There's absolutely nothing – it's not like *Playboy*." '10

It was unfortunate for Michael Heseltine that he'd been chosen by Tavistock Tories just as *Town* was going through one of its periodic girlie phases. 'How would you like a bust in the mouth?' boomed the February issue, over a pretty woman in aggressive karate pose, loosely wrapped in towelling. Both that edition and the following month's contained several topless girls. The pictures were artistically taken and rather grainy, and they could hardly be described as pornographic, but their purpose was obvious. The April issue seemed only to emphasize the new trend, with a cover focusing on a girl's midriff, showing her knickers and a holstered revolver at the top of her thigh – all to promote an item on the thriller-writer Len Deighton.[11]

In the end it wasn't the scantily clad ladies that caused Heseltine the most embarrassment, but *Town*'s satire. One edition contained a harmless skit about a visit Prince Philip had recently made to see the King of Morocco, including a mock conversation between the Prince and the Queen. Unfortunately for Heseltine, it was still an era when Conservatives got upset about the slightest affront to the monarchy.

Perhaps the real problem was the whole glossy, modern style of *Town*. The magazine and its very name summed up people's anxieties about Michael Heseltine: that he was a flashy, trendy, vulgar City-slicker who knew little of the country and its ways. 'A lot of people felt that he wasn't ever going to be terribly interested in this area,' explains one of his critics. 'Everybody knew that he was a very ambitious chap, and we felt that it was just being used as a stepping-stone – which I think it was.'

Grumbles led to plans and plots. A caucus meeting was held. Many of the malcontents were Archie Jack's friends, who hoped to install him in Heseltine's place. Jim Cobley soon concluded there was a serious risk of his candidate being overturned, and quickly alerted him to the danger. As the adoption meeting approached, Cobley says, the two 'were in daily, hourly, minute-ly contact', working out how Heseltine could confound his critics.[12]

Any account of Michael Heseltine's life would be incomplete without the events of Friday 26 March 1965. It was an evening of tension and passion which Heseltine himself acknowledges as a milestone in his career. Many of those present say the young, beleaguered candidate delivered the most powerful, compelling speech they have ever heard. Tavistock's Victorian town hall, with its wood panelling and portraits of past MPs keeping an eye on their potential successor, was packed with 540 people. Just before the meeting started, the anti-Heseltine farming lobby filed in *en bloc* and squeezed into what space was left, pressed against the walls. 'The hall was crammed,' one local paper reported, 'jammed to capacity, with people standing two deep in the aisles.'[13] The large numbers may not simply have been attracted by the prospect of a lively political punch-up: in his youthful enthusiasm,

Jim Cobley had advertised free refreshments, to make it more of a social occasion. There was no thought of checking membership cards, and the heavy numbers probably worked in Heseltine's favour.

The evening also saw Sir Henry Studholme's farewell address, but his testimonial for his successor seemed less than effusive: 'I believe he will make a good MP. I would be glad to have him as my member and I am prepared to give him my entire support.'[14] It was no secret that Heseltine was not Sir Henry's own preference. Nevertheless, the selection panel had made their decision and Studholme's old-fashioned sense of loyalty dictated that he should help the new man all he could. The rebels tried to enlist his help, but failed.

When Heseltine was called to address the assembly, he said he felt like his old headmaster at Shrewsbury when succeeding Sir John Wolfenden. Comparing Sir Henry Studholme to Wolfenden was not the shrewdest move, given the latter's well-known role in liberalizing the law on homosexuality, but Heseltine got away with it, and then confronted his critics head on. 'Let there be criticism and frankness,' he declared, 'because it would be inconceivable that everybody in this room is unanimous without reservation that I am the man for this division – indeed, from some of the things I have heard in the past few days, not inconceivable but miraculous.' But, he insisted, 'At the close of the proceedings, let one thing be clear. Whatever is decided here tonight is the will of the association. Now is the moment of protest – tomorrow there is another job to be done. And, if I am the man you choose to lead you, as from ten o'clock tonight the battle shall commence.'[15]

Turning to farming, the 'time has long since passed', he said, when Tavistock 'could have been considered an agricultural constituency'. Every day new houses were being built around the southern end of the seat for Plymouth commuters 'who have but scant interest in the operations of the price review mechanism'. 'I am not a farmer,' he admitted, 'but then I am not being considered to run a farm.' Rab Butler had not been a teacher when he introduced the 1944 Education Act, nor was Lord Beveridge a doctor when he devised the modern health service. Farming was a part of life 'you will have to teach me'.[16]

'Heseltine told me he had rehearsed the speech fifteen times,' says Jim Cobley, who noticed the candidate's trembling hands as he sat down to great applause. 'I remember Michael picking up the water-jug and shaking. Bits of water were going into the glass and some of it on to the table.'[17]

He was 'greeted with a storm of applause' said one account, which described how Heseltine then displayed his 'art of repartee, ready wit, and quicksilver method of dealing with criticism' in thirty minutes of interrogation. 'Let the questioning be ruthless,' he had insisted, and it was.[18] The wonderfully named Lieutenant Colonel Mervil Stirling-Webb got up brandishing a copy of *Town*, claiming the item on Prince Philip poked fun at the royal family. 'Does he go along with this sort of thing?' Stirling-Webb demanded. 'If he does, I do not think it is right that he should represent us.'

Michael Heseltine had his answer ready. He was a loyal royalist, and didn't think most people would consider the article offensive. 'I really think that if Her Majesty had read the article she would have laughed as well.' In publishing magazines one was bound to be controversial, Heseltine argued, but he was not the editor. 'You either take Lord Thomson's view that you appoint an editor and let him get on with it, or the Beaverbrook view and appoint someone and do the job yourself. I take Lord Thomson's view.' He could not take responsibility for everything in his magazines, since he could not read everything that went in.[19] If he became MP for Tavistock, Heseltine added, he would have to think carefully about attaching his name to such publications. (He was as good as his word. Whereas until that point Heseltine's name had always adorned the title-page of *Town* as 'publisher', it never appeared thereafter on any of his magazines.)

Would he live in the constituency? he was asked. Yes, he and his wife had been house-hunting that very day – though perhaps 'prematurely', he joked. Did he support the Common Market? 'Yes,' and for Britain to join was 'a logical decision we ignore at our peril'. One man suggested that the party hadn't time for Heseltine to learn about agriculture, and that he had clearly been 'pushed upon us' by Central Office.[20]

Then occurred what one account called 'a moment of high drama' as the chairman moved that Heseltine be adopted. 'A hush descended upon the members of the audience as the tall, lone figure of Captain

H. P. Chichester Clark . . . rose from their ranks.' He proposed that the matter be referred back to the selection committee.[21] A local reporter, James Mildren, remembers that Clark spoke in a booming Shakespearian voice 'that came from the back of his throat', and was constantly interrupted by the squealing of his hearing-aid, which he kept trying to adjust.[22] 'Many of us are of the opinion that Mr Heseltine does not have all the qualifications necessary,' he declared. 'We require a candidate from the West Country who is in touch with the intricate requirements of agriculture as well as social conditions.'[23]

There was some applause, but by now Heseltine's critics were doomed. It had been an occasion – all too rare in politics – where the outcome was genuinely decided by a single speech. Heseltine had won the evening with the sheer quality of his defence. Many of the farmers who had come to vote against him were persuaded that someone who could defend his own position so skilfully would also be a good advocate on their behalf.

At the vote, only twenty-seven people supported Clark's amendment, and a mere seventeen opposed Heseltine's adoption. Dick Broad recollects that Heseltine immediately rose to say he would start running at once, 'and he ran from the stage to the door and shook hands with everybody on the way out. It was typical of his dynamism.'[24]

Michael Heseltine had convinced not just sceptical Tories but also the Tavistock press. 'It is doubtful,' declared one editorial, 'if a speech of such frankness, power and purpose has been equalled in the town before.'[25] 'This man thinks on his feet, he can sway with a punch and come back fighting,' wrote another. 'He will be a hard man to stump with a question during an election meeting.'[26]

It was almost a year before voters had a chance to try. Over the intervening period Heseltine rented a local house and spent almost every weekend in the constituency. His usual routine was to leave London at midday on Friday. His agent would collect him from Exeter St David's station around teatime. Then it was frenetic activity through Friday evening and all day Saturday, before Jim Cobley returned him to the station again on Sunday morning.

Chastened by comments at the adoption meeting, Heseltine did a crash course in farming. Betsy Gallup, his party chairman, ran a dairy farm with her husband, Robin, and recalls the time they invited Heseltine to dinner. He sat up half the night poring over their accounts to grasp the minutiae of subsidies and grants, trying to fathom out how they could possibly make a living. There were regular sessions with each of the area's four or five NFU branches, and Jim Cobley arranged for him to spend several days with local farmers, following them as they went about their work and chatting about their problems. The hours spent on the quiet, lush hillsides of west Devon must have seemed light years from the manic world of advertising sales or Tenterden building sites.

In one respect Heseltine refused to bend to Tavistock opinions, remembers Jim Cobley. 'One thing the party workers were always saying was, "Use your influence on Michael – just get him to have his hair cut." He always had a phobia about his hair: he was very funny about it; he would never have it cut. "They've got to like me as I am," he would say.'[27]

In the autumn of 1965 Cobley suddenly announced he was applying to become agent in nearby Honiton, widely regarded as one of the most physically attractive seats in England. 'He looked at me and said, "Jim, I'm going to be Prime Minister one day and you would just love to be the agent to the Prime Minister, so stay with me and you will always be my agent during my time in the House of Commons." '[28] But Cobley could not be persuaded, and, though a new agent was appointed for the March 1966 election, Heseltine ran much of the campaign himself.

Nationally, Labour was widely expected to win a bigger majority, and in Tavistock the Tories were a little nervous about the effect their flashy new candidate might have on the vote. The main threat came from the Liberals, for historically Tavistock had been a Whig/Liberal fiefdom under the patronage of the Dukes of Bedford – the Russell family. But it was a question of geography as well as history, since the postwar Liberal revival had begun with Mark Bonham-Carter's 1958 by-election victory in the adjacent constituency of Torrington. The Liberals had lost that seat at the general election a year later, but Jeremy Thorpe's 1959 win in North Devon showed the underlying strength of Liberalism in the region. In 1964 the Liberals had cut Henry Studholme's majority to half of what it had been in 1959; with another such jump they might take the seat.

Tavistock, then, was one of the Liberals' top twenty target seats, and their leader, Jo Grimond, visited it early in the campaign. More unexpectedly – and this perhaps betrayed his party's nervousness about the Liberal threat – the new Tory leader, Edward Heath, delivered his first speech of the 1966 election in Tavistock. He told the audience he had known the Tory candidate since he was an Oxford student in the early 1950s.

It is striking how much Heseltine tried to appease Liberal voters during the campaign. The man who had borne a National Liberal label in 1959, and whose hero was Lloyd George, claimed at one meeting that his grandfather had known the Liberal premier. Any differences between the Conservatives and the 'new Liberals, the young Liberals, the protestors of 1964' were contrived and artificial. He shared the basic Liberal beliefs in individual freedom, tolerance and a radical approach; and on the fundamental issues – the Common Market, regional planning, restrictive practices and reform of the unions – the Conservatives and the Liberals agreed.[29]

Heseltine fought Tavistock as he had Gower and Coventry North – as if it were a knife-edge marginal. 'It was,' says a former YC official, John Hart, 'somewhat different to have a candidate that went looking for voters over and above the voters that were looking for him.'[30] Remote Dartmoor farmhouses saw Conservative canvassers for the first time in memory, and the party claimed to have covered more ground than ever before. It was still an era when voters expected traditional village meetings, and Heseltine conducted two or three a night, at staggered starting times, with supporting speakers filling in while he swept from one church hall to the next.

Liberals may have hoped to attract Labour voters, but a poll which *The Economist* commissioned as one of a series in a few select seats showed Labour as Heseltine's main challenger in Tavistock, with the Liberals trailing third. The survey appears to have been inaccurate, given the outcome on polling-day, but the Liberals' poor figure may have discouraged Labour voters tempted to make a tactical switch to the centre party.[31]

Nor can Heseltine's vote have been harmed by a photo which appeared in the *Daily Mirror* on election day, showing Anne, dressed in a lace negligée, cradling their second child, Alexandra, who had just been born, a week early.[32] The birth must have come as a relief after a miscarriage the year before. Anne had been absent for the entire campaign, and Michael Heseltine didn't get to see his new daughter until she was five days old.

With the Tavistock result, there was double reason to celebrate:

Heseltine, Michael (Con)	21,644	(49.2%)
Trethewy, Chris (Lib)	13,461	(30.6%)
Middleton, Peggy (Lab)	8,902	(20.2%)
Conservative majority	8,183	(18.6%)

Not only had the Tory majority risen substantially – to 8,183, compared with 5,400 in 1964 – but the party's share of the vote had also increased by 1.6 per cent.

Nationally of course, the picture was grim for the Tories, with a Labour majority of ninety-eight seats – the Conservative Party's worst result since 1945. Michael Heseltine was one of a handful of new Tory faces, and he recognized the personal advantage:

I was lucky in my initiation. To climb the greasy pole of politics most rapidly, it helps to enter the House of Commons when your party has suffered a serious electoral setback and faces perhaps four years in opposition. In 1966 only eleven new boys emerged as orphans of the storm.[33]

Yet the new MP got off to a surprisingly slow start at Westminster – diverted, perhaps, by his expanding business activities. He didn't deliver his maiden speech for more than three months. Then, in a debate on Labour's Prices and Incomes Bill, he gave an interesting exposition of the Heseltine philosophy on free enterprise, and in particular the rather cynical and depressing view that people are almost entirely motivated by self-interest.

'I do not believe,' he asserted, 'that behind the closed doors of human motivation considerations of the national interest weigh in the balance.' In any case, how could one define that 'national interest'? 'Businessmen,' he added, 'will respond to one thing, and one thing only – the opportunity to increase their salaries, their profits, and the capital value of their companies.' While he accepted 'paying higher

unemployment benefits in order to remove the fear of unemployment',
Heseltine was years ahead of his party in suggesting that MPs should
be asking 'what nationalized industries can be denationalized'.[34]

In his early months in the House, Heseltine concentrated on transport issues, and within eighteen months he was one of his party's
unofficial spokesmen on the subject – in those days the Tories' official
front bench was confined to the twenty or so members of the Shadow
Cabinet and a handful of others. The job meant that over the next
three years in opposition Heseltine would work closely with the
two figures who most determined the course of his career over the
subsequent twenty years. One was soon a close friend and ally; the
other would eventually become his most implacable foe.

In 1967 the Conservative transport team was led by Peter Walker,
who had been brought into the Shadow Cabinet at the unusually young
age of thirty-three, after running Ted Heath's successful leadership
campaign in 1965. Heseltine's promotion occurred after Walker had
asked the new MP to organize a tour of the West Country. It went
well, and Heseltine was asked to join Walker in opposing Barbara
Castle's 1967 Transport Bill, a major item in the Wilson government's
programme. Walker was barely a year older than his colleague, and
although Heseltine has never had many friends in the Commons it
was perhaps natural the two should get on. Walker himself dates
their friendship to 1966, when Heseltine was elected, although *Town*
magazine had run a profile of him back in 1961, shortly after his own
election as an MP.[35] The following year Walker even tried his hand
as *Town*'s share-tipster, though his column lasted only one issue.[36]

Both men were surprisingly rare examples of Conservative politicians who had made their own money in business – though Walker
had done so rather more rapidly than Heseltine. Both came from
middle-class homes. Both were modernizing, technocratic Tories who
despised the imperialists and racists on the right and the old-fashioned
aristocrats with their class-ridden prejudices. Both were deeply
ambitious and rather cold creatures. It seems to have been a friendship
more of like-minded politics than of any personal warmth. They
worked together on the Tory front bench for most of the next six and
a half years, and for his early progress Michael Heseltine owes Peter
Walker a great debt.

Heseltine had to lead opposition to those parts of the Transport Bill which nationalized private bus firms into the National Bus Company and also created passenger transport executives (PTEs) in the big conurbations. He proved to be one of the most effective critics of the legislation in committee, though in her diaries Barbara Castle describes with relish the 'blissful moment when I knocked Michael Heseltine off his balance'. Heseltine claimed it was outrageous that PTEs would have the power to manufacture or produce anything they required for their activities. 'I greatly enjoyed,' wrote Castle, 'standing up and reading an identical clause word for word in the 1962 Tory Transport Act!'[37]

In October 1968 Heseltine first came into close contact with another strong-willed woman who would also try to get the better of him. When Peter Walker moved to another post, Margaret Thatcher became Shadow Transport Minister for a year, though she saw it as 'a brief with limited possibilities'.[38] It was during this period that Michael Heseltine first came to dislike Thatcher: not for her politics, but because he saw her as 'embarrassingly rude' and abrasive.

Edward Heath's shadow ministers in the late 1960s were given rather more leeway than a modern opposition front bench. Party spokesmen were more often allowed to assert themselves on other matters, and in 1968 Heseltine revealed himself to be well to the left of his party on two of the most explosive issues of the time.

This was the year when race came to the fore in British politics, as Labour tried to curb both immigration and racial discrimination. On both questions Michael Heseltine took a rather more liberal line than most of his Tory colleagues.

Labour's famous Commonwealth Immigrants Bill was designed to limit the number of Asians coming to Britain, primarily from Kenya. In his 1966 election address Heseltine had maintained 'that all men and women regardless of colour, class or creed are entitled to equality of opportunity',[39] and now he was one of fifteen Tories – most from the left of the party – to join a larger group of Labour left-wing rebels in opposing the bill on the main vote, at its second reading. He also opposed the legislation on three further votes. His argument was both that the bill was based on 'pure naked racialism' and also that Britain should honour past promises made to Kenyan Asians.[40] While Conservative whips had advised MPs to support the bill, at the same time the Tory leadership granted a free vote, allowing individual members to follow their consciences. It was nevertheless a courageous act.

Arguably more rebellious was his stance on the 1968 Race Relations Act, which made it illegal to discriminate on racial grounds in both jobs and housing. 'To my dismay,' says Heseltine, 'the Conservative Shadow Cabinet whipped the party to oppose the new bill's second reading.'[41] He defied the whips, as one of around two dozen Tory MPs who abstained, arguing that the party should say how it would legislate instead.

Only three days before the vote on the Race Relations Bill, Enoch Powell delivered one of the most famous speeches of postwar British politics – the so-called 'rivers of blood' speech, in which he predicted civil strife if coloured immigration continued. In later years Heseltine would always draw 'some satisfaction from the fact that I was one of the first Conservatives to attack [Powell's] speech', though judging from press reports at the time, most of his intervention was a call on Heath to act decisively.[42] 'The Conservative Party is split down the middle,' Heseltine warned. 'The buck has been passed to Ted Heath, who has got to lead the party out of this most difficult and desperate matter . . . I emphasize this to Edward Heath. It is now important that he spells out in detail Conservative policy in order to create the right sort of climate for discussion.'[43]

Heseltine's stand on race issues and his rejection of Powell met considerable opposition in his constituency – an area which had virtually no coloured population or racial tensions. The 'split' Heseltine mentioned certainly existed in his own local party: Powell had many admirers in the area, particularly around the eastern fringes of Plymouth, where there was a strong lobby in favour of the Smith regime in Rhodesia. One Tavistock party committee voted by ten votes to six in support of Powell. 'Many of us feel Mr Powell was speaking for Britain,' said a member. To some, Heseltine's forthright position only confirmed their reservations when he was selected. A few described him as 'pink', while one Tavistock activist suggested the differences with Heseltine went much wider. 'Speaking to Conservatives as one does, one realizes how very opposed so many of his views are to the rank and file of general opinion on many issues, not only race relations.'[44]

A year later Tavistock's MP also fell out with his party on hanging, when the Commons was to decide whether capital punishment should be abolished permanently, following a five-year experiment. Hanging was 'barbaric' Heseltine argued, and he would support it only if there was 'evidence that it acts as a real deterrent, and this evidence doesn't exist'.[45] (In later years, however, Heseltine said he would contemplate hanging for terrorist murders.)

Political differences, however, accounted for only some of the simmering tensions between Heseltine and his constituents. He remained ill at ease with the farmers, despite regular meetings with each of the local NFU branches. Once a year he would meet the farmers' leaders to explain the outcome of the government's annual price review; the farmers, of course, were never happy with it, and the occasions were often fraught. The journalist James Mildren recalls Heseltine coming over to the Bedford Hotel in Tavistock after one such encounter looking exhausted and complaining, 'They were buggers tonight.'[46]

'He very soon impressed people with his grasp of fundamentals,' says John Finnegan, a former NFU official.[47] Others are less sure. At one NFU meeting in Holsworthy a pig-farmer was explaining how there was no longer any money in raising pigs. 'Michael thought about it,' says one witness:

and put his commercial mind to it, and said, 'Dairy farmers are doing quite well in terms of the price review. My advice to you is to turn over to dairy farming and get some cows.' This old man sat there gazing, and got up and said, 'I don't think you know much about farming. Pigs and cows are not the same size. How can you put cows into a pigs' house?'

People also remained unhappy about Heseltine's flashy style, and the way he seemed to flaunt his wealth by racing his Jaguar along the narrow Devon lanes. Betsy Gallup, as Tory chairman for a time, says she acted as 'a little bit like an aunt, and felt a duty to put the brakes on a bit . . . Michael was a bright young man, but he wasn't awfully tactful,' she says. 'Every now and then we had to say, "We don't do it like that down here." ' But advice about his appearance never seemed to get through. 'He always wore rather pale grey suits,' she recalls, 'and appeared with a kipper tie with pale pink and blue chrysanthemums.' This was one place, perhaps, where the Guards tie might have been a better choice. One old lady rang Betsy Gallup and asked her to do something about his ties, since she felt they were a 'disgrace' and not the way people ought to dress in the country. 'Michael Heseltine said to me, "I don't care. Annabel gave it to me for Christmas and I'm going to wear it." '[48]

In a way, Michael Heseltine didn't really have to care. Within months of winning Tavistock it became obvious that it would not be a seat for life. In March 1966 the Boundary Commission issued its recommendations for changes in the parliamentary map of Devon. The number of Plymouth seats, it said, should be increased from two to three, and the new eastern seat of Plymouth Sutton should now include Plympton and Plymstock from the Tavistock constituency. The rest of the Tavistock seat would be lumped together with most of the Torrington division in a new West Devon constituency. In short, Heseltine's area was being carved up between the new seats of Plymouth Sutton and West Devon.

Neither of the new divisions was particularly inviting. In West Devon Heseltine would have to compete for the Conservative nomination with Peter Mills, the member for Torrington, who had a much stronger claim. Not only had Mills been an MP longer – since 1964 – but he actually owned a farm in Heseltine's constituency. Mills was just the kind of gentleman farmer and amateur politician that so many of Heseltine's party members preferred. Plymouth Sutton looked almost as unpromising, not least because it contained several members of the right-wing Monday Club who disliked Heseltine's record on race. (Indeed, in 1972, the Sutton party confirmed their political inclinations by instead picking Alan Clark, at a time when he was saying immigrants should be told not to come to Britain because they weren't white.)

Having only just been elected an MP, Heseltine was careful not to reveal his thinking on the new boundaries. In a way, the changes could prove a blessing, offering the perfect excuse to move to a more convenient seat nearer London. The reorganization was meant to take effect at the next election – due in 1970 or 1971 – but in fact Tavistock was preserved for another Parliament by the Labour government's refusal to implement the changes immediately. As with every boundary review, Labour stood to lose seats, though the Home Secretary, Jim Callaghan, explained that the reason for delay was because it would be foolish to change the parliamentary boundaries until it was clear how local government might be reorganized in the wake of the Redcliffe-Maud commission. Michael Heseltine was in a rather curious position. While his party accused Labour of gerrymandering by not implementing the changes, the delay worked to his personal advantage, postponing the day he would have to look elsewhere.

So Heseltine remained in Tavistock to fight the 1970 election. On nomination day there was a scare when the Labour candidate, Harold Luscombe, and his agent turned up just before the final deadline without his £150 deposit. Luscombe's agent explained that the money hadn't yet come through from Labour headquarters. This worried Heseltine, for, without a candidate, thousands of Labour voters would be bound to switch to the Liberals, and on the 1966 figures his opponents' combined vote would have been enough to defeat him. 'Heseltine came up very condescendingly,' says Luscombe, 'and said, "Look, old chap, if people in the Labour Party can't afford to pay your nomination fee, I'm quite happy to pay it for you." '[49] He even dispatched Betsy Gallup to get £150 in cash from her own bank, before Labour produced a cheque at the last moment. Years later the agent admitted to Luscombe that it had all been a publicity stunt to get the candidate's name in the papers.

By now Michael Heseltine had become enough of a national figure to spend several days campaigning around the country. His absence from Tavistock didn't make much difference: 1970 was a good year for the Conservatives, and Ted Heath unexpectedly took power. Although forty ballot papers in Tavistock were spoilt by having 'Powell' scrawled across them, Heseltine's result was particularly impressive. He secured a swing of 7.8 per cent from the Liberals – far better than the national trend:

Heseltine, Michael (Con)	25,846	(57.1%)
Banks, Mike (Lib)	10,397	(23.0%)
Luscombe, Harold (Lab)	8,982	(19.9%)
Conservative majority	15,449	(34.2%)

Heseltine's majority – which had almost doubled from 1966 – was the largest margin ever recorded in Tavistock, and also the biggest percentage majority there in modern times.

Looking back on it twenty years later, Michael Heseltine saw his first four years in the Commons as 'undoubtedly the most stretched period of my life'.[50] His business activities continued. He had a young family: after Alexandra in 1966, the Heseltines' third (and final) child, Rupert, was born in 1967. Anne regularly travelled down to Tavistock for weekends and summer holidays, though it must have been a hellishly inconvenient journey with three young children. Shortly after the 1966 election the Heseltines had rented Pamflete House on the river Erme, where they had their own private jetty. Anne Heseltine often used the house to entertain party workers and for charity events, though people complained that its location at the southern end of the seat was too remote from most constituents.

Despite all his other commitments, there seem to have been few complaints that Heseltine neglected Tavistock. Problems were tackled assiduously. To supplement his regular surgeries in the major towns, every September he would borrow a caravan and travel round the small rural communities, parking for half an hour by village greens or parish halls so that locals could raise their concerns in person. Heseltine, whose business interests now included a magazine called *Amateur Tape Recording*, was one of the first to use a tiny portable recording-machine. Once he'd appraised a constituent's problem, he would reassure them that something was being done by dictating a letter for his secretary to type up later.

His increasing national responsibilities also took up time, especially after November 1969, when Heath made him official front-bench spokesman on transport – though, unlike Peter Walker before him, Heseltine didn't sit in the Shadow Cabinet. The portfolio required demanding sessions in committee, and lengthy trips abroad. In the autumn of 1969, for instance, he undertook a six-week tour of India, Hong Kong, Singapore, Australia and the United States to study how docks were run in each country; it was in readiness to oppose Labour's bill to nationalize the docks (which was eventually lost when the 1970 election was called).

Heseltine also found time for other party engagements. In March

1968, for instance, he was a guest of the Young Conservatives in Brixton in south London. In the audience that day would doubtless have been a twenty-four-year-old banker, a former chairman of the YC branch, who had left school at sixteen but now had his own thoughts on a parliamentary career. Had Heseltine known the bespectacled banker would one day deny him the ultimate prize, one can only assume he would have been incredulous.

Unusually in those days for MPs – even front-benchers – Heseltine took on a full-time political researcher. Eileen Strathnaver, the daughter of a wealthy New Jersey businessman, had graduated from Princeton and Oxford, where she read history. Officially she was Lady Strathnaver, through her marriage in 1968 to the son and heir of the Countess of Sutherland, Lord (Alistair) Strathnaver. Her husband had caused something of a stir in the tabloids by his decision, after coming down from Christ Church, Oxford, to join the Metropolitan Police, and the couple would eventually divorce after he had a well-publicized affair with a policewoman colleague. Eileen Strathnaver's relationship with Michael Heseltine would prove more enduring: she has continued as his political aide – with a long break while she brought up her children – to this day.

Despite such help, it's still difficult to see how Heseltine managed to juggle so many interests. Throughout this period he continued with heavy daily involvement in his business. Indeed, he based himself at his company offices near Oxford Circus rather than at the House of Commons. He continued as managing director of the firm right up until his official elevation to the Tory front bench in 1969, and didn't resign as chairman or from the board until after the 1970 election.

During the late 1960s Heseltine had quickly laid firm foundations for his future front-bench career: he would spend twenty-two of the next twenty-seven years either as a minister or in the Shadow Cabinet. Yet the period from 1966 to 1970 was also the very time when Heseltine's business really took off, and was transformed into a dynamic and highly lucrative publishing empire.

9. Campaign *Strategies*

If the Tories of Tavistock thought they had found a wealthy business-man when they chose Michael Heseltine in 1965, they were mistaken. While Heseltine gave the appearance of prosperity, and his businesses had an annual turnover of £700,000 and employed fifty staff, he was still burdened with debt from the expensive misjudgements of the early 1960s. The financial position remained precarious.

Town magazine continued to lose money, and editors. In 1966 Heseltine offered the editorship to Julian Critchley, who had lost his parliamentary seat in the 1964 election and had since bought a flat on the top floor of a house the Heseltines had moved into in Chepstow Villas, in Notting Hill. His editions of *Town* look no worse than any others, but its circulation continued to decline. As a result, the contributors' budget was constantly being cut, so Critchley had either to write much of the magazine himself or resort to articles rejected by his predecessors. After a year, and what he calls 'tactics of exclusion and discreet hostility' by Lindsay Masters, he too was fired. Critchley was especially upset that Michael Heseltine did not have the courage to sack him in person, but got Masters to tell him instead. 'Our friendship was over,' he writes.[1]

Julian Critchley had tried once more to push *Town* down the girlie route, only to encounter firm opposition from its proprietor. Heseltine's stance was prompted partly by his puritanical streak, but also by the fear of being labelled a pornographer. And, after events in Tavistock, who could blame him? 'It probably would have made a difference if we'd been able to have some tasteful nudes,' says Critchley's successor, Brian Moynahan – 'not that we had any intention of turning it into *Playboy* or *Penthouse* . . . It was a constraint, but accepted.'[2]

Brian Moynahan's biggest disagreement with Heseltine concerned a cartoon by Ralph Steadman. It involved a 'polyphoto' of the Queen, in which one frame showed a royal corgi taking a pee. 'Michael pulled that, and lost us Steadman as an illustrator.'[3]

Moynahan was given extra funds to spend on television advertising, and claims to have pushed circulation up from 18,000 to more than 50,000, but it wasn't enough. Today, when printing is far cheaper, *Town* could have made money; then it remained a drain on resources.

For much of its life, *Town* was subsidized by the *Directory of Opportunities for Graduates* and the other careers directories, which were still generating tens of thousands of pounds a year. Without them, Cornmarket would never have survived. *DOG* was by far the most lucrative, and by the mid-sixties was being published with a separate cover for each university; the school-leavers' directory also made money, though the overseas editions of *DOG* – in Canada, France and Germany – were less successful. The directories had also spawned highly profitable careers ventures, such as the book *Which University?*

The most important spin-off, though, was probably the Graduate Appointments Register, a very simple idea which was assisted by the advent of the photocopying machine. The register collected CVs from graduates and then sold copies in bulk to subscribing companies, according to category – £30 a month, say, for people with physics degrees. 'I plagiarized it from America,' says Adrian Bridgewater, who initiated the register. 'I remember going to Esso . . . They said, "Well, fine, we'll take a year's subscription for the whole lot!" '[4] By photocopying the CVs with the name and address concealed, it was possible to charge an extra fee whenever a firm was interested in a particular graduate.

At first, says Bridgewater, Heseltine didn't understand how profitable the idea might be. 'I shaped up in the Edgware Road boardroom and did a pretty amateur presentation, and Michael said, "I think we'd better stop that straight away." ' Bridgewater simply ignored Heseltine and carried on with the operation – an indication of the haphazard way in which Cornmarket was run. 'It turned out to be one of the big money-spinners,' he says. 'He didn't understand it.'[5]

Years later, as a minister, Michael Heseltine would constantly stress the importance of good management, with proper systems in government to assess what activities cost and whether they are worthwhile. This was in stark contrast to the way his own businesses were run during the early years. 'He did in those days have the ability to lead a small group incredibly well,' says Adrian Bridgewater, but 'one didn't have business plans, nor was one asked for them'.[6]

It is astonishing, in fact, quite how disorganized Cornmarket was in the early 1960s. 'The whole thing was a shambles,' says Paul Buckley, who arrived as an ad salesman around 1963, 'but it was all rather good fun.' Buckley recalls going into the offices with Heseltine at weekends to hunt through filing cabinets for missing invoices. With no proper management or financial structure, it was quite easy for projects to lose vast sums. 'We never knew what was making money and what was not. It was a hopeless accounting system,' Buckley adds. 'It took a year to find out if anything was making money.'[7] 'They didn't have accurate information about anything,' says Robert Heller, who joined Heseltine's business in 1966. 'It was chaotic; cheques were often not paid into the bank, but left in drawers.'[8]

It remained very much a 'seat of the pants' operation as the partners constantly played with new ideas. Among them were an in-house magazine for Hilton hotels, and new owners' packs for people who bought cars from Rootes or Ford. Heseltine would flit from one scheme to the next, never getting too involved, and often displaying a very short attention span. It was left to others to sort out the detail.

Yet, amid the chaos, Heseltine and Labovitch had several great assets. First, they themselves had imagination and energy, and the precious gift of inspiring those around them. Second, both were superb at talent-spotting, picking staff with the ability and creativity to carry ideas through.

Third, Lindsay Masters had developed a revolutionary way of selling advertising. He operated by strict rules. His sales staff were mainly graduates, and worked by telephone. Rival magazines were carefully combed for potential new advertisers. The sales team were not allowed to take people out to lunch; Masters reckoned that getting prospective clients drunk, and having too much alcohol yourself, was a very inefficient way of selling space. Instead, the team kept possible advertisers' details on cards in boxes. Any new member of the staff would be presented with a box and told to start ringing the numbers; each salesman was expected to call on twenty-five prospective advertisers a day – any more was thought to be unmanageable. The system worked, says Masters, by:

making absolutely certain that the salesmen gave them regular calls once they had made their first call, and made a note on the card of what had happened during that conversation. It always had to have a date on it. That was the date of the next call. And if it was a week hence, or three months hence, it would go into their diary, so that, in theory, if you worked the system properly, the man never got off the hook for ever. You'd got him until he fell, as it were.[9]

Boozy lunches might be banned, but Masters encouraged the idea that selling space should be fun. It became something of a game. 'Every time you made a sale you put a coloured sticker on the board,' says Neil Crichton-Miller, who joined the company around 1966. 'You could see how everyone was doing and whether targets were being met. People who couldn't sell were sacked, and people who could were paid a lot.'[10] They sound basic today, but in the late 1950s and early 1960s such systematic selling methods were novel.

Equally radical were the design features that Tom Wolsey had been pioneering on *Town* magazine, and which remained ahead of their time. Heseltine and Labovitch had some of the crucial ingredients for business success, but so far they had not always applied their creativity and energy to the best kind of publication.

The partners only stumbled on the keys to prosperity through financial necessity. By 1964 things had grown so serious that Labovitch and Heseltine were forced to give up part of their businesses to secure a rescue package. The problem was the mounting debt with their printer, Hazell, Watson & Viney, which was in the process of joining a large new conglomerate, the British Printing Corporation (BPC) (long before it formed the basis of Robert Maxwell's empire). Heseltine was hauled before the BPC managing director and told to sort things out. So, in lieu of payment, BPC was given 49 per cent of the equity in Cornmarket Press, the parent company for Heseltine and Labovitch's publishing concerns. 'It was a tremendous *coup de théâtre* for Michael,' says one former BPC executive:

He was really sent in to be carpeted – 'Look here, what are we going to do about all this?' Anyhow, Michael did a wonderful job of hypnosis, and turned him on to all the wonderful printing that would accrue from working closely with Haymarket. That was turned round by him personally – no doubt about it. I mean, he was in desperate trouble and managed to turn a problem into an opportunity.

It was the classic escape route for a struggling business: to convert debt, which can kill an enterprise, into equity, or ownership, thereby transforming the balance sheet. The risk, of course, is that the new shareholders will have different expectations of the company and will make new demands.

The rescue also resulted in a new name, suggested by the chairman of BPC, Sir Geoffrey Crowther. 'Hazell' and 'Cornmarket' were neatly combined to form 'Haymarket'. (There was the added attraction, though he may not have appreciated it, that Heseltine's ancestor Thomas Dibdin had once managed the Haymarket Theatre.)

The forced marriage with BPC was a turning-point. It meant that for the next seven years Haymarket would be operating, in Heseltine's words, 'on the fringe of this company, this printing and publishing giant, which constantly changed ownership and was constantly renegotiating its deal with us'.[11] Not only did the advent of BPC save the business, it also opened up a whole new field of magazine publishing which the two partners had never seriously considered, and which transformed the whole outlook. If the debts of the early 1960s were created by three misguided ventures, the company's future fortunes were to be built on three outstandingly successful business magazines.

Geoffrey Crowther had reached a basic understanding with Heseltine and Labovitch – 'You find magazines to publish, and we'll print them.' So, from the autumn of 1964, Haymarket began a systematic policy of acquiring new titles. Lists of magazines to be approached, and their company chairmen, were compiled from the media directory *BRAD*. 'It was very simple,' says Heseltine:

We wrote personally addressed letters to the chairman saying, 'We'd like to buy you.' And the fact that we didn't have the money or they were ten times our size, or a hundred times our size, mattered not one whit ... We sent out hundreds of letters, and if we bought two magazine groups in a year that was fine. In fact you only need one a year to make it worthwhile.[12]

Among those acquired this way were such exciting titles as *Amateur Tape Recording* – which published the first circuit diagram for a video recorder – and *8mm Camera*. Each employed two or three staff, and made small but steady profits. Heseltine also bought a group of camping and caravan journals after driving past endless camp-sites on holiday in France and concluding that here must be a growth business. But the first really significant acquisition came in 1965, and it was possible only because of the new partnership with BPC.

Heseltine had sent one of his regular letters to a publisher he'd never heard of called Alf Morgan, and got a message back from Canada: 'We're just about to sell to Thomson and I've got your letter. He's a bit big and I don't want to sell to him. Are you really interested?'[13] Haymarket merely had to pay the same as the mighty Thomson Organization had offered – £250,000. It wasn't the kind of investment Haymarket could afford on its own, of course, but BPC was willing to lend the money.

Alf Morgan's portfolio was diverse, and included leisure journals. But the real assets were the medical magazines – in particular the fortnightly *GP* and the *Monthly Index of Medical Specialities*, or *MIMS*, which keeps doctors informed about branded drugs. Buying these publications involved none of the trouble or risk of launching a new title and hoping it might work. Better still, most of the Morgan publications already made money.

Haymarket's next major breakthrough came towards the end of 1965. Crucially, it showed how to capitalize on the creative skills developed through *Town*. Haymarket learnt that the British Institute of Management (BIM) wanted a publisher to revamp *The Manager*, the magazine it distributed free to members, and who might exploit the rapidly growing market for business advertising. The Thomson Organization was again a front-runner, but Haymarket mounted an audacious rival bid. The following two weeks saw the unfolding of a brilliant operation.

On the business side of the proposal, the new link with Sir Geoffrey Crowther enabled Haymarket to pull in two heavyweight partners – the *Financial Times* and *The Economist* – since Crowther was chairman of both. Not only did the new partners add journalistic and financial credibility, but the arrangement also prevented either publication launching a rival magazine. It was envisaged that Haymarket, *The*

Economist, the *FT* and the BIM would all take equal 25 per cent stakes in the consortium.

But the smartest move came on the editorial side. Heseltine was inspired by a story he'd once heard about Donald Stokes, the boss of the vehicle-makers Leyland, when bidding for a bus contract in Scandinavia. Leyland's rivals had all placed their designs on the interview table, but Stokes had supposedly taken the Scandinavians outside and shown them a model of the bus he proposed. 'I'd heard that story,' says Heseltine, 'and always laughed at it with admiration. So, when I saw what was for us a spectacular opportunity, I said to Clive, "Let's not muck about – let's do it." And we worked over a weekend. We produced a magazine. So when we went in against the other people we said, "There's your magazine!" '[14]

A Haymarket team – Clive Labovitch, Brian Moynahan and a designer, Derek Birdsall – worked flat out to produce a ninety-six-page dummy of the top-quality publication they had in mind. Their principal model was the highly successful *Fortune* magazine in the United States. Called simply *Management*, rather than *The Manager*, the dummy was a glossy which included many of the design features Tom Wolsey and his colleagues had developed so successfully over the years on *Town*. It included headlines, and pictures from *Town*, and chunks of text lifted from recent copies of *The Economist*. Brian Moynahan even wrote one or two articles specially, all to produce a handful of realistic copies, each properly printed and bound in a full-colour cover. The dummies were distributed to a startled and highly impressed BIM committee. 'We actually *showed* them what we could do,' said Clive Labovitch. 'The Thomson Organization just talked.'[15]

The title was eventually changed to *Management Today* (there was already an Irish magazine called *Management*), and to edit it Labovitch turned to Robert Heller, the business editor of *The Observer*. The two men had met when Heller wrote a story for his paper explaining how Haymarket had mounted its successful bid. Heller was reluctant at first, but was impressed by the calibre of the consortium. 'This struggling magazine house,' he says, 'was now allied with some of the biggest publishing partners.'[16] Yet Haymarket was not fully trusted by the *FT* and *The Economist*: no cheques for more than £200 could be signed without their approval.

Serving as editor of *Management Today* opened up a whole new career for Robert Heller, and he soon became an influential management guru. Initially he wasn't impressed by Heseltine (who had repeated his mistake of taking a socialist to the Carlton Club) – especially when the latter began outlining his political ambitions rather than his plans for the new magazine. 'I assumed Heseltine was the front man more than the driving force, and that the driving force was Labovitch,' Heller says. 'The truth was the other way round: that Labovitch was the front man and persuaded the commercial people of the *FT* that he was a serious businessman, but Heseltine provided the dynamic and real entrepreneurial brain.' As for the original coup in stealing the contract from under Thomson's noses, 'That was pure Heseltine, I recognize, in retrospect.'[17]

Management Today had a guaranteed distribution to BIM members, and this circulation was soon increased by a big direct-mail campaign and ads in the *Financial Times*. The first issue came out in April 1966, just two weeks after Michael Heseltine was elected for Tavistock.

Shortly after the launch, Robert Heller recalls passing Heseltine in the corridor at Haymarket. 'He was looking very flushed and excited, and he said, "I've just realized we've produced one of the world's most important magazines." Looking back, it's clear that he'd actually seen that we had just given him the keys to the kingdom.'[18]

Management Today was soon outselling its main rival, *The Director*, and was first in what became a stable of highly lucrative business magazines. The arrangement with the BIM would later become the model for other Haymarket titles published in conjunction with similar bodies – the Institute of Marketing, the Institute of Personnel Management and the British Computer Society. Yet, strangely, Clive Labovitch chose this very period to leave. It was the worst possible timing – just as Haymarket had hit on the formula for success, and as his partner was about to be distracted by a new political career.

Michael Heseltine would later tell people he had spent three days begging Labovitch to stay. But he could not be persuaded, and the two men divided the business between them, as well as their substantial debts. Heseltine retained all the magazines, while Labovitch took the highly profitable careers directories. On the face of it, Labovitch seemed to have got the better deal. But a crucial factor was the way key staff chose to jump. The only important figure to follow Labovitch was Denis Curtis, a brilliant but highly volatile production manager, who was known for juggling all the printing schedules in his head. Lindsay Masters's decision was the most vital. Friends say he calculated that with Labovitch he would only ever be number two, but, with Michael Heseltine increasingly concentrating on politics, he knew he could soon be running the show if he stayed.

The reasons for Clive Labovitch's decision may never be fully understood. He himself said he wanted to concentrate on careers and education publishing. 'The time had come,' he explained, 'when I had to decide whether to devote my career to glossy magazines. It is an unreal world, and if you stay too long you begin to believe in it.'[19] In later years Labovitch would talk of a 'premature mid-life crisis' and of being scared at what the company was getting into.[20] It is absolutely certain, however, that he was not pushed. Heseltine told Labovitch that he was bound to make a success of the business now that he himself would be concentrating on Westminster. Rather than this being an incentive for Labovitch to stay, the knowledge that Heseltine would soon be diverted by politics actually seems to have encouraged his departure.

Those close to events say a crucial role was played by Labovitch's wife, the journalist Penny Perrick. 'Penny didn't think Clive was important enough [as a publisher] and could do better things,' says a Haymarket source. And 'he had an inflated idea of what he could do on his own'. As a vocal socialist, Perrick had never liked Heseltine's politics. Nor was she keen on him as an individual – especially after hearing his best man's speech at her wedding to Clive. 'He welcomed his bank manager,' she once said. 'He welcomed his accountant. He had forgotten that he was at a wedding. It was as if he were at a board meeting.'[21] A close friend of Heseltine says Perrick also wanted a place on the Haymarket board, and was deeply upset when Heseltine would not agree. She was convinced that her husband was the real brains of the business, and that he would be better off on his own, especially if Heseltine was going off to be an MP.

Whatever the reasoning, it was a dreadful misjudgement. The

decision has uncanny similarities to William Heseltine's mistake in 1887, when he split with Hudson Kearley. By 1973, as Michael Heseltine was heading for fame, power and wealth, Clive Labovitch's firm was bankrupt, and his marriage had collapsed too. And, tragically, just like Michael's great-grandfather eighty years before, Clive Labovitch also attempted suicide. Fortunately, he survived.

Perhaps surprisingly, there doesn't seem to have been the slightest ill-feeling between the two men after the split, even though they produced some publications in direct competition with each other. When Labovitch went bust, Heseltine even arranged for him to rejoin Haymarket. And whenever reporters rang Labovitch in later years, hoping he might dish the dirt on his former partner, they would be disappointed. Until his death in 1994, Labovitch always regarded Heseltine as a man of sound judgement and strong nerve, and someone with whom he never had to write things down. 'He was a good person to work with,' he insisted. 'Reliable. He was always entirely straightforward. And kind.'[22]

The story of what happened to Clive Labovitch after the split may help explain his and Michael Heseltine's relative contributions during the ten years they worked together. While Labovitch was undoubtedly a highly creative and innovative *publisher*, he seemed to lack the necessary skills to succeed as a *businessman*. 'It was a big mistake for Clive to go, because he was not a good manager,' says their colleague Paul Buckley. 'He was an ideas man. Michael was much more business-like and entrepreneurial.'[23]

The parting of the two founders did little to instill confidence in the future of Haymarket. 'There was a sense of crisis,' says Neil Crichton-Miller. 'Labovitch had taken away the solid money-spinners and had left Michael with altogether more speculative stuff.'[24] They might have just hit on a successful formula with *Management Today*, but that wasn't yet proven, and only a quarter of its profits went to Haymarket anyway.

The company's precarious position wasn't resolved until June 1967, when Heseltine invited John Pollock, the commercial publishing director of BPC, down to his constituency home in Devon. On a beach, the two men struck a deal whereby BPC would inject a further £150,000 into the firm, and in exchange increase its stake from 49 to

60 per cent. 'John Pollock was not a frightfully strong character,' says a former colleague, 'and was rather taken in by the Heseltinian glamour, I think.'

At the same time, Haymarket would take over the management of twenty magazines owned by BPC, and contribute its publishing expertise. The titles were a mixed bunch, and none was very profitable. BPC had acquired them over the years, often in lieu of bad debts (in much the same way as it had gained its original stake in Heseltine's business). Pollock and his colleagues recognized that BPC were printers, not publishers; in the past the company had taken little interest in the magazines, and left their editors to their own devices.

Overnight, Haymarket's magazine portfolio all but doubled. Nevertheless, the acquisitions cannot have looked too promising: they included *Parents* magazine, *Houses and Estates* and a journal called *World's Press News*.

Without this second BPC deal, many now believe Haymarket would have gone under. Yet Heseltine was taking a great personal risk: he had done what entrepreneurs try to avoid at all costs, and ceded overall control of the business he'd created. Haymarket was now a subsidiary of BPC, and Heseltine was effectively BPC's employee. He and Lindsay Masters kept their places on the board, together with their long-serving colleague Simon Tindall (who was good on publishing minutiae), but they could now be outvoted by four directors from BPC. If things went wrong, Heseltine might easily be sacked. Yet, if the BPC rescue in 1964 had been something of a turning-point for Haymarket, the 1967 arrangement proved to be the start of its real success.

Now BPC had overall control, it immediately took a far greater interest in how Haymarket was run, and would no longer tolerate the chaotic financial procedures that Heseltine had allowed. A new financial director, David Fraser, was appointed to introduce proper accounts and control systems. Heseltine would later admit it 'would have saved me years' if he'd learnt the lessons earlier. 'You must understand the essential disciplines of cash – having it, not having it, accountants, bookkeeping, proper recording of information. It's the commonest failing, I reckon, in starting a business.'[25]

'Fraser cleared everything up on the financial side,' says Neil

Crichton-Miller. 'He was a very able man.'[26] He has remained with Haymarket ever since. An early victim of the new stringency was *Town* magazine, which folded in November 1967 after an eight-year struggle. 'We should have closed it long before we did,' Heseltine would admit years later.[27]

Shutting *Town* was also an important strategic decision. From now on Haymarket would publish only specialist magazines, catering for particular leisure, trade or professional groups. Yet the company had learnt much from its experience of producing other publications. The careers directories had established an efficient operation for selling advertising space, while *Town* magazine had shown the importance of good design. The subject-matter of the latest titles might appear pedestrian, but once they had been redesigned by Haymarket's art team, or given the hard sell by the advertising department, they became popular money-spinners.

Paul Buckley was assigned by Heseltine to go through the diverse BPC pebbles picked up from the Devon beach and decide whether they should be discarded or polished up. *Autosport*, for instance, has been in the Haymarket stable ever since. The attempt to rejig *Flying Review International* was less successful. Heseltine and Robert Heller tried to reposition it as a kind of *Management Today* of the air. 'Michael wanted a more prestigious magazine,' says the editor, Gordon Swanborough. 'It became square-back, larger page size, and had glossy paper, and immediately lost its appeal to the enthusiast. It wasn't the kind of paper the enthusiast wanted.'[28] Without the plane-spotter market, *Flying Review International* flopped and was eventually sold.

On the face of it, one of the least attractive titles acquired from BPC was *World's Press News*. As the name suggests, it had started as a magazine for journalists and the newspaper industry, then gradually it had expanded to cover advertising as well, though it was never a comfortable combination. Based in an office near the Old Bailey, it had a staff of just three journalists, and much of its content consisted of press releases which had simply been reprinted. But Lindsay Masters and Robert Heller – who, besides editing *Management Today*, also had a role in developing future ventures – recognized that here was a potential nugget. With the right polish and presentation, they could make a success of it. Under a new title – *Campaign* – they would refocus the magazine towards the advertising industry.

The origins of *Campaign* magazine, and the credit for it, are still disputed. This is understandable, perhaps, given its enormous success. Over the next thirty years, *Campaign* would be the flagship of Haymarket publications, and would generate a large share of Michael Heseltine's personal fortune. After *Management Today*, it became the second major strand in Haymarket's rapid expansion.

Paul Buckley obtained copies of other advertising journals from around the world. 'I saw *Advertising Age* from America, and I walked into Michael's office and said, "That's it." It was on glossy paper. That was our role model, really.'[29] Lindsay Masters spent a weekend pasting up a dummy on his coffee-table, using cut-up bits of other magazines. Robert Heller produced a mock-up based on the American *Time* magazine.

Haymarket continued publishing *World's Press News* right up until its relaunch as *Campaign* in September 1968, and gradually extra journalists were recruited for the new title. The new editor was Michael Jackson. He was only twenty-five, but had worked both as an advertising copy-writer and as a sub-editor on two Fleet Street tabloids.

Some at Haymarket envisaged the new magazine as an advertising version of *Management Today* – an up-market glossy – but Jackson thought advertising people were looking for something more newsy and gossipy: 'They didn't want to read long analytical articles. What they wanted to know was who's been fired, who's losing accounts, what creative people are on the loose. They really wanted a sensationalist, newsy newspaper . . . but which also had a look of sophistication and urbanity about it.'[30] So the pages were glossy, but *Campaign* was tabloid in size and had news on the front cover. The headlines and articles were presented like a tabloid, though the features and photos were the length and quality of those in an up-market journal.

The magazine was designed by Roland Schenk, a Swiss who'd worked in Germany but was attracted to London by the Swinging Sixties. Schenk's distinctive layout was incredibly simple, with a black bar across the top of each page and headlines restricted to just a few specific sizes of Franklin Gothic typeface. 'This was radical,' says

Schenk, 'in that no other paper had that discipline.'[31] The formula was imposed rigidly on all *Campaign* editors thereafter; almost thirty years on, modern copies of the magazine look barely different from the original.

If Schenk was responsible for the design, Michael Jackson claims credit for the magazine's title. Lindsay Masters had suggested the name '*AdPress*', as an attempt to encompass the markets of journalism, public relations and advertising. Although it would concentrate on advertising, he felt the journal couldn't discard its journalist readers overnight. Jackson instead suggested '*Campaign*', though Heseltine felt it sounded too political. 'I had a hell of a job to persuade them on that,' says Jackson. 'They said, "Let's canvass all the editors in the whole group," and that came out that, yes, "*Campaign*" was the best name.'[32]

Campaign caused a rumpus even before it was launched, when the dummy edition ran an item saying the editor of the *Daily Express* was about to be kicked upstairs. Fleet Street was not used to experiencing its own techniques from a trade paper which refused to wait for official announcements, or which revealed who was being sacked before the individuals had been told themselves. *Campaign* journalists worked hard at making contacts, though often they indulged in the dubious practice of trading information: for example, telling agencies which accounts were coming up for renegotiation, in exchange for news of sackings. In the late 1960s it was unheard of for a trade magazine to be controversial, to embarrass people or to carry the latest rumours and gossip. Yet so often did *Campaign*'s scoops prove to be correct that it quickly became essential reading.

Part of its success came from hiring most of its writers from Fleet Street, not the cosier trade press. Philip Kleinman came from the *Daily Telegraph*, and Peter Elman from the *Daily Mail*. Other staff included Elinor Goodman, the future political editor of *Channel 4 News*. Goodman joined Haymarket as a secretary, and Michael Heseltine was reluctant to let her work as a journalist at first, but she soon became one of *Campaign*'s best reporters.

'We wanted to make the paper as vulgar as we wanted,' admits Philip Kleinman. 'It brought the readers flocking in. It said what previously people only said to each other in bars.'[33] It was Kleinman who drafted *Campaign*'s 'Statement of Editorial Policy'. 'We will criticize as well as praise, undeterred by bluster, unseduced by hand-outs,' it warned. 'We shall tread on corns, set teeth on edge, wake up sleeping dogs.'[34]

And they did. It was not the kind of magazine Michael Heseltine would have written himself, of course, but he and Lindsay Masters appreciated that something radical was needed in the face of the competition. Inevitably there were people who didn't like the new journal; some complained the content was fit only for the scurrilous *Private Eye*. Ralph Steadman again caused trouble, with a cartoon depicting the editor of the *Sun* being presented with a shovel of steaming manure and being told, 'Hold the front page – I think we've got a story!' Some Fleet Street proprietors got so irritated by items in *Campaign* that they withdrew their advertising, though they usually relented. Yet Michael Jackson doesn't recall Heseltine ever interfering editorially: 'He never made me tone it down.'[35]

On one occasion the advertising agency J. Walter Thompson (JWT) tried to apply pressure through a director who was a Tory MP. Heseltine told Jackson that the only way to placate JWT – which was then the world's biggest agency – was to go and have lunch with the board. After a meal of continuous grousing about why *Campaign* couldn't print proper news, Jackson says Heseltine came to his rescue:

Michael said, 'Well, we've heard a lot from you about what a terrible paper *Campaign* is. There's a well-established ad-industry paper called *Advertisers' Weekly* . . . Hands up who reaches for *Ad Weekly* first?' And of course nobody put their hands up. 'Who reaches for *Campaign* first?' And they all put their hands up. It was quite a nice way of dealing with it.[36]

Yet, after only eight months, Michael Jackson was sacked. As with Julian Critchley's departure, it was Lindsay Masters who did the deed, not Heseltine. Jackson believes he was fired because his magazine upset too many people. 'My reading of things is that they tolerated me as long as I was putting the paper on the map. Once it had established itself they could afford to get rid of me, and they could say to all those people in the ad industry, "We've got rid of that nasty Michael Jackson." '[37] The official reason, however, was that Jackson was too disorganized and expensive. Because *Campaign* wanted to protect its scoops, the magazine would leave it to the last moment to confirm stories (so as to stop companies spoiling them by issuing a press release). This meant hiring casual staff on Wednesday nights, and *Campaign* was often late going to the printer, all of which inevitably pushed up costs. 'The trouble with Jackson,' says Robert Heller, 'was in not sticking to budgets, and not coming out on time.'[38]

Robert Heller says the paper was in such a shambles only days before its launch that Lindsay Masters called him in to sort out Jackson's layout. 'If it had been left to him the magazine would probably not have got off the ground, because it was in total chaos.' Yet Heller also acknowledges that 'without Michael Jackson *Campaign* wouldn't have had that Fleet Street edge, and a lot of character'.[39]

The journalists who arrived with the acquisition of the BPC titles, and the new staff recruited for *Campaign*, all increased pressure on Haymarket to recognize their trade union, the National Union of Journalists (NUJ). Michael Heseltine was adamantly opposed to dealing with unions, as he had demonstrated when Julian Critchley wanted to appoint the Marxist Tariq Ali as *Town*'s reviews editor. Heseltine asked Ali what pay he wanted. 'On hearing my response – "An NUJ wage" – he grunted agreement, but warned me in the friendliest possible fashion against any attempts to unionize the outfit.'[40]

By the late 1960s the pressure to recognize the NUJ had become irresistible, and, faced with a strike, Heseltine reluctantly gave in. 'He didn't like the idea of sitting down with them,' says Robert Heller, who had to negotiate for him. 'He didn't like the idea of a union getting between him and his employees.'[41] But few Haymarket journalists would complain that Heseltine was an especially bad employer. Pay and conditions were fairly typical for the industry.

Within about a year *Campaign* had overtaken *Advertisers' Weekly* in its volume of classified advertising. The achievement was celebrated with a brash series of ads in the national press which contrasted the magazines' revenues in detail. In due course *Campaign* would regularly make annual profits of more than £1 million.

Campaign had also forced a radical revamp of Haymarket's advertising-sales department. Despite Lindsay Masters's innovative methods of selling space for the directories and earlier magazines, before *Campaign* Haymarket had never really sold classified ads. This was the big battleground with *Advertisers' Weekly*. Most of the improvements to the sales operation were developed by Josephine Hart, a young Irishwoman who had learnt her selling techniques with the Thomson Organization. Originally Hart was telephone sales manager for *Campaign* – number eight on the magazine's team – but she quickly worked her way up through her organizing skills and ability to motivate people. 'She was quite brilliant at it,' says Masters. 'I had a little thing with her that for every page she sold extra she could have an extra salesman. Finally I had to say, "That's enough," because she had so many.'[42] *Advertisers' Weekly*, in contrast, had just one person to sell its classified space. And Hart was particularly good at teaching new sales staff. 'She was an extraordinarily polished and sophisticated trainer,' says Michael Heseltine.[43]

Under Hart's command the Haymarket sales team became almost entirely female, whereas before it had been mostly men. 'Josephine Hart was a major change,' says Neil Crichton-Miller. 'Previously people had their own box-file of clients. Under her system, nobody had their own clients . . . the sales of classified ads soared once she'd established her system.'[44] Hart would sit at the front of the tele-sales room listening in to team members as they made calls, to make sure they were using the right approach. If they were not, they were soon corrected. Those who didn't sell enough space were sacked if their technique couldn't be improved.

Josephine Hart saw Heseltine as 'a power-house of ideas. He made you feel that everything was possible once you were committed to a course of action.'[45] In time she became a director of Haymarket, though today she is better known as a writer of best-selling novels – among them *Damage* – and as the wife of the advertising man Maurice (now Lord) Saatchi. Indeed, it was at Haymarket during the late 1960s that she first met her future husband. Saatchi, a graduate of the London School of Economics, was then in his early twenties, and spent much of his three years with the company as Michael Heseltine's personal assistant. One of his tasks was to examine advertising patterns, to spot markets for potential new titles. 'I remember this bright-as-a-button guy, really contributing,' Heseltine would later relate. 'His ideas you listened to, and his perception and analysis were valuable. I can certainly remember feeling we had an ace here.'[46]

Maurice Saatchi is sometimes wrongly credited with a role in the launch of *Campaign*. But, as Haymarket's business development manager in the late 1960s, he *was* heavily involved in the third great money-spinning magazine that Heseltine and Haymarket initiated – *Accountancy Age*. Saatchi virtually launched the journal on his own, though the original idea was Michael Heseltine's – what he calls 'a marvellous example of opportunist capitalism'.[47]

The story of *Accountancy Age* illustrates Heseltine's great ability to spot an opening and exploit it straight away. During his systematic campaign of writing to publishers to see if they might sell their titles, he was contacted in the summer of 1969 by a firm called Gee & Co. Gee's letter explained that it was mainly a book publisher, but suggested it might be worth coming for a chat.

As he waited in the company's reception, Michael Heseltine spotted a journal Gee did produce, called *The Accountant*, and he was surprised to see page after page of classified ads. 'What an impressive publishing outfit you've got here to sell that advertising,' Heseltine observed when he was finally ushered in. No, Gee's managing director explained, they didn't have to sell it: the advertising simply turned up in the post. It was 'a remark I shall never forget', Heseltine later related. He didn't waste much time discussing book publishing:

> I realized I was about to make a fortune. And I went back to the office as fast as I knew how, and found Lindsay. Trembling with excitement, I said, 'Look at this, look at this! It just happens! It just comes with the post!'[48]

As a former articled clerk, Heseltine understood the potential market. Maurice Saatchi was assigned to research whether a magazine would work if it were distributed free to every member of the profession. From published directories, Saatchi assembled lists of every accountant in the country, while Robert Heller commissioned a dummy issue. 'We modelled the design on the *Daily Telegraph*,' he says, 'because we assumed accountants read the *Telegraph*.'[49]

But then, while Heseltine was away on a political trip in Singapore and Heller was on holiday in the Algarve, Haymarket suddenly discovered that another accountancy title was also being planned. Its publisher, Morgan-Grampian, somewhat foolishly, had taken space in *Campaign* to announce the new magazine!

Heller was tracked down in Portugal and asked to return immediately. After an intercontinental phone consultation, Heseltine and Masters quickly ordered that the launch date of *Accountancy Age* be brought forward by three months. 'It was typical of his ability to act very fast and decisively,' Heller says.[50] The first edition was prepared almost entirely by freelances; it didn't even have an editor. Philip Kleinman, who knew nothing about accountancy, was roped in to write another 'Statement of Editorial Policy'.

Accountancy Age was an immediate success. 'It cleared the launch costs in four weeks,' says Heller. Unlike *Campaign*, it began churning out substantial profits from the start, and made a six-figure sum in its very first year. As for Morgan-Grampian's accountancy magazine, 'We just got in ahead of them,' says Paul Buckley, 'and I think they were so staggered they didn't go ahead with their launch.'[51]

In 1969 Haymarket made a pre-tax profit of £136,000, compared with just £3,000 the year before. By 1970 the figure had reached £265,000, and the company was on its way to riches. Heseltine could at last justify all the vulgar trappings of wealth he'd enjoyed 'on account'. The family's elegant new home in Wilton Crescent, Belgravia, had separate doorbells for 'Nursery' and 'General', while servants could be summoned by a buzzer hidden beneath the dining-room carpet.

The launch of *Accountancy Age* in December 1969 was Heseltine's last major executive act for the company, before he took up politics full-time. That month, after his appointment as official Tory transport spokesman a few weeks earlier, he became Haymarket chairman, and handed over the managing director's job to Lindsay Masters. Six months later, politics required his resignation as chairman too. The success of *Accountancy Age* ensured that he left with a flourish, having shown the same willingness to go for the jugular that he had done with *Management Today*. It was a quality to emerge again twenty years later, in very public circumstances, as he took on a Prime Minister.

With all three of its main business titles – *Accountancy Age*, *Management Today* and *Campaign* – Haymarket had taken on long-established competition and emerged on top. Just as would happen with Margaret Thatcher in 1990, Heseltine's publishing rivals were victims of their own complacency, and were slow to respond to his threat.

For many years the three magazines would account for the lion's share of Haymarket profits. In two cases – *Management Today* and *Accountancy Age* – it had been Heseltine himself who had noticed the opportunity, and then galvanized his colleagues into challenging established publishers.

Above all, Heseltine had kept his nerve during the traumatic period from 1962 to 1968; and he then played the relationship with BPC with enormous skill. During 1968, before the success of *Campaign*, the talk within Haymarket was that BPC was about to fire Michael Heseltine. Before long, he would be in a position to dismiss BPC.

10. *High Flyer*

The 1970 Conservative government made Michael Heseltine a national figure for the first time. Although he never served in Edward Heath's Cabinet, he managed to achieve a much higher public profile than many colleagues who did. Long before the Conservatives left office in 1974, Heseltine was being seriously mentioned as a future Prime Minister. The Heath years would also see the emergence of several important themes which have continued throughout his political career – the organization of local government, state intervention to aid high-tech industries, prestige projects, and, above all, Europe and the question of European collaboration.

Indeed, there seems to be an unusual coherence to Michael Heseltine's long ministerial record – as if, by some grand design, the government jobs and responsibilities he's held since the Conservatives returned to power in 1979 appear to be a natural progression from the work he did under Heath in the early 1970s.

Few had expected the Tories to win in 1970, and, when they did, Michael Heseltine was sorely disappointed with the rewards. Having served for eight months as the main Conservative transport spokesman, he naturally expected to be made Minister for Transport, conceivably inside the Cabinet (the post had meant Cabinet rank until Barbara Castle left it in 1969). Instead the job went to John Peyton, who had served as a minister in the Macmillan and Douglas-Home governments. Heseltine became Peyton's deputy at Transport, as a parliamentary under-secretary (or PUS – commonly known as 'Pussy'). Instead of being in the Cabinet, or even on its fringes, Heseltine held the most junior position in one of the least important ministries in Whitehall. It must have been all the more frustrating that his close friend Peter Walker, who, at thirty-eight, was only a year older than Heseltine, was the youngest of Heath's Cabinet ministers.

Sir David Serpell, the Permanent Secretary at the Transport Ministry, had expected Heseltine to get the minister of state's job, and the two men had even met before the election, at the instigation of Fred Mulley, the outgoing Labour minister. More than a decade later, Heseltine still seemed to seethe at getting the inferior post. ' "Pussy." That's what they called us. We were the scum of the earth – *tolerated* by the civil servants.'[1]

In fact that was only just true in one respect: some of Michael Heseltine's civil servants barely *could* tolerate him, at least in his early days in government. They found the young junior minister to be brash, overbearing, arrogant and rude. He acted as if his success in running a company entitled him to dictate how things should be done in government. 'He had very much the air of a successful businessman,' says one former colleague. 'He had difficulty relating to civil servants, as he had not worked with them before . . . There was always a degree of impatience with the slow pace of doing things, and a feeling that the Civil Service had its own agenda.' Another senior official recalls his extraordinary boast that 'There is not much wrong with this country that a few businessmen like me couldn't put right.'

Heseltine was particularly dismayed with the calibre of some of his staff. 'In private office I had the nicest but totally inexperienced kids straight out of university. If they went along to some senior civil servant and said, "My boss has asked if you will do this," they were told where to go.'[2]

'I quickly found, to my considerable resentment,' he wrote later, 'that while I was cutting my teeth as a parliamentary secretary my private office was staffed by young civil servants cutting their teeth on me. It was a training ground where the totally inexperienced were sent to find out what the world was all about.'[3] In three and a half years he had seven private secretaries. As soon as any official did start to learn his stuff, and, as important, got to know Heseltine personally, he was immediately promoted.

Heseltine complained about this to Lord Jellicoe, the Cabinet member responsible for Civil Service matters, as well as to senior officials in the transport ministry:

I blew my top. 'You're not going to use me to train your officials. I'm going to have more experienced civil servants to help me do my job. This is *my* private office.' This was a phenomenon – the wilful junior minister who was going to do his job as he best believed it could be done.[4]

In time, most officials got used to Heseltine, and many came to admire him and to enjoy working with him. But during the Heath years civil servants first discovered he had a brief attention span, and hated being swamped with documents. 'On the other hand,' says one official, 'he was annoyed if you did not tell him enough. The art was to tell him exactly the amount of information he wanted to hear.'[5] Heseltine's rule was that any submission had to be summarized in no more than two pages – which wasn't always easy – though officials could also supply as many background documents as they thought appropriate.

It can't have helped Heseltine's attitude that John Peyton confined him largely to dealing with roads, which mainly involved new schemes and handling the outcomes of public inquiries. It was a period of intense road-building, with 210 miles of new motorway completed in 1971 alone, and the minister was often on hand when the ribbons were cut. When he opened the Westway A40(M) in London – almost his first public ministerial duty – he was rather more tactful with angry demonstrators than with Whitehall officials, and expressed 'sympathy' with people whose homes were about to be blighted by noise and pollution.[6] Another Heseltine opening was the section of the M4 west of Maidenhead – five-year-old Alexandra cut the tape and got to keep the special scissors (later swapped for a schoolfriend's comic). The new motorway was, of course, a great help in getting to Tavistock or Swansea, though it was an embarrassment five months later when Heseltine was caught speeding at almost 100 miles an hour along the very stretch he had opened. He was fined £20.

Controversial road schemes, however, generated vast amounts of paperwork, as objectors prepared long, detailed submissions. Heseltine has always preferred oral or visual presentations to hours of reading, though his civil servants have rarely noticed the mild dyslexia he apparently suffered as a boy. As roads minister, Heseltine went for graphics in a big way. Officials were asked not only to pin up large maps of the alternative schemes, but also 'to mark on the maps the homes of all the objectors, and then to give a number to each mark . . . So one very rapidly began to see much more visually the reasons for people's concerns.'[7]

After just four months, Edward Heath announced a radical restructuring of Whitehall. Transport now became part of one of his vast new 'monster-ministries' – the Department of the Environment (DoE). Heseltine was still a 'Pussy', though now of a rather hybrid breed: he retained his transport brief, but quickly acquired certain responsibilities for planning and local government too.

Again he found himself working with Peter Walker, with whom he remained on extremely friendly terms, to the extent that their families would sometimes take holidays together. Once, while out swimming in the sea during a weekend at the Heseltines' home in Devon, Walker says he and his wife were almost drowned by the 'treacherous current'.[8] Kenneth Baker recalls being told by Heseltine during this period that, 'My object in politics is to help Peter get to the top.'[9]

Walker's primary task as the new Environment Secretary was to restructure the whole system of English local government. What became the despised 'Walker reorganization' involved the first substantial changes in local-council structure outside London since Victorian times. The Redcliffe-Maud Commission set up by Labour had recommended that most of England should be covered by new 'unitary' councils, replacing the two layers of local government that then existed in most places. Around Birmingham, Manchester and Liverpool, Redcliffe-Maud proposed a second layer of local administration which would provide strategic direction for each of the growing conurbations.

The Tories rejected Redcliffe-Maud's unitary system, but the changes which Walker introduced in their stead proved to be deeply unpopular, not least within his own party. His successors as Environment Secretary would spend years unpicking Walker's 'reforms' – a process which still continues a quarter of a century later. Indeed, no subsequent Environment Secretary would be more involved in overturning the Walker reorganization than Michael Heseltine. But in 1971 and 1972, as a junior minister, it was his job to promote and defend it.

Three aspects of the 1972 Local Government Bill were particularly contentious. First, various historic counties were abolished – among them Rutland, Westmoreland and the Ridings of Yorkshire. Second, it was proposed to scrap the old county boroughs: these covered more than seventy-nine towns and cities in which, since 1885, services had been run by one all-embracing local council.

One of Heseltine's jobs was to convince local communities that the changes were right. His former Oxford Union president, Peter Blaker, recalls inviting the minister to explain to Tory activists in his Blackpool constituency why the town should lose its county-borough status. 'He made a very big impression,' says Blaker. 'He didn't change their minds, but after Michael's visit, if there was any problem remotely connected with his responsibilities, they said, "Talk to Michael, he'll understand." '[10]

Although the Tories had rejected much of Redcliffe-Maud, they accepted the assumptions of the time. Faced with a predicted population explosion of as much as 14 million people by the year 2000 (a bad overestimate, in fact), the received wisdom was that planning was vital. In the big cities it was felt that existing city and borough councils were too small to handle broader planning issues affecting wider conurbations, so new counties were created in the urban areas of Bristol, Teesside and either side of the Humber, which became Avon, Cleveland and Humberside respectively. Instead of Redcliffe-Maud's three metropolitan counties, Walker now proposed six, adding West Yorkshire, South Yorkshire and Tyne and Wear, to the West Midlands, Greater Manchester and Merseyside. Michael Heseltine was dispatched to Merseyside to persuade local politicians of the virtues of the new county.

But, while the Conservatives accepted the argument for greater planning, political pressures from party activists and supporters pulled in the opposite direction. The expansion of the new metropolitan counties would be at the expense of the traditional, Conservative, shire councils, which were inevitably opposed to the changes. Consequently the boundaries of Merseyside, Greater Manchester and the West Midlands were all drawn more tightly than Redcliffe-Maud had envisaged. Tory activists in neighbouring areas remained happy, but it meant the new councils would be Labour-controlled for most of their existence, and so the 'Met counties' would become all the more unpopular in Conservative circles.

In Parliament most of the reorganization legislation was handled either by Peter Walker himself or by his deputy, Graham Page. When

Heseltine contributed there was no obvious modesty: he once declared that, with the possible exception of Walker, he had 'read more local newspapers on the subject of local government reform than anyone else in the country – I have read virtually all of them'.[11] On one occasion, however, he showed himself to be badly underread, when he said, erroneously, that parish councils are not elected.[12]

The Walker reforms provoked considerable disquiet in Heseltine's own area of Devon. In Plymouth, councillors were particularly upset about losing their county-borough status, which would mean that important services such as education were run from Devon County Council in Exeter, more than forty miles away. 'Michael got a lot of stick, because he was the local MP,' says John Macmillan, his party treasurer. 'One night I had Michael to speak, and he got a very rough ride.'[13]

At the last moment Plymouth City Council – backed by the local Tory MP, the formidable Dame Joan Vickers – voted almost unanimously to suggest an alternative to ministers: a new Tamarside County Council, along the lines of the other new city-based counties of Avon and Cleveland. But the proposed Tamarside would extend well beyond the existing borders of Plymouth to include large chunks of Devon and Cornwall. Tory activists in the Tavistock constituency were divided deeply over the plan: most of the rural areas were resolutely against the further encroachment of Plymouth into Devon, though a few in Plympton and Plymstock, already part of the city, favoured it. Plymouth council allocated £10,000 – then a considerable sum – for its Tamarside campaign, but the idea was never a runner. Heseltine's opposition had pleased most members of his own constituency party, but did not endear him to Tories in Plymouth.

In fact Plymouth's ambitions to expand eastward were a constant source of friction. At one point Plymouth council tried to buy 200 acres of farming land at Sparkwell, well outside the city boundary, to develop more local industry. Heseltine told his constituency officials he couldn't get involved, since he might have to help adjudicate on the dispute. His position as an environment minister, he argued, 'must take precedence over my other constitutional responsibilities as local MP'.[14]

Heseltine's lofty stance infuriated his predecessor. Sir Henry

Studholme lived near Sparkwell and privately told Heseltine in the strongest terms that his first duty was to his constituents. 'It was such an easy mistake for Michael to make when he was in London,' says his chairman, Betsy Gallup. 'A small village on the outskirts wouldn't seem the thing to get het up about. But it had some very vociferous gentlemen in it.'[15]

By now Heseltine was seen less and less in Tavistock; he knew he had no future as a local MP. One of the first acts of the Heath government had been to push through the constituency boundary changes delayed by Labour, and shortly after the 1970 election Heseltine announced he would let his parliamentary neighbour, Peter Mills, take the future West Devon seat, which included most of the old Tavistock. It soon emerged that he wasn't interested in fighting Plymouth Sutton either, which acquired the rest of Heseltine's seat, even though some local activists urged him to stay. 'I remember him standing in our drawing-room,' says John Macmillan, 'and we suggested that he fought Sutton. He made it clear that he wanted to get back to the London area.'[16] 'If he had wanted it, I think he would have got Sutton,' says Betsy Gallup, who was surprised at how swiftly her MP announced his departure.[17]

Heseltine was soon involved in what nowadays is disparagingly called the 'chicken run', as sitting MPs scramble for safe seats in a political version of musical chairs. Parliamentary friends and colleagues are inevitably pitted against one another. Heseltine limited his sights to London and the surrounding counties, and he didn't find it easy at first. The *Sunday Express* columnist 'Crossbencher' suggested he was 'about as popular with Tory selection committees as a coalman in a linen-room'. The paper proposed one solution: 'A haircut.'[18]

Bidding for Mid-Sussex, the area around Lewes and East Grinstead, Heseltine came up against his ministerial colleague Sir Ian Gilmour, but both were defeated by the future Chief Whip, Tim Renton. In Mid-Oxfordshire he was beaten by Edward Heath's political secretary, Douglas Hurd. In Beaconsfield he was dragged into a bitter local squabble as party left-wingers tried to use the minor boundary changes in their seat to get rid of Ronald Bell, one of the most right-wing Tory MPs. Heseltine allowed his name to go forward for the contest, and he joined Bell on the final short list of four, only to withdraw two days before the selection meeting 'in the interests of the Conservative Party'. Bell had the backing of some left-wing MPs, and it seems to have been gently suggested that it was bad form for a minister to challenge a sitting member.[19] Six weeks later, in a neighbouring seat, Heseltine's quest was over. It was his fourth attempt, but worth the wait.

Sedate and prosperous, Henley was the kind of seat any ambitious Tory would dream of. It was situated just thirty-five miles from Westminster, and very safe. From Henley-on-Thames itself – home of the famous Royal Regatta – the constituency swept westward across the Chilterns to the fringes of Oxford. Much of its southern boundary was defined by the meandering river, though the seat carefully avoided Reading. Many inhabitants of the main communities – Henley, Watlington, Thame and Goring – were affluent commuters, divided in their daily commitments between Oxford, Reading and London. The only Labour threat came from a few wards around Cowley in Oxford, home to workers at the British Leyland car plant.

The retiring MP, John Hay, had represented Henley since 1950. He had served as a junior minister under Macmillan, but was left on the back benches by Edward Heath. Although he was still in his early fifties, he had been quite ill, and, after more than twenty years in the House, politics had lost its sparkle for him. The announcement of his retirement naturally aroused considerable interest, and Heseltine was among several MPs who button-holed him for support.[20] In all, 180 people applied for the nomination.

The Henley Tories – who officially called their association South Oxfordshire – also short-listed two other victims of the Boundary Commission. One was William Shelton, the MP for Clapham, who, John Hay recalls, had even bought a home in the constituency. But Heseltine's most serious rival was Norman Fowler, the MP for the disappearing Nottingham South. In the end, however, Heseltine made the best speech and won with a clear majority on the first ballot; this time there was no attempt to get his nomination overturned. John Hay's recollection is that the party had wanted a candidate who was 'fairly rich' – a quality he himself lacked, but Heseltine had acquired. The thinking seems to have been that if their MP was already well-off he would not be diverted by business interests in the way that Hay had been. The Henley party also extracted a promise from their new candidate to live in the constituency, and within a year the Heseltines had moved into a large 1920s mock-Tudor house in Crocker End, near the village of Nettlebed, though they retained their London base in Wilton Crescent.

By the time he secured the nomination for Henley, Heseltine had been promoted. In April 1972 Edward Heath moved him to another super-ministry, the new Department of Trade and Industry (DTI), to become aerospace minister (a title created only the year before). He was now a minister of state, and also ranked as one of the most senior ministers outside the Cabinet. In the official pecking order he was on a par with other long-term leadership rivals such as Sir Geoffrey Howe and Christopher Chataway.

Under Heath, the DTI was a much more interventionist ministry than it is today, of course, and this was especially true after the 1972 Industry Act, which gave ministers considerable new powers. This historic U-turn in government policy was also illustrated by the sacking of the right-wing free-marketeer Nicholas Ridley as a junior minister, and the replacement later in the year of the ineffective Secretary of State John Davies with Peter Walker (pairing him with Heseltine for a third time).

And Heseltine was working with the industry where government intervenes more than almost anywhere else. Most aerospace projects involve research-and-development costs, and there are often important considerations for national security and prestige. Both parties had long accepted that, if British aerospace firms were to compete overseas, government should give a helping hand. This was often through 'launch aid' – state money to pay for initial development costs, and which had to be repaid only when the project went into production. Yet, despite his reputation as a great intervener, it is arguable that during his two years as minister Michael Heseltine didn't make aerospace policy any more 'interventionist' than it already was.

He also quickly discovered that, within the DTI's federal structure, aerospace was almost an independent ministry, with 'something of a life of its own'.[21] Heseltine asked a newly elected MP, Cecil Parkinson, to be his parliamentary private secretary (PPS), or unpaid aide. Parkinson, who had first met Heseltine on an accountancy course in the mid-1950s, protested he knew nothing about aerospace. 'Nor do I,' he recalls Heseltine saying, 'but I want somebody in this department who knows even less than me.'[22]

There was a natural affinity between Heseltine and his new PPS, and if there were any serious ideological differences at that time they weren't obvious. Parkinson was soon impressed by the way Heseltine 'injected a sense of urgency into everything'. The minister liked to operate according to work-plans and regular check-lists; progress was measured at regular meetings:

A typical meeting with the civil servants would go, 'You can have that in three weeks' time.' 'That's no good.' 'Two weeks then.' 'No.' 'OK, one week, if you must.' But in the end they'd be saying, 'You can have it in three days' time.' He just speeded things up. People knew he wouldn't forget things. He definitely quickened up the pace of the department.[23]

Cecil Parkinson adopted many of Heseltine's methods when he himself became a minister seven years later – though with an extra dash of personal charm, one suspects. The future Tory chairman would subsequently remark of Michael Heseltine that 'in his constructive and deliberate unreasonableness he reminds me in many ways of Mrs Thatcher'.[24]

Heseltine's new job plunged him immediately into the task of marketing Concorde. It was inevitably a high-profile role; indeed under Labour, both before and afterwards, the Concorde job was held by a Cabinet minister, Tony Benn. Heseltine's Tory predecessor, Frederick Corfield, had supposedly been sacked for not being dynamic enough, and Heath seems to have hoped that Heseltine – almost twenty years younger than Corfield – would bring some youthful enthusiasm to the task. He was 'a breath of fresh air', says Geoffrey Knight, the former vice-chairman of BAC, the Concorde manufacturers. 'He was, of course, looking for headlines all the time to promote his career, but it so happened that promoting Concorde coincided with that very nicely indeed, so that we benefited from it.'[25]

Selling Concorde wasn't easy. The plane – the world's first supersonic airliner – was beset with problems. Costs had risen from less than £100 million in the mid-1950s, when it was first mooted, to an estimated £1,070 million by 1974, and only part of the increase could be blamed on either inflation or devaluation. It involved a treaty obligation with France, which made it difficult to consider the plane on its intrinsic merits. There was the unavoidable sonic boom, and there were also tricky problems of noise and fumes. Concorde carried only a quarter of the number of passengers of the new 747 jumbos, while its range was frustratingly limited: New York to London or Paris was feasible, but not the short extra distance to Rome or Frankfurt.

By the time Heseltine arrived at the DTI there was little room for resolving these difficulties. The best hope was that an aggressive worldwide sales campaign might recoup some of the vast investment. The Queen, Princess Margaret and Princess Anne were all seen with Heseltine on board the aircraft.

It was unreasonable, however, to expect foreign orders while neither the French nor the British national airline had made firm purchases yet. Early in 1972 there appeared to be a serious danger that Britain's long-distance carrier BOAC (then merging with BEA to form British Airways) might not buy Concorde at all. More than once Heseltine summoned the entire BOAC board to his office. But the directors knew their bargaining position was strong, and argued that they couldn't justify Concorde on the normal commercial criteria under which BOAC was expected to operate. Ministers should underwrite any losses from flying the plane, they insisted. Cecil Parkinson recalls that the airline's board even threatened to resign *en masse*. 'Michael went to work, and two days later I sat listening to the Chairman thanking the government profusely for giving the corporation the opportunity of a lifetime, scarcely able to believe what I was hearing.'[26] Parkinson says of Heseltine, 'That was an example of him at his most effective.'[27]

Whatever the public appearance, however, the aerospace minister had perhaps been outmanoeuvred. The government had to grant BOAC (then state-owned) the money to buy two new jumbos from Boeing, under financial arrangements that probably wouldn't satisfy the National Audit Office nowadays. Moreover, the airline had ordered only five Concordes, compared with the eight for which it had options.

Heseltine's biggest sales effort was a Concorde world tour in the summer of 1972. Model 002 visited eleven countries in a month, including Iran, India, Singapore, Japan and Australia. Heseltine went along for the first two weeks, as far as Singapore. (There were jokes about whether Lee Kuan Yew's authoritarian regime would let him in with such long hair.) Anne accompanied him – to show that Concorde was a family plane – and was rather more diplomatic than Lord Carrington's wife, who had emerged from another trip saying the cabin was 'a bit cramped'. Lady Carrington had touched on a real problem, since the restricted interior was another reason why airlines were reluctant to buy.

Towards the end of the tour the Heseltines flew to Toulouse to rejoin Concorde on its last leg back to London. With a final upbeat press conference at Heathrow, the trip finished with a flourish, though it was completely unjustified. Not a single Concorde was sold as a result of the 45,000-mile journey.

At one point seventeen airlines around the globe had options to buy seventy-four Concordes, though Fred Corfield had expected only thirty sales at best. Then the plane became a victim of the early-1970s recession, environmental concerns and American hostility. The biggest blow came in January 1973, when Pan-Am cancelled its option, and within the hour Pan-Am's main rival, TWA, had cancelled too. Other overseas airlines soon followed.

Eventually, only ten Concordes were ever bought: five each by British Airways and Air France. The last remaining prospect, that the Shah of Iran might buy two or three planes, was finally quashed by the 1979 revolution. Heseltine put in a lot of effort, says the Concorde test pilot, Brian Trubshaw, and generated great publicity, but he didn't make much difference to the plane's eventual fortunes.[28]

Perhaps the strongest criticism of Heseltine over Concorde was not his poor record as a 'super-salesman' but instead his failure both to examine the marketing figures more closely and then to cancel it. 'Concorde was one of the few issues on which Heseltine was indecisive,' says one of his officials. 'Heseltine was much more uncritically committed to the programme than Wedgwood-Benn was,' argues Ken Binning, the DTI civil servant in charge of the plane.[29]

The aircraft was closely tied to Edward Heath's ambitions to join Europe, and in these, of course, Heseltine was an enthusiastic supporter. Indeed, Concorde had been initiated by Harold Macmillan in 1962 as a means of securing French support for British entry to the Common Market (though the gesture proved fruitless). Under Heath, the Number Ten think-tank, run by Lord Rothschild, acknowledged that the project was 'a commercial disaster', but accepted that financial costs were outweighed by European aspirations.[30] Even at the time, Edward Heath did tentatively broach the possibility of cancellation with the French President, Georges Pompidou.

Concorde was a less than glorious episode in Michael Heseltine's career, which may explain why it merits not a single mention in either of his late-1980s manifestos-cum-memoirs, *Where There's a Will* and *The Challenge of Europe*.[31] His work on European cooperation in space, by contrast, is given several pages in each volume.

After visiting the United States, Heseltine had quickly concluded that space was too big a matter for individual European countries. Some American cities had more resources directed towards space research (funded, of course, by the US government) than the whole of Europe. It was absurd for individual European governments to subsidize companies to compete with each other, all in a forlorn effort to match the two giants, America and the Soviet Union, which both had long-established space programmes. Indeed, the USA had just landed men on the moon.

The answer, Heseltine concluded, was greater cooperation and integration on this side of the Atlantic, pooling resources. If Europe combined its expenditure on space, he calculated, it still came to a fraction of the American budget, but would be far more effective than the even tinier sums each country spent alone. In Britain the picture was still gloomier, since money for space research was further divided between several government departments – the DTI, the Ministry of Defence (MoD), even the Post Office, and particularly the Department of Education and Science, through its quango the Science Research Council (SRC). Heseltine made no progress in trying to persuade ministerial colleagues to combine Britain's resources. One close colleague says his unsuccessful battle with the then Education Secretary, Margaret Thatcher, to obtain the SRC's space budget, did much to sour their relations.

In Europe, however, Heseltine had more success, and in 1973 he took a leading part in setting up the European Space Agency (ESA). The ESA combined two previous European space bodies, and countries now agreed to collaborate even at the cost of downgrading or even scrapping their own national space programmes. Heseltine himself abandoned work on Britain's own project, the Geostationary Technological Satellite, and took the highly unusual step for a minister of handing several millions back to the Treasury.

Once the ESA had been established, Britain agreed to rejoin the European launcher project – which it had left two years before – and to work with other Europeans and the Americans on a manned space laboratory. Such cooperation, Heseltine says, 'seemed to me a better use of our national resources than trying to subsidize our national industry – as the official advice to me had originally suggested – in the hope of outdoing the French and Germans'.[32] Civil servants, one should note, deny advising any such thing.

Heseltine was equally convinced of the need for European cooperation in civil aviation. In the face of increased costs and American competition, he argued, 'we must move from *ad hoc* collaboration on specific projects towards an integrated European aircraft industry'.[33] This, of course, would be a recurring theme in his later ministerial career, especially as Defence Secretary in the mid-1980s, and with dramatic personal consequences.

Michael Heseltine's two years covering aerospace inevitably established widespread contacts with industrialists, especially in companies he later handled at the MoD. For instance, he was in almost daily touch with the GEC boss, Arnold Weinstock. The two men had first met when Heseltine was at Transport and horrified his officials by summoning Weinstock to explain in person why GEC's electronic motorway signs didn't work properly. When shipping was added to Heseltine's responsibilities in the autumn of 1972, Cecil Parkinson remembers him saying how pleased he was to be considered capable of handling the extra workload. ' "And there's another little bonus," he said – "Arnold Weinstock has no shipping interests!" At that moment the phone rang. It was Arnold Weinstock. "Oh, Arnold Weinstock *has* got shipping interests." '[34] At first, it seems, Weinstock wasn't impressed with him. 'Arnold's opinion of Heseltine, the

Aerospace Minister, has ... fallen to a low level,' the newspaper publisher Cecil King wrote in his diary after dining with Weinstock in May 1973.[35] Later, however, Weinstock's view improved so much that it produced an important friendship that has survived ever since.

Such close relationships between ministers and the captains of industry were regarded by critics as contributing to the growing corporate state. No British ministry was ever more 'corporatist' than the DTI under Walker and Heseltine; indeed, some observers feel that, during the Heath years, Trade and Industry was as powerful a ministry as the Treasury, under the rather insubstantial Anthony Barber. Michael Heseltine was a great believer in Great Britain Ltd – an economy led by ministers working hand in hand with top businessmen. Perhaps surprisingly for an entrepreneur who had started from almost nothing, it was a world in which small businesses played little part. But then Haymarket succeeded only after it had been rescued by a large industrial conglomerate in the form of BPC.

Heseltine's corporatist outlook must also be qualified. First, he had a low opinion of the calibre of many of the people running British industry. Moreover, one form of 'corporatism' also involves a major role for the trade unions, whereas Michael Heseltine has always shown little interest in consulting union leaders – unlike ministerial colleagues such as Jim Prior, or indeed Ted Heath.

Concorde and space were the biggest items on Heseltine's DTI check-list, but a much smaller high-tech project caused the first serious crisis of his government career. In other circumstances Hovertrain might even have finished him as a minister. In 1973 he was accused of what some regarded as the most serious case of lying to the House of Commons since the Profumo scandal a decade before. He survived because it took several months for the full details to emerge, and, by the time they did, Parliament was then in summer recess.

Hovertrain – as the name suggests – was an improbable-sounding project to develop a passenger train which could run at 300 miles an hour along a cushion of air created by magnetic levitation, powered by linear motors. The vehicle didn't need wheels, but did require a completely new type of track. Since 1967 governments had spent more than £5 million on the idea, channelled through a state firm called Tracked Hovercraft. Six years on, it needed another £4 million to survive, and Heseltine and his colleagues had to decide whether to put up the money.

Early in 1973 rumours began circulating that the Hovertrain was about to be abandoned. The Commons Select Committee on Science and Technology decided to investigate the project, while the Labour MP David Stoddart put down a written question asking the Industry Secretary, 'What further financial assistance he intends to make available for the continued development of the tracked hovercraft train?' Heseltine replied on Peter Walker's behalf: 'The question of the government's providing financial assistance for the continuation of this project is still under consideration. I shall make a statement shortly.'[36]

Two days later, however, Michael Heseltine appeared before the select committee and announced that the government was cancelling Hovertrain. When questioned, he admitted that ministers had taken the decision to cancel on 29 January, two weeks *before* David Stoddart was told that further assistance was 'still under consideration'. Heseltine's two statements seemed contradictory: it was difficult to see how funding was still being considered if the project was already dead. 'I think Michael Heseltine has been lying,' the Tory chairman of the committee, Airey Neave, was heard to remark as he left the room. Neave was so angry that he even approached David Stoddart to emphasize the discrepancies in Heseltine's replies, implying that the Labour MP should pursue the matter.

Stoddart and other Labour members publicly accused Heseltine of lying, although the committee's report, published nine months later, phrased its conclusion more politely: 'Mr Heseltine's answer to Mr Stoddart's question on February 12,' it declared, 'was untrue.'[37]

'I did not lie to the Commons,' Heseltine insisted at a press conference held immediately after publication.[38] He was deeply upset that his integrity was being questioned, but the Chief Whip, Francis Pym, feared problems if it came to a vote of censure, and ordered him to say sorry to the House. Heseltine could have ignored Pym's advice only by resigning. 'He felt that he'd got nothing to apologize for,' says a colleague, 'but that he'd got no option in parliamentary terms. That was a wretched episode for him.'

On the first day that Parliament returned in the autumn, Heseltine delivered a brief statement. 'I realize on reflection,' he said, 'that the wording of my answer on 12 February was capable of more than one interpretation and led to misunderstanding. I apologize most sincerely to the House for the misunderstanding which arose.'[39]

When is a lie not a lie? When it's a 'global' response, it seems, for that is how Heseltine justified his misleading reply to David Stoddart. He claimed that further financial support *was*, in fact, being considered at the time he appeared before the select committee, since he was talking to both Hawker Siddeley and British Rail about how they might salvage parts of the Hovertrain project.[40] Later he even granted them state aid to do so.

Heseltine also claimed to have delayed the announcement because Hawker Siddeley had been bidding to sell the Hovertrain motor to Canada, and a government statement might undermine its chances. This, however, did not square with Heseltine's earlier assertion to the committee that Hawker Siddeley felt cancellation 'will not prejudice their position'.[41]

Heseltine's PPS, Cecil Parkinson, is among those who believe his boss was the victim of Airey Neave's intense animosity towards Edward Heath and anybody to do with him. This dated back to the 1950s, when Heath told Neave he was 'finished' after he had suffered a heart attack.[42] 'If Michael was anything, he was a Ted Heath protégé,' says Parkinson, who suggests that Neave really wanted to grill Heath himself, who probably took the closure decision. 'Various people on that select committee said, "We're not after Michael, he's just the junior minister," ' Parkinson claims.[43]

One Tory member of the committee says that both Neave and another member, the redoubtable Sir Harry Legge-Bourke, looked down on Heseltine as 'new money' and 'brash'. And they disapproved of the way he had cut short his National Service, whereas they, in contrast, had distinguished war records. Legge-Bourke was particularly upset about Hovertrain because its test site at Earith was near his Isle of Ely constituency.

Heseltine seems to have been guilty more of cock-up than of conspiracy. He undoubtedly did mislead David Stoddart, but there's no evidence of any plot to deceive MPs for any personal or political benefit. He may just have been suffering from his relative ministerial inexperience. His private secretary, Tony Lane, says he was an unfortunate victim of the timing of events, and of the Whitehall convention 'that all decisions are said to be under consideration until they're announced'.[44]

Heseltine's swift rebuttal once the select committee's report was published, and his apology to Parliament, stopped the issue gaining further momentum. David Stoddart did not press his complaint, and there was little desire among others to do so. Today, in a different climate, it might have generated a media frenzy over 'Tory sleaze'.

The day after the report, both the *Daily Mail* and the *Express* featured Anne Heseltine and their children in their new Oxfordshire home. The coverage portrayed her husband sympathetically, implying that Hovertrain was just part of the job for a busy member of the government.[45] 'A thing like that would have crushed a lot of junior ministers,' says Cecil Parkinson, who had feared for Heseltine's future.[46]

As with many political rows, the furore over whether or not Heseltine had lied obscured the real question: whether it was right to abandon Hovertrain. The select committee felt ministers had made a serious error, and said the cancellation was both 'premature and unwise'. It also condemned the government over the peremptory way in which staff at Tracked Hovercraft were sacked.[47]

Today, surviving members of the select committee are reluctant to blame Heseltine for the decision: they suspect he would have preferred to continue the project. In the face of what was apparently a unanimous decision by Heath and other Cabinet members, however, there was little he could do. One senior non-government source connected with the project suggests the real reason for cancellation may be far more sinister: that ministers bowed to pressure from the Nixon administration, which was worried by the competition that Hovertrain might have posed to the US transport industry. Heseltine has since said the full story will be told one day, but not by him.[48]

Michael Heseltine had eased his way out of the crisis, and Ted Heath does not seem to have been too worried about the Hovertrain incident. He was upset, however, with what he regarded as Heseltine's lukewarm handling of the bill to establish a third London airport at Maplin Sands on the Essex coast, which, along with the Channel Tunnel, the government saw as a major prestige project. Faced with a revolt from local Tory MPs, there was a serious risk the bill might be defeated. Just before the all-important third-reading vote, Heseltine and other ministers were summoned for a dressing-down by Heath at Number Ten. They hadn't promoted the legislation enthusiastically enough, the Prime Minister said, and were too willing to compromise with the rebels. 'Heseltine came back to the office fairly chastened,' says Tony Lane. 'Whatever thoughts he had about making concessions on Maplin, Heath considered them unnecessary.'[49]

There were other set-backs, too. On one occasion Heseltine embarrassed his colleagues with a disastrous speech at a National Sporting Club dinner to honour Brian Trubshaw and the French Concorde pilot. The TV presenter Hughie Greene had opened proceedings with a light-hearted speech packed with jokes. 'Michael decided he'd do that too,' says Cecil Parkinson. 'It went down like a lead-filled balloon. He'd misjudged it totally. He'd laid a real egg.'[50] Word of his performance soon reached the press, which reported he'd told 'a couple of stories that were pure stag-night material – and lost conviction half-way through'.[51] (Alas, no record of the actual stories survives.) Worse still, Heseltine knew his audience consisted almost entirely of top people from the aviation world, with whom he had to deal every day. 'He came in the next morning,' says Parkinson, 'saying, "I've done this terrible thing." But it was quickly forgotten.'[52]

Overall, however, Heseltine emerged from the tempestuous three and a half years of the Heath government with his reputation enhanced, though he wasn't universally liked. The story is told of a Cabinet Office exercise to handle a mock hijack at a British airport. When the imaginary terrorists demanded a government minister as a hostage, his colleagues unanimously volunteered the minister for aerospace!

More seriously, it helped, perhaps, that Michael Heseltine had managed to avoid the real historic crises of the period – industrial relations and the two coal strikes; disputes over pay policy; and Northern Ireland. Nor had he played much part in the big debate over joining the Common Market.

When Edward Heath called a snap election in February 1974,

Heseltine took his new constituency in Henley with a majority of 8,900.

He'd gained a new seat, but then found himself out of office, for, unexpectedly, the Prime Minister's gamble had failed. In the face of a second miners' strike, Heath had gone to the country on the issue of 'Who governs Britain?' The voters had given the Tories an answer: 'Not you.'

11. *Oh My Darling Heseltine*

Nineteen seventy-four was a momentous year in British politics. The change of government from Conservative to Labour was confirmed only after two general elections. At the second, in October 1974, the new government secured a precarious majority of just three seats, and even that would soon be whittled away by deaths and desertions, though Labour remained in office for another four and a half years. For the Conservative Party, the trauma of two successive defeats would provoke a radically different type of politics.

If the Tories had won either election, Michael Heseltine would almost certainly have joined the new Cabinet shortly afterwards. Instead, in opposition, he began by shadowing his old DTI job, and when Edward Heath unexpectedly moved Peter Walker to cover Defence in June 1974 Heseltine replaced him as the main Tory spokesman on industry, with a place in the Shadow Cabinet. To reach Cabinet level after just eight years in Parliament was good going, though not exceptional. Today, more than two decades later, Heseltine boasts of being the only member of Heath's Shadow Cabinet who is still sitting on the front bench.

Although Michael Heseltine detested the powerlessness of opposition, he still found the job easier than many politicians. In 1974 trade and industry were critical subjects. Labour's new Industry Secretary was Tony Benn, who in opposition had driven his party's industrial policy to the left. Although Labour's 1974 manifestos were greatly watered down from the party's earlier commitment to nationalize twenty-five top companies, Benn still envisaged a substantial extension of public ownership through the proposed National Enterprise Board. Labour also wanted planning agreements between the government and major firms.

Benn's left-wing stance, combined with the evident division in government ranks over industrial policy, and the unpopularity of much of what Labour proposed, were ideal conditions for any shadow minister. Heseltine seized them wholeheartedly. During the summer of 1974 he enlisted a team of more than twenty Tory back-benchers to exploit the uncertainty over which companies Labour might nationalize. Each MP was assigned to a particular industry, with the job of campaigning nationwide on the implications of public ownership in each case.

On the whole, Edward Heath had been good to Michael Heseltine. He'd advanced his career, and it was a sign of their friendly relations that the Tory leader should have attended a party at Heseltine's home in Wilton Crescent to celebrate his fortieth birthday in March 1973. Until the autumn of that year Heseltine was describing his leader as 'our Oliver Cromwell, our Lord Protector', but then disillusionment quickly set in. It may partly have reflected Peter Walker's unhappiness with Heath, first because the DTI lost responsibility for energy after the 1973 world oil crisis, and then over his 'demotion' to Defence. And Heseltine was very upset about Heath's handling of the 1973–4 miners' dispute.

People close to Heseltine say the main problem, though, was Heath's abrasive manner. Quite apart from the dressing-down over the Maplin bill, there was an occasion when the Tory leader reportedly told Heseltine to his face that he was too ambitious and interested only in himself. Heath's adviser Michael Wolff told him not to worry: that was simply how the boss treated people who were close to him, and it was a sign that he was now a major player. But Heseltine complained that he was 'only human' and bound to react to such harsh treatment.

A Conservative leadership contest became inevitable after the October election defeat, in which Heseltine himself had again bucked the national trend and increased his Henley majority by 1,300. His reservations about Heath became obvious a mere ten days afterwards, when he publicly advised his leader to decide on his future before Christmas – a remark his boss can't have found helpful.[1] A month later Margaret Thatcher announced she would run for the leadership.

Though Michael Heseltine was certainly not a Thatcher fan, he, too, had concluded it was time for Heath to go. Like many on the Tory left, however, he hoped Heath's replacement would be the party chairman, Willie Whitelaw. But Whitelaw was far too loyal to challenge Heath himself. The only answer, many Whitelaw supporters calculated, was for Heath to fare sufficiently badly in the opening round of the contest that he would have no option but to resign. Then Whitelaw could honourably stand himself.

Norman Tebbit, who worked in Margaret Thatcher's 1975 campaign team, claims Heseltine voted for her in the first round. 'I recollect John Nott and myself persuading Michael Heseltine, who was a Whitelaw man, that unless he voted for Margaret on the first ballot there would be no second ballot and no opportunity for Willie to stand.'[2] When subsequently asked, Heseltine has refused to reveal publicly whom he supported in the first round, which adds credence to Tebbit's account: he may be ashamed to admit having helped Thatcher to power, whereas if he'd backed Heath why not say so? A close friend is adamant that Heseltine voted for Thatcher, though she herself says her team 'believed him to have been an abstainer'.[3] What seems certain is that the former Heathite didn't support Heath.

Heseltine did briefly discuss the idea of standing himself in the second round. It wouldn't have been a serious bid, of course: like his first run for the presidency of the Oxford Union, he would have just been staking a claim for next time. Wisely, he decided against, for he would probably have garnered even fewer than the nineteen votes obtained by two other long-term contenders, Jim Prior and Geoffrey Howe. Instead, Heseltine joined the Whitelaw camp, though he wasn't very active. In any case, by then it was too late. If Heseltine did vote tactically for Thatcher in the first ballot, he must soon have realized his mistake. With the help of disillusioned left-wingers, Margaret Thatcher had gained sufficient momentum from beating Heath in the first round to take her to victory in the second. Like many of his colleagues, Heseltine had regarded Thatcher's candidacy as a bit of a joke at first, and realized only too late how serious it was. For more than fifteen years he would be saddled with a leader he disliked, though at the time he assumed her reign would be brief.

'Michael was practically white a few hours after it was announced,' says Michael Jones, who worked for him at the time of Thatcher's victory. Heseltine was convinced he would be sacked, and it cannot have reassured him that Airey Neave, his chief critic over Hovertrain, was one of Thatcher's closest advisers. 'He was absolutely shocked when she included him in the Shadow Cabinet,' says Jones.[4] It is said

Thatcher had planned to demote Heseltine or sack him altogether, in which case few people today might ever have heard of him. It seems that a senior figure – possibly Geoffrey Howe – spoke up on his behalf.

There was also a more immediate reason to keep Heseltine – one of those amusing quirks of history. On the very day that Thatcher announced her new Shadow Cabinet, he was leading the Tories against the second reading of the Industry Bill in the Commons. It was hardly the moment to sack the party's industry spokesman. Without this piece of luck, Heseltine might easily have been dismissed, in the same way Peter Walker was in 1975. And, since he was still a relatively minor figure, few people would have noticed, let alone complained. Later, Thatcher would have even greater misgivings about retaining Heseltine as Shadow Trade and Industry Secretary. 'What I did not fully grasp at this time,' she says, 'was how ideologically committed he was to an interventionist approach in industry which I could not accept.'[5]

Whenever Thatcher and Heseltine had dealt with each other in the past – as transport spokesmen, and then over space funding – relations had been strained. Heseltine has always had trouble accepting women in positions of authority. 'I've always in my bones felt Michael's not a "new man",' says a friend who's known him since Oxford. In Tavistock he had problems when the Tories briefly appointed a woman agent. At Haymarket he'd been reluctant to promote Elinor Goodman – 'Secretaries don't become journalists,' she was told firmly – and he later found it difficult to accept the idea of Josephine Hart as a Haymarket director. Jean Taverner and Eileen Strathnaver are exceptions, of course, but over the years Michael Heseltine has never done much for the cause of women. Now, to his horror, he had a female boss.

Yet initially both went out of their way to be conciliatory, and Heseltine began to change his mind about his new leader. If he performed well in the Commons, or on television, Thatcher might send a note of congratulation. Ironically, in view of later events, Heseltine was soon telling colleagues that he felt particular loyalty to her because of the noticeable difference between the way in which she and Heath treated people. 'At this moment I would follow that woman everywhere,' one adviser recalls him saying. Margaret Thatcher's future press secretary, Bernard Ingham, also remembers noticing how enamoured Heseltine seemed of his leader at the time.[6]

But the political differences would inevitably cause friction. They first became obvious during the summer of 1975, when Labour rescued British Leyland with state funds. The natural instincts of Thatcher and her main economic adviser, Sir Keith Joseph, were to let Leyland go under, but Heseltine persuaded his colleagues that too many marginal seats were at stake. 'That was the first acid test,' says Michael Jones. 'Michael was very tough and brave and said: "We can't entertain the idea of letting these companies go bust." Michael had talked the Shadow Cabinet into taking a more realistic position.'[7] (Another factor was that many employees at Leyland's Cowley works lived in the northern part of the Henley constituency.) Publicly, shadow ministers tried to give noncommittal responses to the Leyland rescue and attacked only the details, but Thatcher admits that the 'variation in tone, particularly between Keith and Michael, was obvious to all'.[8]

Although most of the Shadow Cabinet were hostile to what soon became known as Thatcherism, and were broadly on the left of the party, there was no natural affinity between Heseltine and many of the old-style paternalists who shared his politics. The grandees regarded him in much the same way as nineteenth-century Tories viewed the upstart Disraeli. It didn't help, of course, that Heseltine had made his money in businesses that were very 'Sixties' and regarded as vulgar and distasteful, such as fashion magazines and the glitzy world of advertising. Was he entirely sound? Could one altogether trust a man with such long hair, or who wore very expensive suits with linings of crushed scarlet or decorated with pink elephants? Heseltine may never *actually* have worn pink-elephant linings, but it didn't really matter: it was the jibe that did the rounds.

'The sort of man who combs his hair in public,' the new deputy leader, Willie Whitelaw, is supposed to have observed of the Tory industry spokesman.[9] Although Whitelaw had gained his backing in the leadership election, he felt Heseltine could so easily have been a socialist. To Whitelaw the party meant everything, and he was suspicious of Heseltine's obvious ambition and the way he seemed to be using the Conservatives merely as a ladder to power. Yet Whitelaw's feelings were mixed: he couldn't help admiring Heseltine's effective-ness as a politician, and his drive and gutsiness.

In the Conservative Research Department, the director – Chris Patten – and his colleagues would openly talk about there being a 'wobble' to Heseltine, and often joked about his being 'slightly bonkers'. There seemed to be too much dashing around and too little reflection.

Heseltine made little effort to allay people's doubts, or to enable Tory colleagues to know him better. After Shadow Cabinet meetings, most members would hang around and chat, but Heseltine always left straight away; he always had something more pressing to do. Unlike Whitelaw, for example, he was never one to gossip. And, for a man who was so ambitious, Heseltine seemed to have gathered surprisingly few political friends. Two of his advisers, Michael Jones and the MP John Cope, would often suggest he should spend time with back-benchers in the bar. 'He didn't find that he had the character to sit down with Tory backwoodsmen and make them like him,' says Jones. 'He felt it would make them like him less.'[10]

Heseltine reassured himself with the thought that neither Edward Heath nor Margaret Thatcher had been chummy with back-bench MPs either, and it hadn't stopped them reaching the top. As someone who'd been successful in business, he felt that ingratiating himself with parliamentary colleagues was beneath him. Instead, he would make himself well-known and popular in the country, through appear-ing on television and with speeches to the party grass roots. It was a very similar strategy to Enoch Powell's, though the politics were very different, of course. Popularity in the constituencies, Heseltine reckoned, would eventually influence members at Westminster – the people who ultimately elected the leader. And he adopted one basic rule: never turn down an invitation. Unlike most politicians, Heseltine now had the resources to hire a helicopter, if necessary, and fulfil a string of engagements in one day.

Heseltine's exchanges with Labour, both at Westminster and out-side, were often blistering and highly personal. He mocked Harold Wilson, Jim Callaghan and Tony Crosland for their lifestyles – for owning 'luxurious pads that would do credit to the most self-seeking capitalists', for instance.[11] On Labour's plans for public ownership, he accused Tony Benn of lying, and Harold Wilson of 'a travesty of the truth'.[12] Another row erupted when he charged Benn with 'blackmail' and 'corruption' in his use of the 1972 Industry Act, though he later withdrew his words.[13] In turn, Tony Benn said Heseltine and his party had 'systematically lied' about Labour's own industry legislation.[14]

The Shadow Industry Secretary was making a better fist of opposition than many of his colleagues, even though the more experienced Benn often got the better of him in the Commons itself. 'Heseltine made another flayling attack which gets no support from his own benches,' he wrote in his diary after one exchange. 'He is an awful old flop.'[15] Both men would hate to admit it, but in many ways Michael Heseltine and Tony Benn were alike: deeply ambitious, fascinated by new technology (including Concorde), obsessive, and distrusted by their colleagues. The Labour minister had little regard for Heseltine as an individual and thought him intellectually shallow. But Benn admitted he 'did admire him for making the headlines in Opposition which is a very difficult thing to do'.[16]

At the same time Heseltine felt British industrialists did too little to defend themselves. In the face of the attacks from Labour, he suggested, company bosses should actively promote the importance of profits. Nor did he think many businessmen were good at their jobs; he decried 'the sort of slovenly "I'm not responsible", "I can't do it, try somebody else" attitude which you find in far too many companies with which you have to do business'.[17] But, after his period as a Heathite interventionist, Heseltine seemed to be regaining confidence in free enterprise. 'My prolonged exposure to the attitudes of Labour MPs,' he later wrote, 'and my obligation to probe the reasoning behind their nationalization measures, rekindled my faith in the capitalist system.'[18]

Yet 'free enterprise' was usually the term he employed, rather than the 'free market' stressed by the emerging Tory right. When Heseltine extolled the virtues of capitalism – which he did often – he generally meant large public companies, not small businesses. Yet so long as Labour pursued its public ownership plans, and Heseltine maintained his ferocious attacks, his differences with the Thatcherite approach to industry weren't too obvious.

Amid the shock of losing two elections, and a bloody leadership contest, Michael Heseltine soon emerged as one of its few spokesmen able to rouse a disheartened Conservative Party. The first example came in March 1975 at the party's national council meeting – a kind of interim party conference – when Heseltine was reportedly in 'ebullient form' amid the apathy and somnolence. But Heseltine's first really big occasion – one of the landmarks of his career – came that October at the party's annual gathering in Blackpool. It was his first platform speech at the conference, and he spent hours preparing.

'We are involved in a struggle for the very heart of society,' he told Tories assembled in the Winter Gardens:

The threat to nationalize our aircraft and shipbuilding companies is not just a threat and an erosion of freedom for those industries; it is a challenge to us all . . . It is only in a free and dynamic society that there can be any prospect of removing the remaining pockets of hardship and distress that still scar our society. We must give the strong, and those with natural advantages and talent, the opportunity to develop their gifts, for there is nobody else to protect and aid the weak.[19]

Not since Iain Macleod's great platform oratory in the 1960s, or the occasional turn by Lord Hailsham, had a speaker raised the spirits of party loyalists so effectively. They cheered loudly, clapped, and stamped their feet in thunderous delight, and gave Heseltine a standing ovation, which was then an accolade bestowed much more sparingly by conference audiences.

Sarah Hogg, later head of John Major's Number Ten Policy Unit, recalls visiting Blackpool as a reporter for *The Economist*, accompanied by a colleague, Mark Schreiber. Both tried to retain their journalistic neutrality:

Hezza was on flying form. The audience loved it. The applause was deafening. Seeing Mark's unmoved countenance, an empurpled constituency chairman seized him by the lapels. 'Clap, damn you! Don't you believe in England? CLAP!'[20]

Ironically, Mark Schreiber (now Lord Marlesford) is one of Heseltine's closest friends, and if he hadn't advised him what to say on that occasion he has certainly done so at other times.

Heseltine had prepared his speech with his new researcher, Dermot Gleeson. 'We'd divide it into sections,' Gleeson says – 'scribble a bit before handing it over to each other and rewriting it.'[21] Michael Jones, another adviser who helped with speeches, says a lot of the work – too much – involved removing incomprehensible material that Heseltine had included. 'Though he'd have great ideas, there'd be moments when he'd lapse into incoherence. Sometimes he'd do drafts and you'd think, "What *are* we talking about?" '[22]

Nor did Heseltine's reception at the 1975 conference reflect the substance of what he'd actually said, says Dermot Gleeson. 'The standing ovation was to do with the manner of the delivery, not the content. If he'd read out the New York telephone directory with that vigour and style he'd have got a standing ovation.'[23]

Afterwards Heseltine presented Gleeson with a copy of Lord Home's memoirs, inscribed with the words 'If you can get me a standing ovation with your first speech, what will you get with the second?' Now he'd done it once, of course, the new star had to generate a rapturous reception year after year, and the Heseltine performance quickly became a set-piece annual event. Advisers say he would rehearse his speech pacing around his hotel room, and that often much of it would be written at the very last moment. Following Harold Macmillan's advice, he took particular care over the final words, to ensure it ended with a climax.

Every October the final applause had to be longer than in the previous year, but the currency soon became debased as ovations became standard for most Tory front-benchers. It took Heseltine much physical effort, with arms flying and sweat pouring from his body. And Simon Hoggart described another feature:

The fascination lay in the terrible things that were happening to his hair. Something had gone dreadfully wrong with the engineering system holding it up. Great chunks of it crashed down, like cliffs falling into the sea, covering his forehead and sometimes blotting out his eyes.

Now and again he tried to shore it up in mid-speech, but then a bit would sheer off and crash around his ears. By the end the whole noble edifice was in ruins, a sad reminder of the frailty of man-made things.[24]

The old-fashioned Tory grandees privately deplored Heseltine's annual demagoguery as vulgar in the extreme. Nor was Mrs Thatcher a fan – it's said she deliberately avoided being present and having to applaud. Bruce Anderson relates the story of a sketch performed by the candidate Noel Picarda during a conference revue in the late 1970s. Two drunken peers are leaving the platform after a Heseltine speech. 'You can shay what you like about that fella Hesheltine,' says one – 'he can't half find the party's clitoris.'[25]

Heseltine's most notable conference speech, at least in opposition, came in Brighton in 1976. It was a week after Labour's annual gathering had been dominated by the drama of Denis Healey trying to win delegates to his economic policies before flying off to win support for sterling from the International Monetary Fund.

On the very morning that Heseltine spoke, Labour's disarray was compounded by a rise in interest rates to what was then an unprecedented 15 per cent. He pounced upon Denis Healey's crisis with relish. 'He should go,' he declared. 'This government should go; and if it had a shred of pride it would go today.' He went on to deride Labour's claim to support private enterprise: 'The reality lay in Blackpool last week: a one-legged army limping away from the storm they have created. Left, left – left, left, left.'[26]

The audience roared with laughter as Heseltine marched leftwards across the Brighton stage as if he had a limp. He couldn't resist milking it: 'Left, left, left,' he repeated. It had been a great risk, but the gag worked as he proceeded to his peroration and another standing ovation:

Let us make one thing clear. The Red Flag has never flown throughout these islands yet, nor for a thousand years has the flag of any other alien creed. It is only our party that can keep it that way. We must not and we shall not fail.[27]

Curiously, the 'Left, left, left' passage is really the only line that survives in people's memories of Heseltine's great seaside orations of the late 1970s, and that was more knockabout comedy than a point of political substance. Michael Heseltine has never been a great phrase-maker.

The 1976 speech led to speculation that Margaret Thatcher might appoint Heseltine as party chairman in place of the lacklustre Lord Thorneycroft, who was then in his late sixties, and the Tory whips did consider this. There was also talk of his changing places with the Shadow Chancellor, Sir Geoffrey Howe. Neither move was likely. If Thatcher's personal relationship with Heseltine was now civil, if not cordial, politically she grew increasingly anxious about his economic views. He had, for example, attacked Labour for failing 'to agree and develop an industrial strategy' when Thatcher herself didn't believe in such strategies.[28]

In January 1976 Heseltine had put the case firmly for state support to British enterprise:

Industry after industry in Europe is in receipt of government finance, direct or indirect, not only for social reasons such as regional readjustment, but simply because governments have accepted the need to develop their industrial capacity.[29]

Such words were rather more likely to come from Tony Benn, or Benn's successor at Trade and Industry, Eric Varley, than from Margaret Thatcher or Keith Joseph. Thatcher says she soon realized that Heseltine's 'outlook was completely different from mine'.[30] She was even less impressed by an event in May 1976 which caused many Tories – not just free-marketeers – seriously to question Michael Heseltine's judgement.

The 'mace incident' was part of one of the most dramatic episodes in recent parliamentary history: rarely has the Commons witnessed such pandemonium. It occurred during a procedural debate on Labour's latest nationalization measure, the Aircraft and Shipbuilding Industries Bill. The precise details of what Michael Heseltine did that night are disputed, and television had not yet been introduced into the Commons to verify matters one way or the other. But if cameras had been present, MPs might have behaved themselves.

The debate was only the latest skirmish in a war of attrition against the bill that had lasted more than a year and involved a record fifty-eight committee sessions. As the ten o'clock vote approached, Heseltine and the opposition believed they might finally scupper one of Labour's leading manifesto commitments. For Heseltine personally it would have been an enormous coup, though ironically he would have been indebted to Robin Maxwell-Hyslop, his old Oxford University adversary. Maxwell-Hyslop had become an expert in parliamentary procedure, and through clever argument and detailed research he maintained that Labour's measure was what is technically called 'hybrid'. Because the bill excluded one shipbuilding company – though it was disputed whether it *was* a shipbuilder – all interested parties, such as firms about to be nationalized, had the right to put their case to a special select committee. The Speaker, George Thomas, had ruled that Maxwell-Hyslop was right and it was prima facie a hybrid bill. Since committee hearings would be time-consuming, and might jeopardize the legislation, Labour sought to suspend the relevant standing order and allow the bill to proceed as normal.

Earlier, a Tory amendment in support of the Speaker's ruling had resulted in a tie, with 303 votes each way. By precedent, the Speaker was obliged to cast his vote against this amendment. The opposition knew, though, that if the vote on the main motion were the same, then this time the Speaker would be bound to side with them and reject the government's efforts to suspend the standing order. The Tories were ebullient; Labour looked glum.

Then, against expectations, the government won the main motion by a single vote: 304 votes to 303. As Labour MPs taunted the opposition front bench, it emerged that they had won only because a government whip had broken his 'pair'. The whip had made a traditional pairing arrangement with a Tory MP whereby both men had agreed not to go through the lobbies that night, thereby cancelling each other out. He should not have been voting at all.

Heseltine and the Conservatives looked crestfallen: a famous victory had been snatched from them, apparently by Labour cheating. Left-wingers – including the future leader, Neil Kinnock – began singing 'The Red Flag' in triumph. Angry and disappointed, Michael Heseltine picked up the silver-gilt mace which sits on the table between the two front benches. The mace is nothing less than the symbol of the Crown's authority delegated to the House, and Heseltine now advanced with it towards the singing Labour members. If that was the respect they had for parliamentary democracy, he suggested, they might as well take the mace. MPs from both sides were horrified. Heseltine's front-bench colleague Jim Prior quickly intervened:

I now leapt up and grabbed the mace from him. 'You bloody fool,' I shouted, 'give it to me, and get out of the Chamber as quickly as you can.' I put the mace back on the table as Michael departed . . . Thanking me a few days later for rescuing him, he remarked that he had made up his mind to pick up the mace. But he hadn't worked out how to get rid of it![31]

Heseltine's departure didn't calm the chamber. Scuffles broke out between opposing MPs, and the serjeant-at-arms was heard using what one member called 'the most foul language that I have heard outside a barrack room'.[32]

Political folklore has it that Heseltine swung the mace in the air as if doing a tribal war dance, or that he brandished it as if about to club Labour MPs. This is the 'Tarzan' version (though Heseltine had acquired the nickname years before).[33] In the absence of photographic evidence, we can rely only on the accounts of people who were present.

The *Daily Telegraph* reporters said Heseltine 'removed the mace and brandished it towards Labour left-wingers'.[34] According to the *Guardian*'s sketch-writer, Norman Shrapnel, he 'shook it at them like a golden fist'.[35] Jim Prior tells how Heseltine, 'holding it above his head as any good Tarzan would, advanced threateningly towards the chanting MPs on the benches opposite'.[36] The Speaker, George Thomas, says he 'wielded it over his head . . . It looked to me as if he was going to crash it down on top of them.'[37] Heseltine's colleague Tom King insists, however, that the idea that 'he was waving the mace in the air and that he was going to brain a few people' is 'not true'.[38]

'I was *not* swinging or waving it,' Heseltine claimed afterwards.[39] He explained that, when his colleague moved to restrain him, Prior had pulled down on one of his shoulders. The effect, he claimed, was that his other arm shot up in the air, and with it the mace.[40]

Margaret Thatcher was furious. Whatever Heseltine's actions or motives, his moment of fury had distracted attention from an important moral victory for the Conservatives, even if they hadn't managed to sink the bill.

For the second time in less than three years Michael Heseltine had to stand up and apologize to the House. He tried to do it that night, but the Speaker wouldn't let him, since Labour would inevitably have moved a vote to suspend him. Instead, George Thomas adjourned the sitting to let tempers cool. 'I deeply regret my action,' Heseltine told MPs at the start of business the following morning, and he was 'apologizing unreservedly'.[41] 'I shouldn't have done it,' he admitted later. 'I shouldn't have allowed myself to be provoked.'[42]

Many of those close to Michael Heseltine say it's unusual for him suddenly to lose his temper. Some people have even wondered whether the mace incident was planned, since Heseltine is normally such a cautious and calculating man, but then he could hardly have anticipated that Labour would win a vote in such a dubious way. One adviser says that sometimes Heseltine's outrage is feigned, but not on that occasion: 'You could see his veins bulging – he was furious.'

What *is* clear is that, when assessing the likely impact on his reputation, Michael Heseltine felt there were two sides to the incident. 'I think there was some very genuine regret,' says a close colleague, 'but there might have been an undertow of a feeling that this is something that would be remembered and stand out in the headlines.' Kenneth Baker recalls that afterwards older Tory MPs were muttering that Heseltine should resign from the Shadow Cabinet. 'When I told Michael this he laughed, saying, "The House may not like it but the public will love it." As usual Michael had an eye for the audience.'[43]

If Heseltine thought it might do him good in the long term, he was mistaken. The 'mace incident' has been held against him ever since, as a prime example of poor judgement and unbalanced character. For those Tories who abhorred his politics, or who disliked him for snobbish reasons that couldn't be voiced publicly, it provided the ideal excuse to do him down. Nor did it help that Heseltine's accounts of the event, as given to Tory MPs in subsequent weeks, weren't always consistent.

Far from promoting her industry spokesman in the autumn of 1976, Margaret Thatcher instead moved him to shadow Environment, a job he certainly didn't want. At first he firmly resisted the idea of giving up his post to John Biffen, though this petulance only damaged his standing further. Thatcher finally secured his acquiescence through John Stanley, an MP who had worked closely with Heseltine during the first two years of opposition and was now her own PPS.

'Michael,' Thatcher says, 'reluctantly agreed to make way for John Biffen on the understanding that he would not have to be Secretary of State for the Environment once we were in power.'[44]

Thatcher's reasons for the switch were twofold. First, of course, was Heseltine's very different political outlook. Now that the DTI was in the hands of Eric Varley, a much less left-wing minister than Tony Benn, and Labour had completed its nationalization programme, it would no longer suffice to denounce government plans as extreme and Marxist. The time had come for the Tories to explain their own industrial policy. Second, while Thatcher may have concluded that Heseltine was unsound politically, she also recognized him as an extremely effective front-bencher who would make much more impact than the existing Environment spokesman, Tim Raison. Thatcher was convinced from her own time shadowing Environment in 1974 that it could involve several vote-winning policies – notably the right to buy council houses, and reform of the rates.

People who worked with Michael Heseltine during this period say he was 'really hacked off' that Thatcher had 'sidelined' him and 'clipped his wings'. Yet in due course he would spend more than five years in two separate spells as Environment Secretary – longer in the job than anyone else.

For a long time in opposition he took little interest in some of his responsibilities, and seemed bored by the complexities of financing local government. 'I can't be bothered with all this,' Heseltine would tell advisers, adding that there 'were no votes in it'. Reiterating Margaret Thatcher's famous 1974 pre-election promise to abolish the rates, Heseltine pledged 'a system that reflects people's ability to pay rather than the size of the house in which they live'.[45] As to what that system might entail, no clue was given. The Tories' lack of detailed thought on local-government issues would be a serious mistake; the party's failure to find a viable alternative to the rates would ultimately prove fatal to Thatcher.

On selling council houses, Heseltine offered tenants not only the right to buy but a generous scale of discounts, ranging up to 50 per cent after twenty years' tenancy. He described possible Labour plans to cut mortgage tax relief as 'a spiteful class measure', and spoke of limiting mortgage rates through adjusting the tax system.[46] The latter was the typical uncosted promise of an opposition politician, and was quietly dropped long before polling-day.

Like all senior front-benchers, Michael Heseltine was entitled to an office in the Shadow Cabinet corridor at Westminster, but since 1974 he had preferred to work from a small top-floor room in Haymarket's new building at the bottom of Regent Street, a mile from the Commons. This self-imposed isolation in Regent Street symbolized his detachment from his parliamentary colleagues. Most ambitious politicians would not dream of distancing themselves so far from the centre of power, intrigue and political gossip.

In addition to two advisers supplied by the Conservative Research Department, Heseltine employed his own full-time staff and other occasional aides. These included the Earl of Shelburne, a Wiltshire councillor who was now standing in the same seat Heseltine had once fought in Coventry. (Nowadays Shelburne is better known for allowing his friend Prince Charles to use his country home, Bowood House, as a rendezvous to meet Camilla Parker Bowles.) In time Heseltine became a very close friend of Shelburne's wife, Lady Frances. He also seems to like aides with upper-crust backgrounds: his secretary, Elizabeth Lamb, was the daughter of a British ambassador.

In place of Lady Eileen Strathnaver, who was now bringing up her children, Heseltine took on an economics graduate called Pamela Collison. It was an appointment he probably lived to regret. Collison found Heseltine 'very open and honest' to work for, and says his outside obsessions included Pink Panther films and Petula Clark. 'The only time I saw him really angry,' she later told the *News of the World*, 'was when he had tickets for one of her concerts. There was a three-line whip in the House, so he had to vote and miss the show. He stamped his feet in rage.' Collison's job was to read papers for Heseltine, collate statistics, prepare material for speeches, and brief him for questions in the House. 'He was very good at speaking,' Collison said, 'but at the time I don't think he had the reputation as a serious politician. He needed someone to give him more political weight.'[47]

Pamela Collison was perhaps not the ideal candidate for this. After he sacked her, Collison claimed it was probably because she had been 'sleeping around', and her dalliances had become well-known within the party. She was to become better known four years later, when she was accused of helping her boyfriend, Paul Vickers, to murder his wife with a drugs overdose. Vickers was sentenced to a minimum of seventeen years; Collison was acquitted of murder but was convicted of making a false prescription to obtain the fatal medicine.

Officially, Heseltine had been given an office and a car by Haymarket because he was again working for the company. 'I was told his main job was to think of new publishing ideas and bring in entrepreneurial flair,' says the former Haymarket director Robert Heller. 'In fact he did very little, because he was so heavily involved in politics.'[48] Heseltine himself would tell political colleagues how satisfying it was 'to discover his presence did raise performance', but in reality the business remained firmly in the hands of Lindsay Masters and his deputy, Simon Tindall. The range of journals had grown steadily. Perhaps the most important new title was *Computing* magazine, published in conjunction with the British Computer Society, which distributed free copies to its 17,000 members. Very soon *Computing* was contributing as much to the Haymarket balance sheet as *Campaign* or *Accountancy Age*.

In practical terms Michael Heseltine had given up day-to-day involvement in Haymarket's work when he resigned as chairman on becoming a minister in 1970. Nevertheless, he played a part in a series of strategic decisions which ensured that when the company was eventually making millions, by the late 1970s, he took the lion's share.

The most important move, in 1971, involved the 60 per cent stake which BPC had held in Haymarket since 1967. Relations between the two parties had always been strained. One former BPC manager says Heseltine's attitude changed completely after the crucial 1967 deal had been struck:

It was an endless stream of complaints about how bloody awful BPC's printing was and so on. It was cleverly done . . . Most of the board meetings were spent arguing about 'Well, I had late delivery here – I really can't go on using BPC printers when we have this sort of performance.' He changed from an eloquent 'I will transform the world' to what he's very good at – sort of poker-faced nit-picking.

By the early 1970s BPC was in deep financial difficulty, and making regular losses. Spotting this, Heseltine and the two other individual shareholders, Lindsay Masters and Simon Tindall, assembled a consortium of four financial institutions to buy out BPC for £1 million. It was a ludicrously low price, given that Haymarket had made more than £250,000 the year before and was expanding rapidly, but Heseltine says BPC 'needed all the money they could get'.[49] The consortium – Charterhouse Development, County Bank, ICFC, and Wren Investments – agreed to take two-thirds of BPC's shares in Haymarket and to lend the company a further £820,000. With the help of a large personal loan, Heseltine bought the remaining one-third (20 per cent of the total shares issued) himself.

It was an ingenious deal which meant that Heseltine, Masters and Tindall had regained control of the company. Heseltine himself now owned just under 50 per cent of the equity. To complete the complex transaction, all the parties involved gathered with their lawyers and advisers in a large hall in the City. 'The inevitable happened at the end,' says one of the bankers, 'as Michael thought he was president of the Oxford Union again and entered into a grand oration and bored everyone stiff.'

Heseltine had been less shrewd, however, with another promising opportunity that had arisen just before. Having learnt much from working at Haymarket, Maurice Saatchi left the company in 1970 to set up a new advertising agency with his brother, Charles. The Saatchis needed £25,000 launch capital, and Maurice approached both of his old bosses to see if they were interested in backing him. Lindsay Masters invested, but Heseltine claims to have felt inhibited by what he thought were the regulations on conduct for ministers. 'Having read the rules of ministerial behaviour perhaps more cautiously than I should, and wishing to remain 100 per cent within the spirit of them, I thought it would not be right to have been involved.'[50]

Years later, reading the guidelines again, Heseltine said his interpretation of the rules had been 'rubbish', and that it was the sort of investment 'ministers are fully entitled to make'.[51]

Saatchi & Saatchi would, of course, become the biggest advertising agency in the world during the early 1980s. Maurice Saatchi freely admits that his company's phenomenal growth was achieved by copying many of the aggressive techniques Heseltine had employed in acquiring new magazines for Haymarket. The Saatchis' progress was also greatly assisted by favourable coverage in *Campaign*, which would often knowingly carry exaggerated claims of the size of the agency's contracts. Many in the advertising world suspected some complicity between Haymarket and the Saatchis, though it was largely a case of Charles Saatchi being such a good source for *Campaign* journalists.

Lindsay Masters and the other original backers were eventually bought out by Maurice Saatchi, and Masters missed the chance to make an even bigger fortune than he would with Haymarket. Michael Heseltine has since speculated as to what might have happened if he, too, had joined Masters as an original investor:

If I'd had shares in it, would they have actually succeeded in buying us out? If I'd been with Lindsay and there had been two of us, instead of Lindsay on his own, we might have reinforced each other. Whether Maurice would have got away with it – I've often laughed about that.[52]

In 1971, several months after joining the government, Michael Heseltine did what ministers are strongly advised to do, and placed his Haymarket shares in a family trust. The two trustees were his solicitor, Charles Corman, and his boss at the DoE, Peter Walker, who has performed the function ever since.

Two years later Haymarket was on the brink of going public. Since 1969 the group's pre-tax profits had roughly doubled every year: £136,000 in 1969, £265,000 in 1970, £453,000 in 1971 and £704,000 in 1972. In 1973 they were expected to top the £1 million mark. Flotation proposals were prepared by Haymarket's financial advisers, Charterhouse Japhet, but then the 1973 oil crisis caused a dramatic slump in the publishing industry. 'The market collapsed and there was no way we could command the kind of PE [price/earnings] ratios we had been talking about,' says Heseltine. 'So we abandoned the flotation plans, and all of us who were shareholders have been profoundly grateful ever since.'[53]

Whether Heseltine would have benefited from going public can only be conjecture. Market flotation might well have increased the value of his shareholding, but on the other hand he would probably have lost control of his business for ever. Heseltine finally secured a majority stake in his company in 1977, when he and the other three individual shareholders – Masters, Tindall and the financial director,

David Fraser – bought out the 40 per cent share held by the Charter-house consortium.

The deal entailed further personal borrowing at a time when Heseltine had also taken out a substantial loan to buy himself a grand new country house in Northamptonshire. Despite Haymarket's continuing profits, it was a heavy burden, especially when, for a period in 1979, interest rates reached an unprecedented 17 per cent. By then, of course, Michael Heseltine and the Conservatives were back in government.

12. *A Model Thatcherite*

Shortly after Margaret Thatcher's 1979 election victory, Michael Heseltine was asked about the likely direction of her new government. Was he at all worried that the Prime Minister might act as a wild right-winger? No, Heseltine responded, for, while Thatcher might have right-wing instincts, she was very cautious. Nor should one worry about Sir Geoffrey Howe at the Treasury. From their days together in the Bow Group, Heseltine was confident that the new Chancellor was a fairly middle-of-the-road Conservative. Above all, he felt, Thatcher's more extreme inclinations would be restrained by those around her, and she would inevitably be guided by the advice of her civil servants. Moreover, her new Cabinet was still a very Heathite group of men.

Michael Heseltine had enjoyed a good election in 1979. Indeed, on days when Margaret Thatcher was not campaigning, journalists would usually follow him instead. And, despite the victory, Thatcher was none too happy with the way most of her front bench had approached the election. In her memoirs she accuses colleagues of behaving 'more like ministers-in-waiting than politicians' – with 'the exception of Michael Heseltine, always relishing a headline'.[1]

As Thatcher shaped her new Cabinet, there was a brief misunderstanding about Heseltine. In 1976 he had accepted the shadow Environment brief only on the grudging understanding that he would have a different post in government. Thatcher tried to oblige: 'I offered him the Department of Energy – an important job at the time, since the fall of the Shah was sending oil prices sharply upwards.'[2] Heseltine responded that if Energy was the best she had to offer then he'd prefer to stick with Environment, and so David Howell went to Energy instead. Heseltine's reaction was a sign of how much he had grown to appreciate the potential of the DoE. He now had a very clear idea of what he wanted to do there.

The prize, of course, was selling council houses. Heseltine believed the policy was 'capable of generating the great social revolution of our time. Everyone who owns a home has made a fortune out of it – and now we're saying to these people you can have a place in the sun too.'[3] Selling council houses was not novel: it had been pursued with gusto by some Tory authorities since the 1960s, notably in Birmingham. What was new after 1979 was the scale of the sell-off. And, more widely, Heseltine expressed the view that council-house sales could be the start of a programme of denationalization in which, eventually, shares in state industries might be handed out to the public. In this he was far ahead of his time: in 1979 the Tories' privatization plans extended barely beyond the industries Labour had most recently nationalized.

Heseltine's initial inclination on council houses, in fact, had been to go far beyond the manifesto commitment and give them away to tenants. This idea had originally been mooted by Peter Walker from the back benches in the mid-1970s, after his dismissal from the Shadow Cabinet. Walker had argued that some councils would support the plan, since they were spending more on housing maintenance and management than they recouped in rents. But when Heseltine first raised it the Treasury was horrified. Margaret Thatcher thought it would greatly upset people who had just made big sacrifices to buy their homes.

So the man who had had trouble selling a single home in Tenterden in the 1960s now became the biggest house-seller in British history. Just as he had found personally in Kent, however, the sales had to be encouraged by large discounts. Two weeks after taking office, Heseltine issued a circular allowing councils to sell houses for at least a third less than the market value, and to give 100 per cent mortgages.

The legislation enacting the right to buy – the 1980 Housing Act – didn't reach the statute-book until eighteen months after the Tories took office. Heseltine was slow in pushing the bill through Parliament, and the initial deadline had to be postponed. Then, in the summer of 1980, a Lords ambush caused further delay, and he was eventually forced to exclude housing for retired people.

In the past, many authorities – Conservative as well as Labour – had refused to sell council houses, because they didn't want to deplete their stock. And in 1980 the initial response from some authorities was obstructive. Several were slow in processing application forms; others insisted on explaining the possible drawbacks to buyers; one council even threatened to house problem families next to those who bought. So Heseltine took firm action against Norwich, a Labour authority he accused of being especially dilatory, to set an example to the others. The council took the minister to court after he'd used new powers to set up an emergency DoE sales office in Norwich, but his action was upheld, and other opposition soon crumbled.

Many Labour councils quietly acquiesced, partly because they were eager to spend the proceeds from sales. The Treasury wanted the new income to reduce the overall level of public-sector debt, but Heseltine agreed with Sir Geoffrey Howe that authorities could use 75 per cent of the receipts to renovate their remaining housing stock or build new homes. In later years councils felt deeply aggrieved – as did Heseltine himself – when the Treasury restricted further the proportion of housing receipts they could spend.

Of all the measures of the Thatcher government, the right to buy had the greatest long-term social impact. More than a million council houses were sold during the 1980s – roughly a fifth of all local-authority housing. But the rush to buy wasn't simply a case of tenants exercising new freedoms: it was aggressively promoted by Heseltine, who forced councils to double their rents. As rents increased, the prospect of buying became more attractive, especially when in subsequent years the DoE introduced even greater discounts.

In opposing the 1980 act, Labour's Roy Hattersley had argued it would 'diminish the supply of public "rented property" ' and that poor tenants would be denied houses that had been sold off.[4] But by the mid-1980s Labour had decided it could no longer oppose a policy that was so popular with tenants, and the party's 1987 manifesto promised to 'maintain the right to buy'.[5]

The great majority of tenants who bought were delighted, though large numbers suffered mortgage repossessions in the early 1990s. But Labour's concern in 1980 that the right to buy would transform council housing from homes for the working class into homes for the poor has proved true. Overall it was the better semi-detached houses that tenants bought, rather than flats. Inevitably the poorest tenants have become isolated on unattractive inner-city estates, plagued by crime, vandalism and drugs. Equally serious, the right to buy was accompanied by big cuts in investment in new council housing.

Michael Heseltine describes the introduction of the right to buy as 'one of the most fascinating and worthwhile political experiences of my life', and frequently cites it as one of his big achievements.[6] Yet he deserves only limited credit. It was hardly his idea: it had been Conservative policy since the February 1974 election, long before Heseltine took responsibility for housing. The Conservatives would have implemented the measure in 1979 no matter who was Environment Secretary. Much of the preparatory work had been done in opposition by his junior housing spokesman, Hugh Rossi; in government, the detail was relentlessly pursued by his housing minister, John Stanley. (Although the two men had once been close colleagues, it was suspected that Stanley had been 'turned' by three years as Thatcher's PPS, and that he was now a kind of double agent who'd been sent to keep an eye on Heseltine.)

Heseltine's identification with the right-to-buy legislation won Margaret Thatcher's praise at a time when he was not always supportive on wider debates in Cabinet. In later years, Heseltine would even joke about being an early, model Thatcherite. He was fulfilling much of her agenda, not just on housing but in other areas of the DoE, and in ways he could claim *were* distinctively his.

The DoE Permanent Secretary in 1979, Sir John Garlick, has described the transition from his previous Labour minister, Peter Shore, as 'a great contrast from a very conservative Labour Secretary of State to a very radical Conservative Secretary of State'.[7] Like the former Labour minister Richard Crossman, Heseltine believed in making a firm impression with civil servants from the start, partly to keep control of the political agenda. He had worked with Garlick at Transport in the early 1970s, and on his first day as Environment Secretary he took his new Permanent Secretary out to lunch. Heseltine wanted to make his mark on neutral territory, away from the distractions of departmental officials and paperwork.

Over a table at the Connaught Hotel, the man who had once charted his life-plan in an Oxford restaurant now presented the DoE mandarin with a more immediate agenda. Just as in Long John's, twenty-five years before, Heseltine set out his intentions on the 'back of an envelope'. When he retired, two years later, Garlick returned the document as a parting gift; today it hangs in a frame at Heseltine's country home. (It is also reproduced in his first book, though strangely the words 'Connaught Hotel' are blanked out.[8])

For most ministers such a check-list would have comprised party policy and manifesto commitments largely drawn up by Central Office. The Heseltine agenda was divided into four sections, only one of which (albeit the longest) covered the political programme. It was a sign of Heseltine's approach that from the very start he paid such attention to three other areas: office management, departmental management and staffing. As the Whitehall expert Peter Hennessy observes, Heseltine takes a greater interest in the workings of government than any minister since David Lloyd George.[9] (A Philip de Laszlo portrait of the great Liberal premier, a Welshman also known for his flowing hair and oratorical skills, was soon hanging in Heseltine's DoE office.)

The Environment Secretary was keen not to repeat his 1970–74 experience of being given staff he didn't respect. At the start, he asked Garlick to submit three names of possible private secretaries. When Heseltine questioned each of them he made it clear they were expected to remain until he left the department. The official he picked, David Edmonds, quickly became an admirer of Heseltine's style and methods, and the relationship went well. (Heseltine also worked with a great variety of other officials, and was ruthless in moving anybody with whom he was dissatisfied.)

Many DoE staff were nervous about Heseltine's return to the department, but they soon realized that he had matured and mellowed in the intervening years. Gone was much of the former arrogance and impatience; they now found a more relaxed, self-confident minister, who was amusing and fun to work with. Whereas the old Heseltine seemed to believe his staff wanted to obstruct him, the new minister went out of his way, both privately and publicly, to praise their professionalism. 'It seems he had learnt not to be so brash,' says one civil servant who had dealings with Heseltine in the early 1970s – though the official still detected 'a vindictive side, because he doesn't want people to get in his way and he likes exercising power'.

Sir John Garlick says their relationship was closer and more cooperative than he'd enjoyed with any past Secretary of State:

With Heseltine, it was much more his saying 'I want to do this. I have made up my mind, now what do you think and how do you think we ought to set about it?' . . . He adopted a position of 'Let's do these things together,' including talking about his policies . . . We would talk about it in a very equal sort of way, a complementary sort of way; he had one role and I had another, but we saw them as integrated.[10]

Garlick's successor, Sir George Moseley, considered Heseltine to be an exceptional motivator compared with most of the ministers he'd dealt with over the years. He found an unusual ability to inspire and enthuse, coupled with a degree of informality rare in a Secretary of State.

Officials would typically find Heseltine holding court with his tie undone and jacket off, dressed in a blue cashmere pullover, leaning back in his chair with his feet resting on his desk. While some ministers would devour paperwork, Heseltine's preferred method was to spend the day talking and listening. Rather than studying the detailed appendix on page 52, say, he would summon large numbers of officials to explain the problem and bat around the options. Heseltine also insisted on seeing civil servants from lower grades than ministers normally meet. 'You guys know things at the broader level,' he reportedly told his top mandarins, 'but when I ask a question of detail you shuffle your feet and don't know the answer. I want people who know the answers at my meetings.' So more junior staff – the people who'd done the detailed analysis – were wheeled in for their opinion. 'You did the work, what do you think? How did you get there? What's your view?' The young officials loved the chance to shine in front of their superiors, and Heseltine was firm whenever one of their seniors tried to shut them up.

These relaxed 'family-style' meetings seemed fairly 'haphazard' at first, says one civil servant, with large numbers of people competing to speak. Nor could one assume that Heseltine had always read the papers. But in time the official saw that there was method in it: 'Heseltine often had an intuitive feel for the balance of an argument which would lead him to a result at which lesser mortals would arrive by a more pedestrian, if rational, approach.' He believed strongly that one could often gauge the strength of a case by looking someone in the eye.

Heseltine also adopted some practices he had observed under Peter Walker. In particular he instituted a 9.15 meeting every morning with his political colleagues – his six junior ministers, their PPSs and the whip covering the DoE. All officials were excluded. The 'morning prayer' meeting is now quite common practice in ministerial offices, but then it was still novel. It gave an extra political direction to ministers who could easily become overwhelmed by the pressure of departmental business. It was an informal opportunity to alert colleagues to potential pitfalls, and to discuss them. The meetings also enabled junior ministers to take difficult matters to the top, which gave them more authority with officials afterwards.

As his own PPS, or unpaid parliamentary leg-man, Heseltine appointed Tim Sainsbury – on the grounds, people joked, that he was the only Tory MP who was wealthier than himself. But, unlike most of his Cabinet colleagues, he felt no need to employ a political adviser to keep in touch with party feeling. 'Why do I need any political advisers?' he would say. 'I've got six ministers.' But his ministerial colleagues were often too busy to foresee problems, and, since Heseltine rarely mixed with MPs, he sometimes ran into trouble.

In the place of the special adviser with a party background, Heseltine used the position to employ experts in particular fields of policy. Tom Baron, for instance, was the boss of a major house-building company who joined the DoE for six months to suggest ways of stimulating the construction industry. With council-house building at a postwar low, Baron stressed the importance of constructing houses for sale, and suggested simplifying the building-control regulations. Environmentalists complained, however, that Heseltine had simply given the big house-builders, for whom Baron had previously been the main lobbyist, their own voice inside government, at taxpayers' expense.

Michael Heseltine had inherited a huge department, a budget of £14 billion a year, and dozens of government responsibilities. Some of these – such as housing, planning and local government – were complex and highly political. Although the DoE had now lost responsibility for transport, its imposing tower blocks in Marsham Street still controlled numerous other areas, from the condition of British oysters to the Tower of London beefeaters; from air pollution to licensing zoos; from Stonehenge to the new towns. And, as Labour's Denis Howell had once shown, the DoE was both the ministry for sport and, somewhat paradoxically, the ministry for rain.

In 1979 these duties provided work for more than 52,000 people. One of Michael Heseltine's principal objectives – underlined on the Connaught 'envelope' – was to cut staff numbers. Here, too, he was pursuing a central Thatcher objective. The Tories had come to power determined to trim the 730,000 strong Civil Service by 100,000, largely by instituting a freeze on recruitment. Heseltine was advised by one of his junior ministers, Lord Bellwin, who had been leader of Leeds City Council, to follow Leeds's example. There the chief executive or chief personnel officer had had to seek Bellwin's approval for any new appointment, explaining why it was needed.

Heseltine adopted Bellwin's procedure at the DoE. 'I gave instructions,' he says, 'that only one person would in future recruit to the department. That burden would be mine.'[11] It caused problems for the personnel managers, of course, and in the long term the DoE missed a whole generation of new staff – especially among the high-flyer grades.

The recruitment freeze was only a short-term measure. More important was the programme known as MINIS. Here Heseltine was determined to apply the management principles of business to the machinery of government. Sir John Garlick found himself forced on to the defensive when Heseltine wanted to know what monitoring reports he received, as the management obtained in 'any proper business'. Garlick admitted he had nothing of that sort at all. 'Well, that won't do,' he recalls his new minister saying. 'I want to know what the Department is spending its money on, because I suspect there are a lot of things you do here that you do because you've always done them and you haven't much idea how much they cost.'[12]

DoE officials assumed that these were the techniques that Michael Heseltine had used in becoming a publishing multimillionaire: civil servants didn't realize that, for most of Heseltine's stewardship, Haymarket was far more poorly managed than any Whitehall department. Perhaps the nearest Heseltine ever got to good management –

as opposed to smart entrepreneurship – was through publishing *Management Today*.

'The management ethos must run right throughout our national life,' he argued, whether in public or private companies, the Civil Service, the NHS or local government. It was a theme which came to affect numerous British institutions and which has dominated Heseltine's subsequent career:

By management ethos I mean the process of examining what we are doing, setting realistic targets, fitting them to the resources available, and monitoring performance – and then, very important, telling people what the results are so that we can go back to the beginning of the loop and improve from there.[13]

One official recalls Heseltine's boast that MINIS would be the most radical change in government since the nineteenth-century reforms of Northcote and Trevelyan which established the modern Civil Service. MINIS – which stood for 'Management Information System for Ministers' – has been described as a kind of 'Domesday Book' of his new kingdom.[14]

In short, MINIS was about knowing who in his department did what, and at what cost. The idea was that Heseltine could then make judgements on what activities were worthwhile and what areas should be cut, and be armed against the inevitable special pleading. By establishing responsibility for each activity, Heseltine also hoped officials would become more cost-conscious. And he believed MINIS would check the prevailing tendency for government to grow unchecked.

MINIS was a complex process and occupied much of Heseltine's time in his first year. Wherever possible, as a reluctant reader, he had the detail in the resulting reports set out for him in tables and figures. And, in a rare example of openness during the Thatcher years, the documents were made public, though Michael Heseltine is not habitually a champion of freedom of information. In practice, however, most journalists were deterred by the sheer volume of the reports. Paradoxically for an exercise designed to reduce waste, the first round generated a pile of paper four and a half inches thick.

In 1979 the DoE comprised no fewer than sixty-six directorates, most of them headed by a Civil Service under-secretary. Each under-secretary produced a MINIS report on what his or her directorate did, setting out its priorities, expenditure and staff costs, together with an organization chart. They were also asked for their objectives in the six months ahead, and to suggest how their achievement of these might be measured. Heseltine then digested each report before a long series of meetings with directorate heads during the spring and summer of 1980.

MINIS was intended as an evolving process of annual reviews – MINIS 1, MINIS 2, and so on – in which past targets would be compared with actual results. But, of course, it wasn't just about costs and manpower: the operation inevitably concerned policy too – it was a neat way of asking whether the DoE was doing the right things. Over time the exercise was considerably refined, and later rounds emphasized new objectives. Heseltine then gradually passed much of his overseeing role to his senior officials.

Sir John Garlick was initially taken aback by Heseltine's plans, but gradually came to accept MINIS. Most civil servants remained sceptical, however. One confidential memo discussed how to avoid 'further grounds for complaint' from staff, and suggested individuals who were most 'likely to be cooperative'. Staff 'hated it', says David Edmonds. 'They felt it was the Permanent Secretary's job to manage the department, not the minister's. For the Secretary of State to challenge the amount of resource needed, to refuse to believe the range of bleeding-stump arguments, to grill under-secretaries on their management, was anathema.'[15]

Edmonds had a hard job timetabling the necessary meetings to discuss each directorate, and some lasted several hours. Anxious under-secretaries would be summoned to Heseltine's conference room for the big interrogation. The process could have been designed to intimidate.

The under-secretaries sat at a rectangular table directly facing Heseltine, surrounded by the Permanent Secretary and other officials. 'Although my questions were often superficial,' he says, 'the prospect of a dialogue with the Secretary of State usually helped concentrate minds.'[16] Civil servants spent weeks beforehand marshalling their information and arguments; they knew they were having to justify colleagues' jobs, and their own.

Experiences were mixed. Some thought Heseltine was open to argument. In certain cases he was surprised by what people told him, and seemed to change his attitude. But others left thinking the process was merely a charade and that, before he'd heard their case, Heseltine's mind was already fixed on a particular percentage cut, with little thought as to how it ought to be achieved. 'I don't think he took much notice of the work that was done,' says the head of one directorate. 'He had just decided before we went in there. Not once did he say, "Lose something there, or don't put any effort into 'X'." The detail was neither here nor there.'

Staff numbers fell quickly: one in twelve people had gone by the end of Heseltine's first year, and almost three in ten by the time he left the DoE in 1983 – 15,000 jobs. It was a bigger cut-back than in any other Whitehall department. Among areas to suffer the biggest reductions were research, economics and statistics, and the information directorate which employed the DoE press officers.

At times, Heseltine's cost-cutting seemed obsessive. When he discovered the DoE made 40 million photocopies a year, he imposed strict new rules, though 'there was general amazement,' says one senior official, 'that a Secretary of State should spend even five minutes of his time on something so relatively trivial'. Each member of staff was allocated a number of photocopying coupons, which caused problems once they'd run out. The consequence was the return of old-fashioned carbon paper.

When questioned by the Commons Treasury and Civil Service Select Committee, Michael Heseltine confirmed he would introduce MINIS to any other ministry he went to, unless it already had a system that was equally good, which he thought unlikely.[17] The implication was probably intentional: that his Cabinet colleagues were not as effective or cost-conscious in managing their departments as he was. They noticed.

But the committee was impressed with MINIS. So, too, was Margaret Thatcher, and in February 1982 she invited Heseltine to address a seminar in the Number Ten dining-room to outline its virtues to ministers and officials from other departments. One can imagine how his colleagues felt about 'Professor' Heseltine's exposition – especially after his comments to the Treasury Committee.

My fellow Cabinet ministers sat in rows while I explained my brainchild, each with his sceptical Permanent Secretary behind him muttering objections, or so I suspected. Any politician knows when he is losing his audience's attention, and I knew well enough. When I had done, there were few takers and absolutely no enthusiasts.[18]

Thatcher herself spent another twenty-five minutes extolling the Heseltine method, but the gathering remained unconvinced. Few ministers had any desire to become managing directors; politics was difficult enough. Some ministers and mandarins argued that they already had such systems; others said MINIS was appropriate only to a department like Environment. Sir Frank Cooper at the MoD was scandalized by what his senior colleagues in the DoE had to tolerate. In time, however, MINIS would heavily influence the wider Financial Management Initiative which was designed by Margaret Thatcher's cost-cutter, Sir Derek Rayner, and applied across Whitehall.

One of the few DoE civil servants to emerge from MINIS with *extra* resources was Terry Heiser, the under-secretary in charge of local-government finance. Heiser 'took him on', says a witness to his MINIS encounter with Heseltine. 'He looked him steadily in the eye and agreed that Michael Heseltine could cut staff if he was ready for the consequences – which might well mean a failure to secure a local-government financial settlement next time around, in good order and in good time.'

Heseltine knew that cutting Heiser's staff could be dangerous. Of all DoE responsibilities, local-government finance was politically the most sensitive. The Conservatives had come to power promising to reduce public spending. Since defence and law and order were both protected, and social security was bound to rise with increased unemployment, it was inevitable that other areas, like housing and local government, would bear a disproportionate share of the cuts.

Although Michael Heseltine had served as a local-government minister under Ted Heath, it was not a world with which he felt empathy. Neither he nor any of his immediate family had ever stood in a local election, nor would Heseltine ever have considered serving as a councillor. Yet, unlike some Tories, he did not have an instinctive distaste for town halls – indeed, he later extolled the virtues of municipal government. In practice, of course, his own strong inclination is towards greater control and intervention. Whether observing businessmen at work, or civil servants, or council officials – or, later on, service chiefs – Heseltine always feels he could do better.

The 1979 map of local government reflected the unpopularity of the outgoing Labour government. Many councils had changed hands over the last five years and most were Conservative-controlled, including the vast majority of the big-spending counties. Unusually, the Conservatives even ran each of the four main council associations. Because of his political affinity, Heseltine initially believed that most local authorities could be persuaded to cut spending through his cajoling and appeals to party loyalty. According to David Edmonds, 'he felt he would forge an alliance with Conservative colleagues in local government and change performance . . . He felt that by talking he could agree on the level of expenditure.'[19] He would soon feel that they'd badly let him down.

'In my first year I made a mistake,' Heseltine later conceded. 'The local authorities, both Tory and Labour controlled, all assured me that local government had always complied with the overall expenditure guidelines set by central government. "You won't need controls," they said. "We always stick to the guidelines." '[20]

On taking office Heseltine announced that council spending for the current year, 1979–80, would be 1 per cent lower than in the previous one, and that spending for 1980–81 would be a further 1 per cent lower. For several months it was a game of exhortations and threats. But, if councils didn't comply with the new climate of spending cuts, then stern action might be needed. Heseltine's problem, however, was that the existing financial system seemed designed to encourage profligacy: the more councils spent, the more money they got in rate support grant from central government.

After just six months, the Environment Secretary announced that councils he thought were spending a lot more than the government recommended would suffer cuts in their grant. In September 1980 he named the first fourteen 'overspenders' to be penalized. Most were inner-London boroughs, and only one – Hammersmith and Fulham – was a Tory authority. One hundred and fourteen other councils which had also overspent their government targets – many of them Conservative-controlled – were reprieved. Heseltine's list seemed decided more by politics than by economics.

Over the next few years, one grant system rapidly replaced another, as increasingly tough controls were imposed. Labour and Conservative councillors united in denouncing the growing Whitehall interference as a serious attack on local democracy. 'There is an ever-increasing danger,' wrote the Tory leader of Kent, Sir John Grugeon, 'that local authorities will, over time, become no more than local agents for central government.'[21]

The Environment Secretary often met council deputations who came to London begging for leniency. Heseltine was convinced that most local-government leaders knew little about how their authorities were run and simply took the advice of their treasurers and chief executives. 'The treasurers were not allowed to speak at first,' says a DoE official who witnessed many such exchanges. 'Heseltine would go through the budget with the leader to demonstrate that the leader did not know enough about it. Then he'd let the treasurer in. It was an exercise to let Tory councils in particular be aware that they were running large businesses, spending other people's money . . . to make them think there are better ways.'

In effect Heseltine was encouraging councils to conduct their own miniature MINIS exercises. Often he would embarrass leaders by comparing their figures with another authority of similar size: why, for instance, did they need twice as many men to empty the same number of bins?

Heavy Tory losses in the 1980 and 1981 council elections soon meant it was no longer largely a case of convincing political allies. The transformation was symbolized by Labour's takeover in 1981 of the Greater London Council (GLC). A new generation of more radical Labour councillors, such as Ken Livingstone and Tony Banks in London, and David Blunkett in Sheffield, argued that with unemployment soaring towards 3 million they should seek to regenerate their local economies through the creation of organizations such as the Greater London Enterprise Board. Relations between Marsham Street and many council chambers rapidly moved towards confrontation. Heseltine became the Labour bogeyman.

In Michael Heseltine's first two years, councils *had* actually cut their overall budgets. Now spending was set to rise, thanks largely to massive increases by just three of the new Labour councils: the GLC, Merseyside and the West Midlands (the latter being two of the metropolitan counties Heseltine had helped create ten years before).

One recurring problem was that, if the government cut local-authority grants, councils could put up their rates to compensate – if necessary through a supplementary rate in the middle of the financial year. There was little political risk for Labour councils in this, since poorer families – the core of their support – got rate rebates. It was more affluent (and typically Conservative) voters, and local businesses, who paid most of the extra bill.

Heseltine was being squeezed from both sides, since neither Downing Street nor the Treasury thought he was doing enough to restrict council spending. At one point Margaret Thatcher summoned her Environment Secretary and several Tory council leaders to Number Ten to urge greater restraint. Her views were shared by many back-benchers, who muttered that Heseltine was being weak and vacillating; newspapers such as the *Daily Mail* and the *Sun* regularly berated him for not being more decisive. Yet, from the other side, local authorities were pleading with Heseltine, quite truthfully, that they'd already suffered big cuts under Labour. Any further economies, they argued, would damage essential services. It even reached an absurd point where some councils were penalized by Heseltine despite spending *less* than the figure the DoE otherwise calculated they needed to spend.

In the face of aggressive and more radical opposition from local government, ministers searched desperately for new weapons. Heseltine felt the answer was political, not financial. His suggestion was that, if an authority wanted to levy a supplementary rate, the whole council should be obliged to stand for re-election first. This had obvious snags: why, for instance, should councillors who might have opposed the supplementary rate still risk losing their seats?

Heseltine's Cabinet colleagues narrowly rejected his re-election sanction in favour of an alternative appeal to the voters, which had been inspired by recent events in Coventry. The ruling Labour group on Coventry City Council had tried to resolve its internal divisions by holding a referendum on whether to increase the rates or cut services. Coventry voters had chosen cuts by more than seven to one. By obliging councils to hold a referendum before levying a supplementary rate, ministers claimed they would be returning power to the people. But it also involved more centralization: both the wording of the question and the date of any referendum would be set by the Secretary of State.

Within days the referendum plan was savaged by leading Conservatives. Many deplored it as yet another infringement of local autonomy; others abhorred the idea of referendums in principle, and thought it was a risky precedent to give voters a veto on taxation. When Heseltine attended a highly charged session of the back-bench Environment Committee in November 1981, all but four members attacked the scheme. 'Well, I'm not here to break up the Tory party,' Heseltine pleaded with Conservative MPs. 'But we can't do nothing. What else is there for us to do?'[22]

Saddled with an idea that hadn't been his own preference, Heseltine had to defend it from Tory critics on both right and left. A preliminary Commons debate saw the rare spectacle of not a single Conservative back-bench speaker supporting the ministerial line. When nineteen Tories rebelled in the vote and many more threatened to do so later, it was clear that local referendums would never get parliamentary approval. After frantic discussion in Cabinet committee, Heseltine was forced to withdraw his bill. Instead, he took the simpler (though even more centralist) course of outlawing supplementary rates altogether, and imposing even tighter penalties on councils who spent more than the government thought they should.

The collapse of Heseltine's bill naturally raised the spirits of Labour councils. It also showed poor political instinct on his part, and was not the last time he would be forced into an embarrassing Commons retreat. The Chief Whip, Michael Jopling, blamed Keith Hampson, who was PPS to the local-government minister, Tom King. Hampson had promised the whips that there was sufficient support on the back benches.

Such confusion was characteristic of the Department of the Environment's approach to local-government spending. In Heseltine's time, both of his main local-government bills had to be withdrawn from Parliament and then resubmitted. 'A bit of a shambles' is how his Cabinet friend David Howell describes it. 'It wasn't terribly impressive, and there was a general view around that the Environment team were making a bit of a horlicks of it.'[23]

The immediate problems of council spending naturally prompted the wider question of whether to abolish the rates altogether, as Margaret Thatcher had famously pledged in 1974 and Michael Heseltine later reiterated. The 1979 manifesto, however, had deliberately steered away from the issue, saying that income-tax cuts must take priority over rates abolition. The government had already stored up trouble for itself by postponing indefinitely the reassessment of rateable values that was due in 1982. Yet, equally, to have carried out the revaluation would have aroused great discontent. 'We've got this problem,' Michael Heseltine had supposedly told Margaret Thatcher in 1979. 'There's no problem,' she replied firmly – 'we're not doing it.'[24]

The end of 1981 was a frantic period for the DoE's local-government finance directorate. For, as well as considering short-term remedies such as referendums, Downing Street had also forced it into a review of the rates. For several months a DoE team put considerable effort into examining possible alternatives, though some are sceptical as to whether Heseltine ever believed they would really find something better. 'From fairly early on,' says one colleague, 'he felt the 1974 Thatcher promise to abolish rates was a millstone. I think his efforts were to push reform into the long grass.' Nevertheless, the 1981 review was a substantial exercise. Tom King says that he and Heseltine saw every single back-bench Tory between them, to canvass the various possibilities. 'We established there were lots of different views, and always a blocking minority for each one.'[25]

The main runners included a modified property tax, a local income tax, and Margaret Thatcher's own initial preference, a local sales tax. And when the review produced a Green Paper in December 1981 another option was also listed – a poll tax, whereby each local resident would pay the same set sum. At this stage the poll tax was never treated as a serious option by the DoE team: it seems to have been included more for the sake of completeness, and, according to one account, was greeted with laughter at first. 'Try collecting that in

Brixton,' said one official.[26] But the other alternatives all posed serious snags too. 'Probably none of the possible new sources of local revenue could be used on its own as a complete replacement for domestic rates,' the Green Paper concluded.[27] The clear inference was that rates should stay.

This was not what Mrs Thatcher wanted to hear. 'I will not tolerate failure in this area,' she wrote in the margin of the draft Green Paper.[28] Not only were Labour councils – and some Conservative authorities – thwarting her financial strategy with rate increases, she also regarded domestic rates as a tax on home ownership, and owning one's home was something she wanted to encourage. Despite Heseltine's Green Paper, in the summer of 1982 a Cabinet committee under Willie Whitelaw was told to look at the rates issue once again.

Whitelaw's committee, however, arrived at much the same con-clusion as Heseltine's DoE review the year before – that there was no workable alternative. Heseltine would later explain how the poll-tax option 'was dismissed by the Cabinet with hardly a backward glance. I wish that I could . . . say that I won the argument, but in truth there was no argument.'[29] Ministers came close to despair as they floundered for something to satisfy the Prime Minister.

The biggest champion of tougher financial controls on local councils was the new Chief Secretary to the Treasury appointed in January 1981. Leon Brittan had little sympathy either for the DoE or for local government, and firmly believed that rates were taxes, and that council spending was public expenditure, and therefore an important element in economic policy. For two years he and Heseltine would be locked in a fierce struggle, which would have a historic rematch later. The two men 'understood each other's functions' says one official, but witnessing their battles was like 'watching two medieval assassins circling each other with poniards at the ready'. Brittan wrote a paper arguing that ministers should take further powers, this time to limit council rate levels – what became known as 'rate-capping'. Heseltine claimed that rate-capping would be too strong an erosion of local autonomy. He argued that the spending problem was really confined to only a handful of big urban authorities – the GLC and the metropolitan counties – and a better solution would be simply to abolish them. By the time Heseltine left the DoE, in January 1983, it looked as if this sop had persuaded Brittan and the Treasury to forget rate-capping, as it gave them the prospect that the highest spenders would soon be eliminated.

But Brittan persisted, with Margaret Thatcher's encouragement, and when ministers came to agree the Tory manifesto in May 1983 they included, at the very last minute, both abolition of the metropolitan counties *and* the rate-capping measure that Heseltine thought he had killed. 'Michael Heseltine was very much against it,' says his Cabinet colleague Jim Prior, 'and after the election his opposition led Margaret to deliver to him one of the most violent rebukes I have ever witnessed in Cabinet. No doubt, these issues of local government fuelled the disagreement between Michael on the one hand and Margaret and Leon on the other, which ultimately led to their resignations from her Cabinet over the Westland affair.'[30]

The introduction of rate-capping in 1984 was perhaps the most drastic of all the sanctions that Whitehall placed on local government during the 1980s. Central control also increased later in the decade, however, with new government powers over the school curriculum, higher education, housing, and competitive tendering. Today only about 20 per cent of council spending is generated locally, compared with twice this proportion in 1979. Many political activists – Tories included – have decided that being a councillor is no longer worth the effort now that local authorities have so little discretion.

Most experts believe the serious erosion of local-government autonomy began during Heseltine's time at the DoE, though one could argue that the process started under Labour, with the famous warning to councils by his predecessor but one, Tony Crosland, that 'The party's over.' Sir John Garlick once warned Heseltine to take care in cutting local authorities down to size: one day a Labour government might use the changes to do things he didn't like. Heseltine replied that there weren't going to be any more Labour governments.

'The Man in Whitehall Knows Best' approach, which the government seemed to have adopted, was a complete reversal of Conservative promises of the late 1970s. 'We shall reduce and eliminate many of the controls that currently tie Britain's cities to the Whitehall departments,' Heseltine had told the 1978 Tory conference.[31]

Initially Heseltine was reluctant to increase government interference, partly because he had little faith that civil servants could do any better than local councils. After the 1979 election he had initiated a review of central controls, reiterating that 'local councils are directly elected' and answerable to the voters:

They do not need, they do not want, the fussy supervision of detail which now exists. I am determined to clear the way for local action at all levels. I am not going to nanny – and nor are my officers – local authorities.[32]

Some rules were abolished – such as the complex process for agreeing county structure plans, and the need for DoE approval of proposals for municipal crematoria. But one of Heseltine's junior ministers, Geoffrey Finsberg, has admitted that when councils 'started swinging to Labour we stopped doing that!'[33] By the end of the 1980s council powers had been restricted, in one way or another, by fifty separate acts of Parliament.

Michael Heseltine can rightly say that during his three and a half years at the DoE he had successfully opposed the two most controversial measures which came in later – rate-capping and the poll tax. Indeed, if he'd stayed, he might have stopped the poll tax altogether, if not both policies. But the overall pressure towards centralization was probably too powerful for him to resist, even if he had wanted to. Downing Street and the Treasury were determined to control local-government finance, and both were insistent that council budgets were part of public spending. Some economists argue, however, that one doesn't need to include local-authority budgets in a country's overall public-expenditure figures. As Simon Jenkins points out, neither the German nor the American government sees any need to get embroiled in local-authority spending.[34]

Perhaps the greatest irony is that, throughout the 1980s as a whole, town and county halls actually cut their budgets more than central government. Heseltine can argue that this was partially a result of his tight controls, as well as other measures he initiated to make local government more efficient – what one might broadly term acts of privatization. His three years at the DoE saw rules imposed to make council direct-labour organizations more businesslike, and also the first stages in competitive tendering, whereby authorities were obliged to let outside firms compete to provide services such as rubbish-collection. And, just as the MINIS exercise tried to establish at what cost the DoE did things, Heseltine imposed an obligation on authorities to produce quarterly figures showing staff levels for each of their activities. It became possible to compare and contrast the 456 councils in England and Wales, and to find benchmarks of good practice.

Heseltine's most far-reaching innovation, for which he is seldom given credit, was the foundation of the Audit Commission in 1983. Influenced by his accountancy background, he had long been convinced that the relationship between councils and their district auditors was far too cosy; this had first concerned him as a junior environment minister under Edward Heath. The Audit Commission would now supervise district auditors, and often bring in outside accountancy firms to do audits. The commission would also carry out value-for-money studies to show how local government might operate more efficiently. Yet, initially, the Treasury blocked the Audit Commission proposal. Despite its clamour for more council cuts, the Treasury was unhappy with the idea of a financial body operating outside its control. This delayed the commission's creation by two years.

The Audit Commission proved to be one of the most successful innovations of the Thatcher era, yet it is barely mentioned in most accounts of her government. The commission claims its work has saved billions in local-government spending, though it could also be seen as yet another erosion of local autonomy. Under the independent-minded and imaginative leadership of first John Banham and then Howard Davies, it soon extended its scope beyond local authorities to the NHS and the police.

Michael Heseltine's economy and efficiency measures at the DoE, and his part in the struggles with local government, make him difficult to categorize in assessing the wider dramas of the first Thatcher administration. It was a period of intense debate over the direction of economic policy. Within months of the Tories coming to office the Cabinet dissenters came to be known as 'wets' – a term the Prime Minister used to denigrate those Tory paternalists and left-wingers who worried that unemployment was too high and that Thatcherism was causing too much damage. The wets included Sir Ian Gilmour, Francis Pym, Jim Prior and Heseltine's old friend and mentor Peter

Walker, whom Thatcher had restored to the front bench in 1979 (after Heseltine had long urged her to do so).

At the time – perhaps unhelpfully – Peter Walker described Heseltine as 'certainly very much in the wet, left stream of Tory politics'.[35] But the Chancellor, Sir Geoffrey Howe, never thought of Heseltine as a wet, while Nigel Lawson, the chief architect of the Conservative monetarist strategy, saw him merely as 'semi-wet'. 'Contrary to his reputation,' Lawson writes, 'Michael (unlike, say, Peter Walker or Kenneth Baker) has never been an indiscriminate big spender.'[36] Hugo Young categorizes Heseltine merely as an 'outer wet', compared with 'inner wets' such as Walker, Prior, Gilmour, Lord Carrington and Norman St John-Stevas.[37] He never joined their private cabals, and they never quite felt they could trust him.

Margaret Thatcher's close ally Cecil Parkinson also puts Heseltine in a different category to the others: 'Michael would say, "We should spend more on this but take it from there." He accepted the overall need to contain spending. Others were saying that with unemployment at this level we should spend more. He was prepared to nominate areas to cut back.'[38]

At times Heseltine could be quite cheeky in suggesting cuts for Cabinet colleagues. One DoE official recalls being sent to discover how much could be trimmed from the defence budget by abolishing military bands, for which the DoE had no responsibility.

Heseltine played a leading role in economic debates, and often expressed scepticism of the harsher aspects of monetarism. Early on, he was also the only Cabinet critic of one of the most significant economic measures of the Thatcher years, Geoffrey Howe's abolition of exchange controls in October 1979. Nigel Lawson, who was then Financial Secretary, says Heseltine feared 'people would abuse their unaccustomed freedom, and buy villas in the south of France rather than invest in productive assets at home'.[39] Ominously, Heseltine was equally dismayed that the Cabinet hadn't been consulted properly, though this would have been difficult with a measure that was so financially sensitive.

Michael Heseltine also stood out during this period for daring to suggest that ministers ought to consider a freeze on public-sector pay.

It must have seemed something of an idea from a different age – a throwback to the discredited prices-and-incomes policies of Harold Wilson and Edward Heath – though he won backing from one or two Cabinet colleagues.

He particularly advocated freezing pay for government employees during a critical economic discussion in July 1981. Britain was in the midst of deep recession, and unemployment had reached 2.5 million – its highest level since the 1930s. Yet, far from proposing a traditional Keynesian boost to the economy, Sir Geoffrey Howe was demanding another £5,000 million in spending cuts. To most Cabinet members the idea was unthinkable. 'The result,' says Margaret Thatcher, 'was one of the bitterest arguments on the economy, or any subject, that I can ever recall taking place at Cabinet during my premiership.'[40] For once the various types of wet were not only united in the opposition but were also joined by several ministers normally considered 'dry'. According to Hugo Young, Michael Heseltine was among the first to speak out.[41]

As he condemned Sir Geoffrey's plans as disastrous, Heseltine's words would have carried a certain emotional intensity. For his very presence at the Cabinet table had required him to interrupt a three-week trip to Liverpool, where he'd been dispatched in the aftermath of serious rioting.

13. *It Took a Riot*

Be careful, the police had warned: several of the men he was about to meet had been involved in the local riots only a few nights before. One or two, they said, might be carrying guns. And, when Michael Heseltine duly arrived at the community centre in Toxteth, the black leaders insisted they wouldn't talk to him if his Special Branch men were also there. It was agreed that the police would remain outside.

It must have been an incongruous scene inside the small basement meeting-room. Michael Heseltine and his colleagues weren't just representatives of a despised Conservative government: he and his PPS, Tim Sainsbury, were also two of the wealthiest men in politics – if not *the* two – and both multimillionaires. But Heseltine was determined to find out what had gone wrong. 'He began by asking about housing and how the recreational facilities were,' recalls a former DoE official, Paul McQuail, 'and they said all they wanted to talk about was the police. He was quite battered by questions all round, and there were some very emotional contributions. It was the kind of thing ministers normally refuse to listen to, but Heseltine took it for two hours without letting it get out of hand.'[1]

Nineteen eighty-one was the summer both of the royal wedding and of the worst English riots of modern times. Serious trouble had first broken out in Brixton that Easter. In July there were further disturbances in south London, and in Southall, Manchester and several other English cities. Some of the worst violence occurred in Liverpool 8, in the area known as Toxteth, about a mile from the city centre, over a period of two weeks. It was started by young blacks, though they were soon joined by white youths. Molotov cocktails were thrown, buildings were burnt down, and shops were looted. Hundreds of people were injured, and one man was killed. For the first time in mainland Britain, tear gas was used against the rioters, and, according to the subsequent Scarman Report, ministers came close to bringing in the Army. At times the violence had been so intense that the police had had to withdraw.

The government was far more worried about the violence on Merseyside than that anywhere else, for it was an area where the recession had hit hardest. Following a string of factory closures, unemployment in Liverpool had reached more than 20 per cent; among young blacks in Toxteth it was around 60 per cent. Even strict monetarists in the government worried that there might be a heavy social price for imposing tough controls on government spending. Only a few weeks before the riots Cabinet members had discussed a report by the Downing Street think-tank which warned them not to ignore Merseyside's economic problems. It would be politically and socially unacceptable, the document argued, as well as expensive, to allow the area to go into 'managed decline', an approach favoured by many on the Tory right.[2]

After a day's visit to Liverpool herself, Margaret Thatcher decided a minister should go for longer. As Environment Secretary, Michael Heseltine was the obvious choice, though David Edmonds, his private secretary, says there was considerable lobbying for the assignment. Peter Walker also put himself forward, but as agriculture minister he wasn't an obvious contender. 'Heseltine went in hard,' recalls Edmonds, 'and said, "It's my job." '[3] For two and a half weeks most of Heseltine's other engagements were passed to his deputies, Tom King and John Stanley.

Michael Heseltine wasn't a stranger to Liverpool. He'd visited the Shrewsbury School mission as a boy (and paid a quiet return visit in 1981) and had handled Merseyside during the Walker local-government reorganization of the early 1970s. During his first two years as Environment Secretary he also chaired the Merseyside Partnership. This was a scheme started under Labour to channel government money into approved inner-city projects, many of them run by voluntary groups. Partnerships existed in seven cities, and each was chaired by a different DoE minister who would visit three or four times a year. His predecessor, Peter Shore, had picked Liverpool, and Heseltine explains he himself did the same 'because it looked likely to prove the most challenging. It was.'[4]

Heseltine's trip in the summer of 1981 would lead to a continuing personal involvement with Liverpool; by his own admission he acquired 'an affection for that great city'.⁵ To some officials and ministerial colleagues it seemed a bizarre obsession, but it proved to be one of the abiding influences of his political career. 'Merseyside,' he later wrote, 'supplied me with one of those priceless formative experiences from which every politician takes strength; it tested many of my deepest political beliefs and instincts and intensified my convictions.'⁶

He was accompanied by about a dozen officials from several different ministries, including Eric Sorensen, head of the DoE's north-west office. The Environment Secretary regarded the exercise as an opportunity to express his own distinctive alternative to prevailing government thinking, and it was intended as a pilot study, to see how policy might be improved throughout Britain's inner cities. 'Heseltine was absolutely determined from the word go that this was now going to be the opportunity to demonstrate what could be achieved by government pump-priming,' says Sorensen.⁷

The Home Secretary, Willie Whitelaw, sent along his deputy, Tim Raison, to examine the racial dimensions (and to ensure Heseltine didn't interfere with police matters). But the group went with scant idea of what they were actually going to do there. 'We made up the thing as we went along,' says David Edmonds.⁸ After meeting council leaders at the town hall, for instance, Edmonds suggested Heseltine might walk down to the Pier Head and catch the Mersey ferry. And they did. But soon invitations came flooding in, and every day became a rush of meetings and visits, from breakfast until midnight.

As Heseltine toured local council estates, he came to resemble the Pied Piper of Hamelin – reporters, photographers and TV crews dogged his footsteps, along with a particular Liverpool phenomenon, the 'scallies'. Swarms of cheeky young ruffians would suddenly appear wherever he went, waving their arms behind him in the hope of being seen on television. Heseltine says he couldn't help but admire the kids and their spontaneity, even if they were a constant irritant:

You'd do your best to calm them down and make some rather pompous political remark, and some devastating, vicious piece of wit would come out of a sproggins of about three. You just burst into helpless laughter. Their greatest charm and their worst enemies are all rolled into one. They're remarkable people.[9]

Heseltine was keen to find things out for himself. 'Why don't you come and look at the shite we live in?' yelled a woman in Croxteth, and he did.[10] One flat he visited had been flooded a month before, and had been without water or electricity ever since. Worse, the tenants had then had their belongings destroyed by vandals and had been too demoralized to clear up the mess. Heseltine walked through the sad debris of smashed crockery and broken toys. In the back of a van in Kirkby he met local street-children, who'd been brought to see him by community workers.

What he saw often brought out the rarely seen emotional side of Michael Heseltine. He was obviously shocked – not just by the condition of much of the local housing, but by the fear and violence people had to contend with. 'I'd seen problems like these before,' he told one reporter, 'but it's the sheer concentration of problems that is staggering.'[11] Lord Bellwin, who'd seen such things himself as a council leader in Leeds, later expressed surprise that Heseltine didn't seem to know that such conditions existed. 'He was visibly moved,' says David Edmonds.[12] 'Where do you live?' Heseltine was asked by a mother on a dilapidated estate in Croxteth. 'Somewhere rather nice, near London,' he replied quietly.[13]

Liverpool people showed surprisingly little hostility to Heseltine. He came with 'no magic formula', he said, 'no pot of gold', 'no simple, instant solutions'. All he promised was 'the longest period of listening any minister has given an area'.[14] He may have been a representative of a hated government, visiting a strongly working-class area where unemployment was endemic, but locals seemed pleased that anyone should take such an interest. The fact he was wealthy, wore expensive suits, and drove a Jaguar didn't seem to worry people – they rather admired that. Nor did it cause much trouble when the press revealed that he'd interrupted his Merseyside tour to welcome Margaret Thatcher and 400 other guests to a lavish party at his Oxfordshire home to celebrate Annabel's eighteenth birthday party – at an estimated cost of £10,000.

Somehow the two characters – Tarzan and Scouse – mixed rather well. Perhaps the reason was Michael Heseltine's charisma, his presence and, importantly, that he seemed unafraid of the underlying tensions that could so easily have sparked more violence. Maybe it was because he was prepared to listen rather than to lecture. But Liverpudlians like the star name, the big personality, the snappy dresser, the flamboyant spiv. Heseltine was a show-business politician in a show-business town.

His first meeting with black leaders, however, didn't go well. Several walked out because, they said, he refused to discuss the police. Two days later he was invited to a memorable encounter with the Liverpool 8 Defence Committee at a community centre in Toxteth. Heseltine wanted to discuss housing and jobs, but black leaders again insisted the overriding problem was police harassment. He didn't try to admonish anybody for the rioting. At the same time, he impressed his officials with the way he managed to keep the discussion focused, and the temperature cool enough for the meeting to last two hours.

It was followed by a tricky encounter the following evening with the Merseyside chief constable, Kenneth Oxford, over dinner in a private suite at the expensive Atlantic Tower hotel. Heseltine was deeply disturbed by what he'd heard from the young blacks in Toxteth. Even if only a fraction of what they'd said was true, it was clear that some local police were guilty of racism and brutality. Why wasn't there more community policing? Wasn't it inevitable that regular use of stop-and-search powers would eventually cause trouble?

The most dramatic initiative, and certainly that with the highest profile, came towards the end of the three-week tour. Heseltine had been struck by the absence of business leaders who might play a role in Liverpool civic life. People with commercial interests in the city tended to live well outside it, in rural Lancashire, or across the Mersey in the Wirral. Despite its proximity to the city centre, Liverpool 8 was remote from the daily lives of such commuters. Equally, all the major financial institutions were present in Liverpool, but Heseltine saw them as having 'absentee landlords' running affairs from London, or through a regional office in Manchester.

His staff rang round the big banks and building societies to invite their chairmen or chief executives to come to Merseyside and look at the situation for themselves. There was enormous reluctance at first, but when Tim Sainsbury persuaded Robin Leigh-Pemberton, the chairman of the NatWest Bank, to accept, most of Leigh-Pemberton's rivals soon followed. Heseltine hired a coach, provided the party with beer, plastic cups and sandwiches, and drove them round the worst parts of the area. Anne Heseltine went too.

Heseltine hoped that if the financiers saw the situation at first hand it might engender a broader commitment to local communities. Robin Leigh-Pemberton, now Lord Kingsdown, remembers being shocked. On one block, Arkwright Gardens, in Everton, nearly every door seemed to have been kicked in. The only flat that remained untouched belonged to a disabled woman who couldn't leave her home. 'The others are out all day, and when they go the neighbours or whoever just turn up and break in,' he recalls her saying. 'And I thought to myself, "What an appalling indictment of communal behaviour in the 1980s!" '[15]

It was evident that the local authorities had been negligent in maintaining council properties, but the party was also surprised at how unwilling tenants seemed to assume any responsibility as well. Everyone felt 'they' – the council – should do something, without it ever occurring to them that they might do some repairs themselves.

Brian Corby of the Prudential remembers how eager locals were to talk, and seemed 'almost dressed for the occasion'. As a 'man from the Pru', he was more familiar with inner-city life than most men on the bus. 'If anything surprised me it was that Michael Heseltine expressed *himself* surprised at some of the things he heard,' he says. 'I think it was quite a revelation for him that day, and he came away, I'm absolutely certain, thinking that something must be done.'[16]

As the bus tour came to an end, the financiers were wary about what Heseltine would want next. Would he twist their arms to invest some of their substantial funds in Liverpool? No, he decided, that would have been too blatant. Instead, as they gathered for a parting cup of tea in the Adelphi Hotel, he asked each businessman to find a bright young manager who could be seconded to the DoE for a year to work on inner-city problems.

The official outcome of Heseltine's three weeks on Merseyside was a famous twenty-one-page minute circulated to Cabinet colleagues, entitled *It Took a Riot*. The document was never officially published, but a copy was leaked to the Whitehall analyst Peter Hennessy. Heseltine wrote much of the report himself, including the powerful opening:

It took a riot. No sentiment was more frequently expressed to me during the time I spent with Tim Raison in Merseyside. There is no escaping the uncomfortable implications.[17]

The Environment Secretary proposed a six-part strategy:

1. The economic and social decline evident in Merseyside, and other conurbations, requires a new priority for these areas in our policies.
2. A continued ministerial commitment to Merseyside is required for a specific period of, say, one year. A single regional office is needed in Liverpool comprising the main departments concerned with economic development. Similar arrangements should be adopted for other conurbations.
3. Our industrial, regional and training policies should be reassessed within the new context and administered with flexibility.
4. As part of this, we should involve the private sector and the financial institutions to a far greater degree than hitherto.
5. The future of the metropolitan counties and the GLC should be examined quickly.
6. Substantial additional public resources should be directed to Merseyside and other hard-pressed urban areas to create jobs on worthwhile schemes.[18]

'I cannot stress too strongly,' a key passage said, 'that my conclusions and proposals are not based on my fear of further riots. They are based on my belief that the conditions and prospects in the cities are not compatible with the traditions of social justice and national evenhandedness on which our party prides itself.'[19]

Heseltine prepared the ground for his prescription with a quiet dinner for a small group of Whitehall mandarins, including the Cabinet Secretary, Sir Robert Armstrong, and the head of the Civil Service, Sir Ian Bancroft. He took them to Lockets, a smart restaurant in Westminster, and they were impressed with his analysis.

Margaret Thatcher wasn't. The very title *It Took a Riot* seemed to suggest to her that violence should be rewarded. She diverted discussion to an ad-hoc group of ministers, few of whom would welcome the notion that the government should change its economic policy. Neither the Industry Secretary, Sir Keith Joseph, nor the Chancellor, Sir Geoffrey Howe, supported Heseltine. Sir Geoffrey preferred his own free-market solution of 'enterprise zones' – small areas where businesses were given exemption from tax, rates and government regulations. As Environment Secretary, Heseltine had legislated to establish the zones and had helped decide their locations, but he considered market solutions were insufficient in a desperate situation like Liverpool. The Chancellor, however – who had once been a Merseyside MP – believed 'managed decline' was probably the only answer for the area. Nor was Willie Whitelaw much help, even though he had responsibility for law and order as Home Secretary, and greatly admired Heseltine's work in Liverpool (and largely shared his political outlook).

With so little support, the Environment Secretary knew it was futile to press for *It Took a Riot* to be discussed by the full Cabinet: it would simply be rejected even more firmly. Instead he had to make do with a meagre increase in the funds for the urban budget.

But rejection by Cabinet colleagues had done nothing to dampen Heseltine's ardour. His time in Liverpool was 'his Damascene conversion' in the view of a local Tory MP, Malcolm Thornton.[20] And in Blackpool that October Heseltine was quite willing to jeopardize his traditional standing ovation by setting out his new stall at the Conservative conference.

The inner cities needed extra resources, he told the hall, and preferably investment from the private sector. 'But if the case can be made, it may also be from extra public expenditure.' It was obvious he'd been deeply affected by his experiences on Merseyside. 'You have to live there really to understand what 3 million unemployed means.' One couldn't just depend on self-help, he argued, in an obvious dig at the preferred Thatcherite solution: 'Self-help has a limited meaning in an inner-city community, where 40 per cent of the young kids may be without work, and if they are black the figure may be 60 per cent. There is one labour exchange in central Liverpool where 20,000 unemployed people are registered. Eight hundred youngsters applied to just one firm for thirty apprenticeships.'[21]

In previous years Michael Heseltine had roused his audience by telling them exactly what they wanted to hear – often to the private disgust of many senior colleagues. This time he delivered a message many grass-roots Tories would have found unpalatable. In a passage which he thought laid the ghost of Enoch Powell, he insisted the large urban immigrant communities were here to stay:

Let this party's position be absolutely clear. They are British. They live here. They vote here. However tight the immigration legislation – and in everyone's interests it should be tight – there will be a large black community in this country tomorrow, just as there is today. There are no schemes of significant repatriation that have any moral, social or political credibility.[22]

It was a courageous thing to tell an audience which has never been known for liberal sentiment. When it prompted loud applause, tears came to Heseltine's eyes. 'I will and do condemn the handful of blacks that rioted,' he continued. 'But I condemn just as strongly the whites who rioted alongside them.'[23] The standing ovation was as rapturous as ever, and the biggest for any minister that week, apart from Margaret Thatcher. Of all the conference speeches Heseltine has delivered, he would later say that 1981 was the one of which he was most proud:

There was something that had to be said, and risks that had to be taken, and positions that had to be adopted, very clearly; and I spent many hours, sat up very late the night before that speech, preparing certain parts of the speech, so that they were indelibly expressed in black and white. No one would have the slightest doubts where I stood ever again.[24]

Heseltine had set out a very distinctive approach compared with the new breed of Thatcherites who had just joined the Cabinet. It was an obvious contrast to Norman Tebbit's famous 'bike' speech, delivered just three hours later. 'He didn't riot,' Tebbit said of his unemployed father in the 1930s. 'He got on his bike, and looked for work.'[25]

Margaret Thatcher had rejected *It Took a Riot*, and deplored its economic message, but her more pragmatic side recognized that Heseltine would do a good public-relations job in Liverpool. Shortly before the Tory conference she accepted his suggestion of greater government commitment to the area, and announced his appointment as Minister for Merseyside for twelve months. A thirty-strong task force was assembled to assist him, comprising civil servants and a dozen managers seconded by local employers – among them Royal Insurance, British Rail and United Biscuits. Significantly, it included nobody from any of the local councils, and, unusually for a government initiative at that time, the officials came from three different ministries – the DoE, the DTI and Employment (though not the Home Office) – in an attempt to coordinate their existing efforts. Heseltine had first argued for greater cooperation between government departments over the setting up of the European Space Agency in 1973; the problems of government compartmentalization would become a growing theme of his.

For the next fifteen months Heseltine spent a day in Liverpool almost every week. Generally he went either on Friday or on Monday, when he might have driven himself up from his country home the previous night, before starting with a working breakfast. Quite often he drove round on his own, and refused police protection when he visited Toxteth. 'He used to love going to Liverpool,' says Roger Bright, his assistant private secretary. 'Here were practical problems for him to try to get his teeth into and make an impression on.'[26] The work was a continuation of his initial visit – chasing progress on several schemes that were devised then, holding meetings, generating ideas, striking deals, persuading businessmen and councillors to work together. Above all, he delighted in unblocking log-jams. It could be described as a process of political entrepreneurship, ideally suited to Heseltine's skills.

Eric Sorensen became director of the task force, and his deputy was Colette Bowe, a DTI official who'd been brought up in Liverpool. Heseltine, she says, was 'one of the most effective politicians I've ever had anything to do with', and particularly adept at getting the official machine to do as he wanted. 'He's very good at knowing how to use various kinds of guile and charm, and then quite harsh, tough questioning as well,' she adds. 'If a Cabinet minister says, "Come to a meeting with me," people come. And he'd say things like, "Given that such a high proportion of the population of this city is not white, why do you only ever see white shop assistants?" It was a good combination of using his own personal clout and being unafraid to ask them pretty hard questions.'[27]

While Heseltine faced initial hostility from the Labour-controlled

Merseyside County Council, he was greatly assisted by the Liberal group which still ran the city of Liverpool itself. Its leader, Sir Trevor Jones, had earned the name of 'Jones the Vote' by developing the idea of 'pavement politics' and running successful Liberal by-election campaigns in the early 1970s. Jones and Heseltine soon established a close working relationship. 'We agreed to cooperate,' says Jones. ' "You don't attack me and I won't attack you," we said. So we never had public rows, but we had plenty of private ones.' Not all Liberals were too happy with Jones's close dealings with a Conservative minister. 'I got into trouble,' he says, 'with the younger ones basically saying, "He's Heseltine's lackey. He's a Tory." '[28]

Jones and Heseltine were similar figures in many ways – men who'd run their own successful businesses before going into politics. They were both aggressive, flamboyant, slightly roguish characters who courted publicity and enjoyed the grand gesture. They had a common Welsh ancestry and, although they came from different parties, had similar views on most issues. Privately, Heseltine felt Sir Trevor and his Liberals were a far more effective opposition to Labour in Liverpool than the local Tories. Often the two men would talk late at night over a drink in the minister's hotel suite. It's an example of how Heseltine has few qualms about working closely with people from other parties. Sir Trevor claims that Heseltine could be quite indiscreet and even admitted on one occasion that he was himself a Liberal at heart but could never have sat on the sidelines, deprived of power, as the party leader, David Steel, did.[29] Heseltine thought of Jones as a model for the type of civic leader who should be encouraged: the Environment Secretary hankered after a return to the nineteenth-century tradition whereby successful local businessmen applied themselves to build the great cities. He lamented that 'the great names that would foregather in the Victorian days to discuss the problems, have gone'.[30] His best example was Joseph Chamberlain in Birmingham.

Although Sir Trevor's party officially ran Liverpool City Council between 1981 and 1983, the Liberals never enjoyed an overall majority, so they needed to strike deals with Labour or Tory councillors. A good example of how Jones and Heseltine operated well together concerned the Liverpool Garden Festival, which eventually took place in 1984.

Heseltine had initially been alerted to the idea of garden festivals by the back-bench MP Philip Goodhart, who pointed out how the Germans had used *Buntesgartenschauen* after the war to help revive their flattened cities. Once Heseltine had initiated the scheme in Britain, several cities applied for DoE funds and approval to host the first festival, but the Environment Secretary decided it would be an excellent initiative for Liverpool. He and Jones inspected the derelict and polluted site of an old military fuel reserve alongside the Mersey. 'Good God, Trevor, do you think anything will grow here?' was Heseltine's initial reaction.

The land was owned by the city council, and, although he was leader, Jones knew it might take months to cobble together the necessary support from other parties. Without an overall majority, Jones said, 'the council would still be arguing over the colour of the railings'.[31]

But Sir Trevor Jones wasn't just the leader of the city council: he was also a director of the Merseyside Development Corporation (MDC), a body Heseltine had earlier set up to regenerate the Mersey docks area. Jones therefore persuaded his council colleagues to hand the site over to the MDC; the development corporation duly applied for the festival, and Heseltine chose Liverpool ahead of a stronger bid from Stoke-on-Trent. 'I was sorry for Stoke,' Heseltine later admitted. 'They were entitled to feel that my decision went against them because I was concerned for Merseyside, and there was an element of truth in their suspicion.'[32]

Heseltine wanted a big project, a quick colourful return for all his efforts on Merseyside, and the festival had an obvious appeal to him as a passionate gardener. Trevor Jones was equally keen, because the proposed site was in his council ward. But hopes that the scheme might help local unemployment quickly foundered when it was discovered that the landscaping firm was based in Manchester, and bussed its workers from there every day. 'You can just imagine,' says John Hamilton, the then local Labour leader. 'Liverpool people standing around, unemployed, watching Manchester men doing this job for them – that they could have done. Whilst the idea was right, you can imagine the psychological effect that had!'[33] Given the traditional rivalry between Liverpool and Manchester it was a serious

19. With Diana Solomon, a teenage sweetheart from Swansea.

20. On his engagement to Anne Williams in November 1961.

21. As an ITN television presenter, interviewing the 1963 Miss World.

22. Not every voter's cup of tea: he was defeated in Coventry North in 1964.

23. Heseltine became MP for Tavistock in 1966, but only after thwarting attempts by some local Tories to drop him.

24. Every summer Heseltine toured constituency villages with his mobile surgery. When the Tavistock seat disappeared under boundary changes, he was glad to move nearer London.

25. Receiving a constituency delegation protesting at the inclusion of Plympton and Plymstock in the City of Plymouth.

26. As Aerospace Minister, Heseltine's prime job was to sell Concorde. Despite an energetic campaign, he failed to get a single new overseas sale.

27. With Rupert, Annabel, Anne and Alexandra at their new home near Nettlebed, Oxfordshire. Heseltine had promised Henley Tories he would live in the constituency, but four years later moved to a country estate in Northamptonshire.

28. 'The man who bought his own furniture.' And assembled it, too.

29. With Anne and Annabel outside Henley Town Hall, listening to results from the February 1974 election.

30. The Pied Piper of Liverpool, 1981. Heseltine quickly struck up a rapport with the swarms of boys his visits attracted. 'They are so friendly, witty and alert,' he said.

31. Escorting a busload of City businessmen round the worst parts of Merseyside. Many were shocked by what they saw; so was Heseltine.

32. In his office with the de Laszlo portrait of Lloyd George, Heseltine's political hero. He had to give up the picture when it was discovered that, coincidentally, it belonged to the grandson of William Heseltine's nineteenth-century business partner.

33. Greenham Common cruise missile base, 1983. Heseltine claims he simply borrowed the combat jacket because it was raining. Others recall discussions over whether it would be a good PR gesture. It was.

34. After his Westland resignation in January 1986, he took to the air with a TV film presenting the case for a European consortium to save the helicopter company.

mistake, though locals were employed later on other aspects of the project.

More than 3 million people attended the festival in the summer of 1984, and it did much to improve Liverpool's image and self-esteem. It was followed, however, by disputes over who should then take responsibility for the site, and the initial developer went bust.

The garden festival was typical of how Heseltine's interest and involvement could quickly make something happen. Local councillors and DoE officials quietly chuckled over the way that Liverpool projects which had previously been firmly rejected for government funding suddenly got approval when resubmitted. When Heseltine found that other cities had failed to spend their full allocation from the government's Urban Programme, he quietly shifted the remaining funds to Liverpool. Even so, Merseyside was only getting back a fraction of the money Heseltine had had withdrawn in rate support grant from councils in the area. (For technical reasons, both Merseyside and Liverpool had suffered far more severely from such cuts than most local authorities.)

If the garden festival was temporary, a more permanent tourist attraction has been the renovated Albert Dock, which now contains a maritime museum, the northern arm of the Tate Gallery, shops, restaurants and offices, as well as the Liverpool studios of Granada TV. 'Heseltine was very much the prime mover', says Trevor Jones. Jones also credits the Minister for Merseyside with the regeneration of a site in front of the Anglican cathedral which had lain derelict for years. Heseltine initiated an architectural competition which eventually turned the area into housing cooperatives and accommodation for students.

Another achievement was the Wavertree Technology Park on the site of an old railway sidings three miles from the city centre. Heseltine pumped in £10 million of government money to reclaim the land, and enlisted the help of Plessey, which owned a factory next door, to attract new high-tech businesses to the location. Heseltine saw it as a prime example of partnership between private and public investment.

Further afield, in Knowsley – a borough notorious for its poor housing, much of which was thrown up to accommodate postwar overspill from clearing Liverpool's slums – Michael Heseltine was also involved in the transformation of Cantril Farm. Known locally as 'Cannibal Farm', this was the least popular estate in the whole borough. Built only in the 1960s and early 1970s, it was a planning disaster – a jungle of tower blocks, grey maisonettes, deck-access flats, passageways and subways that seemed to be designed for criminals, vandals and drug-dealers. More than 300 properties were empty, and many had been so badly vandalized they were unlettable. The local school had been burgled 248 times in one year. Knowsley's leaders, led by Jim Lloyd – an old-fashioned, right-wing Labour 'boss' – were desperate to know what to do with the estate. They were quite willing to forget their political differences with the government if Heseltine could find a solution.

The Minister for Merseyside turned to his former housing adviser, Tom Baron, and twisted his arm to produce a plan in just a few weeks. Baron roped in the builder Laurie Barratt, and Clive Thornton of the Abbey National Building Society. Their answer was radical, and hardly likely to win support from most Labour authorities. They proposed that the estate should be taken out of council hands and sold to a trust set up specially to run it. About a third of the properties would be knocked down; the rest would be rehabilitated. Barratt would also build 600 new houses for sale, and Baron insisted that certain rules had to be waived – he wanted, for instance, to evict the most troublesome tenants. The funds would come from the Housing Corporation (the government body that assists housing associations), the DoE's Urban Programme, and a raft of loans from the Abbey National, Barclay's Bank and Knowsley Council, though the contribution from the public sector was far greater than the private investment.

It was a sign of the desperation of the Knowsley Labour group that it gave Baron unanimous backing for his scheme. Today, under its new name of Stockbridge Village – a title Baron chose himself – the estate is far more attractive than it ever was as Cantril Farm. Three in ten of the houses are now owner-occupied; the area is well maintained by the trust's fifty staff; and, instead of vacant properties, there's a waiting-list of more than 700 families. To Heseltine, not only was it a chance to extend the right to buy, it also showed that a trust could manage social housing better than local authorities. It was also an example of what Labour councils and a Conservative government could do when they cooperated.

If Michael Heseltine managed good cooperation with two metropolitan boroughs – Labour Knowsley and Liberal Liverpool – his time on Merseyside almost certainly spelt the end of the metropolitan counties. Not only was Heseltine furious with Merseyside's spending policies after the county had turned Labour in 1981 – which made his struggles with the Treasury all the more difficult – he also felt it had taken a negative, party-political approach to his attempts to revive the area. Many voices in Liverpool – including Trevor Jones and the city council's chief executive, Alfred Stocks – were quick to tell Heseltine that the concept of a Merseyside County Council hadn't worked. They argued that instead, where provision had to extend beyond borough boundaries – with the Merseyside police and fire services, for example – it could be managed by a joint board with representatives from all the councils involved. This, after all, was how the Mersey tunnels were run. Heseltine hardly needed convincing. Although abolition of the metropolitan counties did not become Tory policy until the 1983 election, he was seriously thinking about it as early as the summer of 1981. Alfred Stocks even offered to draft the bill!

The minister's exasperation with the metropolitan counties was partly fuelled by his growing view that they should have done much of the strategic work he was having to do. If Merseyside County Council, and the GLC in London, had been more effective, he believed there might have been no need for the two urban-regeneration bodies he initiated – the Merseyside and London Docklands Development Corporations.

The Merseyside Development Corporation (MDC) had been established against the will of both Labour and Conservative members of Merseyside County Council. Earlier, in fact, Heseltine himself had firmly rejected the idea of a development body for the Liverpool docks area. Before the 1979 election, the Tory leaders of Merseyside had been negotiating to take over the derelict parts of Mersey docks themselves; it was exactly the kind of strategic planning scheme for which metropolitan counties had originally been created. Merseyside Tories feared, however, that Labour ministers might push the county council aside and set up their own government body instead. Their concern was even addressed during the 1979 election, in a speech in Liverpool, by Heseltine himself:

No doubt the Prime Minister [Labour's James Callaghan] would find some scheme which would involve spending more of the taxpayer's money to set up some government agency or, knowing that the Merseyside County Council were on the threshold of an agreement, he could muscle in on their plans to redevelop the South Docks area. It would be much better for him to let the council get on with the task and complete their scheme.[34]

Heseltine, of course, now did exactly what he had accused Labour of being likely to do – he set up an agency involving taxpayers' money. It was nothing less than a blatant U-turn. The decision was all the more strange since the government was officially committed to culling quangos rather than creating them.

Heseltine carried out the move in a quite ruthless manner. The Tory chairman of Merseyside County Council, Sir Kenneth Thompson, learnt the news only when Heseltine rang him at home one morning while he was having breakfast, at the same time as the DoE was briefing the press. The conversation was heated, and Thompson eventually slammed down the phone. Sir Kenneth, a former Tory minister, was furious that he had not been consulted by Whitehall. His council's own plans for the site, by now well-advanced, suddenly had to be abandoned. Thompson promised to oppose the new body at every step, denouncing it as 'faceless' and a 'quango'.[35] (Nevertheless, he later became an MDC director.)

Urban development corporations (UDCs) had been an important item on the 'envelope' Heseltine had given Sir John Garlick at the Connaught Hotel. Authorship of the idea is keenly disputed, however. Peter Walker claims to have dreamt up the concept when he was Environment Secretary.[36] The former Labour planning minister John Silkin has also claimed credit.[37] Crucially, though, it was Heseltine who persuaded more free-market colleagues – such as Thatcher, Howe and Joseph – that the idea was worth trying.

Everyone's basic model for the UDCs was the new-town corporations which were set up by the Attlee government after the war to plan and build the new towns. Local councils, it was thought, were too bureaucratic and political to be effective developers. The UDCs were given both government money and wide-ranging powers – to acquire land and reclaim derelict sites, to build factories and houses, to grant planning permission, and to invest in local industry. Whereas Sir Geoffrey Howe's enterprise zones in principle involved a *withdrawal* of government controls, the UDCs took a very different approach. More than any other body, in fact, they epitomized the Heseltine style of government. They were interventionist, using government funds selectively to generate local activity; they involved partnership between the private and public sectors; they invested in big symbolic projects, such as the Albert Dock, which were designed to bring back a sense of local pride. Above all, the UDCs involved central government coming in to act decisively and directly, bypassing normal democratic procedures and elected politicians in the form of local councils.

Michael Heseltine's initial intention was just one development corporation to cover much of London's docklands, where a joint committee of local authorities had failed over many years to agree on concerted action. It was born of his experience as aerospace minister in the Heath government, regularly travelling to the site of the proposed new London airport at Maplin:

The way I used to go was in a small aircraft flying all over the East End of London, and there was a desert. You just looked down and you couldn't believe the prosperity that ended more or less at the Tower of London could be so iron-curtained away from what was happening further east. And that was one of the things that made me so determined to try and bring a new opportunity to this area.[38]

Earlier still, as a junior DoE minister, Heseltine had conceived the idea of a new authority to coordinate development along the banks of the Thames, and he had even commissioned some exploratory work.

The London Docklands UDC covered a far larger area than that for Merseyside, and faced very different circumstances. The City of London, which was close at hand, was already overcrowded, and rents in the Square Mile had been climbing sharply. Financial institutions were looking to move out, but needed to stay close to the City; Docklands was an obvious location. Heseltine was inspired by the

American examples of Boston and Baltimore, where private capital had regenerated the dilapidated city waterfronts, so most of the people Heseltine appointed to the boards of his UDCs were businessmen. Often they had property interests, like Nigel Broackes, the chairman of Trafalgar House, who became the first chairman of London Docklands. Broackes admits he had never even visited the area when Heseltine asked him to do the job, and had to look it up in the *A–Z London Street Atlas*.[39]

A big mistake with Docklands was not to build good access roads at the very start. It was a lesson Heseltine should have learnt by now, as his Tenterden development had suffered exactly the same problem twenty years before, though on a much smaller scale, of course. He did secure £77 million from the Treasury to build the Docklands Light Railway – no mean achievement in a climate where public investment was discouraged – though critics said he chose the wrong train system.

Overall, however, he took far less personal interest in London Docklands than he did in Merseyside – 'He'd come perhaps twice a year,' says Broackes, 'and we'd go round in the bus.'[40] It was far easier to secure private funding beside the Thames than it was on the banks of the Mersey: the ratio of private to public capital in Docklands was about nine to one during the 1980s, whereas in Liverpool it was roughly even. Indeed, business interest in London Docklands was so great that by 1986 there was what the *Evening Standard* called an 'orgy of property development', with the construction of office blocks and more than 2,000 private houses a year.[41] And that was before the deal to build the great Canary Wharf complex. With the 1990s recession, however, Canary Wharf's original developers went bust at considerable cost to the government, and many houses in the area remained unsold. When property prices collapsed in the early 1990s, owner-occupiers in Docklands lost more heavily than perhaps anywhere else.

Because of its location, London Docklands was always going to be attractive to investors, and was therefore likely to provide few lessons for urban regeneration elsewhere in Britain. The Financial Institutions Group – the people seconded to the DoE after Heseltine's Liverpool bus trip – spent a year trying to devise ways in which City investors might get more involved in other decaying inner cities. They visited the United States and Europe, and held an all-day brain-storming session with Heseltine in the rather inappropriate setting of a hotel in prosperous Hertfordshire. The main product of their work was the urban development grant – for certain projects, Whitehall would top up private investment by the amount required to make a scheme viable.

Heseltine's visits to Liverpool 8, however, had shown that the area's problems weren't just financial. In 1982 Heseltine gave his junior minister, Sir George Young, an extra brief to look after racial issues, to the disquiet of the Home Office. He also sought an adviser to liaise with urban black communities. The role would inevitably be contentious, and it proved impossible to find a black person who held the respect of all sides. In the end the job went to one of the most unusual people ever to have served as a ministerial adviser, particularly to a Conservative Secretary of State.

Ed Berman was one of the few remaining representatives of the 1960s 'alternative society'. Born in America but now a British citizen, Berman had made his reputation from his community theatre group, Inter-Action. He had also made headlines in the late 1960s and early 1970s as head of the Santa Claus Union, when he was arrested during demonstrations outside major London stores against the 'exploitation of children's fantasy'.

Heseltine had first met him on a ministerial visit to Berman's inner-city training and business centre in Kentish Town, London. Berman lived on a nearby cooperative, where the members ate communally, shared the chores, and had the same set allowance of £28 a week. Before he could work for Heseltine, his cooperative had to meet to approve his new role, and the DoE bureaucracy was flummoxed by Berman's request to be paid the same £28 as his weekly co-op allowance. This was unheard of. Special advisers were senior members of staff, and the Civil Service pay scale dictated a salary of more than £200 a week. Not even the cost-conscious MINIS process could handle such an unorthodox spending cut. The dilemma was resolved only when the department agreed to pay Berman's salary direct to his cooperative. He then continued getting his weekly £28.

It was a sign of Heseltine's open-minded approach to problems that he was willing to employ such an unconventional, eccentric character. Berman's value to Heseltine was, first, that he enjoyed good connections with inner-city black communities through his touring street theatre. And, second, he had a refreshing, lateral approach to problems. 'He threw some good ideas into the pot and gingered us up,' says Roger Bright.[42] Another colleague was somewhat less impressed: 'I thought, "What the hell's Michael doing with this twit?" ' Heseltine, too, later expressed doubts about the appointment.

Much of Berman's work involved visiting inner-city areas and persuading Labour councillors to apply for grants from the DoE's urban budget, which by 1982 was seriously underspent. 'Michael said, "See how much of this money you can get out there, and see that it's not mistreated," ' he recalls.[43] Berman says he almost had to beg local authorities to spend from the one area of the DoE budget where financial stringency didn't appear to apply, and which had political favour. Even though there were tens of millions of pounds to dispose of, it was something of a struggle. Northern Labour bosses were understandably suspicious when an American with a Trotsky-style beard turned up and claimed to be Michael Heseltine's aide. Municipal leaders were even more bewildered when Berman urged them to dream up inner-city projects which the DoE could finance. It seemed bizarre to them, when Berman's boss was being so hard on the rest of local government spending.

Ed Berman also arranged for more than a dozen people from various ethnic backgrounds, and from different cities, to serve on advisory committees at the DoE – 'people who would otherwise refuse to go into a Whitehall building'.[44] Rastafarians found themselves sitting next to public-school-educated civil servants and the chief executives of building societies. After one committee meeting, Berman even arranged for Heseltine to meet four 'burners' in his room at Marsham Street – young blacks who claimed to have been involved in the riots in Brixton, Bristol and Manchester. Heseltine was fully aware of their background, but wanted to know what had motivated them. Margaret Thatcher, had she known, would have been horrified.

Ironically, given his initial disdain for the job, Michael Heseltine's time at the DoE was easily his most active and successful period in government. He later described it as 'four of the happiest years of my

life'.[45] The right to buy, the battles with local government, MINIS
and Merseyside are obviously the heart of his record, but, given the
ragbag of DoE responsibilities, his stewardship involved a host of
other significant achievements.

The 1981 Wildlife and Countryside Act, for instance, protected
many of Britain's endangered species and their habitats. Heseltine
was especially proud of his record on conservation and heritage issues.
He vetoed plans for the 'Green Giant' – a vast skyscraper on London's
South Bank – and initiated the architectural competition for the
extension to the National Gallery, though the winning entry would
famously be described by Prince Charles as a 'monstrous carbuncle
on the face of a much-loved friend' and was never built. Heseltine
also established the Queen Elizabeth II Conference Centre on an
unoccupied bomb-site opposite Westminster Abbey. This involved a
long tussle with the Treasury, who refused to fund infrastructure
projects. Heseltine had promised to secure private investment, so
Margaret Thatcher was extremely upset when none was forthcoming.
As the project had already been announced, and was so prestigious,
it couldn't be scrapped. The Treasury had to pay after all.

Responsibility for the DoE's ancient monuments and historic sites
was hived off to a new semi-autonomous agency, English Heritage,
under the chairmanship of the former motoring correspondent on
Town, Lord Montagu of Beaulieu. It must have given Heseltine some
personal satisfaction when his old OUCA enemy Robert (Robin)
Cooke also agreed to become his ministerial adviser on the upkeep of
the Palace of Westminster.

Liverpool, though, remains the interest for which Heseltine's first
spell as Environment Secretary is principally remembered. But, for
all the time he devoted to the city, many argue that Heseltine's
impact was only cosmetic. 'A lot of money was spent,' says a former
Merseyside Labour councillor, George Bundred, 'lots of trees were
planted and goodness knows what, but at the end of the day it
didn't bring any employment, and that was the real problem – these
youngsters on the scrapheap.'[46]

Margaret Thatcher concurs. Heseltine's role on Merseyside 'made
a great impression, which was undoubtedly politically helpful to us,'
she says. 'Though for the most part his efforts had only ephemeral

results, I would not blame him for that: Liverpool had defeated better men than Michael Heseltine.'[47]

Michael Parkinson, professor of urban affairs at Liverpool's John Moores University (and not to be confused with the former *Town* journalist), is the foremost expert on the city's recent development. Ten years ago he was sceptical about the likely long-term impact of Heseltine and the task force, but he now gives them considerable credit. Quite apart from the five or six very visible large-scale projects in the area, Parkinson says, several positive developments in British inner-city policy can be traced back to Heseltine's Liverpool period. 'Most of the things that are happening now, he set in motion,' he argues.[48] Among these are moves to coordinate ministerial departments through regional offices, the assigning of ministers to look after specific regions, the encouragement of housing associations and cooperatives, and the channelling of government aid through business-led agencies rather than local government. Above all, most of the 'experiments' (Heseltine's own word) on Merseyside involved the idea of partnership between government and private enterprise. Partnership was surprisingly uncommon in the early 1980s, but has since become widely accepted by all parties (and is pursued with particular enthusiasm by Labour's John Prescott).

'There are things on Merseyside today,' says the city's former Liberal leader Sir Trevor Jones, 'that wouldn't be there if he hadn't come. I think that is testament enough.'[49] More than a decade afterwards, Margaret Thatcher's Minister for Merseyside still remains popular in the area, even if his party isn't. The Conservative vote fell to just 15 per cent at the 1992 election, and the party now holds only one of the ninety-nine seats on Liverpool Council, but Michael Heseltine is acknowledged as one of the few national Conservative figures to have expressed genuine concern for the city. Liverpool's former Labour leader, John Hamilton, says he 'meant well, but he was ineffective'. But he adds, 'Most Liverpool people, they say, "Oh well, he's a Tory – and we don't think much of Tories – but I'll give credit to Heseltine: he was the only Tory that did something for us." '[50]

14. *Defence Battles*

The thought of Michael Heseltine as their boss horrified the top brass. Some tried to stop him. In September 1982 the Defence Secretary, John Nott, had announced that he was leaving politics at the next election to return to business. Since defence was expected to be a big issue in the forthcoming campaign, it made sense to install his replacement as early as possible. Heseltine had been tipped for the job for months, but the Sunday before Christmas there were press reports that service chiefs were lobbying to block his appointment. Instead, it was said they were 'rooting' for the Scottish Secretary, George Younger, whom they saw as a more amenable candidate.[1]

The first three years of the Thatcher government had seen considerable upheaval at the MoD, quite apart from a war in the South Atlantic. The Chief of the Defence Staff, Sir Edwin Bramall, later admitted that the service chiefs had then 'hoped for a period of consolidation in which the lessons of the Falklands could be absorbed, new equipment brought into service, and a new strategy developed. This was not to be.'[2] Following the newspaper speculation, Bramall and Willie Whitelaw, the Deputy Prime Minister, issued strenuous denials that they'd discussed how to stop Heseltine.

The party chairman, Cecil Parkinson, and the outgoing Defence Secretary both thought Michael Heseltine was the right choice, while Margaret Thatcher felt he was 'clearly restless' after three and a half years at the DoE.[3] Heseltine was on holiday when the Prime Minister rang with the news; he was out alligator-spotting in the wilds of Tobago (though the tabloids all missed the obvious headlines about 'Tarzan in the jungle'). She told him to expect to be at Defence for several years.

The apparent disquiet among the military chiefs would only have convinced Thatcher that Heseltine was the best choice. His cost-cutting record at the DoE suggested he would have few qualms about attacking the far greater inefficiency at the MoD, or challenging the vested interests of the three armed services and the defence manufacturers. Moreover, Defence would also remove Heseltine from the economic and social arenas where he and the Prime Minister seldom agreed – or so Thatcher might have thought. Perhaps to be on the safe side, she filled the simultaneous vacancy of Permanent Secretary at the MoD with her principal private secretary, Clive Whitmore; he was supposedly such a favourite of hers that 'Ask Clive' had become known as a Thatcher catch-phrase. Some saw the move as similar to John Stanley's arrival at the DoE in 1979 – as a means of keeping tabs on Heseltine (and five months later Stanley followed him to the MoD).

Thatcher's most immediate requirement, however, was a Defence Secretary who had enough profile to confront the burgeoning peace movement. 'John Nott was not interested in campaigning on nuclear deterrence,' says a ministerial colleague. 'We had the greatest difficulty even in getting him to make a speech on it. Now we had a Secretary of State who really believed in getting the message across.' The debate with anti-nuclear protestors could not be avoided. Britain had ordered a new Trident nuclear weapons system, and American cruise missiles were soon to be stationed at air-force bases in England. In the face of this, the Campaign for Nuclear Disarmament (CND) had grown from 3,000 members to 100,000 in three years, and its mass demonstrations were making considerable impact.

CND had been around for a quarter of a century, having grown from the mass marches to the nuclear research station at Aldermaston in the late 1950s. But it had been moribund for years, and the organization which emerged so rapidly in the early 1980s was a very different animal. Following the election of Thatcher in the UK and Reagan in the United States – who were both given to hawkish rhetoric about the Soviet Union – there was a real public fear that the West might be willing to use nuclear weapons. CND combined detailed analytical work about defence strategy with many of the tools of direct marketing to build a large-scale campaign that was credible, broad-based, and well-informed. And many of its arguments against Trident and cruise were shared by former military chiefs, and even some Conservatives.

Once more Heseltine was being brought in as a highly visible, flamboyant salesman, to shake things up after a lacklustre performance from his predecessor. In 1972 he'd been told to sell Concorde; from 1976 it had been council houses; now it was nuclear weapons.

For his first five months as Defence Secretary, until the June 1983 election, the battle against CND took up most of Heseltine's time. Before his arrival, this had been the responsibility of the minister of state, Peter Blaker (Heseltine's old Oxford Union colleague), who had worked with two or three civil servants on the presentation of the government's 'deterrence' policy. Heseltine acted quickly to beef up their work.

Initially he considered an idea mooted by John Nott – to spend £1 million on publicity to explain the reasons for nuclear weapons. This proved to be a bad mistake, since the mere revelation by Heseltine that he was thinking of spending taxpayers' money in this way prompted a rush of contributions to CND. Heseltine soon modified his approach. At the start of March 1983 he established a new division within the MoD known as Defence Secretariat 19, or DS19 – a small team of public-relations specialists and defence experts. Its purpose was to counter CND and promote the government's view on nuclear deterrence. DS19 prepared literature, briefed MPs, made films, and provided Michael Heseltine with speech material. It also collated the results of outside opinion polls, and planned to issue counter-publicity if the peace movement mounted demonstrations against Heseltine.

Although it comprised only seven staff, DS19 acquired a sinister status on the left and among peace activists. Its very existence inevitably raised serious constitutional issues. Civil servants are often involved in explaining and promoting government policy – that, after all, is what departmental press officers spend much of their time doing – but DS19 was thought to touch the limits of propriety. Many leading MoD officials had serious concerns about whether they were really being asked to promote the Conservative Party.

Heseltine's strategy was based on the fact that the opinion polls seemed to be delivering conflicting messages. For instance, a Marplan survey conducted a few days after his appointment showed majorities of more than two to one against both cruise and Trident. Yet the same poll showed that fewer than one in four of those questioned wanted Britain to abandon its nuclear weapons altogether.[4] So Heseltine deliberately steered away from arguments about the merits of cruise and Trident; instead he concentrated on wider ideas – of a 'strong' or 'weak' defence; the need to protect concepts such as freedom, democracy and security; and the Atlantic alliance.

Above all, Heseltine wanted to simplify the language of the debate. From his first television interview onwards, he always avoided the term 'unilateral disarmament'. 'For God's sake, stop using stupid words like "unilateral"!' one admiral recalls him exploding. 'He said, "Go down to the pub and say something's unilateral and they'll think you're off your rocker. If you mean one-sided, call it one-sided!" Every now and again he had a flash of brilliance – the common man's flash of brilliance.'

The head of DS19, John Ledlie, suggested that Heseltine should take journalists on a press trip to Greenham Common, one of the US airfields where cruise missiles were to be sited. This, Ledlie argued, would help him 'to take the initiative and demonstrate the safety of the base'. The visit, for which he was accompanied by his wife, Anne, was the famous occasion when Heseltine was seen wearing a combat jacket (sometimes wrongly called a flak jacket). How he came to don it is disputed. The Heseltine version – backed by a senior colleague – is that 'It was raining and I hadn't got a coat and it was early morning and it was cold, and some military chaps put this on my shoulders.'[5] John Ledlie, however, recalls long discussions beforehand about whether or not Heseltine should wear the jacket. Ledlie felt it might be seen as too militaristic, and be a 'red rag to a bull'. In hindsight he admits Heseltine was right: it provided a powerful image for the cameras, which was even picked up by cartoonists.[6] The Defence Secretary thereafter wore combat jackets for other visits to military bases.

Another publicity trip came on Good Friday 1983, when tens of thousands of peace demonstrators were due to link arms all the way round Greenham Common. The same day, Heseltine went to West Berlin and looked out across the wall towards the Communist East. But perhaps the most significant incident – albeit unplanned – occurred in February, when Heseltine went to address local Conservatives in Newbury, not far from Greenham Common. A crowd of peace protestors surrounded the town hall, and as he arrived he fell over in the mêlée. The incident was portrayed in the press as the Defence Secretary being 'roughed up', while *The Times* reported that 'a woman dragged him to his knees'. Heseltine himself was quoted as saying he 'was pulled to the ground'.[7]

The fracas received extensive coverage in the press and on TV, and enabled Heseltine to take the moral high ground. Later he claimed it had been one of the peace movement's most serious mistakes, and the crucial turning-point in the propaganda battle, though he conceded that CND hadn't been responsible for the trouble. 'I don't think CND wanted that,' he said. 'It was bad luck from their point of view. We know the consequences: the British people don't like that.'[8] Strangely, accounts by Heseltine only a few months afterwards differed markedly from what he was originally quoted as saying had happened. Instead of being pulled down by the Newbury protestors, his explanation now was that he had fallen or stumbled.[9]

Almost from the start, Heseltine was determined to portray the peace movement as politically motivated, emphasizing its contacts with Communists and the Soviet Union. In doing so he was also quick to associate the Labour Party with CND – which was hardly unreasonable, since party policy was against all nuclear weapons. But this, of course, cleverly linked Labour with the Soviets.

The work of DS19 was highly sensitive, and arguments about its activities continued for years afterwards. The first important issue was whether the unit should use material obtained from the intelligence services. John Ledlie admits that some ministers 'were sometimes pretty cavalier in their attitude to these matters', but insists that Heseltine would have regarded it as foolish to risk being accused of using MI5 information against CND.[10]

The Tory chairman, Cecil Parkinson, had earlier said it would be 'manifest nonsense' to suggest that 'CND is dominated by Communists and other left-wingers', but when Heseltine contradicted him nobody spotted it.[11] In April 1983, two weeks before Margaret Thatcher announced a general election, Heseltine stepped up his attacks on the political links of leading CND members. He wrote to Conservative MPs and candidates with information assembled by the Tory MP Ray Whitney on the political background of the organization's top officials. Heseltine warned that a majority of CND's National Council were either on the left or extreme left:

They are an organization led and dominated by left-wing activists ranging through the Labour Party to the Communist Party.

Many people attracted to the peace movement will just not want to believe that behind the carefully-tuned phrases about peace lies the calculating political professionalism of full-time Socialists and Communists.[12]

The next day, in the marginal seat of Exeter, Heseltine claimed that, at its most extreme, CND's purpose 'was to argue the cause of the Soviet Union at the expense of the free societies of the West'.[13] He pointed out that the organization was about to send a delegation to the international conference of the World Peace Council, which was regarded as a Soviet front organization.

Many of the biographical facts in Heseltine's letter to candidates could quite easily have been obtained from public sources, though some of the details were factually wrong, and one person even threatened libel action. It was widely suspected that much of the material had been obtained from the intelligence service MI5.

Two years later, a former MI5 officer, Cathy Massiter, revealed that in 1981 she had been asked to gather details on leading CND members. Among other means, these had been obtained through telephone taps and an MI5 agent inside the organization's headquarters. As CND grew in popularity in 1982 and 1983, the demands upon Massiter became more intense. She says that, after Heseltine took over, her branch director was approached by a senior official from DS19 who 'requested information about the subversive political affiliations of leading members of CND'. Although MI5 bosses had decided 'that we could not give information from any secret or classified sources', Massiter did assemble material on the left-wing links of CND leaders, and her report was passed to DS19.[14] 'It did begin to seem to me,' said Massiter, 'that what the security service was being asked to do was to provide information on a party political issue.'[15]

The Observer later alleged that Massiter's work was passed from DS19 to the defence minister, Peter Blaker, and that Blaker helped Whitney compile his April 1983 dossier.[16]

Even though the MI5 bosses had refused to release details obtained from *secret* sources, supplying any information for political purposes was a clear breach of the rules governing the work of the service. A directive dating from 1952, and signed then by the Home Secretary, Sir David Maxwell Fyfe, laid down that the security service should be kept absolutely free from any political bias or influence.

Despite his new aggressive stand against the peace movement, Michael Heseltine consistently rejected its requests for a public debate. The CND chairwoman, Joan Ruddock, had even suggested the Albert Hall as a venue. The candidate who had regularly challenged his Labour opponent to a debate in 1959 was now careful to avoid such exchanges. (Heseltine said privately in 1996 that he would have been at a disadvantage against an attractive female opponent like Ruddock.) He did, however, allow his more knowledgeable deputy, Peter Blaker, to debate with CND.

In the 1983 election the Conservatives won an overwhelming victory. They ended up with a majority of 142 seats, and Labour was almost pushed into third place, in terms of the popular vote, behind the Liberal–SDP Alliance. Much of the Tory success was attributed to the victory in the Falklands War and to the reviving economy. Defence and the nuclear issue also played an important role in the Conservative campaign, though Labour probably suffered more from its obvious divisions on the issue than from its opposition to cruise and Trident. 'Michael Heseltine at our press conference and throughout the campaign was devastating in his criticisms of Labour's policy,' says Margaret Thatcher.[17] But then it was relatively easy to be effective when Labour's deputy leader, Denis Healey, and the former Prime Minister, Jim Callaghan, had both indicated that they didn't support party policy.

Michael Heseltine was given and took most of the credit for the peace movement's defeat. One close participant says, however, that much of it should have gone to Peter Blaker, who had liaised between the many pro-nuclear groups which operated on the fringes of both government and party. 'While Heseltine attracted the publicity,' he says, 'Blaker really did the work.' Another of those involved says Heseltine brought much more attention to the anti-CND campaign without doing much that was new: just as with Concorde, he attracted

coverage simply through being a flamboyant figure. 'I've found somehow the publicity almost seems to find me,' Heseltine once mused,
'whatever my part in the process is.'[18]

DS19 was disbanded just three months after the election, and
much of its work passed to the MoD's 'Holocaust Desk' instead. 'I
set the task,' Heseltine said of DS19. 'The task was, I think, dealt
with and that is the moment to close it down.'[19] The decision seemed
only to underline that DS19 had been created as a political device to
win the election, especially considering that the really significant event
– the actual arrival of cruise missiles – wasn't due until the end of
1983.

Heseltine had stopped CND in its tracks. Nevertheless, for the
rest of his time at the MoD he remained the object of noisy and
forceful demonstrations when he addressed university meetings,
replacing Enoch Powell and Keith Joseph as the new bogeyman of
the student left. He seemed to revel in the drama of such occasions,
and in running the gauntlet of protestors. 'When you got through,'
he later related, 'the atmosphere in the audience was electric, and
from the moment you began to speak the overwhelming majority of
students, who were on one's side and wanted to hear the message,
erupted spontaneously to almost anything that you said.'[20] On several
occasions he made headlines after being pelted with eggs or paint,
though it was perhaps fortunate for Heseltine that another unruly
demonstration went virtually unnoticed. When it was reported that his
student daughter Annabel had thrown an egg at Greenham Common
protestors, he was lucky that the story was published long after the
event.[21]

Michael Heseltine also relished the formal aspects of being Defence
Secretary, such as taking the salute at the Royal Tournament; his
Guards tie enjoyed more outings than ever. But when he entertained
a party of new Tory MPs, just after the 1983 election, they were
struck by how little Heseltine spoke of defence and how much he
enthused about his newly acquired office furniture. His octagonal
table and bookcase, he explained to visitors, had belonged to Winston
Churchill during his two spells at the Admiralty. 'The first thing
Churchill said when he returned to the Admiralty as First Lord was:
"Where's my octagonal table?" ' Heseltine explained. 'I can see why.

It's a beautiful piece.'[22] And he then showed guests a crack in a panel of his mahogany bookcase, supposedly caused when Churchill kicked it in a moment of rage.

The implication was obvious, especially when his room also housed the de Laszlo portrait of another Prime Minister, Lloyd George, which Heseltine had brought with him from the DoE. Despite his attachment to the picture, the Defence Secretary eventually had to relinquish it. Somebody had noticed the painting in a photograph of Heseltine, and recognized it as a long-lost family heirloom which had been lent to the government's picture collection years before and then forgotten. By an astonishing coincidence, the owner of the portrait was Viscount Devonport, the grandson of Hudson Kearley, the business partner of Heseltine's great-grandfather.

Another wall of Heseltine's sixth-floor office displayed an enormous chart depicting the extent of his new ministry. As he had once promised, Heseltine decided in his first week to introduce a version of MINIS to the MoD. He later related his first exchange with his new Permanent Secretary, Clive Whitmore: ' "I wonder if by chance you've heard of the MINIS system?" "Yes, you may remember that I was in No. 10 when you did that presentation." "Ah yes, I'd like to introduce it here." "I thought you might." '[23]

As the conversation suggests, most MoD officials viewed MINIS with scepticism: some had already told the Commons Treasury Committee it was not suited to their department. They felt their existing 'Management Audit' system, which forecast costs over the next ten years, was perfectly adequate, but 'there was no question of arguing with him' says a senior official. A MINIS expert from the DoE was seconded to Heseltine's new department, though MoD officials had already made inquiries about the system well before the new Defence Secretary arrived, in anticipation of his appointment.

Michael Heseltine knew the Ministry of Defence was a far more complex organization than even the DoE, with a budget of £17 billion – 5 per cent of the national product – and more than half a million employees – 246,000 civil servants, and another 320,000 in uniform. This massive organization was beset with divisions and tensions which often developed into bitter feuds – either between the three services or between the civilian and military wings. When Heseltine asked for the organization chart for his office, it took months to design, and then it came on four large sheets which officials had some difficulty fastening together. The very process of drawing the 'wiring diagram' illustrated many of the ministry's structural problems; this, of course, had been Heseltine's intention.

A senior MoD official who worked closely with Heseltine believed MINIS never worked as effectively there as it had at the DoE – partly because the Secretary of State couldn't give it anything like the same attention. 'We would schedule all the MINIS meetings,' the official explains, 'and then they got shortened or cancelled. He was trying to do too much on top of highly political issues.' The new Defence Secretary didn't seem to allow for the sheer size of his new dominion. Whereas the DoE had been divided into 66 directorates, the MoD was broken down into 156 blocks for MINIS purposes, each headed by an under-secretary or an officer of two-star rank.

It would have been all but impossible for Heseltine to spend time considering each section individually, as he had at the DoE, and, when he was inevitably diverted by other priorities, cynicism developed about the MINIS process and the sixteen-inch brick of paper it produced. 'I don't think it was so effective,' says one particip-ant, 'because people would spend months preparing the MINIS document and then he only spent twenty minutes on it. "So that was it?" people would say.' Sir Edwin Bramall, the Chief of the Defence Staff, was among many who regarded the whole process as highly cumbersome. 'The effort was disproportionate to the result.'[24]

Michael Heseltine, like many ministers, struggled to cope with the constant stream of documents. Some officials accused him of reading only those briefs in which he was especially interested. Sir Clive Whitmore – with whom Heseltine got on well – often had to press him to clear his in-tray. But Heseltine was determined to take as much time as he needed to decide an issue, and not to be bullied (though he wasn't averse to a bit of bullying himself). 'When he was told the department wanted a decision by Friday,' says one colleague, 'he'd ask how long the department had had to look at it, and when told six months, say, he'd insist he had six months too.' The Heseltine rule was that only certain individuals could send him paperwork. Nearly everything that came to him, he insisted, had 'first of all been looked at either by senior military or civilian advisers, or by one of my ministers'.[25]

MoD civilian numbers fell by 20,000 during Michael Heseltine's three years there – about one job in every twelve. He also encouraged a 'tail to teeth' policy, of moving civilians into backup jobs being done by soldiers – the so-called 'tail' – which enabled him to push 4,000 more men into the front line – the 'teeth'. There were also steps towards privatization, such as in the provision of food, warehousing, vehicle maintenance, and even the department which manufactured dentures. Heseltine's biggest privatization was of the Royal Ordnance factories, while the Royal Dockyards at Devonport and Rosyth were also transferred to private management.

The most controversial issue of Michael Heseltine's tenure – at least internally – was his reorganization of the department. He regarded the process as a continuation of the historic trend whereby the three services – Army, Navy and Air Force – had gradually lost their independence in the interests of an integrated defence organization. It had begun with the appointment of Earl Mountbatten as the single Chief of the Defence Staff in 1958, above the chiefs of each service. Mountbatten had then recommended setting up the unified Ministry of Defence in 1964. 'I looked to see how deep into the ethos of the organization that reform had gone,' says Heseltine, 'and I was persuaded it hadn't gone anything like as far as it should have done.'[26] The most recent development, in 1981, had been to abolish the three separate Army, Navy and Air Force ministers, in favour of two new ministers of state: one to look after the armed forces as a whole, and another for equipment procurement.

In 1983 the MoD was still a highly federated structure. Each of the three services had its own extensive planning staff who worked on policy for its particular field. In addition, there was a fourth secretariat for the Chief of the Defence Staff, though this was weaker than those of the individual services. The three service chiefs did not report directly to the Chief of the Defence Staff, but instead to a Chief of Staff Committee, which reached decisions by consensus. Heseltine thought the system daft. Many activities were carried out in triplicate, and it encouraged rivalries between the services to the detriment of the overall defence effort.

Heseltine says he drew up an outline for reorganizing the MoD on his own, while travelling on a RAF VC10 on his way back from a trip to Kuwait.[27] His basic concept was that, instead of an MoD structure largely divided between Navy, Army and Air Force, the future structure should be based on function. This obviously weakened the clout of the individual services and the men who ran them, and centralized power in Whitehall. The planning sections of the three services would be brought together in a new combined Defence Staff. Each service chief would effectively lose his policy role, and answer instead to the Chief of the Defence Staff. Other activities were combined, too, as the old khaki, navy blue and light blue merged in some areas to become an inter-service purple. In the place of three separate lorry fleets, for example, there was a new joint fleet. Equally important, though less contentious, the MoD acquired a new Office of Management and Budget.

This, of course, was exactly the kind of disruption the top brass had feared when Heseltine's appointment was first mooted, and they fiercely resisted it. Didn't the success in the Falklands, they argued, show how well the existing system worked? The counter-argument was that the war in the South Atlantic had shown precisely the need for service integration in waging modern warfare. Heseltine himself would later admit his decision to 'stand so apart' from Sir Edwin Bramall and his colleagues 'was without doubt the least comfortable position I adopted in government'.[28]

Bramall felt he had been bounced into accepting the reorganization. In the same way as the Merseyside County Council chairman, Sir Kenneth Thompson, had been among the last to hear about the new Merseyside Development Corporation, so Bramall was shown Heseltine's defence blueprint only a few hours before it was made public. 'I was on three days' leave in Cornwall, and on Friday night he rang up and said, "I have this report and I have to release it to the press on Monday or else it will leak." ' Bramall managed to look through the plans and make a few changes. 'But you can only claw back so much,' he says. 'The trouble was, we're all public servants and we have to do what we're told.'[29]

Heseltine admits he pushed the changes through 'ruthlessly'.[30] He feared that, had he consulted Bramall and his colleagues sooner, they would have rallied opposition in Parliament and the press. It's a habit of defence ministers, says Bramall, to treat the chiefs with 'wariness' in case they take up entrenched positions. 'He no doubt thought that if he revealed his plans earlier, [I] would be in duty bound to inform the other chiefs and this would make it more difficult for him to achieve what he wanted.'[31]

Heseltine's opponents waged a three-month campaign, partly through the letters columns of *The Times* and the *Daily Telegraph*. A former naval chief, Admiral Sir Henry Leach, said it was time Heseltine was told 'For God's sake *stop*.' The new system, he warned, would make it easier for the Defence Secretary 'to get the military advice he thinks he *wants* but it may not always produce the *best* advice'.[32] But opposition in the Commons was limited, partly because very few Labour MPs were interested in how the MoD was organized. Bramall and his colleagues secured some modifications to Heseltine's proposals, such as leaving each service chief with a small executive staff, but they remained unhappy. Heseltine reminded them there was one means of appeal – direct to the Prime Minister.

Some chiefs hoped that Margaret Thatcher's known antipathy to Michael Heseltine might help their counter-attack. But she completely supported her Defence Secretary. After the chiefs had secured a few safeguards – such as their continued right of access to Downing Street – Bramall declared that they could 'live with the new system and make it work'.[33] It took effect from the start of 1985.

The Chief of the Defence Staff and the Defence Secretary didn't always disagree, though. Sir Edwin Bramall admired Heseltine's 'great drive' and his 'style, energy and vision about Europe', but he also thought he was 'cavalier' and 'more interested in the political short term than the long term'.[34] And Bramall felt able to speak bluntly to him – particularly over the inconsiderate way Heseltine treated people, and his notorious time-keeping.

If his brief period of National Service had taught Heseltine anything, it should have been the military emphasis on punctuality. Yet he so often failed to keep his appointments at the agreed time that Bramall soon began provoking him by wearing a placard round his neck saying 'On Call'. The Chief of the Defence Staff might arrive in the morning, for example, to be told Heseltine wanted to see him quickly. A meeting would be arranged for 11 a.m., and so Bramall's other engagements were then delayed or cancelled. But Heseltine would be too busy at 11, and postpone the appointment until 12.15, and then to 4 p.m., and again until later still. Bramall, meanwhile, would spend his day juggling all his other plans. 'At seven I'd see him in his jersey with his shoes off, and he'd say, "What are we seeing each other about?" '[35]

Bramall's patience eventually snapped: 'I flew at him. I said, "All my life I have been raised to think that you cannot lead anyone unless you respect those below you. You so often treat people with contempt." He would then say, "I'll try to do better," and then of course . . .'[36] Yet Michael Heseltine was supposed to be a minister who believed in efficiency.

It is a cherished MoD tradition that, when they retire, senior officers above a certain rank are entitled to a final meeting with the Secretary of State. The departing Second Sea Lord, Admiral Sir Desmond Cassidi, found his farewell appointment with Heseltine postponed repeatedly. When Cassidi was finally ushered in, the Defence Secretary didn't even bother to look up or invite his guest to sit down. 'I'm sorry,' Heseltine reportedly said, 'but I'm already late for another appointment.' 'I'm sorry about that, minister,' Cassidi replied, 'but on my last day I'm exercising my statutory right to give you my views on what is wrong with the Service.'[37] And so he did.

Admiral Cassidi, needless to say, was not a fan of Michael Heseltine. Nor were other top brass. 'I have so little regard for Mr Heseltine,' one Royal Air Force chief responded when approached for this book, 'that I would find it distasteful even to discuss him.'[38] Says one former admiral, 'He is the most self-centred senior politician I have met, and I think as far as he was concerned Defence was somewhere between a stepping-stone and a necessary chore to get where he wanted to get to.'

On one occasion, however, the Defence Secretary seems to have been put in his place, though the story may well be apocryphal. At one meeting, Heseltine was so exasperated with his officials and expert advisers that he reminded them that by the age of forty he'd made a million pounds three times over. What, he demanded, had they done by that age? There was an embarrassed silence, until one scientist piped up that he had detonated three nuclear bombs.

Heseltine's three years as Secretary of State saw little difference with his ministerial colleagues on the broader issues of strategic policy. The Foreign Secretary, Sir Geoffrey Howe, found him 'an imaginative and effective partner in our frequent double-acts on the NATO or WEU stage'.[39] Both men were keen on developing the Western European Union for greater defence cooperation.

When President Reagan invaded Grenada in 1983, Heseltine was as angered as Thatcher by his failure to consult Britain properly. On East–West issues, Heseltine sided with Howe in urging the Prime Minister to be more conciliatory towards the Soviets. And when the Reagan administration became increasingly keen on its Strategic Defence Initiative (the so-called 'Star Wars' programme, which involved a complex anti-missile system in space) Heseltine was far more sceptical than Thatcher, and initially opposed it as a dangerous escalation in the arms race. He did eventually sign an SDI agreement with the US, but it was motivated entirely by commercial consider-ations, and because he feared the Americans would steal a march in new technology. In 1985, when the US Defense Secretary, Caspar Weinberger, hosted an SDI conference at Ditchley Park in Oxford-shire, Heseltine made his feelings known by initially declining an invitation. He then arrived late, and the next day he didn't show up at all.[40]

On the controversial domestic and civil-liberties aspects of defence, Heseltine generally took a hard line. As one would expect, he backed wholeheartedly Thatcher and Howe's decision in 1983 to ban trade unions at the government spy-satellite headquarters, GCHQ. He supported the prosecution of the Foreign Office clerk Sarah Tisdall for leaking his own public-relations plans for the arrival of cruise missiles in 1983 – not that they involved anything startling.[41] Later, Heseltine fully approved – and by some accounts pushed for – the prosecution of the MoD assistant secretary Clive Ponting for leaking documents about the sinking of the Argentine cruiser *General Belgrano* during the Falklands War.

Arguments over the *Belgrano* had arisen well before Michael Hesel-tine arrived at the MoD. The Labour MP Tam Dalyell suspected that the ship had been deliberately sunk to sabotage peace negotiations which the Foreign Office had been conducting through Washington and Peru. A long string of inconsistencies had been shown up in ministerial accounts of events leading up to the attack, and further inaccuracies were exposed when new details came to light. To put it bluntly, ministers had been lying.

A new book, *The Sinking of the Belgrano*, by Arthur Gavshon and Desmond Rice, published in the spring of 1984, led Dalyell and the Labour Defence spokesman, Denzil Davies, to probe deeper.[42] The two critical issues were when the *Belgrano* was first spotted and whether it then reversed its course away from the British exclusion zone around the Falklands. Heseltine decided he had to establish for himself what had really happened in May 1982. 'I want to be quite sure that there is not a Watergate in this somewhere,' he reportedly told people (prompting the question of whether he saw Thatcher as filling Richard Nixon's role).[43] The task was assigned to Clive Ponting, one of the MoD's most able young civil servants, who had more in common with Heseltine than either man would care to admit. Ponting had spent the first four years of the Thatcher government working with the Downing Street efficiency adviser, Sir Derek Rayner. Like the Defence Secretary, Ponting had impressed the Prime Minister with his attempts to cut government waste; he even had the unusual honour of being asked to address the full Cabinet on one occasion, and was later awarded the OBE for his work. Heseltine's private secretary, Richard Mottram, gave Ponting four days to draw up 'a detailed chronology of the events leading to the sinking of the *Belgrano*'.[44]

Ponting's account, which was twenty-five to thirty pages long, and covered around eighty separate events, later became known as the 'Crown Jewels'. A series of high-level meetings took place on Friday 30 March 1984 and the following Sunday, to consider the report and decide how to respond to Dalyell and Davies. On the first occasion, Ponting and all the senior ministers and officials spent three hours in the Defence Secretary's office. The fact that it was such a long meeting by Heseltine's standards reflected the atmosphere of crisis; by the end, several delayed visitors were left queuing outside. It was clear from Ponting's work that MPs had been misled about the *Belgrano*. The question was, Should ministers now release further details, so correcting previous accounts?

Both Clives – Ponting and Whitmore – argued for greater disclosure, in particular to reveal that the *Belgrano* had been spotted a day earlier than admitted until now. Ponting claims this was firmly resisted by the minister of state, John Stanley, who was thought to be monitoring the *Belgrano* issue for Margaret Thatcher. Heseltine, however, accepted Ponting's argument for 'openness'. 'After Tisdall, I can't face another secrets case,' Ponting quotes him as saying.[45] At a second three-hour meeting in Downing Street on the Friday afternoon – another sign of just how sensitive the issue was – Thatcher was persuaded that Denzil Davies should be sent a letter about the earlier sighting of the *Belgrano*.

Heseltine, however, still had to answer a detailed list of questions from Tam Dalyell about the cruiser's movements. Ponting drafted a reply which would have stated for the first time that the *Belgrano* had suddenly reversed course and moved away from the British exclusion zone, eleven hours before it was torpedoed. The civil servant says both intelligence and naval sources told him there were no security reasons for this not to be released.

This time, however, both Thatcher and Heseltine rejected the idea of being more frank. Instead, the Prime Minister wrote to Tam Dalyell accusing him of simply pursuing his contention that the government had tried to wreck the Peruvian peace plan. Heseltine himself told Dalyell that, following Thatcher's earlier letter to Denzil Davies, 'There is nothing that I can usefully add.'[46]

During his years at Environment, Michael Heseltine had been fairly liberal about the release of information: senior officials were allowed to talk directly to journalists, and his MINIS reports were publicly available. Initially he had accepted Ponting's case, and was reluctant to use arguments about national security to suppress the facts. But, according to Ponting, John Stanley went behind Heseltine's back to get Margaret Thatcher to insist that the Defence Secretary adopt a more restrictive approach. As a result, Heseltine withheld information not just from Tam Dalyell but also from the Commons Foreign Affairs Committee, which had just started its own inquiry into the *Belgrano* affair. The minister who had once misled MPs over Hovertrain was now involved in suppressing the truth over a far more serious matter, and evading his constitutional responsibilities to Parliament.

Later, in explaining his stance to the Foreign Affairs Committee, Heseltine resorted to the 'security' excuse he had wanted to avoid. 'If we were to move down the road of a detailed analysis, which was being requested of the Ministry in questions to me,' he argued, 'we would end up with yet more requests for yet more information . . . we would move into realms of questioning which we could not answer because national security interests would not permit it.'[47] In short, it was the 'slippery slope' argument.

Clive Ponting was disgusted. He felt Heseltine, Stanley and Thatcher were perpetuating a cover-up simply to avoid political embarrassment. 'I had never come across anything so blatant in my fifteen years in the Civil Service,' he later wrote. 'It was a deliberate attempt to conceal information which would reveal that ministers had gravely misled Parliament for the previous two years.'[48] However, Michael Heseltine later claimed that Ponting himself had initially advised that, for security reasons, it would be best to tell MPs nothing more about the *Belgrano*. As for the blocking answers given to Tam Dalyell, Heseltine claimed that Ponting had made no protest at the time.

Six days after Heseltine's unhelpful letter to the Labour MP, Ponting sent Dalyell an anonymous note telling him the response had been written 'against the advice of officials but in line with what John Stanley recommended'. Suggesting other questions he might pursue, Ponting added, 'You are on the right track. Keep going.'[49] Three months later he sent Dalyell two crucial MoD documents which exposed the *Belgrano* cover-up.

When the MoD police traced the leak to Clive Ponting and secured his confession, they took the view, perhaps surprisingly, that his offence was not worth prosecuting. But the Solicitor-General, Sir Patrick Mayhew, thought this would be wrong, especially after the recent secrets conviction of Sarah Tisdall. A senior MoD official travelled to Heseltine's country home, where he was on leave, and presented the conflicting views on charging Ponting. A minute of the meeting recorded, 'The Secretary of State said he was shocked by the flagrant breach of confidence by a senior officer who must have been fully aware of the potential consequences of his action. He had been in no doubt that the decision to prosecute Miss Tisdall under the Official Secrets Act was right. If the decision was his, he would prosecute Ponting.'[50] But, despite several subsequent phone calls between staff at the MoD, Mrs Thatcher and the Law Officers' department, Heseltine later assured MPs he was 'not involved in the decision to prosecute'. Nor, he claimed, did he have 'any contact, directly or indirectly, with the Law Officers or their officials in that context'.[51]

When Clive Ponting appeared at the Old Bailey in January 1985, neither Michael Heseltine nor John Stanley was called as a prosecution witness, despite being intimately involved in the affair. Instead, to the anger of many MoD staff, it was Heseltine's private secretary, Richard Mottram, who had to endure an eleven-hour cross-examination in the witness-box. Ponting's acquittal came as a shock to everyone – not least himself. No one was more upset than the Defence Secretary.

Michael Heseltine was passionate about Ponting. He felt personally betrayed by the way his official had been briefing a political opponent, Tam Dalyell, at the very same time as he was advising his minister how to answer the MP's questions. A year later, Heseltine walked out of a *Channel 4 News* studio, while the programme was on air, when he heard that a recorded interview with Ponting was about to be shown on the same programme. And in a Commons debate only a week after Ponting's acquittal Heseltine delivered one of the most stinging attacks a government minister can ever have made on a civil servant. His seventy-minute speech – which some described as a second prosecution – contained a detailed account of his relations with Ponting. From the political point of view it was a brilliant parliamentary performance, and perhaps the most effective speech Heseltine has ever made in the House. It did much to raise the spirits of Tory MPs and to diminish the government's embarrassment after its defeat in court.

Although Heseltine had undoubtedly participated in efforts to keep the truth from MPs, it is clear that he was nowhere near as hard-line on the issue as John Stanley. In the Commons debate Labour tried to portray his deputy, rather than Heseltine himself, as the main villain of the piece, and called for Stanley's resignation alone. Unlike the Hovertrain affair a decade before, Michael Heseltine could not this time be accused of saying anything which was actually untrue. Instead, he had refused to give answers which would have corrected previous false information.

Heseltine was even less frank with MPs, and did come close to lying, over another important issue – a decision by NATO defence ministers at a meeting in Montebello, Quebec, in October 1983. It soon emerged, mainly through the United States Congress, that the ministers had agreed to update NATO's short-range and battlefield nuclear weapons. On dozens of occasions MPs asked ministers whether such a decision had been taken at Montebello. Again and again Heseltine or his colleagues produced answers such as 'My colleagues and I did not endorse any specific proposals for modernization.'[52]

To most people the answer would have suggested that ministers had not agreed any modernization programme, but the key word was 'specific'. The meeting had, in fact, agreed to modernize *in principle*, but had not decided on the precise details. Heseltine's responses were highly disingenuous and deceitful, though in most cases he left it to colleagues such as John Stanley to answer. After he left the MoD, a journalist asked Heseltine about Montebello and the *Belgrano*, and how he justified lying to Parliament. 'If you want to find out who's been lying,' Heseltine chuckled, 'you should talk to John Stanley.' The conversation was quickly ended.

The fact was that Britain found the Montebello decision politically embarrassing. NATO was claiming at the time to be cutting back on its short-range nuclear arsenal, and the peace movement was still politically powerful – especially in Germany, where the weapons would be used. In America, the administration was much more open about Montebello. In March 1985 the US Assistant Defense Secretary, Richard Wagner, was asked in Congress why Heseltine and British ministers were so reluctant to acknowledge the decision. Wagner agreed it was probably 'for home consumption'.[53]

In hiding the government's nuclear plans from Parliament, Heseltine could cite plenty of precedents, of course. In November 1985 Labour's Defence spokesman, Denzil Davies, suggested that any decision to modernize short-range nuclear weapons should be debated by MPs. Heseltine taunted Labour that the Callaghan government had not consulted anyone in the late 1970s when it had instituted the Chevaline project to update Britain's Polaris nuclear missiles. As for the suggestion of a Commons debate on nuclear modernization programmes, Heseltine asserted, 'It was unthinkable.'[54]

The irony was that, just seven weeks later, Michael Heseltine would resign from office in protest at the manipulation of the decision-making process and a lack of proper consultation which he felt was 'an affront to the Constitution'.[55] He would be referring to Cabinet government rather than parliamentary business. Yet in deceiving MPs as Defence Secretary over the agreement reached at Montebello, and allowing Parliament to be misled over the *Belgrano* – not once, but on numerous occasions – he himself was guilty of a far more serious breach of constitutional duties.

But ministerial commitments have always been far more important to Michael Heseltine than the rights of Parliament, as he had shown in his row with his predecessor in Tavistock, Sir Henry Studholme, over the proposed industrial development at Sparkwell. Indeed, the very fact that he physically bases himself away from the House of Commons whenever he is out of office suggests a disdain for the institution. Michael Heseltine has never been a great parliamentarian.

Principles had their limits. Michael Heseltine's wider political ambitions would always override any short-term commitment to improve MoD efficiency and introduce better management. Politics would ultimately prevail over economics and financial common sense. In June 1985, during the Brecon and Radnor by-election, for instance, Heseltine suddenly cancelled the proposed closure of an Army camp at Crickhowell in the constituency. However, the move was not enough to save the Tory candidate from defeat a few days later. More political still was Heseltine's handling of a proposal for a combined Defence School of Music.

Military music was an area where Heseltine had suspected there was room for economies even while he was at the DoE. Previously each of the three services had enjoyed its own music school, which obviously involved considerable triplication. Combining the three schools was exactly within the spirit of his organizational reforms. The tricky question, as ever, was where the new school would be sited. Before his work on the *Belgrano*, Clive Ponting had been asked to investigate. He calculated that the cheapest option would be at Eastney, near Portsmouth, which would save about £4 million in capital costs and roughly £250,000 in annual operating expenditure. But he learnt that the Defence Secretary had wider aims:

The meeting lasted exactly three minutes. Heseltine as usual lounged on his sofa, idly flicking through the papers. Before any discussion he announced his decision. 'I'm fed up with all these bases in the South-East. You can go anywhere you like as long as it's north of Birmingham.' . . . This was obviously Heseltine in his 'Minister for Merseyside' role.[56]

Officials soon found another site, near Edinburgh, even though it was more expensive than Eastney. Ultimately, however, the decision was delayed, with both the Scottish and the south-coast options thwarted by a strong lobby to preserve the Royal Marines Music School at Deal in Kent. The Defence Secretary quietly forgot ideas of improving efficiency, or pursuing regional policy. The MP for Deal, Peter Rees, was the Chief Secretary to the Treasury – a powerful figure in Cabinet spending battles. And his seat was a marginal one.

Heseltine was inevitably involved in serious spending battles with Peter Rees and the Treasury, though his budget was to some extent protected by a commitment made by NATO countries in 1979 to increase defence expenditure by 3 per cent a year until 1986. During his struggles at the DoE, Heseltine had become a stern critic of the Treasury and its apparently indiscriminate drive for economies; at one point at the MoD he accused them of 'a Gatling-gun mentality' on spending cuts: 'They just sweep the arc and see what falls off the trees.'[57] After the 1983 election, the new Chancellor, Nigel Lawson, demanded emergency spending cuts, and Defence was a prime target. What Lawson describes as 'a tense meeting' between himself, Heseltine and Margaret Thatcher, secured an MoD reduction of £240 million.[58] It was highly embarrassing for Heseltine, since only the day before he had heralded his previous budget in the annual White Paper on defence. He suffered a similar cut the next year, and also had to accept an end to growth after 1986 when the NATO commitment expired.

Critics say Heseltine should have given far more thought to the way in which this long-term squeeze on MoD resources would affect defence policy. Contrary to the common view that Heseltine doesn't pay enough attention to detail, some colleagues felt he was obsessed by the minutiae of running the department rather than concentrating on broader questions of whether Britain's defence commitments were sustainable. One admiral says:

He was always fiddling around with the wrong things, when there were really quite important decisions to be made – about the overall level of expenditure, about our policy in NATO, and about various procurement things. He had this absolute fixation with the organization of the Ministry of Defence. He shouldn't have fussed himself with that at all. He had a highly competent Permanent Secretary to run the department for him.

It was a widely voiced criticism, but Heseltine's response was that defence policy didn't need great change. John Nott had already carried out a review in 1981, he explained. 'It's interesting, isn't it, that people always want you to change, review our defence policies. Why? Our defence policies are working.'[59] Yet Heseltine showed no concern, either, for the complexities of military strategy. 'I put strategy papers up to him ad infinitum,' says Sir Edwin Bramall, 'and he just wasn't interested.' When Bramall asked about plans for five years ahead, he says Heseltine responded, 'Don't tell me about five years, tell me about five months.'[60]

Margaret Thatcher, too, accuses Heseltine of short-termism. The specific example she and many of her supporters cite is the case of the early-warning plane Nimrod, which had been under development for more than a decade, to replace the fleet of Shackletons which was now forty years old. Eleven months after Heseltine left the MoD, his successor, George Younger, cancelled Nimrod in favour of buying American AWACs planes, after Britain had spent £660 million on the Nimrod project. Thatcher says the affair 'constituted a unique – and uniquely costly – lesson in how not to monitor and manage defence procurement. A minister has to be prepared to work through the details if he is going to come to the right decisions and this Michael was always unwilling to do.'[61]

As the MoD approached 1986, when the NATO 3 per cent growth guarantee expired, the budgetary gap between the ever-growing costs of increasingly sophisticated weapons systems and what the Treasury was willing to pay was bound to widen. In 1985 the Commons Defence Committee, chaired by his former Cabinet colleague Humphrey Atkins, accused Heseltine and his officials of giving 'vague and evasive answers' to questions on the issue. They predicted a shortfall of nearly £1 billion for 1987–88, which would entail a cut of more than 6 per cent. The committee expressed the 'strongest suspicion that there will indeed be considerable difficulties leading to cancellations, slowing-down of acquisitions and the running-on of equipment beyond its economic life-span.' The situation 'will require some hard decisions', it concluded, warning that Heseltine's approach 'may result in a defence review by stealth'.[62]

Heseltine's answer was that improved efficiency and competition would resolve the problem. The former businessman who knew all the tricks of delaying payments was also a great believer in 'slippage' – letting equipment programmes, and hence their bills, slip from one year to the next. Critics suggested that the slippage was political, not financial: as with Nimrod, Heseltine deferred difficult problems in the expectation that someone else would have to deal with them.

In the summer of 1985 the political commentator Hugo Young reported on a lunch Heseltine had recently attended with journalists. Once again he charted the future on an envelope, this time sketching out the defence budget for the years ahead:

He drew the graph line of future expenditure and the graph line of future revenue, and managed to demonstrate that, up to a certain point in time, they could be reconciled. 'And after that,' he added, with the smile of the conjuror completing his final trick, 'I'll be gone.'

And when exactly did the Defence Secretary think that might occur? In 1986.[63]

15. *No Place for Me with Honour*

The company at the heart of the Westland affair was not especially large. Yet it led to the resignations of two Cabinet ministers, two tense debates in the Commons, and even a threat by the Attorney-General to send the police into Number Ten. 'I may not be Prime Minister by six o'clock tonight,' Margaret Thatcher was heard to say at one moment.[1]

The Westland crisis marked the turning-point for her government. Although she was to win a third election, and served for nearly five more years, Thatcher never carried quite the same authority after the extraordinary events of December 1985 and January 1986. The episode eroded her reputation for integrity and tough, decisive leadership, and gave her a more pro-American, anti-European image. After Westland, most things her government did seemed to go wrong. The poll tax and entry to the European Exchange Rate Mechanism were the most notable examples, but there are a host of others.

Some see Westland as a catalyst which provoked the eruption of tensions and emotions which had been simmering in the Thatcher and Heseltine camps over many years. It is true that neither politician trusted the other, and their politics were markedly different. But until 1985 both had managed to contain their differences. Much that Michael Heseltine had done had met with Thatcher's approval – council-house sales, MINIS, Liverpool, defeating CND, the reorganization of the MoD, and greater competition in defence procurement. Relations with Downing Street were 'excellent' says a close MoD colleague. 'Generally the Prime Minister did not cause us trouble.'

For Heseltine's part, he had enjoyed his two jobs under Thatcher – though Environment more than Defence. She, in turn, had largely left him to get on with things. He disliked the manner in which Thatcher ran her government, but had simply devised techniques to deal with it. It was important to be firm with her, he told friends –

to stand your ground and fight back. Then you got on with her. It was a rough world, but he knew how to survive. Heseltine was also confident that Thatcher wouldn't dare sack him, unlike some of the earlier wets. She knew he would cause more trouble on the back benches. The one thing Heseltine dreaded was the Jim Prior solution – banishment to Northern Ireland. Ulster was a job it was politically impossible to refuse.

Heseltine would tell people how he found Cabinet meetings an embarrassment. 'There's no point in speaking,' one official recalls him saying, 'because she won't listen.' Thatcher was at her worst on Europe and often delivered the most petty, personal comments about other Community leaders. He was also frustrated to have been kept away from economic responsibilities. He remained astonished that so little blood had been shed over the advent of 3.5 million unemployed. Privately, Heseltine felt the way in which British industry had been allowed to decline was immoral, and yet Thatcher seemed indifferent to it.

Not once since 1979 had the Cabinet discussed industrial strategy, but then Thatcher didn't believe in such a thing. But Heseltine was as keen as ever on taking responsibility for Trade and Industry, and it wasn't as if the chance had never arisen – the DTI job had changed hands almost every year, as a procession of colleagues – mainly right-wingers – took their turn: Sir Keith Joseph, Patrick Jenkin, Cecil Parkinson, Norman Tebbit and now Leon Brittan.

But Michael Heseltine knew that the MoD, too, could play a role in supporting Britain's industrial base. His initial wish to site the Defence School of Music in the north had shown economic concerns beyond balancing the departmental budget. The Ministry of Defence spent £17 billion a year – 5 per cent of the British economy. Procurement accounted for about half of that, and 90 per cent was spent in the UK; 10,000 British firms depended on military orders, and 700,000 jobs. Some believe that, in the absence of any industrial policy from his DTI colleagues, Heseltine decided to pursue a one-man industrial strategy from within the Ministry of Defence. Indeed, one can argue that Heseltine 'intervened' more in British industry during his three years at Defence than he has ever managed during his spells at the DTI.

Heseltine's primary policy on weapons procurement was to secure better value for money. While the cost of defence equipment tended to rise as technology improved, Heseltine believed the whole procurement system was appallingly inefficient, and far too cosy. Instead of a typical commercial arrangement of a fixed price agreed in advance, defence contractors were often paid on a 'cost plus' basis – whatever the product cost to make, plus an agreed amount for profit, which was often calculated as a percentage of the cost. This, of course, provided little incentive for quality, punctuality or cost control. Some MoD suppliers were thought to be defrauding the department, and cases of abuse regularly emerged. Heseltine believed this whole process needed greater competition. Then there was the additional problem of 'gold-plating': the natural desire of the services for the best possible performance, and the most up-to-date, and often most expensive, technology.

A central role in Michael Heseltine's attempts at reform was played by Peter Levene, the chairman of a leading MoD contractor, United Scientific Holdings (USH), which he had built up from a small business. Levene was originally appointed by Heseltine on secondment to the MoD as a special adviser – a post normally filled by aspiring politicians, but which Heseltine preferred to assign to non-political experts. Then, in 1985, the Defence Secretary promoted Levene, and made him more permanent, by appointing him Chief of Defence Procurement.

It was one of the most controversial appointments made during Margaret Thatcher's term in office, and was badly mishandled by Heseltine. First, Levene was being brought from outside the Civil Service to fill an existing position; the incumbent, David Perry, was pushed sideways. Second, there was the evident risk of a conflict of interest, since Levene's former firm, USH, would continue as an MoD contractor, and these concerns only deepened when Levene was succeeded as USH chairman by Sir Frank Cooper, the previous MoD Permanent Secretary. Special arrangements had to be made to ensure that Levene never took decisions on USH contracts.

But the greatest disquiet concerned Levene's salary. From bringing in an outsider to the DoE who wanted only £28 a week – Ed Berman

– Heseltine now took on an expert who required sixty-five times as much. Heseltine proposed to pay Levene £95,000 a year, plus £12,000 in pension contributions. It was a third less than Levene had been getting at USH, but twice as much as the MoD Permanent Secretary, Sir Clive Whitmore, earned, and much more than the Cabinet Secretary (or, come to that, the Prime Minister). The Civil Service Commissioners, who oversee Civil Service procedures, were so outraged that they threatened to resign *en bloc*. They objected both to the appointment itself and to the way it was made. Heseltine employed the same last-minute bouncing tactic he had used with MoD reorganization: the leading commissioner was told about the appointment only the day before it was announced. It was said that even Sir Robert Armstrong, the head of the Civil Service, only learnt of it earlier the same day.[2] The decision was opposed by both Armstrong and Whitmore, but again Margaret Thatcher ensured that Heseltine got what he wanted.

The fact that Levene's appointment was 'bungled', argues Peter Hennessy, 'distracted attention from the value of it, which was considerable'.[3] Influenced no doubt by his own business experience, Heseltine was convinced that if he was going to make an impact on the contracting process he needed somebody on his side with commercial experience of winning defence orders. When he first met him, Levene completely concurred with his analysis of what was wrong. 'Here was the poacher urging on the gamekeeper,' Heseltine writes.[4] Levene expected to save a staggering 10 per cent from the equipment budget (and by 1989 claimed to have done so).[5] Even if it was only 8 per cent, Heseltine later suggested, 'he will have paid for the Trident programme single-handed. Not a bad achievement for one entrepreneur!'[6]

'There was a feeling abroad,' Peter Levene later said of the MoD before his arrival, 'that to have a contract for the Ministry of Defence was a pushover, and that really you could almost name your own price.'[7] Levene abolished 'cost plus' on the grounds that it gave contractors no incentive to restrict costs: indeed, if their extra profit was a calculated percentage of the costs there was an obvious incentive to *boost* them. Also, the number of MoD contracts put out for tender almost doubled over the next two years. Where competition was difficult because there was only one British supplier – with Trident submarines, for instance – then new rules increased competition among that firm's subcontractors.

But competition had its limits. Heseltine, unlike some of his Cabinet colleagues, was mindful of the effect of procurement decisions on Britain's industrial base. A telling example concerned a £280 million order for two new Type 22 frigates. The former Minister for Merseyside was insistent that at least one of the ships be built by Cammell Laird in Birkenhead, who had made Type 22s before, but now had nothing left in their order book. Without the contract, the firm would almost certainly have to close, with the loss of 1,700 jobs – another severe and symbolic blow to Merseyside. However, Norman Tebbit, the Industry Secretary (seen increasingly as a rival of Heseltine for the future Tory leadership) wanted both ships to go to Swan Hunter on Tyneside, which would be cheaper. It was a paradoxical situation, with Heseltine, as Defence Secretary, putting forward the industrial and social arguments that other ministers might usually have raised. Most of the Cabinet's Economic Affairs Committee agreed with Tebbit.

Heseltine felt so strongly about the frigate that in January 1985 he told Thatcher he would quit if he didn't get his way. The then junior employment minister, Alan Clark, who dealt with Heseltine over the issue, saw him as having an 'infatuation with Liverpool'. He wrote later, 'it was all bound up with him showing his mettle to the crowd. He gabbled over the phone, was wild-eyed in the lobbies. Apparently threatened to resign. Why not? Get lost, she should have said, *then* give the contract to Cammell's.'[8]

'I was astonished that he could seriously contemplate resigning over so trivial a matter,' writes Nigel Lawson. 'I had not previously realized the extent of his frustration with Margaret.' Thatcher preferred that both frigates should go to Swan Hunter, but wasn't prepared to lose Heseltine over a minor issue. She seized on Heseltine's argument that awarding one Type 22 to Merseyside would reward men at Cammell Laird who had crossed picket lines to continue working during a recent strike. So one frigate went to Birkenhead, at an extra cost of £7 million to the defence budget. 'She did not show it,' says Lawson, 'but she was seething. Michael had humiliated her:

from then on, she was as determined to do him down as he was determined to run his own department in his own way.'[9]

In many cases, of course, the cheapest option was to buy defence equipment off the shelf from America. This was usually urged by the Treasury, who sought to save money, and also by the service chiefs, who wanted equipment that was proven and likely to arrive quickly. In July 1983 Heseltine bought British Aerospace's ALARM anti-radar missile for the RAF, rather than its cheaper American rival, HARM, which the Treasury preferred. Nine months later, however, when considering an anti-submarine missile for the Royal Navy, he chose the American Harpoon rather than the Sea Eagle proposed by British Aerospace. Significantly, while the former announcement was made by Heseltine himself, he left the latter to his minister of state, Geoffrey Pattie. The Harpoon decision prompted a thinly coded public attack from his maverick colleague Alan Clark. On the BBC programme *Question Time*, Clark said it was unwise to become increasingly dependent the Americans – which echoed Heseltine's own views, of course – but also added that it took 'a very strong Secretary of State to resist recommendations from civil servants even though these are often quite narrowly founded'. According to Clark, Heseltine made great efforts to get him sacked, but Norman Tebbit and Margaret Thatcher came to his defence.[10]

Nor did the Defence Secretary's crusade for value for money in procurement always sit easily with his long-standing belief in European collaboration. Heseltine argued that competition between European suppliers was wasteful, and allowed the market to be dominated by American firms which were supported by enormous orders from the Pentagon. He believed an imbalance between European and American work on NATO defence contracts would have serious implications for European industry, and could ultimately endanger the whole future of the Atlantic alliance. He reasoned that, if America took most of the orders, it could foster European resentment towards the US and equally reduce American respect for Europe.

Yet Heseltine's experience of Concorde should also have illustrated the disadvantages of collaborative ventures. Research costs tended to be much higher, and, because of the multinational agreement, such projects were far harder to cancel.

Heseltine's most significant collaboration, which preceded the famous Westland saga, was his 1985 success in establishing a joint venture with Germany, Italy and Spain to develop the European Fighter Aircraft (EFA) – the plane now known as Eurofighter 2000. The idea was to build on the cooperation which Britain, Germany and Italy had first established in the late 1960s in developing the Tornado fighter-bomber. The four countries agreed on a feasibility study for a project which might eventually involve the production of up to 1,000 planes, and an estimated £20 billion of business. Although the project had been long mooted, Heseltine played a leading role in brokering the final agreement, particularly in persuading the German defence minister to accept a lighter plane than he initially wanted. 'That was Heseltine getting up early in the morning,' says Sir Edwin Bramall. 'He was in constant touch with Manfred Woerner.'[11]

Yet many people were far from convinced that the European Fighter Aircraft was the best option, or even necessary. Once again the initial Treasury line was to buy American. Others argued that missiles would gradually replace planes in future warfare. One former senior MoD official believes Heseltine seized the EFA as 'manna from heaven', as a chance to press his distinctive views on European issues. The idea had, he says, previously been rejected by John Nott 'as too expensive, too risky and not necessarily required militarily'. The most Nott had been willing to fund was a demonstration model to show that British firms were world leaders in aerospace. But Heseltine, according to this source, reversed Nott's decision in a manner that was 'blatantly political', picked up the European option, and 'bulldozed it through the Treasury and everywhere else'.

Sir Geoffrey Howe, however, sees the EFA deal as a 'notable coup' which left Heseltine's confidence 'riding high'. This was partly, he suggests, because one of his opponents had been Margaret Thatcher, 'who had wanted an Anglo-American or all-British aircraft'.[12]

Norman Tebbit also believes the EFA agreement had a major influence on what was to follow, but for very different reasons. Heseltine had been keen that, unlike Tornado, the EFA consortium should also include France. But the French aerospace company Dassault had a prototype it had already built for a fighter aircraft. Heseltine made considerable efforts to secure a compromise which would enable

France to join the team, but without success. Tebbit says 'the Cabinet had refused to allow the dilution of the specification of the proposed European Fighter Aircraft to keep the French, who wanted a less capable aircraft, in the consortium'. Because of this, he believes, 'Michael was still sore.'[13]

It was nevertheless a considerable achievement to overcome the postwar Franco-German special relationship and secure Germany's participation without France. The August 1985 Turin agreement on the European Fighter Aircraft was said to be the biggest industrial development ever approved by a British government.

Only eight weeks later Michael Heseltine was also involved in the biggest arms deal in British history, when Saudi Arabia agreed to buy 132 Tornados, at a cost of £4 billion, much of it to be paid in oil. Heseltine put particular effort into defence exports; he often travelled abroad, and made three or more trips to Saudi Arabia, at least one of which was secret. 'We had to beat the Americans,' says Sir Colin Chandler, the head of MoD sales:

and the Saudis wanted the Tornados quickly, so we had to take them off the RAF. We had to cut red tape like mad! The Americans wanted cash – we were prepared to take oil. They wanted restrictions – we didn't impose any, except the nuclear capability, of course . . . The Chief of the Air Staff learnt that we had nicked ten of his aircraft. No one told him.[14]

As for the oil element of the deal, the Energy Secretary was none too pleased either, according to Chandler: 'Peter Walker went absolutely nuclear. But we said, "Sorry, it's in the national interest." No one was consulted. It was just done.'[15]

The following year Heseltine's Tornado deal formed part of the much wider and highly controversial Al Yamamah contract with the Saudis. This, combined with a second agreement in 1988, was reckoned to be worth a staggering £40 billion in all. The Al Yamamah deals have subsequently become the subject of intense investigation. In particular, journalists have been fascinated by the question of whether middlemen earned a rake-off – a traditional way of doing business in the Middle East – and by the role played by the Prime Minister's son, Mark Thatcher. When Michael Heseltine announced the September 1985 Tornado contract he especially praised the role of Margaret Thatcher. 'One cannot overstate the Prime Minister's contribution in the sale,' he said.[16]

Heseltine's two big negotiations during 1985, with the Saudis and over the EFA, may explain why it took him so long to take much interest in the problems of a much smaller player on the aerospace scene. Like many defence contractors, the Westland Group was in a delicate position when it came to dealing with Whitehall: while the DTI was officially its 'sponsoring' ministry, and often granted launch aid, the MoD was by far its biggest customer.

Westland was a relatively small firm: because of a drop in civil helicopter sales, by 1985 it had fallen to around the 500 mark in the Stock Exchange rankings. Yet the company had a broader strategic and industrial significance. The Falklands conflict had shown the increasing role of helicopters in modern warfare, and Westland was Britain's only manufacturer. And almost three-quarters of its 11,000 workforce was concentrated in one town – Yeovil.

Heseltine and his colleagues first learnt that Westland was in serious trouble in October 1984, more than a year before the political crisis broke. Westland's hopes rested on two possible deals for its W30 helicopter: one from India and the other from the British Army. The first depended on British overseas aid, while the second required the MoD rapidly to find money from its increasingly stretched resources. During the spring of 1985, the then Industry Secretary, Norman Tebbit, expressed concern about Westland's empty order book:

I approached Michael Heseltine to see if the Ministry of Defence could help with any orders to fill the gap. I met not only a flat refusal – in view of the tight defence budget, that was understandable – but a complete indifference as to whether Westland survived. With helicopters available from America, France and Germany the survival of Westland was a matter of industrial not defence policy I was told by MoD.[17]

In April 1985 Heseltine told Cabinet colleagues what he had told Tebbit: that the MoD had no need for Westland helicopters. Although the company was close to bankruptcy, the Defence Secretary was unsympathetic – he regarded it as inefficient, badly managed and too soft on its unions. In June, Margaret Thatcher chaired two meetings to consider government aid; Heseltine was willing to inject £30 million, provided the Treasury paid half. Unsurprisingly, the idea was turned down.

Towards the end of June, at the suggestion of the Bank of England (which was looking after the interests of Westland's banks), the company appointed a new chairman, Sir John Cuckney, a former MI5 officer. He was a seasoned 'company doctor' – a specialist in salvaging businesses which found themselves in trouble – and he had never lost a patient. He also enjoyed superb contacts in the City, in politics and in the military world. Cuckney was brought in with only one purpose – to devise a rescue package by the time the next annual results were announced, in December – and his appointment had Heseltine's full support.

It was immediately obvious that Westland's future depended on an international partnership, and within five weeks, by August, Cuckney had proposed the solution which would eventually lead to Michael Heseltine's resignation: a tie-up with the American firm United Technologies Corporation, which was the world's biggest makers of helicopters through its subsidiary Sikorsky. Westland had worked with Sikorsky – through joint ventures – for almost forty years.

Cuckney and Sikorsky were quickly lobbying both the MoD and the DTI for support. Michael Heseltine was slow to react, and Cuckney later reported him as saying 'he did not particularly mind if Westland went into receivership', since British Aerospace and GEC would inevitably pick up the pieces.[18] But Heseltine's opinion changed after a visit in late September from the Sikorsky boss, Bill Paul. He now realized that, if the American firm was linked to Westland, the MoD would come under intense pressure to buy Sikorsky's Black Hawk helicopters. Sikorsky planned that Westland would make the craft under licence, which Heseltine felt would turn the British company into 'merely a metal-bashing operation'.[19] Three days afterwards, Heseltine scrawled on a report about Westland, 'No option except receivership to be discussed without my express authority!'[20] Yet 107 days later he felt the company's survival was so important as to be a matter for resignation.

The second important ministerial player in the Westland story was Heseltine's old sparring partner Leon Brittan, who had just been demoted to Trade and Industry from the Home Office. Sir Geoffrey

Howe suggests 'Leon's self-confidence must have been dented by his move,' in marked contrast to Heseltine's ebullience after his big deals of the summer.[21] Brittan was 'obviously shaken', says Thatcher, 'and determined to make his political mark. As a result he proved oversensitive about his position when the Westland affair blew up. All this made for errors of judgement when facing a ruthless opponent like Michael Heseltine.'[22] Yet initially Leon Brittan, too, took a very different line from the one with which he became so strongly associated. In early October, Brittan wrote to Thatcher urging that a European option for Westland should also be explored. 'For God's sake, give the Europeans a chance!' he is supposed to have said at one stage.[23] Heseltine would later claim that the Industry Secretary even suggested that a European solution was *preferable*, though Brittan hotly denied this.[24]

It wasn't until mid-October, after Sir John Cuckney and the Westland board had spent several months working on the Sikorsky option, that Michael Heseltine offered to explore the idea of rescue by a European consortium. The Defence Secretary argued that Cuckney had no experience of European collaboration, whereas he himself, he told colleagues, was probably more familiar with such deals than anyone. Other ministers, including Leon Brittan, were happy for him to go ahead. The companies in the proposed European consortium – the French firm Aérospatiale, MBB of Germany, and Italy's Agusta – were not brought together by Heseltine, however, but initially approached each other for commercial reasons. They feared the Americans would simply use Westland as a foothold to sell the Black Hawk in Europe. Sikorsky, meanwhile, had now enlisted the Italian firm Fiat, which gave its bid a European dimension.

The official British government position, soon expounded by Leon Brittan, was even-handedness and that the final outcome was up to the Westland directors and shareholders. Although Heseltine had been allowed to explore a European solution, he didn't take active steps until late November; then he soon went well beyond the government's official neutrality. Through the close relationships he had built up in Europe over the years, particularly during the EFA negotiations, Heseltine arranged an important meeting in his office at the MoD. The gathering involved the national armaments directors (NADs) –

Peter Levene and his equivalents – from Britain, Germany, France and Italy, together with representatives from the three members of the proposed consortium. For much of the five-hour talks Heseltine was away at a meeting in Essex; by the end, the NADs had agreed to recommend that for certain classes of helicopter their governments should buy only those designed and built in Europe. This was thought to exclude anything from a possible Sikorsky–Westland combination.

Thatcher and Cuckney saw Heseltine's initiative as an act of sabotage: the NADs' decision, they felt, had been engineered to scupper the Sikorsky rescue. Thatcher, who heard about the meeting not from Heseltine but through Cuckney, says 'this was more than a blatant departure from the government's policy of maximizing competition to the best value for money: it also placed Westland in an almost impossible position'.[25] Leon Brittan, who now seemed much less enthusiastic about a European option, would describe the NADs' recommendation as a 'pistol pointing at the company', and a 'monopolistic, anti-competitive and coercive directive'.[26] The Treasury, too, felt the restriction ran counter to the drive for value for money – something Heseltine normally championed.

On the other hand, it could be seen as an outstanding example of the kind of cooperation in military equipment which European states had long discussed; it was a natural follow-up both to a 1978 agreement on helicopter cooperation and also to the EFA deal. The Commons Select Committee on Defence later described the NADs' declaration as 'an extraordinary *tour de force* by Mr Heseltine. If it had been implemented in full it would have been a major advance in European collaboration in defence procurement.'[27]

The decision of the European national armaments directors transformed the Westland issue from an industrial problem into a full-blown political crisis. As Magnus Linklater and David Leigh note in *Not With Honour*, their comprehensive account of the Westland affair, of all the turning-points in the unfolding drama, the NADs' meeting was 'the most critical. From it flowed actions which were to end in political turmoil.'[28]

In the first week of December, Margaret Thatcher held two ad-hoc meetings with her most senior Cabinet colleagues, including Heseltine, Brittan, Tebbit, Howe, Lawson and Willie Whitelaw. Thatcher and

Brittan argued that the NADs' recommendation should be rejected, and reiterated that Westland should decide for itself which option to choose (which would almost certainly be Sikorsky). Heseltine argued that the issue could not just be left to market decision-making: the government was Westland's biggest customer, and it would be wrong to let the company fall into foreign hands. The argument went to the heart of Thatcher's and Heseltine's differences over economic and industrial policy. But Sir Geoffrey Howe was sympathetic to Heseltine, and so too was Norman Tebbit, who felt that a stronger European option would give shareholders more of a choice. With ministers divided, Thatcher deferred matters to the Cabinet's Economic Affairs Committee – code-named 'E(A)' – on the following Monday, 9 December.

Unusually for a Cabinet committee, part of the E(A) meeting was attended by two outsiders – Sir John Cuckney and one of Westland's financial advisers. Yet Cuckney's case failed to convince ministers. Heseltine said later that 'virtually every colleague who attended the enlarged meeting and thus came fresh to the arguments supported me'.[29] Colleagues refute this. But, rather than make a final decision then, Margaret Thatcher agreed that her Defence Secretary should have a few days to iron out the European bid. If Heseltine and the consortium did not produce 'a package which the Westland board could recommend' by 4 p.m. on Friday 13 December – just four days later – ministers would repudiate the declaration by the NADs. 'Do you realize,' an exasperated Thatcher was later quoted as saying, 'we have spent three hours of precious time discussing a company with a capitalization of only £30 million? What is the world coming to?'[30]

Heseltine spent the rest of the week frantically firming up the Europen bid, which British Aerospace and GEC had now joined. For a minister to drop everything to mount a company rescue was unusual, but for the Defence Secretary to do so rather than a DTI minister was unheard of. Heseltine's eight-page proposal went to the Westland directors, who quickly decided still to back Sikorsky. They felt his alternative lacked the right legal and financial support.

Michael Heseltine had set to work believing that the E(A) committee would reconvene to discuss his plans. He later claimed that Thatcher had said at the Monday meeting, 'We shall meet again on Friday at three o'clock when the Stock Exchange closes.'[31] Others, however, say that this intention was superseded by discussions during the Monday gathering. Heseltine was deeply aggrieved that no second meeting ever took place for him to convince his colleagues that the European consortium was viable, and that they should endorse the NADs' decision. Thatcher's account, backed by some colleagues, was that since ministers had agreed on a policy on the Monday – letting Westland decide its own fate – a second meeting was unnecessary. Yet later it emerged that two ministers, Nicholas Ridley and Lord Young – both Thatcher allies – had put the Friday engagement in their diaries, and that Number Ten had phoned round on the Wednesday to cancel it.

As the Defence Select Committee noted afterwards, it was odd that Heseltine was given no chance to report back on his work; in fact, he could report only to the directors of a private company. Discovering that the expected meeting would not now take place was a critical point for Heseltine. 'The moment that that decision was taken to cancel the opportunity for a collective judgement, I knew that something very wrong had happened,' he later claimed.[32] For the first time over Westland, Heseltine threatened resignation. 'I did tell the Prime Minister,' he said, 'that if she refused to allow those matters to be discussed, ventilated, explored at full Cabinet, I would resign.'[33]

The Defence Secretary also alerted several colleagues, including the Deputy Prime Minister, Willie Whitelaw; the party chairman, Norman Tebbit; and the Chief Whip, John Wakeham. He couldn't put up with Thatcher's shouting-match style and her inability to decide issues on the basis of rational argument, he warned them. At the weekly Thursday Cabinet meeting before the Friday deadline, Heseltine protested that it was 'intolerable' that the second E(A) meeting had been cancelled. Thatcher insisted that Westland was not on that morning's Cabinet agenda, and that he should have given notice to raise it. Kenneth Baker, the Environment Secretary, recalls:

Michael pressed on, insisting this was a matter for the Cabinet. When Margaret interrupted him he said, 'Don't interrupt me.' Margaret then said that her decision as to what could be raised in Cabinet accorded with tradition – 'That's the position. I'm sorry.' Michael replied, 'You're not in the least sorry.' There was cold anger on both sides, and I had never seen such a bitter exchange between colleagues, certainly not in front of a full Cabinet. I thought to myself that this issue would run, and that Michael was taking on the Prime Minister in a very personal way.[34]

When nobody came to Heseltine's aid, Thatcher curtailed the 'short, ill-tempered discussion'.[35] Heseltine demanded that his dissent be recorded in the minutes, and when his protest was subsequently not noted this only fuelled his suspicions of a conspiracy. He had a heated row with the Cabinet Secretary, Sir Robert Armstrong, who claimed the omission was merely an error and would be corrected. 'Such an error and correction,' Heseltine said later, 'was unprecedented in my experience.'[36] He believed the E(A) meeting had been cancelled because Thatcher feared he would win.

Four days later, on Monday 16 December, Leon Brittan told Parliament that the government would not interfere with Westland's decision. Heseltine sat on the front bench glowering with obvious disapproval. He then provoked the Prime Minister's anger when two days later he promoted the European bid before the Commons Defence Select Committee; it was a private meeting, but details inevitably leaked. Heseltine won considerable backing from the committee's members, most of whom were Conservative. That Thursday the Cabinet discussed Westland in full session for the very first time – albeit only for about ten minutes. Heseltine was heavily reprimanded as Thatcher told him to stop campaigning for the European bid. Ministers affirmed that the decision lay with the Westland board and shareholders, and that none of them should lobby for any option.

What seems extraordinary about the whole Westland episode is how badly Michael Heseltine handled his Cabinet colleagues. Two of them – Norman Tebbit and Geoffrey Howe – had initially been sympathetic. Several others – including Peter Walker, Tom King and Norman Fowler – were friends and allies of long standing. Yet Heseltine seems to have made little effort behind the scenes to shore up support or win ministers over, especially among his more senior colleagues. Although he is a great one for business deals and for assembling financial consortia – be it for *Management Today*, or buying out BPC's majority in Haymarket, or the EFA – Heseltine has never been adept at gathering political allies. Instead, he prefers a wider, more public, strategy.

So it was with Westland. Michael Heseltine would not accept defeat. He was 'absolutely looney, completely hyped up with the thing', says a ministerial colleague who suspected he had 'persecution mania'. Another noticed signs of strain. 'A bone twitched in his cheek and his knee would bounce during ministerial meetings.' Michael and Anne cancelled a New Year holiday in Nepal, and instead he spent the break fighting for the European option, the terms of which had been considerably enhanced just before Christmas.

Much of the battle was waged in the media, assisted by the seasonal absence of other news. It was increasingly presented as a gladiatorial combat between Heseltine on the one side and Brittan on the other, with the latter portrayed as Thatcher's stooge. The principal weapons in this fight to the death were the 'briefing' and the 'leak', of which Heseltine was as guilty as anyone – or at least of letting others do it for him. It was strange for a government that had recently prosecuted Sarah Tisdall, and (unsuccessfully) Clive Ponting for divulging secrets. 'The Official Secrets Act has been in ribbons,' said *The Economist*. 'At one point, irate ministers were reading whole chunks of Cabinet papers directly to journalists.'[37]

As 1985 turned into 1986 the frenzy intensified, with volleys of letters back and forth. To counter the idea that a Sikorsky deal would wreck Westland's business in Europe, Downing Street suggested that Sir John Cuckney should write to Thatcher seeking clarification. The Prime Minister prepared a draft reply reassuring Cuckney that Westland had nothing to fear, but when Heseltine saw it he thought the letter was inadequate. On the pretext that ministers might be legally liable if any of the advice was later shown to be wrong, he consulted the Solicitor-General, Sir Patrick Mayhew (acting as Attorney-General while Sir Michael Havers was ill), who agreed that Cuckney should be told more about European anxieties about Sikorsky. So Heseltine proposed some extra material for Downing Street to include, setting out the nature of the risks. His wording was ignored, however, and Thatcher's final letter contained only a general reference to European concerns. She also reassured Cuckney that the government would resist any discrimination against Westland from Europe, and would still regard the company as British.

Angry that his much stronger warning had been ignored, Heseltine was then responsible for the concoction of an exchange of letters with David Horne of Lloyds Merchant Bank, who was advising the Europeans. His staff even rang Horne's office and dictated three questions for the banker then to write back and ask. When Horne's letter duly arrived, Heseltine's response was dispatched within the hour, enclosing the very same wording he had proposed for Thatcher's letter to Cuckney but which had been rejected. This warned that European governments and companies would treat a link with Sikorsky as 'incompatible with participation' in various European helicopter projects.[38] Heseltine's letter was promptly given to the press.

Michael Heseltine had consulted neither Downing Street, the DTI, nor Sir Patrick Mayhew before sending his letter. This was a blatant breach of Whitehall protocol, and the most serious challenge yet to Thatcher's authority. The effect on her and Leon Brittan 'can have been nothing short of incendiary', said the Defence Select Committee.[39] Thatcher told Brittan to his face that Heseltine was now running circles round him. Yet the curious question is why she didn't now sack Heseltine, or indeed had not done so already. His campaign was clearly a serious assault on the stated policy of non-involvement, and arguably went against collective Cabinet responsibility. Brittan had already urged Thatcher to dismiss Heseltine in mid-December, and she discussed the idea with friends at a Christmas party. But the Chief Whip, John Wakeham, cautioned against it. Thatcher even spent two and a half hours with ministerial colleagues composing three successive drafts of a letter threatening Heseltine with dismissal. But her press secretary, Bernard Ingham, not normally a timid man, advised her that Heseltine might use the ultimatum as good reason to resign – something she felt she couldn't afford politically.

It might seem out of character, but Thatcher was frightened. Past ministers she'd pushed aside – St John-Stevas, Gilmour, Pym and Prior – had posed surprisingly little threat from the back benches. Heseltine was different. 'Michael was at that time a popular and powerful figure in the party,' she admits in her memoirs. 'No one survives for long as Prime Minister without a shrewd recognition of political realities and risks.'[40] Outside, he would pose a formidable challenge to her leadership. Inside the Cabinet, he might still be contained.

Michael Heseltine's letter to Lloyds Merchant Bank prompted what was perhaps the most disgraceful act of the entire Westland affair. Margaret Thatcher suggested that the Solicitor-General should be consulted again. Sir Patrick, judging only from a copy of the letter he'd seen in that morning's *Times*, said it did appear to contain 'material inaccuracies'. It was then suggested that Mayhew ought to write to Heseltine, pointing out these errors and asking him to send a new letter to Lloyds correcting them.

Sir Patrick's letter to Heseltine arrived in ministerial offices at lunchtime on Monday 6 January. Within two hours a distorted account was leaked to the Press Association by the Department of Trade and Industry, though only the two most damaging words – 'material inaccuracies' – were given out verbatim. The DTI information officer given the unpleasant job of leaking was Colette Bowe, Heseltine's former colleague from the Liverpool task force. Mayhew himself was equally embarrassed. As an old friend from their days at Oxford, he had warned Heseltine in advance that he would have to write to him. After the leak, he wrote a second note expressing his 'dismay' that the letter had been disclosed 'in a highly selective way', and the rules 'flagrantly violated'.[41]

To leak the advice of a law officer, without his knowledge or blessing, was a far more serious offence than even the wide-scale disclosures of the previous few weeks. Mayhew's letter had been marked 'Confidential' – the same classification as the material Clive Ponting sent to Tam Dalyell. Leon Brittan would soon admit that he had authorized Colette Bowe's leak, and years later he revealed that he had received 'express approval from Number Ten' – from Thatcher's two most senior advisers, Bernard Ingham and Charles Powell.[42] (As befits a QC who once specialized in libel, Brittan is very precise in what he says; his use of the word 'express' refuted the official explanation at the time that he had misunderstood Downing Street's wishes.)

Number Ten and the DTI later produced spurious arguments about the need to get Mayhew's letter into the public domain before a Westland press conference that afternoon. In the event, Heseltine was able to supply Mayhew with extra papers to back his case and which seemed to satisfy the Solicitor-General, though

this fact was largely ignored amid all the fuss. The true purpose of the leak was obvious: to damage Michael Heseltine. The
Sun took the bait, emblazoning the words 'YOU LIAR!' down its
front page.[43] It later apologized and made a gift to charity in lieu of
damages.

Leon Brittan's clumsy leak had given Michael Heseltine the moral
high ground, and yet he chose to let matters cool down. But Margaret
Thatcher, still furious about his letter to Lloyds, was determined to
assert her authority. 'I now knew from Michael's behaviour,' she says,
'that unless he were checked there were no limits to what he would
do to secure his objectives at Westland. Cabinet collective responsibility was being ignored and my own authority as Prime Minister was
being publicly flouted. This had to stop.'[44] At Chequers on the first
Sunday in January, she, Wakeham, Whitelaw and other advisers
devised a solution to shut her Defence Secretary up. And they decided
that George Younger should take over if Heseltine carried out his
threat to resign.

Events came to a head at the regular meeting of the full Cabinet
on Thursday 9 January, almost three years to the day since Heseltine
had first taken charge at the MoD. Twenty-one ministers attended
that morning – Lord Hailsham was abroad – of whom no fewer than
ten have already published memoirs. Most of them give the meeting
considerable coverage, though their accounts differ markedly. Let us
piece together the fragments.

Westland was the first major item on the agenda. Unusually,
Thatcher read from a prepared statement, and began by reiterating the
existing position, warning that if things continued thus the government
would have no credibility left. She even quoted some of the damaging
newspaper headlines from the previous few weeks. Then both Leon
Brittan and Michael Heseltine put their cases.

Heseltine patiently argued that there had been no proper collective
Cabinet discussion of Westland. 'He spoke quietly,' says Nigel Lawson, 'and not at all aggressively, and sought to find some compromise
arrangement.'[45] Yet Heseltine had already lost the few allies he had
once had. 'The earlier validity of his argument,' says Geoffrey Howe,
'for there had been some, seemed to grow less and less as Michael's
presentation became more apparently obsessive. The more he seemed

faintly reminiscent of Tony Benn, and occasionally he did, the less he commanded our sympathy.'[46]

The Prime Minister said that, pending the imminent decision by Westland shareholders, it was important that ministers did not intervene. Heseltine went along with this. Thatcher then deployed the Chequers solution. Henceforth, she insisted, all answers to questions on Westland should be cleared through Sir Robert Armstrong and the Cabinet Office. Nigel Lawson believes that, following her climb-down over the Type 22 frigate almost a year before, Thatcher had 'now set out to humiliate Michael, in the full knowledge that this would almost certainly lead to his resignation . . . Indeed she had already decided whom she would appoint Defence Secretary in his place.'[47] Yet Heseltine accepted this restriction – at least initially.

But then came a decisive move from Nicholas Ridley, the Transport Secretary. Despite being a close political ally of Thatcher, Ridley was also a friend of Heseltine, and had been a regular guest at his drinks parties. Both men shared an interest in gardening, and they even used to swap plant cuttings before Cabinet meetings, though not that day. With Ridley's intervention, says Kenneth Baker, 'new life was breathed into the whole issue'.[48]

What, the Transport Secretary asked, was the status of things people had already said about Westland? There followed several exchanges between Heseltine and Ridley, who was backed up by the Agriculture Minister, Michael Jopling. The position was firm, said Thatcher: everything had to be cleared. 'Heseltine silenced,' the Social Services Secretary, Norman Fowler, wrote on his pad; as a former journalist, he realized that the press would present this development as a 'humiliating defeat' for his colleague.[49] It was ridiculous, Heseltine argued, to have to confirm with the Cabinet Secretary statements he had already given journalists, and he proceeded to list some of them. 'I suspect that no one present saw this as anything other than a ruse,' says Thatcher. 'No one sided with Michael. He was quite isolated.'[50] Eight or nine ministers contributed, but Whitelaw, who might have been a conciliator, sat silent. So too did Geoffrey Howe and John Biffen, who would themselves become victims of the Thatcher way of doing things. Only Norman Tebbit tried to mediate, but without success.

The Prime Minister began to sum up, though as usual she simply restated her own views – in this case on the need to restore collective responsibility. Suddenly Heseltine snapped.

There had been no collective responsibility over Westland, he retorted, and constitutional practices had been ignored. The precise words that he said next vary from one account to another:

'I cannot accept this decision, I must therefore leave this Cabinet.' (Nicholas Ridley)[51]

'If this is the way this government is going to be conducted, I no longer wish to be part of it.' (Nigel Lawson)[52]

'There has been a breakdown of collective responsibility and I must therefore leave the Cabinet.' (Kenneth Baker)[53]

'Prime Minister, if this is how it is to be I can no longer serve in your Cabinet.' (Lord Young)[54]

The next day, several papers reported yet another version: 'I am afraid I shall have to leave.'[55] Whatever Heseltine's exact remarks, everyone agrees that he gathered up his papers, closed his red ministerial folder, and walked out. Nobody tried to stop him.

It was a historic moment of high political drama – the first such resignation since Heseltine's municipal hero, Joseph Chamberlain, walked out of Gladstone's Cabinet in 1886, exactly 100 years before (over the much bigger issue of Home Rule) – yet Heseltine's colleagues carried on as if it was quite normal for ministers to march out of Cabinet meetings. Peter Walker says he regrets not following Heseltine and asking his friend to come back and thrash things out: 'If the Prime Minister had said, "Just sit down and don't be silly. Let's talk about this," I am sure he would have done so. Everyone was so staggered to see him walking to the door, we remained breathless.'[56]

At first, some members of the Cabinet weren't even sure that Heseltine had resigned. He hadn't actually used the word 'resign', and those who thought he had said 'this Cabinet' wondered if he was simply leaving that particular meeting. 'A lot of people just thought that he'd been a bit rude, and then gone out to the loo,' wrote Alan

Clark, who wasn't actually present himself.[57] Cabinet ministers had 'resigned' before, and then been talked out of it – George Brown, the Labour Foreign Secretary, being a notable example. But any chance of saving the situation was dashed by the presence – unusually – of a few journalists in Downing Street; in those days the press didn't normally bother to hang around for the outcome of most Cabinet meetings. Having straightened his hair and his Guards tie in the Number Ten washroom, Heseltine marched through the front door. 'I have resigned,' he told an astonished BBC cameraman who barely had time to switch on. 'It would be wrong for me to say anything at this instant. I have resigned from the Cabinet and I will make a full statement later today.' With that, Heseltine strode off down Downing Street.

'If the cameras had not been there,' says Peter Walker, 'one of us would have phoned him and asked him to come back and talk it through.'[58] MoD officials thought much the same thing when they suddenly discovered that Heseltine had returned from Downing Street two hours early. His private secretary, Richard Mottram, had thought when Heseltine set off for Cabinet that morning that there was a risk of a resignation. When his minister told him the news, Mottram's immediate concern was whether his position could be salvaged. His heart sank when Heseltine revealed that he'd already announced it on camera.

The normal constitutional convention when ministers resign is for them to explain their reasons to the House of Commons. It again illustrated Heseltine's attitude to Parliament (before the Commons was televised) that, instead of waiting for the House to return, four days later, he should have summoned a press conference for four o'clock that afternoon. More unorthodox still was that he delivered his resignation statement, which included a strong attack on the Prime Minister, in a hall at the MoD – on government property. And Defence officials had even helped Heseltine draft his statement. Approval for this had been granted by the Permanent Secretary, Sir Clive Whitmore (for which, it's said, Thatcher never forgave him, and it may have tipped the balance in favour of Robin Butler when she chose a new Cabinet Secretary two years later). Afterwards Heseltine always felt bad that Whitmore had endangered his own career on his behalf –

not just with the press conference, but with his support throughout Westland.

For twenty-two minutes Michael Heseltine delivered a closely argued account of what had led him to resign, explaining his view that constitutional procedures had broken down. In complete disregard of the Official Secrets Act, he gave a rare glimpse of the inner working of government; it was a story of intrigue, duplicity and manipulation, by both ministers and their officials. The statement ran to some 3,000 words and took up almost two-thirds of a page in the next day's broadsheets. 'To be Secretary of State for Defence in a Tory government is one of the highest distinctions one can achieve,' he concluded:

To serve as a member of a Tory Cabinet within the constitutional understandings and practices of a system under which the Prime Minister is *primus inter pares* is a memory I will always treasure.

But if the basis of trust between the Prime Minister and her Defence Secretary no longer exists, there is no place for me with honour in such a Cabinet.[59]

Some saw the statement as a suspiciously quick piece of work – especially for a man who avoids the written word. Moreover, Heseltine had even managed to get home for a quick lunch with his wife, Anne, who accompanied him to the press conference. And the fact that this was held only five hours after he left the Cabinet meeting inevitably raised the question of just how spontaneous his resignation had been. His friend Anthony Howard is among those who say it 'wasn't possible' to write so much in the short time available: 'That statement had been written well before the walk-out.'[60]

Richard Mottram insists it had not been worked on beforehand. 'He prepared it after returning from Cabinet, in the normal way he would for any major speech. It went through a number of versions within the time available. We had a real problem in that it was still being corrected when the press conference started.'[61]

There is strong evidence, however, that Heseltine had been contemplating resignation for some months, and well before Westland arose. Apart from Hugo Young's account of Heseltine's not expecting to cope with the defence budget beyond 1986, the commentator Peter Jenkins had reported the previous October on his friend Heseltine's 'alarm at the way things are going, especially in the cities'. Jenkins suggested he 'could even be brewing up towards a spectacular resignation'.[62]

Heseltine could not see any satisfactory way to move on from Defence. He knew that Thatcher was very unlikely to promote him – and especially not to an economic post. Resignation might be the best way out of an increasingly difficult situation. It would put him in a good position to win the leadership if the Tories lost the next election, which the polls suggested was quite possible.

However, during the week of the fateful Cabinet meeting the possibility of resigning seemed to have receded. Heseltine felt he had done his bit, and it was now down to the Westland shareholders. The evening before his resignation, at a gathering with friends, Anne Heseltine had told her husband, 'I think you may have to do it tomorrow – after Cabinet.' But Michael Heseltine felt that the crisis had now settled. 'I think we'll get through all right,' he reportedly said.[63] So Anne was rather surprised the next morning when she heard the news in a call from a Press Association reporter, Chris Moncrieff.

From early December, as Michael Heseltine felt increasingly victimized by Thatcher and the government machine, it is reasonable to suppose that the arguments for resignation, and the explanations he might give, had been churning through his mind. When the moment came, it is probably true that there was no prepared statement. Yet, because he felt so strongly, the detailed justification burst forth like waters held back by a dam.

But only three months before Heseltine had been quite happy to see Westland fall into receivership. How had it suddenly become a resigning matter? Partly it was the momentum of the whole affair. As Westland's future was increasingly portrayed in the media as a battle between Heseltine and Thatcher, and as a question of leadership – hers or his? – minor matters were greatly magnified and positions became entrenched. And Heseltine successfully widened the relatively trivial arguments about Westland itself into a range of much more substantial differences – economic, industrial, strategic and constitutional.

It is hard to dismiss the view that Michael Heseltine was in the market for an issue on which he could make a dramatic exit from the government, and that Westland was the best on offer. 'At the time,' Nicholas Ridley later wrote, 'I came to the conclusion that he was obsessed by his desire for the European solution. I now think I was wrong. I think in retrospect he was determined on taking a course of action that would lead to a spectacular resignation . . . The difficulty was that no real issue of principle was around, so he decided to elevate Westland into one.'[64]

Heseltine's explanation is that if he had given in to Thatcher on Westland he would have been 'a broken reed' thereafter. He feared being slowly marginalized, like several of her past Cabinet critics. Before long, the fateful call might have come to do his duty in Stormont, followed by the drip, drip, drip of disparaging lobby briefings from Downing Street. Moreover, having threatened to resign, Heseltine felt he couldn't give way. He told *Panorama*:

If, at the end of the day, at any stage, I had backed down from that, they would know that I was a man of straw, a man who threatens but has not the steel to stand by his word . . . If the people with whom you are doing business – the Prime Minister, senior colleagues – know that in such hypothetical and future circumstances you protest and you say perhaps you'd have to threaten to resign, they would all look at you and say, 'Oh yes, oh yes, we've heard it all before – we don't need to worry about him.' And if I ever thought they thought that of me I could never face the responsibilities of this job that I used to have.[65]

It was a revealing comment, though it barely stood up to examination. Politics and government are inevitably about compromise, and about stepping back from previous positions. Resignation threats should be used sparingly. If colleagues might no longer respect Heseltine for backing down, the question also arose as to what people would think of a Prime Minister who caved in to colleagues who threatened to resign, which in his case she had done once already, over the Type 22 frigate order.

Heseltine believed equally that his own reputation with European defence ministers depended on the outcome of Westland. It would, he felt, also be taken as a measure of how serious Britain was about future cooperation. 'It would be no exaggeration,' the Defence Select

Committee later concluded, 'to say that British policy on helicopter collaboration had become a touchstone of British policy on defence collaboration.'[66]

Michael Heseltine had undoubtedly become obsessive, if not fanatical, about Westland, and had blatantly broken the rules of ministerial conduct, but others should also shoulder blame for what happened. 'It was grievously mishandled by the centre of government,' says a senior MoD official. John Wakeham was in contact three or four times a day during the crisis, yet failed to prevent the Defence Secretary's departure. Willie Whitelaw regrets not recognizing that Heseltine had a genuine grievance, and not stressing to him the importance of collective responsibility. Though he feels the European consortium would never have secured a Cabinet majority, Whitelaw thinks that Thatcher should have at least given Heseltine a chance to explain his views. 'I was always rather sad that she never allowed him to put his case to everybody when he wanted,' he says. 'Ted Heath would have let the case be put.'[67]

Michael Heseltine would always claim to have no doubts about what he'd done, though he now faced life in the political desert. '[Even] if everyone thought I was wrong,' he said, 'if it was a life of wilderness, I would have resigned, because I believe that there was an affront to the constitution.'[68]

16. *Where There's a Wilderness*

Michael Heseltine's five years as a political outcast are the most fascinating period of his career. It was the one time during three decades in politics when he could reveal something of his true self. Without the restrictions of front-bench solidarity, or government office, he was able to say much more of what he actually believed, and speak about anything that took his fancy. Yet, as his ambition burned more brightly than ever, he needed to tread a fine line. To become Conservative leader, Heseltine had to present a distinct alternative to Thatcherism while also being careful to avoid further accusations of disloyalty.

Heseltine had followed his resignation with a media blizzard. Over the next five days he was interviewed by all the main TV and radio news and current-affairs programmes – usually live and at some length. He even resumed the role of television reporter for the first time in more than twenty years, making a short film for *Channel 4 News* advocating the European bid for Westland. And he continued to play a leading part in the dispute, not least in events which forced Leon Brittan's departure from office only two weeks after his own.

In his resignation statement, Michael Heseltine had accused Brittan of collaring the chief executive of British Aerospace, Sir Raymond Lygo, and leaning on him to withdraw from the European consortium. Brittan vehemently denied the charge, saying he had merely used a chance visit by Lygo to the DTI to warn the company not to be seen as anti-American; if the accusation were true, however, it would destroy the Industry Secretary's claim to be even-handed. On the Monday after his resignation, Heseltine rose in the Commons to ask Brittan 'whether the government had received any letters from British Aerospace giving its views of the meeting'. It was a brilliant trap, based on a tip-off from within the company, and the prey walked into it. Brittan's immediate response was simple: 'I have not received any such letter.' MPs were suspicious, and pressed him further. Had any other member of the government received a letter from Lygo or from British Aerospace?' 'I can only speak for myself,' said Brittan. 'I am not aware,' he added later, 'of any letter from Sir Raymond Lygo to anyone else either.'[1]

His responses had been phrased with all the skill of a good lawyer, but had been just as disingenuous as some of Heseltine's parliamentary answers in the past. Later that evening Brittan returned to the Commons to say he apologized if he had misled MPs. The Prime Minister, he revealed, had not received a letter from Lygo, but had received one from the *chairman* of British Aerospace, Sir Austin Pearce. He had not wanted to reveal the fact earlier, since the letter had been marked 'Private and Strictly Confidential', but he was now free to do so.[2] Brittan's behaviour did little for his reputation, and he was eventually torpedoed by an inquiry by Sir Robert Armstrong into the leak of the Solicitor-General's 'material inaccuracies' letter, which confirmed that Brittan had authorized its disclosure. Suffering from falling confidence on the Tory back benches – and a touch of anti-Semitism – Brittan was forced out.

Of the key ministerial players in the affair only Margaret Thatcher survived. On the day of the crucial Westland debate, 27 January 1986, she, too, had speculated to colleagues that the affair might bring her down. She was saved by a long-winded prosecution speech by the Labour leader, Neil Kinnock, which, by his own subsequent admission, 'let Mrs Thatcher off the hook'.[3] Michael Heseltine then spoke almost as if there had never been any problem. 'I do not believe that the House has listened in a decade to a worse parliamentary performance,' he said of Kinnock's speech. The man who only eighteen days earlier had attacked Thatcher for a breakdown in constitutional procedures, now praised her for admitting it was wrong to leak Mayhew's letter, and he called on Conservative MPs to unite. 'We shall be in the Lobby together with one purpose – to maintain a Tory party in power in this country and to keep the Labour Party out.'[4]

Despite Heseltine's campaign, the European bid was eventually defeated. The initial meeting of Westland shareholders ended in deadlock, but a second gathering accepted Sikorsky's offer by 68 per cent to 32. There had been frantic buying of Westland shares on the

Stock Exchange, and it became clear that some were being bought for motives which were not simply financial. Companies owned by Lord Hanson and Rupert Murdoch – both admirers of Margaret Thatcher – acquired holdings, and a further 20 per cent of Westland was purchased by six mysterious buyers operating through various nominee companies around the globe. The Commons Trade and Industry Committee later had 'substantial suspicions which, however, fall short of proof' that these buyers were secretly and illegally acting together in what's known as a 'concert party'. Sir John Cuckney himself suspected as much, though he spoke of a 'fan club'.[5] The buyers clinched the deal for Sikorsky, but who they were and what motivated them have never been established.

What was also not explained fully at the time was why Sikorsky was so keen to take a stake in the British helicopter company, or why, apart from her well-known pro-American sentiments, Thatcher seemed so eager to assist it. One theory, which emerged only several years later, linked Westland with the massive Al Yamamah arms deals with the Saudis, in which Heseltine himself had been involved as Defence Secretary. In a 1993 court case in America, a former Sikorsky executive, Lieutenant Colonel Thomas Dooley, alleged that the firm saw Westland as a route by which it could sell Black Hawk helicopters to Saudi Arabia at a time when Congress – under pressure from the strong pro-Israel lobby – prevented US defence firms from selling complex weaponry to the Saudis.[6]

One aspect of his departure which Heseltine must have found depressing was how little support he got from fellow ministers – even from those he considered friends. Sir Geoffrey Howe, who had torn loyalties, having worked closely with Leon Brittan, accused Heseltine of drawing 'a wholly exaggerated and misleading picture'.[7] Yet when Howe himself eventually resigned, five years later, he would articulate very similar concerns about Margaret Thatcher's style of government.[8] Unlike the practice after some previous resignations – such as Peter Thorneycroft's over financial policy in 1958, or Lord Carrington's at the start of the Falklands War – no other defence ministers chose to go with Heseltine. The minister of state for defence procurement, Norman Lamont, who had enjoyed working with Heseltine, had a quick word with the junior procurement minister, John Lee, as soon as the news broke. 'As it was essentially a personal resignation rather than a departmental one,' says Lee, 'we didn't feel any obligation to follow him.'[9]

Heseltine's outrage over Westland was not entirely convincing. His talk of it being an 'issue of fundamental constitutional principle' was a great exaggeration.[10] Ministerial diaries have shown that Prime Ministers and officials have long been guilty of manipulating the Cabinet agenda and tailoring minutes. Moreover, Heseltine himself had never gone overboard to consult people as a minister – whether council leaders or service chiefs. Nor had he ever shown much respect for Parliament's constitutional rights.

Nevertheless, opinion polls suggested that the public supported Heseltine's stand by a margin of around two or three to one.[11] Surveys of his parliamentary colleagues were more ambiguous. More than three in five Tory MPs backed the European option, but roughly the same proportion also approved of Margaret Thatcher's handling of the affair. And most MPs thought Heseltine had damaged his chances of one day becoming leader. He undoubtedly had.

For many, Heseltine's resignation simply looked like another temper tantrum, similar to the mace incident. The overall impression was summed up by his puppet on the *Spitting Image* programme – a long-haired, manic-looking figure with wild, revolving eyes, clutching a model helicopter. Westland had given him the air of a fanatic who had caused havoc over a relatively trivial issue. 'To resign in a fit of pique is understandable,' said the right-wing MP Michael Fallon, 'but what's not forgivable is to kick the milk-bottles over on the doorstep as you go out.'[12]

Over the next five years there was regular talk of Heseltine being brought back, but he always conceded there was no chance of that while Margaret Thatcher was Prime Minister. Moreover, Willie Whitelaw also seemed to have turned against him. Heseltine was by no means confident of his future. (Throughout his career, contrary to his public image, he has often lacked confidence about his future prospects.) There were too many recent examples of ex-ministers who had quickly faded from view. One close parliamentary ally was convinced that Heseltine would soon go the same way, losing his political momentum and being forced to return to business life. At one point Heseltine even asked Lindsay Masters whether he might return to Haymarket as joint chairman. 'No,' said Masters, who made it clear he would quit if Heseltine insisted on coming back. Instead, Masters gave him a token consultancy, at a reported salary of a more-than-token £100,000 a year.

Yet history showed it was possible to resign from office and still become Prime Minister. There were two postwar examples in Anthony Eden and Harold Wilson. But throughout his years on the back benches Michael Heseltine would regularly be flattered by another precedent – Winston Churchill, who had spent the 1930s sniping at the Baldwin and Chamberlain governments over both India and the threat of Nazi Germany. Heseltine was only too conscious of the parallel:

No Conservative of today can draw anything but pride from the foresight and persistence of Winston Churchill who warned those governments of their folly. He preached an uncomfortable message. He was scorned, distrusted, dismissed as 'a man without judgement'. But he was right and his critics wrong; and he was rewarded in time by his fellow countrymen's recognition of his wisdom and of their debt to him.[13]

Like Churchill during his wilderness years, Michael Heseltine used every available resource to remain a public figure. Constantly gathering political intelligence, he would identify the best opportunities to intervene against the Conservative leadership. He would keep a certain distance from the House of Commons, speaking only in debates on major issues and when he could be most effective. He would exploit his personal reputation to draw on the best advice and expertise. He would publish extensive writings, employing a team of assistants to carry out his research. Like Winston, he would fight and he would survive.

Heseltine's initial coup was a request to address the annual conference of the Young Conservatives (YCs) due to take place a month after his resignation. The YCs were then under the control of Tory left-wingers, and their chairman invited Heseltine without consulting either his national committee or Central Office. The party chairman, Norman Tebbit, was furious.

'Let me say what is easier said outside the government than inside it,' Heseltine told the YCs. 'There is hardly any perception of the scale of this nation's decline over the postwar years.' Warning of the 'cancerous' effects of having 3.5 million unemployed, he called for a 'new impetus' and 'an altogether more dynamic approach' to industrial policy. In short, he wanted the party to embody 'caring capitalism' – a phrase he adopted to point up his differences with Thatcherism.[14] Thatcher later responded with her own 'popular capitalism'.

It was the opening salvo in what he knew would be a long campaign. Two weeks later he joined Tory back-bench protests over DTI plans to sell off British Leyland to the American car firms Ford and General Motors. The dispute raised similar issues to Westland, though this time Margaret Thatcher was eventually forced to back down since, she admits, the government was then 'at our most vulnerable' because of the earlier controversy.[15]

'I hold the assassin's knife,' Heseltine admitted to a friend, and yet he was also acutely aware that he had to temper his opposition – especially with a general election on the horizon. Publicly, he used another phrase: 'He who wields the knife never wears the crown.'[16] History, however, suggested notable exceptions – and none better than Thatcher herself, who had wielded the knife in 1975 and taken Edward Heath's crown.

Deprived of office in both senses, Heseltine initially worked from a small cramped study in his London home, which was now in Chapel Street in Belgravia. He had the services of a secretary, and help from his daughter Alexandra, but sometimes answered the phone himself – disguising his voice against unwelcome callers. Soon he got Haymarket to acquire a small suite of offices on the sixth floor of an old-fashioned block in Victoria Street, a few hundred yards from the Commons. In the main room Heseltine sat at a large desk with a Thomas Dibdin painting over his shoulder. In the outer room sat his secretary and Eileen Strathnaver, his personal assistant from the late 1960s, who had now returned.

Strathnaver, who still works for Michael Heseltine, has a reputation as a superb organizer rather than a source of political ideas: she knows how he will react to any proposal, and always has to hand whatever material he needs. 'Her great value,' says a former colleague, 'is that she knows his mind very well and is terribly loyal – like a platonic mistress.' Journalists fishing for indiscreet stories from her are wasting their time. Indeed, Strathnaver is so loyal to Heseltine that she will deliver the official line even when his closest allies ring to give him an ear-bashing. Some compare the closeness of the relationship with that of Harold Wilson and Marcia Falkender, but without the intrigue. Anne Heseltine, however, is not a fan. 'We've got that boring secretary of Michael's coming down, I'm afraid,' she announced when Strathnaver visited their country home one weekend.

Two other people who quickly became semi-permanent fixtures in the Victoria Street entourage were the Tory MPs Keith Hampson and Michael Mates. At Westminster, they soon became known as Heseltine's two most loyal lieutenants.

Hampson wrote most of Heseltine's speeches and articles – a job he'd once performed for Edward Heath – and claimed credit for coining the phrase 'caring capitalism'. Earlier in his career, observing him from afar as a back-bench MP, Hampson had disliked Heseltine and thought him too flashy. He rapidly changed his mind while serving as Tom King's PPS at the DoE after 1979, when they came into almost daily contact. After the 1983 election Heseltine took Hampson to Defence as his own PPS.

Hampson was a distinctly damp Conservative who showed no inclination to trim with the times and had always been overlooked for ministerial office. As a former university history lecturer with a PhD from Harvard, his presence gave some intellectual weight to the Heseltine ship, though he was used more as a presenter of ideas than as a significant policy thinker.

Michael Mates was very different, and in truth the two lieutenants never really got on well. Widely known as 'the Colonel', Mates had spent twenty years in the Army. After being elected to Parliament in 1974, he became a leading member of Willie Whitelaw's team in the subsequent leadership contest. He, too, was frustrated at having been passed over by Margaret Thatcher. Mates only really got to know Heseltine during the Westland crisis, through his membership of the Commons Defence Select Committee, and didn't actually join his team until after the committee published its report on the affair in the summer of 1986.

Heseltine's lieutenants urged – as others had before – that he should get to know more Tory MPs if he ever hoped to secure their votes. He did appear a little more frequently in the Commons tea- and dining-rooms, but never felt comfortable. 'I'm not a very clubbable person,' he once admitted, 'sitting around with a drink and people coming up to you.'[17] Long-standing MPs were so unused to his presence that it looked exactly like the calculated gesture it was. Nor did it help his reputation when, on one early tea-room visit, he sat down at the table reserved for Welsh Labour MPs. As he'd planned in the mid-1970s, however, the big effort would be made on the public stage.

For the next five years Michael Heseltine toured constituencies on the rubber-chicken circuit – so called after the inedible food that is mythically served on such occasions. Rarely was an invitation turned down; his diary was soon full for six months, and his office was booking dates eighteen months away. By July 1986, six months after Westland, he claimed already to have addressed 117 meetings, and the very fact that he was counting suggested something of a campaign.[18] But local reporters expecting further attacks on the government were usually disappointed: the usual fare was a 'loyal' topic such as defence, with plenty of rousing Labour-bashing.

Michael Heseltine was almost as big a star attraction as Jeffrey Archer, with larger gatherings than he'd ever seen as a minister. Local parties found the profit from a Heseltine lunch or dinner could run to thousands of pounds. Very quickly he was building up a pile of IOUs from MPs who were grateful that his visit had raised enough money, for instance, to pay their agent's salary for several months.

His general rule was to try to get home on the night of a visit, but when the venue was too far away he might stay with the constituency member. It was a more effective way of getting to know parliamentary colleagues than any stilted chat in the tea-room, and some were tickled by the thought that a future Prime Minister might have stayed with them. Michael Brown, for instance, despite being a right-winger, willingly put Heseltine up at his home after a speech in his Brigg and Cleethorpes seat, and the following morning gave his guest a tour of the garden. The next week, some Heseltine plant cuttings arrived at Brown's office at the Commons.

Nevertheless, Heseltine had to overcome a bad reputation for being cold and aloof with his parliamentary colleagues. Steven Norris recalls the time in 1983 when Heseltine paid a campaign visit to his Oxford East constituency, next-door to Henley. Norris says his visitor barely seemed to care who he was.

He strode across the car park, would have walked straight past me if his agent had not steered him in my direction, shook my hand wordlessly, with a quite obvious lack of enthusiasm, and, turning on his heel, continued his royal progress . . . I do remember how popular he was with my campaign team thereafter. Indeed, when we relaxed after hours with the occasional game of darts in the Cowley Conservative Club, one of his campaign posters came in rather handy.[19]

Not many politicians could have afforded to run this American-style presidential campaign, of course. Heseltine hired his old ministerial driver, Andy Godfrey – 'my first act of privatization' – and installed a fax machine in the back of his Jaguar to keep in touch with his office.[20] One MP was getting a lift with Heseltine when, he recalls, an editor rang to ask if the former minister would write something for that Sunday's paper. Heseltine already had some material to hand, and the editor was astonished when it was faxed through immediately. When necessary, Heseltine would fly to speaking engagements – by helicopter, of course. He admitted he could never have managed it if he had been poor – the freedom to do so was partly why he had acquired his fortune.

Heseltine now had the chance fully to expound the *noblesse oblige* Toryism that is the essence of his philosophy – the paternalistic idea that with wealth and power comes responsibility to help the less fortunate. 'By background and experience I'm wholly committed to the benefits of the capitalist system. But I'm a Tory. And I believe that with the privileges that come to those who benefit most from the capitalist system there are obligations.'[21]

There was no shortage of high-profile speaking opportunities to develop his ideas. On return trips to Liverpool, for instance, he argued for extra subsidies for small firms in deprived areas, and for a new Urban Renewal Agency to encourage private investment, along the lines of the development agencies that had worked successfully in Scotland and Wales. The theme was always that regeneration could not be left to the free market. 'There are no known ways,' he said, 'to restore activity and hope to these places that [are] not led by the targeted use of public funds.'[22] Later Heseltine suggested that councils should sometimes compete for central-government money: those with the best schemes would get the grants.

On the economy, Heseltine joined those Tories who argued that spare cash should be devoted to public spending, instead of being earmarked for tax cuts. And £3 billion of receipts from council-house sales, which had been frozen by the Treasury, should be released for new investment.

Freed from the chains of office, Heseltine's true feelings about the last seven years of Thatcherism now erupted: 'We've blown North Sea oil; we've sold the assets. We're a society too anxious to consume; and an economy too reluctant to invest.'[23] He began arguing that the DTI should be strengthened at the expense of a 'significant diminution of the role of the Treasury, which I think is a historic anachronism within this country'.[24] Heseltine is a stern critic of the Treasury, and believes it has an anti-industrial bias which is promoted by the tax system – a view shared by Labour 'modernizers' such as Will Hutton. Tax relief on mortgage interest and pension contributions, for example, simply diverts investment into property and government bonds instead of industry. Mortgage tax relief should be restricted to first-time buyers, Heseltine argued, while pension relief should be redirected to industrial activity. If the Treasury was one obstacle to manufacturing growth, and guilty of short-termism, another was the City of London – an institution for which Heseltine had felt contempt since his days as an articled clerk. 'The whole psychology of the City is profoundly anti-industrial,' he said.[25]

Two months after his resignation, Heseltine signed a book deal with the publisher Century Hutchinson. Rather than spilling the beans on his ministerial career, which might have damaged his political ambitions, it would be a personal testament based on his time in government: 'my look at tomorrow in the light of the past', he called it.[26]

The typescript was due in six months: a challenge for most authors, but especially difficult for a man who didn't find writing easy. He approached the book as something to be overcome, just like previous hurdles. At school he had made himself into a high-jumper; at Oxford he practised endlessly to become a good speaker. He'd turned himself into a wealthy businessman; as a minister he'd learnt how to generate new policy ideas. Now he'd turn his energy and resources into producing a successful book. In truth, the book was not written but made – proof, perhaps, that British manufacturing was not yet dead.

It was a team operation, run by Julian Haviland, the former political editor of ITN and *The Times*. The fact that Haviland wasn't a Tory – 'centrist' is how he describes himself to colleagues – didn't seem to matter. Haviland and Keith Hampson quickly decided what chapters were required if the work was to be taken seriously, and then recruited experts to help Heseltine formulate his ideas. It was like being a minister all over again, as a stream of specialists came to Victoria Street to mull over the issues of the day. They included academics, businessmen, City economists and financiers, and fellow politicians. Just as in Whitehall, Heseltine enjoyed pitting one voice against another, pushing people to defend their corners (a technique often employed by Margaret Thatcher). Then he would decide for himself. 'I became conscious of his having an acute political intelligence in terms of listening to advice and then following his own line,' says his editor, Richard Cohen.[27] 'He's got the equipment of a well-read man without being well-read,' says another adviser. 'He acquires by social intercourse the knowledge that other people acquire by reading.' People he consulted were often surprised how receptive he was to fresh thinking – especially for a politician. Though Heseltine could never be called an 'intellectual', he loves playing with new ideas.

Here, Michael Heseltine was exploiting his 'star' quality. Just as Winston Churchill had found when out of office during the 1930s, people responded to his invitation. He wasn't any former Cabinet minister, but one who had taken on Margaret Thatcher and left the government in celebrated circumstances. Even those who weren't Conservatives – which included many of those he consulted – couldn't resist the call. 'It's always flattering to be asked by a public figure for an opinion,' says one. Others appreciated that Heseltine could command an audience and was likely to be listened to if he adopted and promoted their ideas. Better still, he might one day return to office and put them into practice.

In some cases Heseltine persuaded friends to set up discussions. One recalls, 'He would say, "I want you to have a lunch and invite those five people. I'm writing a book and I want to hear their views." ' The exchanges were then taped and typed up. On the basis of such discussions, and after gutting many of Heseltine's old speeches, Julian Haviland began writing sections of the book. Other chapters were farmed out. That on housing, for instance, was drafted by his former private secretary, David Edmonds, who was now running the Housing Corporation; Keith Hampson and Michael Mates worked respectively on education and defence; the chapter on race was originally written by Heseltine's research assistant, Praveen Moman, and then revised by Edward Bickham, who at the time was political adviser to the Home Secretary, Douglas Hurd. Early drafts were then sent to specialists for reactions. 'In the end,' says one of those involved, 'it was a combination of wise people's opinions.'

Eric Sorensen and Tom Baron were among the former colleagues who perused the text. His friend Mark Schreiber gently warned of the political consequences of what he was saying: 'Had he thought what the right would make of this?' Generally he had, and it stayed. 'What amazed me,' says one participant, 'was the number of people of high calibre who were willing to read and comment.' When the responses flowed back – and they were often substantial – Heseltine would scribble his own thoughts in the margin. Then each chapter would be discussed again with groups in the office.

Heseltine tried to write the foreword himself. It was awful, he was told bluntly. 'But it's what I believe,' he reportedly pleaded. 'It read like a headmaster's speech-day address,' says someone who saw it. 'It was full of platitudes – perfectly acceptable ones, but ones which were blather. He would have been laughed at if it had been left in that untreated form.'

Towards the end, Julian Haviland reworked the whole manuscript to give it one voice and make it more readable. 'He was very good at putting things just the way Michael would have said them,' a colleague observes. Then it was re-edited by Richard Cohen, a veteran of Barbara Castle's and Tony Benn's diaries, though best known for having edited many of Jeffrey Archer's novels. 'Although the words were somebody else's,' Cohen says of Heseltine's book, 'the views were his, and he read drafts and asked for them to be changed, and asked for his views to be considered. And he kind of stage-managed the operation of getting it together.'[28] It was authorship by entrepreneurship.

Where There's a Will sold 6,000 copies in hardback, and spent several weeks in the *Sunday Times* best-seller list, although the publisher did not recoup its £30,000 advance. Heseltine said he didn't care if it only sold a thousand copies, provided they reached the readers for whose opinions he cared. 'You know,' he told people, 'I've always dreamt of being able to hold in my hands a book that I've written.'

Despite its multifaceted production process, *Where There's a Will* is a personal manifesto, the clearest exposition of the Heseltine philosophy:

I hope in this book to dispel the false belief which has misled too many in my party, that there is a heresy called 'intervention' to which unsound Conservatives have in the recent past been prone but which sound Conservative administrations eschew. The *laissez faire* idealists may hold that all government action, to the extent that it inhibits the free exercise of the citizen's will, must threaten his liberty and weaken his spirit. This is too romantic and impractical a guide for men and women who hold public office, and it has nothing to do with the Tory party.[29]

To his critics, Heseltine only confirmed that he was an old-fashioned corporatist when he argued, for instance, that 'The capitalist system works best when owners, managers, employees and government understand a common interest and work as a team to that end.'[30]

Although the book drew extensively on his experience, Westland was carefully avoided. Compared with most books on policy written by politicians, it read well – largely because it was spiced with personal anecdotes. Reviewers were positive. Of political books of its kind, wrote Hugo Young, 'it is the most impressive I've read by a modern Conservative'.[31]

During the 1987 election campaign Heseltine visited around 100 constituencies, and generated more publicity than prominent Cabinet ministers such as Sir Geoffrey Howe. He even employed researchers to attend each of the party's morning press conferences and then fax him reports on what had been said. With his regular attacks on Labour he appeared the model of loyalty, even if he rarely managed to praise his leader, or mention her. Any thoughts he might have entertained of contesting the leadership after a Tory defeat, however, disappeared when Margaret Thatcher won a handsome majority of 101. Amid the election-night celebrations, she appeared to address one of Heseltine's central concerns with her remark 'We must do something about those inner cities,' though some suspected she simply meant reversing the Conservative decline in urban seats.

The 1987 Parliament was dominated by a policy which proved to be Margaret Thatcher's greatest blunder, and her eventual undoing. The poll tax, or community charge, was a measure that Michael Heseltine could always say he had never approved as a minister. Indeed, he'd been a vehement opponent of it while at the DoE, during the two Thatcher-instigated reviews of the rating system in 1981 and 1982. By a fortunate coincidence he had even avoided the measure on the single occasion when it came to Cabinet – 9 January 1986. It was that morning, of course, that Heseltine walked out over Westland. Ministers approved the poll tax an hour or so later.

From the back benches, Heseltine initially voted to introduce the poll tax in Scotland, but then, when it came to England and Wales, became one of its strongest critics. At the second reading in the Commons, Heseltine delivered what he would later tell people was the 'best speech of my life'. The community charge would become 'known as a Tory tax', he warned MPs. He denounced its 'crude regression which seeks to make equal in the eyes of the tax collector, the rich and the poor, the slum dweller and the landed aristocrat, the elderly pensioners living on their limited savings and the most successful of today's entrepreneurs'.[32] Despite his opposition, Heseltine personally benefited financially from the policy, and, taking his various properties, he stood to save several thousand pounds a year from the abolition of the rates. (Later he himself paid the poll-tax bills of more than a dozen staff and dependants on his country estate.)

Heseltine only abstained at the second reading, rather than join Edward Heath and sixteen other Conservative rebels in the opposition lobbies. He was always extremely cautious about being seen as too much of a rebel: the only time he voted *against* the government on the poll tax was over a critical amendment proposed by his colleague

Michael Mates. This put forward a system of banding, whereby poll tax would be graduated according to the highest rate of income tax one paid. The Mates amendment provoked one of the most threatening rebellions of all Margaret Thatcher's years in office, though she eventually got through with a relatively comfortable majority of twenty-five. The whips approached the vote in an atmosphere of crisis, spreading the idea that Mates was a stooge in a Heseltine plot and that the rebels were the nucleus of an anti-Thatcher faction which would eventually challenge her leadership.

Michael Heseltine was in regular contact with poll-tax rebels such as Peter Temple-Morris, but Mates himself has always played down the extent of any collusion with Heseltine. 'We were doing a number of things together at this time,' he has said, 'but this was not one of them.'[33] One certainly can't say the rebellion was initiated by Heseltine, or organized from Victoria Street. An active approach is never his way when being disloyal. Plots are not hatched; orders are not given; roles are never assigned. Instead, he contents himself with being fully informed about what his allies are doing, and they understand that they have his support simply through his inquiries. No Heseltine fingerprints are ever found.

Apart from his daily dealings with Hampson and Mates, there were no cabals of other supportive MPs. 'It was extraordinary how little was done,' says one back-bench ally, William Powell.[34] 'He always took the view,' says another, 'that he should have no group around him, as he didn't trust the House of Commons. He knew people gossiped a lot and it would get out.' Heseltine was extremely nervous of being seen to foment opposition to the government, though when it came to elections for Tory back-bench committees he happily took the 'whip' of the left-wing Lollards faction, and even attended meetings to cast his vote.

His opposition to the poll tax again brought him into direct conflict with the Environment Secretary, Nicholas Ridley. Relations between the two had become increasingly acrimonious since Ridley's decisive intervention at the Westland Cabinet meeting. Ridley described the resignation as a 'gross betrayal of his loyalty to his colleagues', and from a previous position of friendship he soon became the most acerbic of Heseltine's critics.[35] From around 1988 they also locked horns over 'green' issues.

The so-called 'Lawson boom' of the late 1980s put enormous pressure on the green belt of the South-East – not least in and around Heseltine's own constituency in Henley. Whereas Nicholas Ridley preferred a free-market approach to new construction, and attacked NIMBYism – those who said 'Not In My Back Yard' to development – Heseltine tapped growing public concern about encroachment into the countryside. 'Wherever I drive in southern England today,' he wrote to Ridley, 'the place is being torn up and torn apart.'[36]

Heseltine admitted that during his own time at the DoE he may have been too lenient with the developers: indeed, one new development that he approved in Berkshire had aroused so much opposition it was dubbed 'Heseltown'. But, whereas he had granted only 30 per cent of planning appeals, under Ridley the figure had risen to 40 per cent. Heseltine attacked Ridley's estimate that 500,000 new homes would be needed in the South-East by the year 2000, and in particular he opposed a development of 6,000 homes planned at Stone Bassett in his own Henley constituency. Curiously, he was most emphatic when challenged about his own record as a developer in the 1960s. 'I think you will find,' he told Dominic Lawson of *The Spectator*, 'if you look at my time as a property man, that I never built on green-field sites. Never.'[37] What was Turners Fields in Tenterden, if not a green-field site? Maybe Heseltine was misquoted.

Heseltine's new campaign to conserve the South-East countryside dovetailed neatly with his long-standing emphasis on giving more help to the regions, by measures such as transferring more civil servants away from the London area. But his argument was perhaps undermined by his own record as an MP who had abandoned Tavistock for Henley; nor had Haymarket ever shown any inclination to disperse staff around the country.

His battle with Nicholas Ridley was partly symbolic, of course. Ridley was closer to the Prime Minister than any other member of the late 1980s Cabinet. In championing both the poll tax and the virtues of the free market, and in his opposition to further European integration, the Environment Secretary was sometimes more Thatcherite than Thatcher herself. Heseltine, explains one of his advisers, 'was attacking her by attacking her surrogate, Ridley'.[38] He was an easy target. Nicholas Ridley was an unsympathetic, irascible character who had become a public hate-figure by espousing so many unpopular causes, and yet didn't seem to care about his image.

Long before the Green Party achieved an astonishing 15 per cent share of the vote in the 1989 European elections, Michael Heseltine was among the first to spot how the environment was pushing itself on to the political agenda. Concern about the costs of economic expansion was just one reason; others were the 1986 accident at the Chernobyl nuclear plant and growing worries about both global warming and the depletion of the ozone layer.

Seeking advice on green issues, Heseltine was told that the environmentalist most likely to cooperate with him was Tom Burke, a former director of Friends of the Earth who now ran another pressure group, the Green Alliance. Burke says he went to see Heseltine partly out of curiosity. 'It was love at first sight, really,' he adds. 'I agreed to go away and write speeches for him. The key point was his shrewdness in seeing that the environment was an issue that was winding up the Tory grass roots, and that this was a flank on which Thatcher was vulnerable.'[39]

Yet Tom Burke was by no means a Conservative himself. He had once been a Labour activist, and was now a leading player in the Social Democratic Party (SDP). When he began helping Heseltine, he was also writing speeches for the SDP leader, David Owen. Burke even saw himself as creating a certain competition between the two politicians. He quickly learnt to tailor his work for their different speaking styles and idioms, but the arguments for both were broadly similar. Nobody seemed to notice.

Burke also wrote a very 'green' chapter on environmental issues for Heseltine's second book, *The Challenge of Europe: Can Britain Win?*, which was published in May 1989, just before the European elections. Although it was only about two-thirds of the length of *Where There's a Will*, it involved an even more carefully organized team operation.

One chapter, on education, was farmed out to Richard Jameson, a former civil servant and Conservative councillor who had vaguely known Heseltine at Oxford. Jameson recalls going to Victoria Street to present him and Keith Hampson with the draft manuscript.

He turned over the pages for a few minutes and then said to Keith, 'How much do we owe this man?' Keith said he thought £500 was the going rate; and Heseltine at once took out his chequebook and wrote me a cheque for £500. As he handed it to me he said, 'Mind you declare it as income for tax purposes.'[40]

About 80 per cent of Jameson's text was used in Heseltine's book; many paragraphs were printed word for word.[41] But material was also added, and only about a third of the final chapter can actually be ascribed to Jameson. To a reader, it sits uneasily with the rest of the book – it is much more heavily researched than other chapters, and has the feel of another pen.

Much of the Europe book resulted from a series of special seminars. For instance, Lord (Tom) Boardman – a former ministerial colleague from Ted Heath's DTI, who was now chairman of the NatWest Bank – convened a group of experts on European economic and monetary union (EMU). Boardman himself was sceptical about EMU, but he brought in Christopher Johnson, the chief economist of Lloyds Bank, who is a keen advocate of EMU and the single European currency. Johnson supplied Heseltine with background material, and seems to have played a significant role in convincing him of the case for monetary union.

Among others asked for advice were two high-level diplomats, Sir Nicholas Henderson and Sir Antony Acland. Heseltine was also in close contact with Jacques Delors, the French socialist who was President of the European Commission. Delors was himself preparing his historic report which would recommend three stages towards the achievement of EMU. This was due to be published only a few weeks before Heseltine's work, and on one occasion Delors spent three hours at the Victoria Street office. Heseltine was concerned not just with hearing what the European President was likely to say in his report, but also to ensure that nothing in his book clashed with it. Before long, of course, Margaret Thatcher had conferred 'ogre' status on Delors in Conservative circles. Had it become known quite how keenly Heseltine sought Jacques Delors's advice during his wilderness years – and why – it would have been quite damaging.

The Challenge of Europe was a dull read in comparison with *Where*

There's a Will. Despite, or perhaps because of, being serialized in the *Sunday Times*, it sold barely 2,000 copies in hardback, but then a book on Europe was never likely to be a best-seller. What most pleased Heseltine was that he won the Adolphe Benticke prize of £10,000 which is awarded for books that advance the cause of European unity. The judges particularly commended the quality of the writing. Perhaps the prize should have gone to the people who wrote it, but then all good *communitaire* works are produced by committee.

The book's theme was that, with the advent of the single market in 1992, Britain should embrace Europe wholeheartedly. Heseltine was 'convinced . . . of the advantages for Britain and her partners of moving towards a united Europe', though he didn't see the need for a rigid timetable.[42] He concluded that 'to pick and choose from the constituent parts of Europe's programme, to dine *à la carte*, is to risk quenching the enthusiasm that British managers must display if the opportunity of 1992 is to be grasped'.[43] Which suggests that he didn't envisage the two opt-outs that John Major negotiated for Britain at Maastricht in 1991 – on the social chapter of the Maastricht Treaty and on joining a single currency.

In the late 1980s the big question was not about the single currency, but whether Britain should join the Exchange Rate Mechanism (ERM) of the European Monetary System, thus tying the value of the pound to other currencies, effectively the German mark. Since 1985 a debate had raged inside government. On the one side were the Chancellor, Nigel Lawson, and the Foreign Secretary, Sir Geoffrey Howe, who were both in favour of ERM membership. On the other side was Margaret Thatcher, closely advised by her guru Sir Alan Walters, who was firmly against. Heseltine argued that Britain should join the ERM as 'a step which will strengthen her economic armoury and intensify the fight against inflation', yet he also made it clear that he wanted to go well beyond the ERM (in contrast to Lawson).[44] Heseltine never actually states baldly, 'I want a single currency,' but that is the whole thrust of his treatise, as he dismisses concerns about the loss of sovereignty it would entail. 'No truly unified market can exist without a single currency,' he claims in his book.[45] Quoting a comment by the former chairman of the Stock Exchange, Sir Nicholas Goodison, that 'the momentum is such that economic and monetary union in

Europe are now on the agenda for practical action', Heseltine says that Goodison 'spoke there for much of British business, and he was right'.[46]

On the social aspects of Europe, and the minimum conditions of employment proposed in the then social charter (which preceded the milder Maastricht social *chapter* from which the UK opted out, and included measures such as a maximum 48-hour working week), Heseltine gave his qualified support. 'Britain has legislation in virtually all the relevant fields already,' he wrote in 1989, suggesting the government should sign the charter.[47] However, he felt Britain should 'fight to prevent the more excessive elements', though his writings imply that the battle was not worth pursuing to the last ditch. He also advocated greater involvement for company employees – not something ever noticeable at Haymarket – but told MPs, 'It would be a disaster to try to impose mandatory workers on the boards of British industry.'[48]

Heseltine's most radical proposal was for a new European Senate to supplement the existing chamber of the European Parliament, to consist of members nominated by each of the national governments or parliaments. His cheekiest comment was that 'Margaret Thatcher proclaimed Britain's European destiny in her speech at Bruges.' That certainly wasn't how most people interpreted the Prime Minister's famous Bruges declaration.[49]

In the immediate aftermath of Westland, Michael Heseltine had said surprisingly little about Europe, even though the crisis had partly been about European collaboration. But, as Britain's role in the Community became an increasingly hot issue as the decade drew to a close, Heseltine became the standard-bearer for pro-European Conservatives. Yet his view of Europe is rather different from that of other ardent Euro-enthusiasts such as Edward Heath or Kenneth Clarke. For them European unity is an ideal, whereas Heseltine sees Europe in more practical terms – as the only means for Britain to exert some influence in the world. Much more important, Heseltine regards Europe as the best way for United Kingdom plc to prosper. 'I belong to the "Britain first" school of politics,' he wrote. 'Our markets are increasingly European and, in responding to the process, unashamed national self-interest has to prevail.'[50] Hence the patriotic subtitle of his Europe book – *Can Britain Win?*

Unlike some pro-European politicians, Michael Heseltine never behaves or thinks like a European. His notion of Europe is political and economic, not cultural or emotional. In contrast to Roy Jenkins, Edward Heath or Denis Healey, for instance, he has few European friends. He is not a good linguist, nor does he own a holiday property in Europe or even take many Continental holidays. Civil servants say Michael Heseltine always shows the greatest reluctance even to cross the Channel for ministerial gatherings. Heseltine's Europeanism is entirely pragmatic.

The other big issue Heseltine pursued during his wilderness period was unemployment. It was not something he had to worry about as a constituency MP – Henley's jobless rate was the twelfth lowest in the country – but an interest developed from his days as Minister for Merseyside. He now feared that, with the 'Lawson boom', ministers might become complacent about unemployment levels which were still abnormally high by historic standards. If the then national total of about 2.5 million jobless continued for another ten years, Heseltine warned in a speech in 1988, then the growing 'sense of injustice and anger' might be 'explosive'. 'I simply cannot think it right for politicians to go on making speeches about how things are going to improve if by that they mean we shall gradually move from levels of 3 million to levels of 2 million out of work.' That is, of course, pretty much what has happened since. 'The market unaided,' he maintained, 'does not look like it will possibly find jobs at the speed or on the scale the crisis demands.'[51]

Heseltine's particular concern was the million people classified as long-term unemployed – those without work for more than twelve months. Both of his books called for an experiment with 'workfare', the American system which insists that unemployed people should do state-sponsored activity in return for their welfare benefits. 'When every year the old die of hypothermia, is there some moral superiority about a society that pays the unemployed in a community to stay at home rather than to drop in with a cup of tea?'[52] It was one of the most controversial points in his two books, since the measure was then regarded as right-wing and draconian. It was a sign of how eclectic Heseltine was in his shopping for political ideas: he was quite happy to take policies from both left and right.

Heseltine was also interested in the Swedish example – the policy that, rather than passively providing cash benefits to people without work, the state should devote more money to temporary jobs or training. If an unemployed person refused one of these jobs, or a place on a training scheme, then after ten months he or she automatically lost benefit. Christopher Johnson had introduced Heseltine to the Employment Institute, of which Johnson was the chairman, and to Richard Layard, a professor at the London School of Economics who was carrying out research for the institute on how Sweden and other European states tackled long-term unemployment. The plan was for the institute to publish Layard's findings in a pamphlet under Heseltine's name. 'It was, if you like, a ghost-writing job,' says Johnson, 'but very much the line he wanted to take.'[53] Heseltine's involvement ended abruptly with the political turmoil of November 1990, though the pamphlet went ahead without him.

Heseltine's interest in unemployment was unusual for a senior Conservative politician. Through the Employment Institute, whose staff helped write much of Heseltine's 1988 speech, he was again working closely with non-Conservatives: the majority of the institute's supporters were left-of-centre. Richard Layard himself, like Tom Burke, was then an active member of the SDP, though he now advises the Labour Party. Indeed, one Employment Institute source says Heseltine 'sounded very much what you would now describe as "New Labour" . . . He wasn't a million miles from where Blair is now.'

That could apply to much of what Michael Heseltine was saying in the late 1980s, not just on unemployment but on other major issues – Europe and entry to the ERM, industrial strategy, the poll tax and the inner cities.

During the first part of the decade Michael Heseltine had been a bogeyman to the left, with his attacks on council spending, his campaign against CND, and the prosecutions of Sarah Tisdall and Clive Ponting. After Westland, however, he quickly became the left's favourite Tory. Many Labour people had some admiration for the way he had resisted Thatcher, and as Neil Kinnock's Labour Party moved rapidly to the centre it found much in common with Heseltine.

Perhaps because of this, he was quick to show his right-wing credentials whenever possible. In 1987 Heseltine teamed up with Norman Tebbit, who had served briefly as his unofficial PPS in the 1970s and had left the Cabinet after the election. Together they persuaded ministers to abolish the Inner London Education Authority (ILEA), and responsibility for inner-London schools was instead transferred to the boroughs. It was a natural progression, of course, from the abolition of the metropolitan counties – and with similar reasoning, since the ILEA had almost always been Labour-controlled.

Heseltine also backed the government's market-led changes to the health service, and wrote a pamphlet urging water privatization (partly to secure more investment for environmental improvements). He delivered regular warnings about the Soviets, and ritual attacks on Labour defence policy. He also supported Margaret Thatcher's effort to ban the book *Spycatcher*, written by the former MI5 officer Peter Wright, and opposed parliamentary attempts to reform the Official Secrets Act. And his call for the Bank of England to be given independence from the Treasury found support from people on the right who wanted stricter financial management, though for Heseltine it was also a building-block towards a European central bank.

When Margaret Thatcher celebrated the tenth anniversary of her premiership in May 1989, a few brave friends suggested it was an obvious moment to retire. She would hear none of it, primarily because she feared the dreaded Heseltine taking her place. Kenneth Baker says that 'at that time the succession contest would have been between Geoffrey Howe and Michael Heseltine, and she didn't think that Geoffrey would win. She was not prepared to hand over the party to Michael, who in her view represented all the things from which she had saved her country and her party.'[54]

Officially, the Conservative leader is elected every autumn, though usually the incumbent is returned unopposed. That autumn, however, Thatcher faced the first challenge to her leadership in almost fifteen years – from the elderly back-bench MP Sir Anthony Meyer, an ardent pro-European. Though he was far from a credible candidate, he nevertheless garnered thirty-three votes, while another twenty-four MPs spoilt their ballot papers. Meyer says he ultimately wanted Michael Heseltine to succeed Thatcher, and, though he had no direct contact with his favourite, he asked Keith Hampson if he thought the challenge would be damaging to Heseltine's eventual chances. Hampson thought not.

On polling-day, Heseltine made 'a very noisy abstention', Meyer claims, 'ostentatiously walking up and down the corridor making it plain he was going to abstain'.[55] Heseltine was one of three MPs not to vote at all, which meant that sixty Tory members in all – almost one in six – had failed to back Thatcher. Dozens more made it plain that their future support was conditional. Tristan Garel-Jones, the Deputy Chief Whip, says he warned Thatcher of a hundred more 'lurking in the bushes' who wanted 'to engage in the daylight assassination of a sitting Prime Minister'.[56] Black clouds were closing in on her premiership.

Afterwards, says Meyer, Heseltine suggested it was now 'best to let the thing stew'.[57] Privately, his inclination was not to mount his own bid. Publicly, in response to ever-persistent questions, he uttered the carefully crafted response that he 'could not foresee the circumstances' in which he would challenge Thatcher.[58] This left open all sorts of possibilities, of course, even though Heseltine often added that 'I have always said that the Conservatives will win the next general election and Mrs Thatcher will lead them into it.'[59]

Opinion polls indicated that, of the leading Conservative alternatives to the Prime Minister, only Michael Heseltine was likely to bring any substantial improvement to the party's popularity. One survey at the time of Meyer's challenge suggested that Conservative support would fall if Geoffrey Howe, Norman Tebbit or Kenneth Baker became leader, but Heseltine's elevation, according to the sample, would cause a 13 per cent rise in the Conservative rating – more than enough to overtake the lead that Labour then enjoyed.[60]

In the British political system, where so much emphasis is placed on front-bench figures, it had been a remarkable achievement for Heseltine to remain in the public eye. His public appeal was vital, for he might pose a serious challenge for the leadership only by appearing a convincing election-winner to fellow MPs who feared for their seats.

In later years Michael Heseltine would often thank journalists, individually and collectively, for keeping him visible during this period of exile. Most people took it as a joke, but it contained an element of truth. Perhaps because he is a former publisher, Heseltine has an acute appreciation of how the media work – especially the tabloid press. Some politicians barely skim the newspapers, but he devoured them greedily each morning, to read what they were saying about him, to test the political temperature, and to size up potential opportunities to intervene.

The Heseltine camp also enjoyed excellent media relations. Keith Hampson is popular with journalists, and is married to the television reporter Sue Cameron. Michael Mates's son James works for ITN, though the MP can often be brusque with reporters. Heseltine's former employee Elinor Goodman now covered politics for *Channel 4 News*; an old Oxford friend and Haymarket employee Robin Esser had become editor of the *Sunday Express*, while Anthony Howard was deputy editor of *The Observer*. Heseltine also saw a lot of the columnist Peter Jenkins, as well as John Cole, the political editor of the BBC.

At that time, of course, Heseltine and many journalists had a similar unstated goal – knocking Thatcher. Perhaps Heseltine's two closest press contacts were Tony Bevins of the fledgling *Independent* and Alastair Campbell, a young political correspondent with the Mirror Group. Heseltine appreciated that both enjoyed mischief-making, which invariably meant upsetting the government. During the most intense political periods, Heseltine was in almost daily contact with the two reporters – by phone or in person – exchanging information, sounding out what the press was thinking, and seeking the latest political intelligence – for instance, on what Bernard Ingham was saying in the private Downing Street lobby briefings.

Alastair Campbell and his partner, Fiona Millar, who wrote for the *Sunday Express*, produced several sympathetic profiles of Heseltine, and Campbell claims to have 'regularly offered help and advice to the great man'.[61] It was a peculiar relationship for someone who was also a close adviser to the Labour leader Neil Kinnock, and has since become Tony Blair's press secretary. Politically, of course, it was understandable for a Labour paper like the *Mirror*, since anything which promoted Michael Heseltine was likely to undermine the Conservative Party, at least in the short term.

But Heseltine was careful in his collusion. He weighed up journalists carefully before he trusted them. Even then, relations were always based on unstated assumptions and understandings, rather than any explicit talk of 'how to get Thatcher'. When *Panorama* proposed making a film about Heseltine in 1989, he entertained the producer to lunch at his country home, flattering him with the full silver service and a butler on hand. The two men went into considerable detail about how interview questions should best be worded so that Heseltine could push the boat out as far as possible, though this was a somewhat unorthodox procedure for television. Heseltine made it clear that if anything touched on his loyalty he would have to clam up.

The resulting interview carefully avoided any mention of Margaret Thatcher, apart from one clever question: 'Would you describe yourself as a Thatcherite?' He had built up a business from almost nothing, Heseltine replied, and had initiated the selling of council houses. Then he paused: 'So you could say I'm the original Thatcherite.'[62] The pause had been rehearsed endlessly, and the question required several takes before both sides were satisfied. Heseltine was especially pleased with that answer.

Having filmed Heseltine's responses, the *Panorama* crew then carried out the usual television procedure of filming, for editing purposes, the questions being asked over again, but without answers.

'Do you want to be Prime Minister?' the interviewer said. Now off-camera, Heseltine nodded furiously.

17. *Country Life*

Anne Heseltine had certainly been warned. Having been paraded as Michael's newly acquired fiancée at the selection meeting in Coventry, she could hardly complain that politics was suddenly thrust upon her. 'Every wife of a politician has to bear a very great burden in forgone opportunities and lost leisure time,' Michael Heseltine once observed, 'so at least I'm always able to say, "Well, it was on that basis." '[1]

Anne Williams also knew she was marrying not just an ambitious politician, but a thrusting, workaholic, risk-taking businessman as well. Within just a few months of their wedding the couple faced financial disaster. The story has echoes of the events which brought his Tory colleague Jeffrey Archer close to ruin twelve years later. On the very evening that Anne told her husband she was pregnant with their first child (Annabel), Michael Heseltine announced that his business might go under, with debts of £250,000. Though he had been ever optimistic, she had some warning that things were not going well:

We used to go into the office every Saturday morning, scour through the post, yelp with excitement when there was a cheque and groan when there was another bill, and practically burst into tears when somebody threatened solicitors. At that stage one was very, very frightened . . . We didn't have money stashed away in the bank. We didn't have rich parents we could call on. Michael had to find it from somewhere, and he did. He found every single penny, and every single debt was paid.[2]

Anne Williams was the fifth child of a solicitor – in her words, the 'tail-end child of a large family, born as a substitute for a lost daughter'.[3] Although they had Welsh ancestry, the Williamses had lived for several decades in south London – John Major territory. Anne was born in Streatham in 1934 – her parents had been married at St Matthew's in Brixton, the same local church where John and Norma Major would be wed – but before long her family moved to

319

Amersham in Buckinghamshire. It was quite late in life for William and Edna Williams to have another child: her mother was almost forty when she had Anne; her father forty-eight. 'When her parents came to school functions they looked so much older than everybody else's,' says a schoolfriend, Elizabeth Hayes. 'Possibly that was why she was rather mature; she was never a silly, giggly schoolgirl.'[4]

Because her brothers were already grown up and away fighting in the war, Anne was effectively brought up as an only child. 'I was shy and led a very protected life,' she once said.[5] At the age of thirteen, her parents sent her to boarding-school – St Helen's in Northwood, Middlesex – where she flourished. She proved to be a talented actress who played major parts in school plays, and she was eventually appointed head girl.

'Paradise' is how Anne Heseltine describes her days at St Helen's: 'it was the first time I had anything to do with children of my own age'.[6] After classes she went riding, and she has maintained a love of horses ever since. On one occasion she took a leading role in a debate against the nearby boys' school, Aldenham, on the motion 'The Equality of Women has Gone Too Far'. Anne led the opposition but lost the vote.

Having failed to get into Oxford, Anne Williams went instead to London University, and got a second in modern languages at Bedford College. She also studied briefly in both Innsbruck and Poitiers, and says her 'first ambition, actually, was to be an academic'.[7] A secretarial course followed, at a college in London, where a fellow student was a friend from the local pony club in Buckinghamshire: Sonia Edelman (the daughter of Maurice Edelman, Michael Heseltine's Labour opponent in Coventry in 1964). The two travelled up together every day on the Metropolitan line. 'I do remember she seemed quite lonely in a way, and her parents seemed very remote compared with mine . . . She always struck me as rather self-possessed, and she seemed to me very good-looking and well groomed.'[8]

For a spell, Anne Williams worked for the publisher Victor Gollancz, where, in an era before political correctness, she was known as 'Superbeaut'. She initially acted as what would nowadays be called a PA, and then moved to editorial duties, writing reports on unsolicited manuscripts. 'She was working for a left-wing publisher, so if she

dissented from those politics I never heard her express it,' says
Gollancz's nephew Hilary Rubinstein. 'But it didn't surprise me when
she left to work in an art gallery.'[9] The gallery, in Knightsbridge, was
owned by Andras Kalman; Anne worked there for three years, and
Kalman says she was an 'exceptionally competent associate, and
brilliant at writing letters'.[10] Anne credits her father with encouraging
her love of art: as a child, she says, she was allowed to visit London
museums and galleries on her own.

It was while at Kalman's, in 1961, that she first met Michael
Heseltine, at a party given by a former boyfriend. On their first date,
she dragged him off to the Tate Gallery, which he'd never visited
before. Within a few weeks, says a friend, she was regularly spending
the night at his flat. She was soon drawn into the world of politics
which went with Heseltine's developing career, and marriage followed
in 1962. But it was not easy being married to an ambitious politician
who was also running a business. The couple had three children in
four years, and Anne also had at least one miscarriage. Michael
Heseltine was frequently away, leaving his wife to look after their
homes and young family. But at least they could afford help – although
they seem to have had problems holding on to their nannies.

Quite apart from Heseltine's extensive and high-pressured commitments at Haymarket and Westminster, his then distant constituency,
in Tavistock, didn't help either. Anne and the family were expected
to put in regular appearances at party engagements down in Devon;
she also opened up their constituency home at Pamflete for charity
events, and regularly addressed local gatherings on Michael's behalf:

I made perfectly adequate speeches on a pretty simplistic level, and I'd get
into a terrible state beforehand. Eventually, Michael said, 'Don't do it, it's
not necessary.' . . . I was spending the day trolling along behind him, adding
nothing to the occasion, while some poor soul had to look after me, and
there were things at home I wasn't doing.[11]

Politically, Anne has said that before meeting Michael Heseltine
she had only ever voted once. Despite seeming to enjoy the expensive
high life even more than her husband, there are signs that her politics
may be slightly to the left of his. She is a fan of the socialist writer
George Orwell, and her friend Ann Mallalieu, a Labour peeress, feels

Anne's political outlook is closer to her own, possibly because of her background and friends in the art world. 'I would say that she was perhaps more tolerant than Michael in some ways – perhaps readier to listen to and take in other people's points of view.'[12]

In the early years the Heseltines led the sort of lifestyle that causes many political couples to divorce. By the early 1970s Anne had decided she was no longer willing to be a political wife. She found politics boring, particularly at local level. She hated the endless constituency duties, where she had to be nice to people with whom she had nothing in common. Michael Heseltine once explained how it eventually came to a frank talk:

Like all sensible married couples, we discussed the direction of our life and we reckoned that our whole lives had become dominated by politics, and we thought this was not what we wanted, and that it was time consciously to change that direction. All our social activities . . . ceased to be so concentrated on the political world.[13]

But while Michael Heseltine was serving in the Heath government in the early 1970s, Anne increasingly found herself alone for long periods. So she made a conscious decision to strike out on her own. 'I'm not the sort to sit at home with a boiled egg,' she said. 'If someone asks us to dinner and Michael can't go, I say I can . . . I could not just sit on my bottom; that would be frightfully boring.'[14]

In theory, the move from Tavistock to Henley should have made life easier. It didn't. As the children grew up, they began to share Anne's interest in horse-riding; the girls were given ponies, practised show-jumping and dressage, and spent many of their weekends at local shows and gymkhanas. 'Michael is bored stiff by horses,' says a friend, who adds that the years living near Nettlebed were a 'horrible time' for the couple. Anne's equestrian diversions, and some of her friendships in the local horsy set, put a severe strain on the marriage.

Things improved when the Heseltines took the decision to move out of the Henley constituency and buy a large country house. In this they were taking a risk, since Michael Heseltine had promised his 1972 selection meeting he would live in his seat. Anne was glad to get away from constituents and their day-to-day grievances, but it always surprised her that they didn't receive a single letter of protest from anyone in the local party.

Michael Heseltine set about finding their dream home as if mounting a military campaign. 'I advertised. I did Ordnance Survey recces. I went through Pevsner. There was nothing I didn't do to find what I wanted.'[15] The story goes that Anne even appealed for help through the pages of *Country Life*. 'At a time when every house seems to be for sale, we still cannot find the one we want,' she is supposed to have written in 1976. What they sought was a 'period house of particular architectural quality preferably stone built and in the Palladian manner'. It had to have stables or outbuildings, a couple of cottages, and at least thirty acres for their animals. 'We actually enjoy restoring with our own fair hands, and won't be put off by dilapidated condition – unless riddled with dry rot,' she added.[16]

When they eventually succeeded, about a year later, the property was well worth the trouble. It was situated in the hamlet of Thenford in southern Northamptonshire, just across the border from Oxfordshire, four miles east of Banbury.

Ever since the days when he employed his own chauffeur – yet couldn't really afford to – Michael Heseltine had never hidden his social aspirations and the desire to escape his comfortable but plain middle-class background. Now he could live the life of an eighteenth-century English country gentleman. If his political career was the *oblige*, here was the *noblesse*. Behind their monogrammed gates, Michael and Anne Heseltine would accumulate fine art and antique furniture. They would entertain the highest in the land, from the worlds of politics and academe. And Michael would design and build a great garden and arboretum which would stand for centuries – a permanent, personal memorial should his political ambitions ultimately fail.

Thenford House stands in large grounds with lakes, and is surrounded by farmland. A fine Georgian building which is mentioned in Pevsner's guide to the buildings of England, it was built in 1765 by Michael Wodhull, the descendant of a medieval aristocrat.[17] A 1946 article in *Country Life* describes Wodhull as 'tall and handsome, a man of liberal, even radical views for his time', and it adds that 'as a school-boy at Winchester he was called "the long-legged Republican" '.[18]

The wide front of the house consists of a centre block with a cupola, and pedimented wings linked to it on either side. When the Heseltines bought the property the garden already had many large trees, and the surrounding woodland attracted wildlife such as badgers. Inside, the house has several distinctive features, including a library, fine plaster ceilings, and good fireplaces. The wood panelling on the top floor dates from an Elizabethan house which previously stood on the site. The building also contains a reconstructed mosaic which was unearthed from the remains of a nearby Roman road and moved there by the previous resident, Sir Spencer Summers.

Summers was a former steelworks owner who had served as Tory MP for Northampton and then Aylesbury (overlapping in Parliament with Heseltine from 1966 to 1970). Michael Heseltine had long had his eye on the property, and kept a copy of the 1946 *Country Life* feature. In 1976, when he learnt that Sir Spencer had died, he approached his widow, Lady Jean, through their son, Martin. 'He rang me; he was very correct,' says Martin Summers. 'He said, "Should you ever wish to sell, please consider me." '[19] Having decided that it was no longer practical to keep the house, the Summerses concluded a private deal. The price was never disclosed, though one estimate put it at £750,000.

Heseltine is thought to have spent almost as much again on renovating the property, which only increased the personal debt he had already built up to secure his majority stake in Haymarket. Lindsay Masters, who as Haymarket chairman was still minding the Heseltine publishing assets, had also acquired a large country property, in Hampshire. Both men were keen to reduce their debts, but without diluting their personal shareholdings in the company. The solution, agreed in 1980, was simply to sell off several of Haymarket's most lucrative titles – including *Accountancy Age* and *Computing* – to the Dutch company VNU. The transaction realized about £17 million – half of which went to Heseltine – but it also involved Haymarket losing about a third of its activity. Many observers, both inside and outside the firm, believe the deal was a grave error. *Accountancy Age* and *Computing* cover two of the fields that have seen some of the greatest economic expansion since then – financial services and information technology. Moreover, the loss of such a major part of its business, and some of its most talented staff, seemed to take the stuffing out of Haymarket. Employees were demoralized, and saw the deal as a sign that the firm had lost its dynamism and ambition.

After their extensive renovation of Thenford, the Heseltines invited local villagers to come and look round the building. Under the Summerses, the house had been the focal point of the community in a traditional, paternalistic, almost feudal fashion. Summer fêtes were held on the front lawn, and there were Christmas parties for local children, harvest-home suppers for estate families, and theatre trips for the workers' wives. The arrival of Michael and Anne Heseltine marked the end of an era. While they still hold the odd event for villagers, the Heseltines are rather more distant than the Summerses, even though they now own many of the local cottages. Over the years, they have also acquired several farms in the area, though for tax reasons they are formally owned by a Haymarket subsidiary, Thenhurst Agricultural Ltd.

Local people say Michael Heseltine occasionally stops to talk when passing through the village. He also attends the thirteenth-century Thenford church about twice a year – generally at Easter and Christmas (though he calls himself a 'sort of anxious-to-be-converted agnostic'[20]). After the annual carol service the Heseltines invite the congregation back to the house for festive drinks.

He may have been called 'Michael Philistine' at university, but Heseltine is not a politician one could accuse, in Denis Healey's famous phrase, of having no 'hinterland'. Although he has never taken any interest in literature, and by his own admission is 'not musical',[21] Anne has encouraged an interest in art and architecture. And Thenford gave him a bigger opportunity to pursue his 'obsessions' of gardening and birds.

The pattern was quickly established whereby Anne Heseltine would leave London for Thenford early on Friday, while Michael made every effort to get back to Northamptonshire that night, even if it meant driving – or being driven – from some far-flung political engagement in the early hours of Saturday morning.

'The first thing he'll ask when he comes home,' said Anne Heseltine, 'is, "Have my birds laid any eggs?" He's not a great talker.'[22] Thenford was soon the site of an impressive aviary of more than 100 species – geese, swans, pheasants and, his favourite, ducks. He couldn't explain his love for ducks, he once said: 'I happen to like the look of the things. I spend a certain amount of time, as a matter of fact, wandering round St James's Park looking at the varieties there . . . It just so happens I find that ducks come top of the list.' He has conceded that there is an obvious conflict with his occasional habit of shooting birds, but confesses to 'a growing disinterest and distaste' for the sport.[23]

The other diversion at Thenford was to restore and develop the gardens, which over the last twenty years have become another Heseltine grand project. If he's remembered for anything in 200 years' time, he hopes it will be for 'one of the greatest arboretums of the second half of the twentieth century . . . I have walked round some of the great arboretums, and think about the guys who planted them in the eighteenth century. Think of the people who will look at mine in the twenty-second century!'[24]

In the garden, Heseltine tends to avoid herbaceous borders, finding them fussy. Instead, he prefers informality – areas of rough grass with trees and shrubs. He's a great believer in taking advice, and over the years he has tapped some of the biggest names in horticulture. The American Lanning Roper was brought in to advise on the design of the garden around the house, and greatly influenced its development. Before he died, in 1983, Roper had moved on to the parkland beyond the formal garden, where there was still a lot of space, and begun to extend the Thenford tree collection. Heseltine also approached the expert Roy Lancaster, who advised that a small valley, then occupied by a series of animal enclosures, could be improved with the presence of water. 'He obviously thought about that,' says Lancaster, 'and created what must be one of the best water-garden features in the country.'[25] Heseltine took out scrub and shrubbery, and dug out a series of pools. These were connected by a stream down the length of the valley, flowing into a large lake at the bottom.

Roy Lancaster, who acted for several years as Heseltine's consultant on tree-planting, describes him as a 'great admirer of the sort of trees you need space for – parkland trees, trees of ultimately noble proportion – and therefore he loves the oak, he loves the limes . . . He has a very good collection of both, which makes it difficult for people who want to give him something.'[26] Oaks are particularly responsive to the site.

Over the years, Michael Heseltine has searched the world for new exotic species for the arboretum. He treats the project in an almost academic way, seeking out the rarest varieties in the hope that scientists might one day find his collection useful. He acquires many of them as gifts: on a ministerial trip to Italy, for instance, he was given some of the trees which had appeared in the Italian display at the Liverpool Garden Festival. Others come from botanic gardens; some come from international seed-exchange systems, or from overseas expeditions which Heseltine occasionally sponsors financially. A black market in seeds exists, but Lancaster says Heseltine 'won't support anything that's not legitimate'.[27]

'The relationship between me and my trees is very clear,' Heseltine says, with a touch of Prince Charles. 'I'm the one who does the talking.'[28] 'It is very much a personal collection,' says another expert he consults, John Simmons, a former curator at Kew Gardens. Simmons adds that Heseltine is especially keen on willows and viburnum, and 'gives individual attention to the trees to the extent of engraving their labels himself'.[29] He does the work meticulously. Originally each of the 3,000 varieties of tree or shrub was logged on a card-index, with details, for example, of where it came from, or how big it was when planted. Recently, Heseltine transferred the information to a computer database which was created specially for him, known as 'Tarzan's Treetops' (privately, Heseltine quite enjoys his nickname). Intriguingly, he has a second program with details of his Cabinet colleagues, and known as 'Politician's Friends'.

Experts agree that the arboretum is now one of the best private collections in the country, especially considering how recently it was established. Heseltine loves showing people round the fifty-acre site, but it's strictly 'invitation only'. He promises one day to write a book about the venture.

But, in cutting back some of Thenford's previous woodland, Heseltine has driven away some of the natural wildlife. This certainly didn't please Lady Summers, who carried on living at Thenford Lodge until her death in 1995, and who had once enjoyed sitting in a tree-hide observing the local badgers.

Anne Heseltine has been an important influence on the design of the garden, especially the formal features. 'She's a guiding light,' says Roy Lancaster. 'There are various areas he'll take you and say, "That was Anne's idea." She is a great fan of Lanning Roper: you can see his influence must have rubbed off on to Anne Heseltine. But on the wider landscape, especially parkland, that's Michael's.'[30]

Anne Heseltine's sense of design, and her love of art and fine antiques, obviously helped when it came to furnishing the house, as did knowledge acquired from taking fine-art courses at the Courtauld Institute and at Christie's, where she even wrote an unpublished thesis about Thenford. Occasionally the Heseltines enjoy driving round the Cotswolds and neighbouring counties, browsing in antique shops and spending lots of money.

Alan Borg, the director of the Victoria & Albert Museum and a friend of the Heseltines, says, 'They have some wonderful things at home: very fine pictures and porcelain. She is personally very interested in art history and she collects books.'[31] Michael Heseltine is a collector, too – of Swansea porcelain, suitably enough, and old English banknotes. According to Christopher White, the director of Oxford's Ashmolean Museum, 'Anne has got very good, very clear tastes. One can see the kind of things she would like. I suppose the art in their house can be attributed a bit more to her than to him, but they discuss things together.'[32] Visitors rarely fail to notice the wall of framed political cartoons of Heseltine, the Margaret Thatcher loo-roll holder, and the Gladstone and Disraeli salt and pepper pots. (In 1996, when Labour complained about the Conservatives' notorious 'Demon Eyes' poster against Tony Blair, Heseltine responded that if he had been the butt of it he would have obtained the artwork and displayed it in his lavatory.) But for many years visitors noticed the lack of books on his extensive shelves.

The Heseltines also commissioned the controversial neoclassical architect Quinlan Terry to build a new summer-house at Thenford, in the Palladian style. 'I thought the flamboyant Corinthian order was appropriate for both of them,' he says.[33] It has a swimming-pool in front, and is a place where the family and their regular guests can relax and escape the telephone.

At one point Anne Heseltine commissioned a detailed ceramic four-foot model of Thenford House for her husband's Christmas present. The model-maker, Hugh Colvin, says, 'It was all hush-hush and I was measuring up the front of the house when Michael Heseltine came out and said, "What are you doing?" He knew she was up to something, but wasn't allowed to ask, so he invited me for a cup of tea, and half an hour later we were wandering round the estate discussing trees.' Later, Colvin did some tree-planting for Heseltine, and also made further models. He recalls telling him about a business project with Wedgwood that he had in mind. 'We were having tea and he was surrounded by red boxes at the time, and he said, "Well, I am the President of the Board of Trade – I'll write you a letter!" When I arrived at Wedgwood, in my grotty van, I was met by no less than five directors.'[34]

In 1979, by which time the children were in their teenage years, Anne Heseltine's artistic interests took her into a business venture with Lady Jane Abdy, an old friend and art dealer. The two set up the Bury Street Gallery in St James's, which specialized in nineteenth-century Continental paintings. Running a London gallery proved to be a time-consuming job, however, and after four years Anne was forced to pull out of the partnership. There were too many other demands which took her away from the capital: the house, ministerial trips abroad, political commitments in Henley, and the family. There were also her continuing equestrian interests.

At Thenford, Anne bred Hanoverian horses. She also joined the local Bicester Hunt, and at one time was chasing foxes several days a week, though her hunting was curtailed after a couple of riding accidents. She still occasionally rides with the Devon and Somerset Staghounds when she goes to stay in the Heseltines' third property, a thatched cottage in the village of Exford, in the heart of the Exmoor National Park.

Anne Heseltine had managed to carve out an independent life away from politics, though she would often join her husband for important occasions. Indeed, Anne's presence is a good yardstick of the significance of an event to Michael Heseltine – she attended the Liverpool bus tour and the Westland resignation press conference, for example. But in the early 1980s she was deeply upset by press reports about Michael's close friendship with the Countess of Shelburne, who was ten years younger than he. The daughter of the Earl of St Germans, she was the wife of another earl, Heseltine's former occasional political adviser Charley Shelburne, though the marriage was effectively over. Although the Shelburnes still lived together, the Earl had a steady girlfriend and the couple had agreed to go their own ways without a formal divorce.

Frances, or 'Fanny', Shelburne was often seen lunching with Heseltine in Waltons Restaurant in Chelsea, and among her family he soon acquired the nickname 'Friendly'. 'I have lunch with him from time to time,' she said, 'and ours is an absolutely straightforward friendship.'[35] She denied any interest in politics. People close to Michael Heseltine say that by the time Lady Shelburne did finally divorce her husband, in 1987, his friendship with her had drawn to a close.

Friends say that at one time Anne Heseltine genuinely feared for her marriage, and was frantic with the thought that her husband might leave her. It would have caused severe problems for the Heseltine investment in Haymarket if he had, since a third of the family's majority stake is in Anne's name. In the last decade, however, Michael and Anne Heseltine's relationship seems to have grown much closer. 'I don't think sexual infidelity is a reason to end a marriage,' she once remarked. 'Of course, if you get a partner who's a philanderer, that's something else again. But who knows why these things happen?'[36]

Towards the end of the 1980s, with the children grown up, Anne Heseltine began taking on new, semi-public, commitments. In 1988, she met Christopher White of the Ashmolean, who was looking for somebody to head the museum's fund-raising committee, as part of the university's Campaign for Oxford. 'It took me six months to persuade her to become chairman . . . and when she agreed it was incredible,' he says.

The next day she went off like a rocket, as it were. She worked really flat out at helping the museum, and during the next three or four years we spoke on the telephone every day. She was extremely dynamic, very helpful, she's got great charm and determination – just the sort of person one needs in fund-raising. I had started to try and do it by myself and got nowhere, as an academic. She knew the right people. She got Michael's advice. It was amusing that he always pretended he did nothing about it, but I knew full well that he did.[37]

Although she had no experience as a fund-raiser, Anne Heseltine's committee collected nearly £10 million in four years. Her connections helped, of course. 'I have learnt that after you have met somebody at a dinner party,' she once revealed, 'you have to move very quickly. A letter must be on their desk within forty-eight hours.'[38] One major Ashmolean development was funded by the charitable family trust run by Tim Sainsbury, her husband's former PPS. The Heseltines also gave money themselves.

Christopher White thrilled Anne by also asking her to do some scholarly work at the museum, updating an outdated catalogue of Dutch and Flemish still-life paintings. As well as having a seat on the Ashmolean governing body, she also acts as a trustee of the Imperial War Museum, for which she chaired the British side of the appeal for the American Air Museum at Duxford in Cambridgeshire. In addition, she has advised the Hayward Gallery, and acts as a trustee of the Oxford University student radio station, Oxygen.

Over the years the Heseltines have been known as great hosts, and they have the resources to welcome people on a grand scale. In the 1970s and 1980s their Belgravia home was the venue for regular drinks parties for friends and political colleagues, though they entertain less frequently in London nowadays.

The prime venue, of course, is Thenford. Quite apart from the two coming-of-age parties, for Annabel and Alexandra, the Heseltines hold grand celebrations at the house each time either of them reaches a new decade. And they regularly have guests for the weekend.

The usual practice is for two or three couples to turn up on Friday night and stay until Sunday afternoon, in the traditional country-house manner. These house guests will be supplemented by others invited simply for lunch or dinner, for which twenty or so people might be present. In summer, lunch is often held out in the Quinlan Terry pavilion. Heseltine invariably takes visitors on a full tour of the garden and arboretum, and they can also entertain themselves by swimming or playing tennis. Saturday afternoon might involve a small expedition – possibly to an interesting church in the vicinity, or to the good second-hand bookshop in the nearby town of Brackley.

Partly due to Anne's work for the Ashmolean, guest lists have a strong academic flavour, with a sprinkling of heads, or former heads, of Oxford colleges, such as Anthony Smith of Magdalen, Lord Windlesham of Brasenose, Asa Briggs, the former provost of Worcester, and Marilyn Butler of Exeter, whose husband, David, is the distinguished psephologist. Guests from Westminster tend to be politically congenial, and of Cabinet rank – Geoffrey Howe, Douglas Hurd, William Waldegrave, Tom King and Roy Jenkins, for example. Thatcherite visitors are rare. And notably absent are the several MPs who are regarded as Michael Heseltine's closest political allies. Keith Hampson and Michael Mates have only ever been to Thenford two or three times; one of Mates's visits was to exchange some ducks, a passion he shares with Heseltine. Another lieutenant, Peter Temple-Morris, has never been at all.

Not all visitors to Thenford are successful and distinguished, however. In 1986, at the start of his wilderness period, Heseltine went to see a Youth Training Scheme (YTS) landscaping and reclamation project in Oldham, and on the spur of the moment he invited the teenagers there to come down and visit his own landscaping scheme in Northamptonshire.

The party travelled from Lancashire on a coach paid for by Heseltine himself. It was like visiting another planet for the seventeen trainees, most of whom came from poor and deprived backgrounds. 'Some of them had never been to the other side of Failsworth, never been anywhere,' says one of the organizers, Kenneth Eckersley. 'One girl had on a neatly ironed donkey jacket, because she had no other clothes. The sheer joy on her face was quite touching.' After showing them round the grounds, the Heseltines treated the teenagers to a lavish buffet lunch in the summer-house, and then invited them to spend the afternoon by the pool. When he learnt that nobody had brought any gear, 'Michael sent out for several pairs of swimming trunks,' says Eckersley, 'and they had a fantastic, fabulous time.'[39]

Other visitors have been less welcome – such as the embittered miners who invaded the grounds in October 1996 and dug a large hole in his lawn in protest over pit closures and the spread of open-cast mining.

Michael Heseltine tries to set aside the whole of Saturday and Sunday for life at Thenford; Sunday TV programmes that want to interview him have to take cameras and satellite links to Northampton-shire. There he switches off from the political pressures by gardening and physical labour. 'He just goes very silent on me,' Anne once said, 'and he goes off down the garden and digs or hacks down trees or looks at his beloved birds.'[40] These are solitary activities, of course. So, too, is his other hobby – fishing. They reflect Michael Heseltine's own very private character: he is a man who walks by himself.

None of the Heseltine children has ever really known a time when their father was not a prominent politician. 'He always kissed us goodnight,' says Annabel Heseltine, 'even if, after a late-night sitting in the House, his shadowy presence was announced by the dawn chorus.'[41] Inevitably, it was Anne who bore most of the responsibility of raising them, though the family could afford lots of help. 'She very much laid down the law about how they were brought up,' observes one of Annabel's former teachers. All three children initially attended schools in Oxfordshire, not far from home: Annabel and Alexandra went to Tudor Hall, just outside Banbury, while Rupert went to prep school in Oxford, and then to Harrow.

Annabel used to react badly to taunts about her father's political life. 'I threw the entire contents of a girl's bed out of a first-floor window,' she says of one such occasion, before she learnt to turn the other cheek.[42] She later spent two years in the sixth form at Stowe, the public school in Buckinghamshire. There she found it hard to fit in, and was fairly unpopular for flaunting the family wealth. She would be ferried to and from school by the Heseltine chauffeur rather than be taken by her parents, even though Stowe is barely ten miles from Thenford. And she was also known for her extensive, and expensive, wardrobe – with a particularly costly outfit made for her famous eighteenth-birthday party in 1981, the summer she became a 'deb'. 'She wasn't very sociable,' says one old Stoic. 'I think she felt awkward, and other people were put off because of who she was – and also the dresses, which didn't go down well.' Nor did it make a good impression when the Heseltines appeared to treat Annabel's housemistress as if she were the family maid.

Annabel's greatest impact at Stowe was on the stage; and if Michael Heseltine couldn't see her in a proper performance he would try to get to a rehearsal. He was especially keen that Annabel should follow him to read PPE at Oxford, but when the university turned her down she read economic history at Durham instead. During her student days and early twenties Annabel was an outrageous self-publicist who had no compunction about exploiting her father's fame. While still a student at Durham she began appearing regularly in the gossip columns, often in the company of 'Hooray Henry' types, and happily exposing generous parts of her body to tabloid photographers.

There was a spot of modelling for Norman Parkinson, and then Annabel landed the post of woman's editor of the *Hong Kong Tatler*, though a later attempt at fashion writing for the *News of the World* prompted one former editor to comment, 'She can spell – that's about all I can say about her.'[43] Said another ex-colleague, 'She was a disaster. On her first day she arrived very late and all her copy had not only to be rewritten but actually typed for her.'[44] Then came a spell with an advertising agency, a bit-part in a low-budget film, a stint on satellite TV, and PR work for various restaurants (which on one occasion involved clambering over an elephant). She now works as a freelance journalist, and her wild days seem to be behind her – though she did recently embarrass her father by writing that she was 'leaning increasingly towards the opinion that legalizing drugs might be the answer'.[45] She didn't just mean cannabis, but hard drugs like heroin, too.

The Heseltines' younger daughter, Alexandra, seems rather more conventional. After taking a fine-arts degree at London University, she spent three years at Christie's, where she met her first fiancé, a former Irish Guards captain who had once been rusticated from Eton. The engagement seems to have been as tempestuous as that of her parents thirty years before; Alexandra called it off twice, before eventually marrying Nicholas Williams, a former barrister who now works in the City. The wedding, in 1993, took place in the church at Marston St Lawrence, the village next to Thenford, and included a Welsh male-voice choir. Michael had tears in his eyes.

Rupert is by far the quietest and least public of the three children. Like his father, he suffered from mild dyslexia at school, to the natural anxiety of his parents. (Indeed, it was the diagnosis for Rupert which led the specialist to suggest that Michael must once have suffered the same problem.) After school, Rupert was initially keen to join the Army (unlike his father) but instead he read business studies at Oxford Polytechnic. After being made redundant by an advertising company in 1992 – they blamed the recession, not him – he was given a job in the family firm, and in 1996 he was appointed head of advertising for *Sky Sports*, a new Haymarket magazine published in association with Sky television.

The Heseltines have always been a close family, and Michael and Anne are proud that, even now the children are grown up, they all still take holidays together. Invariably they go to remote and unspoilt parts of the world – often to islands such as Papua New Guinea, Tobago, Fiji or Tahiti. This is partly to indulge Michael Heseltine's passion for exotic birds and plants. He'll rise before dawn and go out alone with his binoculars, hoping to spot rare species before it gets too hot. He also loves snorkelling and scuba-diving.

All three children still regard Thenford as home, and Annabel and Alexandra both have cottages in the village. At least two of the three are likely to be there at any weekend, and Michael Heseltine treats with especial reverence the family get-together over a traditional Sunday joint. 'Their children are tremendously supportive; they're there when needed and around a lot,' says their neighbour Lady Wardington. 'He totally relaxes in the presence of his children.'[46]

Anne and the family are quick to tease Michael about his political work, and prick any tendency towards pomposity. One evening, when a journalist friend began mocking him for a minor political embarrassment earlier in the day, Anne quickly joined in the ribbing. When she once performed in a pantomime for the Bicester Hunt, she happily delivered several lines which raised great laughs at her husband's expense. None of his children show signs of political ambition, and they have always pretended to be unimpressed by his grand titles or career advances.

When the children were still young, Michael Heseltine complained, somewhat tongue in cheek, of an element of 'them against me'. They were developing into 'minor shop stewards', and one child, he said, was 'a very definite militant' with 'negotiating skills' (Annabel, one suspects). 'But it's very good for one,' he confessed. 'It works as an arrangement . . . I think we're a very happy family.' Then he revealed:

We try to run the family as a sort of democracy – but democracy with an authoritarian streak. Most decisions are discussed, all views are canvassed, and then a decision is made – by me, if I can get away with it.[47]

It sounded familiar.

18. *Stop Heseltine!*

In the summer of 1990 Michael Heseltine must have been pretty fed up. His summer holiday in Tahiti had been curtailed by the recall of Parliament following Saddam Hussein's invasion of Kuwait. Moreover, the confrontation with Iraq seemed likely to drag on for months, and, as Margaret Thatcher stiffened George Bush's resolve to threaten military action against Iraq, her position looked increasingly secure. Surely one could hardly challenge a Prime Minister when the country was about to go to war.

Yet, only a few months earlier, things had been looking bad for Thatcher, and therefore promising for Michael Heseltine. The economy was showing early signs of the 1990–92 recession, while in March Labour took the once safe Tory seat of Mid Staffordshire with a swing of 21.4 per cent – its best by-election result in half a century. Polls suggested that Margaret Thatcher had become the most unpopular Prime Minister since surveys began. With voters in England and Wales about to receive their first poll-tax bills at the start of April, the Tories were expected to suffer further humiliation in the upcoming May local elections.

People who met Heseltine during the early part of 1990 noticed a new spring in his step, as if he felt the Prime Minister's days were numbered. 'One got the sense he was going to challenge Thatcher, because of his body language,' says one of his party officials. 'He had at that time what I call "cocktail-party eyes": he's talking to you, but his eyes are looking to see who else is there.' Once the local elections were over, Heseltine planned to mount a new assault on the poll tax.

Then suddenly it all went wrong again. Heseltine was held at bay, not by good results in the local elections, but by a public-relations coup by the Conservative chairman, Kenneth Baker. In what has ever since been cited as the model of outstanding 'spin-doctoring', Baker and his advisers made an overall triumph out of two excellent Tory results in Westminster and Wandsworth (both councils had issued low poll-tax bills thanks to generous assistance from Whitehall). A net loss of 200 seats was nothing like as bad as the 600 some had predicted. The press swallowed the Central Office line and Michael Heseltine seemed to have missed his chance.

He abandoned his planned speech on the poll tax, but nevertheless went ahead with an attack in the pages of *The Times*. At the time his article was treated as a Heseltine manifesto, but in retrospect his critique seems mild. Tactically, he knew that a call to abolish the poll tax would be treated as a full-frontal attack on Thatcher. So instead he spoke of 'a lingering sense of injustice', and proposed reform. The poll tax should be banded according to income – a modification of the Michael Mates amendment. In another reworking of an old idea, he suggested that councils which spent above certain limits should be subject to re-election – the same proposal the Cabinet had rejected back in 1981.[1] He also argued for a return to the old single-tier county boroughs which, as a junior minister, he'd abolished in 1972, and for directly elected full-time mayors on the American model.

On the BBC's *Question Time* a week after the local-election results he conceded that 'Mrs Thatcher would lead the Conservatives into the next election', and that she would win it; for the next six months Heseltine remained unusually quiet.[2] As the Gulf crisis reinforced the Prime Minister's position, Labour's daunting lead in the polls gradually diminished. At the Conservative conference in Bourne-mouth in October the party seemed to be over the worst, thanks in part to the success of the new Chancellor, John Major, in finally persuading Margaret Thatcher to take Britain into the ERM. Worse still for Heseltine, Major was quickly emerging as a fresh leadership rival, alongside the Foreign Secretary, Douglas Hurd.

Michael Heseltine couldn't decide whether or not he should chal-lenge Thatcher that autumn. In July, over post-dinner drinks late one evening, he had confided to the *Sunday Times* editor, Andrew Neil, that he was 'of a mind' to got for it. 'I've only got one bullet in my gun,' Neil reports him saying. 'I can't afford to miss.'[3] A steady stream of MPs quietly urged him to stand – among them Steven Norris (despite his unfriendly treatment by Heseltine), John Lee, Jerry Hayes, and even the arts minister, David Mellor. But it looked as if their pleas would be in vain. At a lunch at *The Observer* at the end of

October, Heseltine told journalists he had 'spent four hard years building up a position unique in modern British political history. He did not propose to throw it away at this stage.'[4]

Just as fortune had rapidly deserted Michael Heseltine with the spring local elections, so it reappeared very quickly with two unexpected events following the conference. First there was the disastrous loss of the Tory stronghold of Eastbourne in another by-election. Then came the most astonishing thing Sir Geoffrey Howe ever did.

What was perhaps *not* surprising was that Sir Geoffrey should have resigned from the Cabinet. He had long been unhappy with the way Margaret Thatcher ran her government, and was increasingly at odds with her over Europe. In the middle of 1989, Howe had been moved from the Foreign Office to become Leader of the House. It was a humiliating demotion, and he had been placated only with the additional title of Deputy Prime Minister, which Downing Street made abundantly clear *was* only a title.

The immediate cause of Sir Geoffrey's resignation was Thatcher's Commons performance in the wake of a European summit in Rome. Departing from a statement she'd agreed with Howe, she cried 'No! No! No!' to a series of proposals Jacques Delors had made, and condemned the idea of a single European currency. Sir Geoffrey's was the third major resignation in five years (following Heseltine himself and Nigel Lawson), and each time there were similar reasons – the Thatcher style and her hostility to Europe.

Howe had been one of the few Cabinet ministers with whom Heseltine had remained in close touch during the wilderness years. The Howes made occasional trips to Thenford, and the Heseltines had visited the Foreign Secretary's official residence, Dorneywood. Heseltine now told Howe he was still inclined not to stand against Thatcher, but he felt the resignation deserved a response from him, especially since it reflected his own feelings so closely. He adopted an old-fashioned device often used by politicians, though not by him before, of sending a 'letter' to his constituency party. 'The crisis is one of confidence,' he told Peter Owen, his association chairman:

It must be quickly restored. There is only one way to preside over and lead a democratic political party, and that is to pay proper regard to the myriad of opinions and, indeed, prejudices that go to make up its support . . . We cannot countenance the sacrifice of Tory seats, needlessly lost in spite of the effort to win and nurture them.[5]

It was the strongest attack Heseltine had delivered on Thatcher since Westland. Yet, as his supporters later admitted, it was an ill-judged move, hastily concocted while also preparing for an imminent trip to the Middle East. It was widely interpreted as a kite-flying exercise, to test the climate for a challenge. But many ministers were angered by Heseltine's implication that, unlike him, they were all ciphers who had failed to stand up to Thatcher.

Nor had Heseltine reckoned on a reply to his letter. While he was abroad, visiting King Hussein of Jordan and the Israeli Prime Minister, Yitzhak Shamir (a sign of his status overseas), the officers of his local association met at Peter Owen's house just outside Henley. It was unusual for a constituency party to respond to an MP's public letter, and still more uncommon for them to do so under the watchful eye of Central Office, for the Conservative regional agent, Donald Stringer, had also chosen to attend.

Michael Heseltine had not always treated his constituency as a priority. After Westland, for instance, there was some resentment in the local party that it was more than a week before he returned to Henley. 'Everybody talked to him apart from his constituency,' says the Henley association president, Raymond Monbiot. 'He was helicoptering around the country and his constituents felt it was high time he came to speak to them directly. We felt we really needed to have him down here to see where he stood.'[6] Few could complain about Heseltine's record of serving his constituents – he never misses a surgery and he always answers letters – but his commitment doesn't compare, say, with John Major's, whose seat in Huntingdon is even safer.

They didn't take a vote, but the nine Henley officers were against Heseltine's statement by a margin of five to four. Afterwards it would be claimed that Donald Stringer had helped them draft the reply to their MP, though both he and Monbiot deny this. 'The suggestion that he was responsible for the composition of the letter I regarded as an insult,' Monbiot says. 'Stringer behaved impeccably at the meeting. He didn't try to influence it in any way. At one point we asked for an alternative word to go into the script which he then supplied.'[7] The party chairman, Kenneth Baker, says Stringer's presence was 'quite unbeknown to me', but the way the document emerged, and was then treated by the Tory high command, had striking echoes of the famous anti-Heseltine 'material inaccuracies' letter which Margaret Thatcher had persuaded Sir Patrick Mayhew to send during the Westland crisis.[8]

Subsequently, several of the Henley officers were deeply resentful about what had happened. The Henley chairman Peter Owen sorely regretted letting Donald Stringer attend the meeting and felt that he and his colleagues had been manipulated into making a reply that was not necessary. The officers also realized they'd been naïve in not thinking carefully enough about how their wording, which was meant to be neutral, would be interpreted. Where Heseltine's letter had been a lengthy six pages, theirs was terse – a mere ninety-seven words – which made it appear even more of a rebuke. 'This association supports the leadership of the party,' it declared, while adding an apparently balancing point that 'events unfolding in Europe' needed 'discussion and debate'.[9] It was transmitted to Heseltine in the Middle East and then released to the press.

Heseltine's constituency party was understandably divided by conflicting loyalties to its MP and to its leader. The Conservative town mayor of Henley urged him to challenge Thatcher, and one branch official nearly resigned over the way Heseltine had been treated by the party officers. A week later, after meeting their MP, Henley officials issued a second statement saying their first response was 'not intended by them to criticize Mr Heseltine's letter'.[10] By then the damage had been done. Heseltine's hasty missive, followed by his absence abroad, had endangered his careful strategy of not being forced into a leadership challenge.

But if Michael Heseltine had acted foolishly, Downing Street's response was even more crass. It is possible that if Margaret Thatcher's press secretary, Bernard Ingham, had kept his mouth shut she might have survived. In one of his confidential briefings for lobby journalists, around Guy Fawkes Night, Ingham accused Heseltine of lighting the blue touch-paper and running. 'Of all the nails that Ingham inadvertently hammered into his mistress's coffin,' says Nigel Lawson, 'this was the most decisive.'[11] Ingham's version, written with the benefit of hindsight, is that 'I was probably in a minority of one among my friends and colleagues in Number 10 in believing that Mr Heseltine would not fight because he knew he could not win.'[12]

Ingham denies telling Heseltine to 'Put up or shut up', though the words were widely attributed to him and repeated by Conservative newspapers. 'Does He Have The Courage?' asked the *Mail*'s front-page headline.[13] 'If Mr Heseltine fails to throw his cap into the ring,' taunted *The Times*, indelicately, 'he will thoroughly deserve to have it stuffed down his throat.'[14] The Labour front bench joined in.

The pressure on Michael Heseltine to stand had intensified when Thatcher and the party Establishment suddenly brought forward the leadership-election timetable by two weeks, deliberately to bring speculation to a head. He had just eight days to make up his mind. It was almost a test of virility. A sign of how the pressure was affecting him came after the normally sympathetic *Daily Mirror* responded to the Thatcher initiative with the headline '*You* Tarzan, *Me* Clever – Jungle queen Maggie lures Heseltine into leadership poll trap'. 'Tarzan the Tory Ape Man has made a right monkey of himself,' added the paper's editorial.[15] In the Members' Lobby at Westminster, Heseltine loudly berated the story's author, the *Mirror*'s political editor, Alastair Campbell, for swallowing Downing Street's propaganda.

The irony about the rush of events of early November 1990 – the prelude to the great Conservative leadership battle – is that several major players acted in ways that contributed to an outcome they didn't want. Michael Heseltine with his Henley letter, and both Downing Street and Labour's leader, Neil Kinnock, in provoking him, all helped increase the momentum which would ultimately result in Margaret Thatcher's replacement by John Major.

In Israel, Michael Heseltine had merely reiterated his line that he expected Margaret Thatcher to lead the Tories to victory at the next election. 'I have said it so often that I am embarrassed to repeat it.'[16] And Heseltine had good reason to be embarrassed, for by the time he returned from the Middle East the possibility of a challenge had turned from unlikely to probable. It seemed like 'now or never'.

The rules governing Conservative Party leadership elections are complicated. The electorate is comprised entirely of Conservative MPs, and to win outright on a first ballot a candidate needs a majority of 15 per cent of those entitled to vote (unlikely for a challenger against the party leader). Other candidates can also join the contest if the first ballot is inconclusive, though in later rounds only an absolute majority is needed to win. The opportunities for bluff and deception are enormous, and the dynamics of the whole process are complex. Heseltine's advisers were deeply divided over what he should do. Between them, they saw three possible scenarios.

The other astonishing aspect to the events of 1990 was that nobody within the Heseltine team was really pushing him to stand. His two closest aides, Keith Hampson and Michael Mates, both wanted him to keep his powder dry. If Thatcher staggered on she might be forced out by the summer of 1991, by the simple pressure of events. They felt that whenever Michael Heseltine stood he would probably get only one shot, but feared that if it was now, then Thatcher might beat him. Even if he wounded her sufficiently to make her stand down after the first ballot, he would then inevitably have to face other contenders. It was possible, though, that Heseltine's early momentum might carry him through, just as Thatcher's had in 1975. But the danger was that, in wielding the dagger, Heseltine would subsequently be handicapped by the charge of disloyalty.

Over the next few days he and his lieutenants frantically canvassed MPs as to whether he should now stand. (This wasn't always helpful: some supporters of Douglas Hurd or John Major urged Heseltine to stand so that he would act as a 'stalking-horse' for their man.)

The better scenario, from Heseltine's standpoint, was to find a stalking-horse of his own, although this would require a more substantial figure than Sir Anthony Meyer. If an initial challenger could wound Thatcher so gravely that she was forced to quit, then Heseltine could enter the fray and slug it out with other top-rank contenders on more equal terms. Suggested stalking-horses included Heseltine's old Oxford friend Sir Peter Tapsell and the Westbury MP Sir Dennis Walters. Both were highly respected at Westminster, but neither was a public figure.

The most obvious stalking-horse, of course, was the man who had just resigned as Deputy Prime Minister. Sir Geoffrey Howe was always more ambitious than was generally realized, but he had already told Heseltine he had no intention of standing against Thatcher. Instead, he did something almost as damaging.

It was not Sir Geoffrey's style to hold a dramatic resignation press conference. Instead, he waited almost two weeks to make a statement to the Commons. It was the best speech of his life, and one of the most devastating parliamentary interventions of modern times, though Thatcher called it a mixture of 'bile and treachery'.[17] Mocking the Central Office line that his departure was over 'questions of style', he related his increasing disagreement with the Prime Minister on European policy. To growing gasps, he concluded:

I have done what I believe to be right for my party and my country. The time has come for others to consider their own response to the tragic conflict of loyalties with which I have myself wrestled for perhaps too long.[18]

His closing words were interpreted by Margaret Thatcher and most other observers as a call to Heseltine. Howe himself has always said they were directed at remaining Cabinet ministers, and an attempt to make Thatcher think again; he didn't expect anybody to oppose her. Although the two ex-ministers had kept in contact, when Heseltine rushed back from an engagement in Germany especially to hear Sir Geoffrey, he had no warning of what he might say. It came as much of a surprise to him as it did to everyone else. But he knew the implications immediately. 'Well, I've got to go, haven't I?' he reportedly remarked.[19]

That evening Cecil Parkinson held a pre-arranged meeting with Heseltine in a room at the Commons. It was a final effort to dissuade him. 'Cecil, she is finished,' Parkinson relates Heseltine responding. 'After Geoffrey's speech she's finished.'[20]

The timing was not of Michael Heseltine's choosing, but he'd been pushed into it, by friend and foe. Ideally, he would have waited until Thatcher was forced out by the pressure of events. Yet now it was *he* who was being pressurized. If Heseltine didn't stand he'd be for ever taunted as the man who'd been frightened. He'd blown it, Bernard Ingham and Neil Kinnock would no doubt say: he was a busted flush. Later that evening the two Michaels, Heseltine and Mates, met in Chapel Street to draft his fateful announcement.

344

It was delivered to expectant reporters and cameramen on the steps of his home the following morning. With Anne at his side, her fingers crossed, Michael Heseltine declared he would be a contender for the leadership: 'I am persuaded that I would now have a better prospect than Mrs Thatcher of leading the Conservatives to a fourth electoral victory.'[21]

In interviews that day, Heseltine had some explaining to do. The 'unforeseen circumstances', he said, were Sir Geoffrey Howe's resignation. Yet only the previous week – *after* Howe had resigned – he'd been repeating his line that he expected Margaret Thatcher to lead her party into the election. But now more than 100 MPs had urged him to stand, he said, and others were flocking to his cause by the hour. He also placed great emphasis on polls which suggested that he was best placed to win back voters who had deserted the Tories.

The secret ballot would take place six days later. There were 372 Conservative MPs entitled to vote, and the 15 per cent rule meant that either candidate would need a margin of 56 votes to win on the first round.

Histories of the first part of the 1990 leadership election naturally focus on the shortcomings of the Thatcher campaign. Many Tory MPs were never spoken to by the Prime Minister's team, or, if they were, it was so obliquely that they did not realize they were being canvassed. And the leadership camp is always susceptible to lies or misleading answers. Steven Norris, one of the MPs privately urging Heseltine to stand, was asked if Thatcher could count on him. 'Absolutely no problem,' Norris says he told her PPS, Peter Morrison. ' "Jolly good", he said, "that's another one." '[22] Thatcher's official campaign manager, George Younger, was diverted by duties in Edinburgh with the Royal Bank of Scotland. And Peter Morrison was so complacent about the result that Alan Clark found him snoozing in his office on the afternoon before polling.

Yet her opponent's campaign, too, was ill-prepared. When Heseltine spoke of having more than 100 supporters, it was probably true, yet until the last few days there had been no list: the names were simply stored in Heseltine's head. At various points over the previous few years, both his *chef de cabinet*, Michael Mates, and Keith Hampson had begged him to start mapping out where his likely support lay.

Heseltine feared that if anything were put on paper the fact would cause fatal damage if it leaked. It was a sign of just how cautious he was during the wilderness period. Whenever MPs had urged him to stand against Thatcher, Heseltine would regularly stress that the idea was theirs not his; he made no inducements to them or promises. His constant fear was being set up by a Thatcher *agent provocateur*.

Once the campaign started, however, Heseltine's private intelligence poured forth from his memory in astonishing detail: who had whispered what to him, and when, and whose constituencies he had visited. Michael Mates then drew up a chart in the new election headquarters in Victoria Street, marking MPs with blue or red pins depending on whether they were supporters or not.

Heseltine had all the momentum, especially having canvassed dozens of MPs the previous weekend. But the calibre of his team was remarkably poor. There was obviously no question of securing ministerial supporters, let alone matching Thatcher's proposer and seconder – Douglas Hurd and John Major – but there was no shortage of *former* ministers languishing on the back benches. Heseltine tried to get David Howell, who had urged him to stand, to nominate him, but Howell thought their differences on Europe might be embarrassing. Geoffrey Howe wouldn't act as a proposer, as he didn't want his resignation to be dismissed as an attempt to catapult Heseltine into the leadership. Peter Walker would doubtless have obliged, but his support would have deterred votes from the right.

In the end, Heseltine was proposed by Sir Neil Macfarlane, his junior sports minister from DoE days. He was seconded by Sir Peter Tapsell, an anti-monetarist Euro-sceptic who had always been disappointed not to get government office. Macfarlane's move caused particular distress in Downing Street since he had played a leading part in Thatcher's election in 1975 and was a long-standing golfing chum of Denis's.

Macfarlane convened the daily Heseltine campaign meetings, the first of which was held after the ten o'clock vote on the evening that battle was declared. They were held in Committee Room J in the House of Commons basement – Guy Fawkes territory – the same room that Willie Whitelaw's team had used in their unsuccessful battle against Thatcher fifteen years before. The candidate himself

didn't always attend the meetings; they were chaired either by Macfarlane or by Sir Dennis Walters.

Heseltine's main day-to-day organization was run by Michael Mates
and Keith Hampson, though MPs say they weren't the ideal choice
for winning over parliamentary support. 'Neither counted for a bean
here,' says one of their campaign colleagues. Other key players were
Peter Temple-Morris and William Powell, who, like Michael Mates,
had both been drawn to Heseltine over Westland and also liked what
he'd been saying on Europe.

Hampson concentrated on policy presentation, ghosting newspaper
articles, preparing a speech for Heseltine for a by-election rally in
Paisley, and thinking through answers for broadcast interviews. Mates
spent much of his time handling the press, though he was perhaps
not the best person to do this. He's 'too much of a thug', says another
from the Heseltine team. 'While he can be very charming, he can also
be very aggressive, especially with journalists.' Peter Tapsell did TV
interviews, along with Peter Temple-Morris, whose lighter touch
made him ideal for the more knockabout broadcasts. Other activists
included Quentin Davies, Anthony Nelson and John Lee. Lee had
been a junior minister with Heseltine at Defence, but later resigned
to concentrate on his seat in Pendle, which he thought was at risk
because of the poll tax.

William Powell acted as a kind of whip for the operation, gathering
intelligence around the Commons. He had an encyclopaedic knowledge of his parliamentary colleagues, and, having been elected in
1983, was especially good on the newer, younger, members – an area
where the team was notably weak.

On policy, Heseltine's shrewdest move was to commit himself to
'an immediate and fundamental review of the poll tax', the prime
cause of the government's unpopularity, which imperilled so many
seats.[23] Thatcher was obviously more constrained than Heseltine, and
when she raised the idea of holding a referendum on a single European
currency it only fuelled the charge that she made policy on the hoof.
Heseltine firmly rejected the referendum proposal:

That's the way Harold Wilson got out of his difficulties over Europe. I don't
believe you can put the issue of a single currency, with all the sophistications

347

and complications, and the impossibility of designing a question of that sort, to the people.[24]

Even before his challenge to Thatcher, Heseltine had shown signs of toning down his earlier enthusiasm for EMU. 'No one knows whether the economies of Western Europe can be so linked together that confidence would permit a single currency,' he had said.[25] Moreover, he reassured people, it would not be an issue for another ten years or more: the decision would not have to be made until 'perhaps three parliaments from now'.[26]

Thatcher's most powerful intervention came during an interview with the editor of *The Times*. Her opponent would 'jeopardize all I have struggled to achieve', she warned, while jabbing a finger at passages from Heseltine's writings:

If you read Michael Heseltine's book, you will find it more akin to some of the Labour Party policies: intervention, corporatism, everything that pulled us down. There is a fundamental difference on economics and there's no point in trying to hide it. Those of us who sat with Michael on economic discussions remember full well . . . Look, you've seen the crumbling of the more extreme forms of that philosophy in the Soviet Union.[27]

Thatcher's vituperative comments backfired badly, making *her* look the extremist, and not Heseltine. They were 'misjudged' and 'damaging', says Kenneth Baker.[28] Heseltine's obvious retort was to ask why Thatcher had employed him as a minister for more than six years if his views were so outlandish.

Although he had habitually distanced himself from Westminster before, Michael Heseltine now spent hours roaming the corridors and approaching MPs (though his aides feared there were many he didn't recognize). 'Michael stands in the centre of the Members' Lobby,' Alan Clark wrote in his diary, 'virtually challenging people to wish him good luck. He gives snap "updates" to journalists, and greets suppliants who are brought along for a short audience by his team. The heavier targets he sees in his room.'[29] 'It was virtually impossible not to meet him at least two or three times a day,' says Cecil Parkinson.[30] The Prime Minister, in contrast, was so confident of winning that she spent the last thirty-six hours before the ballot at a summit meeting in Paris. It was there, on 20 November, that she heard the news that was to spell the end.

Margaret Thatcher secured 204 votes in the first ballot, on 20 November, compared with 152 for Michael Heseltine. Though apparently a good majority, sixteen abstentions meant it was four votes short of the necessary 15 per cent margin. Within minutes, the Prime Minister emerged from the British embassy in Paris to confirm she'd stay in the fight.

This was excellent news for Heseltine. His team were confident that dozens of MPs would switch next time, when only a straight majority was needed to win. Many members – particularly ministers – had voted for Thatcher out of loyalty, but some made it clear that they had now fulfilled their obligations. Nominations for the second round had to be in by midday on Thursday, forty-two hours later. The Heseltine camp were now in the rather strange situation of hoping that Thatcher would hold on. While she remained, other candidates such as Douglas Hurd and John Major, who would be harder to beat, would stay out of the contest out of loyalty to her.

The following day, Wednesday, Margaret Thatcher returned from Paris and reiterated in Downing Street, 'I fight on. I fight to win.'[31] The Heselteenies, as they'd become known, couldn't hide their delight. Alan Clark wrote how 'that mad ninny Hampson is dancing around on his tippy-toes calling out to passers-by, "Tee-hee, she's standing. We've made it. We can't lose now, etc." '[32] But by late afternoon, it was clear that MPs were deserting the Prime Minister in significant numbers. As she met her Cabinet one by one that evening, she suffered what she later called 'treachery with a smile on its face'.[33] Only a handful of ministers pledged their unqualified support. This was now bad news for Heseltine.

The intriguing and paradoxical question is whether Michael Heseltine could have done anything to persuade Thatcher to stay in the fight. Perhaps his campaign should have arranged for some supporters to announce that, while they had backed him in the first round, the interests of party unity dictated that they support the leader next time. It would have been difficult to pull off, and highly Machiavellian, but deviousness is what leadership elections are all about. A more realistic course might have been to remind people of the precarious nature of Heseltine's first-round support. Many people in the first ballot had voted tactically – not so much *for* Heseltine, as *against* Thatcher – knowing that other candidates might join the contest in round two. These tactical voters might easily have returned to Thatcher once it was clear she refused to quit and there would be no alternatives on offer. Had the drift of opinion looked at all ambiguous – or been presented as such – then Thatcher might have been persuaded to battle on.

In fact some Thatcherites have since alleged that the Heseltine camp actually tried to build up momentum by getting people to say they were switching from Thatcher to Heseltine when in fact they had been his supporters all along. Nobody has ever produced any hard evidence that his team did this, but if they did it was highly foolish. What is clear is that Michael Heseltine's forces hadn't thought out their tactics properly.

In particular, they damaged his cause by some of the things they said. For instance, Heseltine managers reminded the press that it needed only eighteen MPs to desert Thatcher for her to lose her majority. Some of the most unhelpful comments came from the men who were meant to be Heseltine's main strategists. 'We have the momentum going for us,' declared Neil Macfarlane.[34] 'I have taken soundings,' said Michael Mates, 'and there are MPs who supported Margaret Thatcher in the first round who will support us now . . . the tide is moving our way.'[35] No doubt there was some euphoria at the thought that they would finally topple Thatcher, but this was the worst moment to sound triumphant. While there was a possibility that Thatcher might withdraw, the Heselteenies should have done everything to convince the Prime Minister that she still had a chance of winning. The time to build momentum was *after* nominations had closed, when the contest had been confirmed as another two–horse race between Heseltine and Thatcher.

On the Wednesday night, Michael Heseltine told his colleagues to keep their fingers crossed that Thatcher didn't drop out on the following day. So long as she remained in the contest, he rightly felt he'd win. But the Prime Minister was slowly reaching her decision to step down. The clinching argument came not from her closest allies but from Cabinet members on the left, including Chris Patten,

Kenneth Clarke and Malcolm Rifkind. They persuaded her that she would almost certainly lose to Heseltine if she fought on, while William Waldegrave warned that 'It would be a catastrophe if corporatist policies took over.'[36]

The following morning Michael Heseltine heard the historic news on his car radio while travelling to a tree-planting ceremony at London Zoo. His heart sank. He later admitted it was the moment he knew he'd lost.

The second critical decision – which Geoffrey Howe believes ended Heseltine's chances – was taken around the Cabinet table later that morning. After she had tearfully delivered her resignation statement, the Prime Minister extracted an agreement from her colleagues to 'Stop Heseltine'. Cabinet members would work to ensure that she was succeeded by one of themselves, and both John Major and Douglas Hurd were soon confirmed as candidates. (The theory was that Heseltine would suffer more defections if MPs faced more choice.) 'The unity of the party is crucial,' Kenneth Baker quotes Thatcher as saying, 'and that's why I am giving up. I couldn't bear all the things I have stood for over the past eleven years being rejected. The Cabinet must unite to stop Michael Heseltine.'[37]

It is striking how her wishes met with no dissent. The Education Secretary, Kenneth Clarke, for instance, was no Thatcherite, but he willingly complied with the 'Stop Heseltine' understanding. Though the two men shared similar views, especially on Europe (and a common interest in bird-watching), they had never been close personally. Like many ministers, Clarke thought a Heseltine leadership would be highly divisive. 'I couldn't see how he could be leader. For the regicide to take over the leadership, not only would it not have won the election but it would have taken years to put the pieces back together again.'[38]

In reality, only two or three Cabinet members were potential Heseltine supporters in the second round. The Defence Secretary, Tom King, had been the guest of honour at Alexandra Heseltine's lavish coming-of-age party in 1986, and Heseltine had once told a friend that King would be his campaign manager when he eventually stood for the leadership. But King was deeply upset with Heseltine for provoking a leadership election when British troops were about to go to war in the Gulf. 'I had my own responsibilities, and it wasn't helpful,' he says. 'It was also quite clear after the trauma of Margaret Thatcher's departure that it would have been enormously divisive within the party if Michael Heseltine had taken over the leadership.'[39]

Heseltine made a brief effort to persuade King to nominate him, but by then the Defence Secretary had already agreed to propose Douglas Hurd. Heseltine also approached Cecil Parkinson, who, despite their long friendship, now made it clear he could hardly lend his support, since he had just spent several days explaining why Heseltine *shouldn't* be Prime Minister. Another of whom Heseltine had high hopes was the Chief Secretary to the Treasury, Norman Lamont, who'd been one of his junior ministers at Defence. Lamont certainly admired some of Heseltine's more right-wing populist features and thought his interventionist streak could ultimately be contained. Alan Clark even reports Lamont saying at the time 'that he could conceive of Michael as being quite an "effective", *tolerable* (sic) Prime Minister' (Clark's emphasis).[40] (In contrast, Thatcher quotes Lamont as telling her that Heseltine would jeopardize 'everything we had achieved on industry and Europe'.)[41] But, instead, Lamont became John Major's campaign manager, though they had never been great friends; he may have calculated (quite correctly) that he had a good chance of succeeding him as Chancellor if Major was elevated to the premiership.

The fact was that very few of the 1990 Cabinet had ever had close dealings with Heseltine, or knew him very well. Only four – Hurd, King, Parkinson and Wakeham – had sat with him round the Cabinet table for more than a few weeks. Generally people who work with Michael Heseltine come to admire and respect him (although there are exceptions – including several defence chiefs). Those who see him only from afar tend to be more suspicious.

In the end Michael Heseltine recruited only one Cabinet member to his cause, and then it may have been by accident. David Hunt shared his views on Europe and was already pursuing an interventionist economic strategy as Secretary of State for Wales. Hunt also admired Heseltine's past work on Merseyside, where he was a local MP. He had been absent from Thatcher's farewell Cabinet meeting, on a ministerial trip to Japan, and therefore wasn't aware of the 'Stop Heseltine' pledge.

When Thatcher heard that David Hunt might be backing Heseltine, she rang him at home to ask if it was true. He confirmed that it was. Thatcher pointed out that it was against the Cabinet agreement, and when Hunt claimed that he knew nothing about such a decision she told him to phone Heseltine and ask to be released from his pledge. She would ring back in twenty minutes. Hunt duly called Heseltine and explained what Thatcher had said, adding that he didn't want to withdraw, and didn't expect to be released. Heseltine confirmed that he would not let him go. When Peter Morrison rang back on Thatcher's behalf, the Welsh Secretary explained why he was sticking with Heseltine. He now wanted the next strongest leader after Thatcher, whom Hunt claimed – to the surprise of many MPs – to have supported in the first ballot.

Almost a third of the parliamentary Conservative Party were the so-called payroll vote – either ministers or PPSs – and the immediate effect of the Cabinet agreement was to consolidate the bulk of this block against Heseltine. Its members looked upon him as an 'outsider', and he had done himself no favours by his constant implication that ministers had let themselves be bullied by Thatcher (especially since there was some truth in it). On one occasion he had begun a *Wogan* interview by retelling the famous *Spitting Image* joke about Thatcher ordering dinner with the rest of her Cabinet. 'The vegetables, Prime Minister?' a waiter asks. 'Oh yes, they'll all have the same.'[42]

With the multiple crises of Margaret Thatcher's resignation, the Gulf conflict, and the government's unpopularity, these were uncertain times; ministers felt that Heseltine might put everything in jeopardy – not least their individual jobs (though he promised to keep both John Major and Douglas Hurd in their existing posts). There was also a collective sense of Cabinet guilt that it had been their advice which finally persuaded Thatcher to quit.

Only five ministers openly backed Heseltine, three of them from the Welsh Office – David Hunt and his two deputies, Sir Wyn Roberts and Ian Grist. The environment minister, David Trippier, who was also deputy chairman of the Conservative Party, quickly became an active member of the campaign, doing TV interviews and canvassing MPs on lists supplied by Heseltine. The most surprising ministerial recruit was Edward Leigh, a staunch Thatcherite who'd held office for only three weeks.

Michael Heseltine had more success with past members of the government – winning eleven former Cabinet ministers, including the three men who between them had run the Treasury and the Foreign Office for most of the Thatcher premiership. Sir Geoffrey Howe not only issued a detailed press statement as to why he backed Heseltine, but also obtained the support of Nigel Lawson and the former Foreign Secretary Lord Carrington (though he had no vote). Lawson's support was perhaps the most unexpected, given his obvious differences with Heseltine over economic policy. Together the three grandees deliberately timed their announcements for the Sunday papers, but by then it was probably too late. Other ex-Cabinet supporters included Peter Walker, David Howell, Sir Ian Gilmour, Norman Fowler, Geoffrey Rippon, Jim Prior, Norman St John–Stevas and Paul Channon (to whom Heseltine is said to have made noises about the Speakership of the Commons). The Heseltine camp also had Edward Heath down as one of theirs, though the former leader never disclosed publicly how he voted.

Heseltine's success in enlisting so many of the old guard illustrated the generational bias of his appeal. Many of his voters were of his age, and had sat with him in the Commons since the 1960s. A study by Philip Cowley of Hull University shows that on average Heseltine supporters were two years older than Major voters, and had been MPs for about sixteen years, compared with twelve years for those who backed Major.[43] In his youth Heseltine had faced most criticism from older, long-serving Tories who disapproved of his past misjudgements. Now the situation was transformed: Heseltine's backing was strongest among the older MPs – people from his generation (many of whom had been around to witness the 1976 mace incident).

Overall, however, Heseltine hadn't done enough advance preparation to win a majority of his parliamentary colleagues. The former MP Robert Hayward, a shrewd observer of his fellow Tories, believes he did far too little, either before or during the campaign, to court the so-called 'tea-room vote' – non-ideological middle-of-the-road MPs like himself – and to reassure people who had doubts about his character. 'There was this disdain for members in the tea-room and the dining-room which was crucial,' Hayward says. John Major, in contrast, was an assiduous tea-room attender, as one might expect of a former whip. So, too, was Douglas Hurd. Hayward was also surprised that in the first round 'the Heseltine team didn't do anything to persuade me to vote for their man'. It was especially strange, he says, 'when it must have been common knowledge to supporters of Michael Heseltine that I had been critical of Mrs Thatcher. I ultimately abstained.'[44]

It seems odd that a man who had been standing in elections all his life should be so detached from the voters who could deliver the ultimate prize. Despite the investment which Heseltine had made in running for the post, precious little thought had been given to the mechanics of a leadership bid, or to what was needed to be successful. For a politician who prided himself on efficiency, good management and first-class organization, Heseltine's 1990 campaign was remarkably haphazard.

'It was not a military operation,' admits William Powell, who says the team were 'all amateurs'. Typically, in business or politics, Heseltine has always excelled at marshalling his forces to deliver a quick hit – from the launch of *Accountancy Age* to the writing of *Where There's a Will*. Heseltine had been contemplating this moment for five years, if not forty-five: one would have expected him to be better prepared. 'There was a degree of chaos,' Powell recalls, 'with no kind of structure. Dennis Walters and Neil Macfarlane told Michael, "You've got to organize this a bit more." '[45]

The canvassing of party grandees and former Cabinet ministers was left to Heseltine himself (with a little help from Geoffrey Howe), and only he ever had a complete idea of how things were going. If anyone dared ask Heseltine how the grandees had responded, he tended merely to say, 'It's looking good.' William Powell says that Heseltine created the impression that 'this was a great man, and you could not tell him what to do'.[46]

There were other handicaps, too. His chief strategist, Michael Mates, was absent for five days – Thursday to Monday – on a trip to the Middle East with the Defence Select Committee, which he chaired. And Heseltine's camp also seemed to lack the camaraderie and team spirit evident among those working for John Major, who were based at a house in Gayfere Street, near the Commons. Major's team comprised several overlapping circles, such as Treasury people, the

Cambridge Union set, and the East Anglian mafia, which all helped when it came to pulling in further votes. The Heseltine forces, in contrast, merely seemed to be a group of individuals and misfits – 'the dispossessed and the never possessed', to borrow a term John Major later used in a different context. Many, like Neil Macfarlane, had lost their jobs as ministers, or, like Peter Tapsell, had clearly deserved ministerial office but had always been denied it. His aides didn't always get along either: the two main players, for instance, Keith Hampson and Michael Mates, were not great friends. There was no sense of the Heseltine campaign being a joint effort in which people could say, if only privately, 'It was me who advised him to do that.' Nor did Heseltine appear very grateful for help. Several of his team note that they were never properly thanked, even though in some cases they took great risks and upset their local parties. 'He was a very cold person to work for,' says one MP.

Heseltine's voters tended to be more public-school-educated, more university-educated and more Oxbridge than Major supporters. As one might expect, Heseltine gained strong backing from MPs on the Conservative left, winning 80 per cent of those whom Philip Cowley terms as 'wet', and 40 per cent of his 'damp' category, but together these groups comprised less than a fifth of the parliamentary party.[47] 'The most important issue driving voting', says Cowley, was Europe. Pro-Europeans were far more inclined to back Heseltine, while John Major picked up most of those who would now be called Euro-sceptics.[48]

Yet, significantly, Heseltine also won the backing of several right-wingers, though they tended to be of the populist type. Some, such as Tony Marlow and John Wilkinson, had grown disillusioned with Thatcher, and supported Heseltine in the first round. Others were Thatcherites who, having supported her to the bitter end, now saw him as the best person to continue her decisive style of leadership. In some cases they were people who refused to vote for anyone from the Cabinet since they suspected senior ministers of a coup in persuading Thatcher to go. At least Heseltine had 'stabbed her in the front', said Edward Leigh, who had first worked with the former Defence Secretary fighting CND in the pro-nuclear Coalition for Peace Through Security. Other right-wing switchers included Jill Knight,

James Pawsey, John Carlisle, Michael Brown (the recipient of plant cuttings from Thenford) and David Evans.

Evans, the blunt-speaking former chairman of Luton Town Football Club, said he wanted 'someone who can restore the morale of the party. Someone who understands the economy.'[49] He also admired the fact that Heseltine was a successful entrepreneur, just like himself. (Indeed, Evans had been among the first to bid for the privatized council refuse contracts which Heseltine had pioneered in the early 1980s.) The MP played an active role in the Heseltine campaign, but came under enormous pressure to switch to John Major, including twenty minutes of arm-twisting by Thatcher in her room.

For a while after Thatcher's resignation the expectation had been that Heseltine's momentum from the first ballot might just carry him through. But, within hours of declaring his candidacy, John Major had seized the initiative. By that evening his camp already claimed the support of 130 MPs.

John Major cleverly portrayed himself as the man who had worked his way up from poverty, and he pledged himself to create 'a classless society' (even if this was pretty bogus, since his children went to a mediocre private school instead of the first-class comprehensive in Huntingdon). His remarks seemed primarily to be directed at the Old Etonian Douglas Hurd, who had to protest that his father had been a mere 'tenant farmer'; but his class strategy also damaged Heseltine, who was by far the wealthiest of the three, and the only one with a country mansion. It was not Heseltine's wisest move, therefore, when he held a 'photo opportunity' in the grounds of Thenford for the second weekend in succession. The image of the patrician, wealthy, landed Tory did not play well against that of the meritocratic boy from Brixton.

Major also succeeded in trumping both of Heseltine's best cards. First he quickly matched his pledge to review the poll tax. Then, to general surprise, he managed to emulate Heseltine's potential as an election-winner. A series of eight polls over the weekend before the second ballot all suggested that Major would do almost as much to restore Conservative popularity as Heseltine. It was a remarkable turnabout, given that just two weeks before fewer than one in twenty voters had named Major as their preferred Tory leader.

357

These polls finally scuppered any chance Michael Heseltine might have had. 'Not so many in the party really want to vote for Heseltine, for himself,' wrote Alan Clark. 'The bulk of Michael's support comes from his so-called election-winning powers. People have guilt about condoning what he did to Her. Once they have a real reason to do so, they'll abandon him.'[50] The polls now provided that reason. The challenger who'd long thrived on popularity ratings was ultimately thwarted by them.

Also important was the anger in the constituencies about Margaret Thatcher's demise. Michael Heseltine might have spent years courting local parties with his speaking engagements, but many grass-roots activists were deeply upset that his challenge should have ousted the Prime Minister, and they also worried about his likely effect on Tory unity. A survey of local party opinion showed that an overwhelming 485 associations backed Major, compared with just 65 for Heseltine (and 22 for Hurd). Such strength of feeling must have influenced wavering MPs. Members who came out openly for Heseltine took some risk with their local parties, and several subsequently faced attempts to deselect them, including Michael Mates, Julian Critchley (who played no part in his campaign), Ivor Stanbrook, Cyril Townsend, Emma Nicholson, Charles Wardle and the right-winger Barry Porter.

In addition, Margaret Thatcher herself exerted great personal pressure on MPs, telling those who were tempted to vote for Heseltine where their true loyalties should lie. Her heaviest cajoling was reserved for ministers. They were firmly reminded who it was who had given them a government job and kept them there, and in some cases who had got them their seats originally. Forced to admit their debt, ministers were told they could now repay Thatcher by voting for her preferred successor, John Major.

The outcome was clear well before the result was declared. 'It's slipping away,' Heseltine told one of his team on the day of polling. The final tally was:

John Major	185
Michael Heseltine	131
Douglas Hurd	56

Of the 204 MPs who had voted for Thatcher in the first ballot, one study calculates that almost three-quarters – around 150 – switched to Major. No more than 20 Thatcher votes are reckoned to have transferred to Heseltine. And of Heseltine's original 152, 40 or so deserted him: around 11 are thought to have gone to Hurd, and 30 to Major. 'It was the switchers from Heseltine who helped create the decisive lead,' concludes the politics professor Philip Norton.[51] The switchers included some of those who had originally pressed Michael Heseltine to stand: Jerry Hayes and David Mellor both moved to Major, for instance, while Steven Norris preferred Hurd.

John Major was two votes short of the necessary 187 needed for an outright majority, but neither of his opponents was going to quibble. Michael Heseltine heard the news by telephone, and as soon as it was announced on television a few seconds later, he and Anne went out on to the doorstep of Chapel Street to address the cameras. Heseltine congratulated John Major, and announced he was withdrawing in his favour. As she watched her husband, Anne looked devastated.

When Michael Heseltine stepped back inside his front door, a poetry book was waiting for him. His children had laid it open at a verse by the Victorian poet Arthur Hugh Clough: 'Say not the struggle naught availeth.'

19. *Here We Go Again*

A week after the result was announced, Conservatives gathered to anoint John Major. He was already Prime Minister but this was his formal coronation as Tory leader, and every member of the parliamentary party, together with peers, MEPs and other party big-wigs, was invited. The ceremony took place in the Queen Elizabeth II Conference Centre at Westminster, a project Michael Heseltine had initiated when Major was still an unknown back-bencher. As the defeated man sat watching, it must have hurt. The new leader had been only a Lambeth councillor when Heseltine first became a minister, and an obscure parliamentary under-secretary when he walked out of Cabinet over Westland.

Michael Heseltine had impressed people – not least John Major and his supporters – with his generosity after the result. 'We are about to see the dawn of a new era of Conservative administration,' he had declared, as he congratulated the new Prime Minister from his Chapel Street doorstep.[1] But what if that administration had been his?

Heseltine's overriding consideration would have been to restore party unity. His position would have had few precedents. Not since Andrew Bonar Law in 1922 had a Prime Minister come straight from the back benches, and in Law's case he had previously served ten years as Tory leader. Even Winston Churchill in 1940 had spent the first eight months of the war as First Lord of the Admiralty. Compared with John Major, it would have been far more difficult for Heseltine to claim the mandate of the last election, since he had been on the back benches at the time. Some friends say that, like Anthony Eden on assuming the leadership in 1955, Heseltine would have held an election as soon as possible, though Christmas and the looming war in the Gulf would have made timing difficult. One possibility would have been the first Thursday in January, with a short campaign break over Christmas, though a more probable date would have been March, once the Gulf conflict was over. Heseltine would have faced accusations of cashing in on the success of the war, but then the most famous 'khaki election' was held by his great hero, David Lloyd George, in 1918, after the First World War.

The personnel of a Heseltine government would not have been very different. He had already made it clear that both of his rivals, John Major and Douglas Hurd, would have kept their places at the Treasury and the Foreign Office. Given his oft-stated belief in strengthening the DTI, a political heavyweight would have been installed there – possibly Chris Patten. Sir Geoffrey Howe could have had a job if he'd wanted one, and might have gone to the Home Office, as a prelude to getting the Lord Chancellorship after an election. Peter Walker would have been invited to rejoin the Cabinet; though, having retired from government seven months earlier, he may not have accepted. And David Howell might have been brought back too. The other likely newcomer would have been Sir Peter Tapsell, possibly as Chief Secretary to the Treasury. Heseltine might also have fulfilled his long-standing desire to see a Minister for Europe in the Cabinet.

Casualties would probably have included Kenneth Baker, who had put the power of Central Office behind the Thatcher campaign, and Michael Howard, who had been particularly vituperative during the leadership election, describing Heseltine as 'the most divisive figure in the party for the past five years'.[2] Others likely to have left would have been the Home Secretary, David Waddington, and Cecil Parkinson (who retired anyway).

Overall, the Heseltine reshuffle would probably have been no more radical than John Major's. His main purpose would have been to stress continuity, and there would have been no sudden influx of Heseltine men. Among his biggest supporters, Michael Mates might have been made a minister of state – most probably at Defence or Northern Ireland – while Keith Hampson could have been granted his wish to become minister for higher education; but Heseltine has never been good at rewarding his friends and supporters.

The reality, however, was that John Major was Prime Minister, and, when he announced his new ministers, some in the Heseltine camp were extremely upset that their man hadn't insisted on jobs for them. Michael Mates, who voiced his displeasure in the strongest terms, did eventually become minister of state at the Northern Ireland Office, but not until after the 1992 election. Nor did Heseltine do anything to stop the dismissal of one of his few ministerial supporters, Ian Grist, from the Welsh Office. And Emma Nicholson got no joy when she asked Heseltine if she could be his PPS. 'I was on the brink of deselection in the constituency,' she says. 'Of all his supporters, perhaps I had stretched myself furthest for him. He rejected my offer curtly.'[3] She should have known that Heseltine was unlikely to accept a woman acting as his antennae at Westminster.

Almost immediately after the leadership result, John Major had rung Heseltine and asked him to join his Cabinet. The offer was accepted at once. But what job would Major give his rival? Many assumed he would be made Home Secretary, including Cecil Parkinson, who spoke to Heseltine just before the new Cabinet was announced. 'I said to him, "Well, it's the Home Office for you." "I know what they're up to," he replied. "It's a political graveyard. I don't want it." '[4] His comments were highly revealing, for they showed just how much ambition Heseltine still harboured. (He was probably unaware just how bad a 'graveyard' the post was: the last Conservative Home Secretary to become Prime Minister was Sir Robert Peel.) Perhaps John Major was already aware of Heseltine's feelings, for Kenneth Baker, who got the job instead, says the premier told him 'that he had definitely not offered the post of Home Secretary to Michael'.[5]

Ideally, Heseltine wanted the DTI, but once again this would have been too sensitive politically. In any case, Peter Lilley had held the job for only four months, and Heseltine was among the fiercest critics of the rapid turnover of Industry Secretaries (seven in seven years). Instead, after a handshake of reconciliation on the Downing Street doorstep – in front of the cameras – Major returned Heseltine to the job he'd first held eleven years before, and the ministry he'd originally occupied two decades earlier. Many saw the move as poetic justice. The one overwhelming task at Environment was tackling the poll tax. If Heseltine failed, the Tories would almost certainly lose the next election.

The new Environment Secretary was given a free hand on the poll tax by John Major and the Cabinet: his refrain was that 'no options are ruled in and no options are ruled out', and that included outright abolition.[6] Heseltine had also secured approval for a fundamental examination of other aspects of local government, including its management and structure. This would enable him to pursue many of the ideas he had been propounding during the wilderness years, such as elected full-time mayors. Heseltine argued (from personal experience) that local-government reform had suffered in the past from being carried out piecemeal. He shared a widespread view that, if the system was going to be reformed, the financial and organizational aspects ought to be examined together. Within the DoE they called it the 'all-singing, all-dancing review'.

When he announced his wide-ranging examination, a week after his appointment, MPs heard a rather more emollient Environment Secretary than the Michael Heseltine of 1979–83. He seemed to be seeking a more cooperative relationship with councils, and appeared to have acquired a new respect for local government as an institution. 'I cannot escape the fact that some of the greatest moments in British history have coincided with the times of resolve, civic pride and municipal initiative in our great towns and cities,' he said.[7]

He also surprised MPs, and blunted opposition attacks, by inviting the other parties to take part in his review, to explore how much they could 'establish common principles for the future role and direction of local government'.[8] Heseltine privately said it was 'a good joke', and knew he couldn't lose: if the opposition parties joined him they would become part of the process; if they stayed out they could be blamed if things went wrong. His offer certainly wrong-footed Neil Kinnock and his colleagues, who weren't sure how to respond but eventually refused to take part because Heseltine wouldn't guarantee to abolish the poll tax. The Liberal Democrats did participate, and promoted their long-cherished plans for a local income tax, though their contributions were largely ignored.

A senior civil servant who had worked closely with Heseltine in the past found the new Environment Secretary 'more Olympian and detached' this time round. 'He was more relaxed, had confidence and had matured. It all showed in his general bearing. He had been in many Cabinet storms, and probably felt that nothing could happen that he couldn't relate to from some previous experience.' Another who knew him in previous DoE incarnations describes Heseltine as 'more autocratic and grand in manner' and 'less hands on', though still 'restlessly stirring things up'. His role in recent historic events seemed to have given Heseltine a new aura. Officials were dealing with a man whose place in history was now assured. More than ever, Heseltine enjoyed a 'presence' in meetings, and fully exploited his heavyweight reputation.

Much of the poll-tax work was delegated to Michael Portillo, the local-government minister, whom Heseltine had inherited. Since his appointment the previous May, Portillo had been chief cheerleader *for* the tax, and had even told the Conservative conference that it was 'a courageous, fair and sensible solution. Far from being a vote loser . . . it will be a vote winner.'[9] Portillo now seemed perfectly willing to do an apparent volte-face, though privately he claimed he had never been keen on the measure and it certainly wasn't an issue of ideological principle. Heseltine had specifically asked for Portillo to be kept on. He was keen to have someone who was familiar with the figures, and he also knew that having a die-hard Thatcherite in charge of the poll tax would serve as a shield against those on the right who still defended it.

Just as John Stanley had been largely responsible for the detail of council-house sales in the early 1980s, and Peter Blaker had fought much of the war against CND, it was now Portillo and the deputy local-government minister, Robert Key, who primarily wrestled with the community charge. Heseltine, says Key, 'called Michael and myself into his office and said, "Right, boys, Cabinet has decided you've got to go away and get rid of the poll tax and introduce something else. You've got three months – and make sure it works." ' Heseltine even dubbed his deputy 'the A A man' (borrowing a phrase from a current T V commercial): although he himself might not know the detail, he knew a man who did – Portillo.[10] Despite dealing with local authorities during three different spells at the DoE, Heseltine has never shown much interest in the intricacies of local-government finance. Frankly, who can blame him?

The two Michaels got on surprisingly well, even though their politics were very different. Portillo was the coming man of the Tory right, a former adviser to both Cecil Parkinson and Nigel Lawson who was already seen by Thatcher as the one to carry forward her true flame. With Heseltine still harbouring leadership hopes, their rival ambitions might have clashed, but nobody has ever suggested there was much disharmony between the two. 'The personal relationship was excellent – to my amazement,' says an official who worked closely with both, 'and civil servants are pretty good at spotting when ministers don't get on.' Perhaps it was because each knew precisely where the other stood. Heseltine was happy to delegate, and Portillo was happy to do the graft.

One civil servant says Portillo seemed to drop any political allegiances in the interests of finding a solution to what looked like an intractable problem – both politically and financially. He treated it almost like an intellectual exercise, at the end of which the possible options were presented to Heseltine. Another official says Portillo 'behaved like a very senior civil servant, in that he presided over things very objectively. It was never my impression that there was any attempt to direct the Secretary of State to any particular outcome.'

It would be wrong, however, to present the two Michaels as bosom pals: it was more a relationship based on mutual respect, across a twenty-year age gap. Michael Portillo's biographer notes a 'lack of warmth' between them, and says that in private conversation he would call his boss 'Heseltine' rather than 'Michael'.[11] Heseltine admired his local-government minister's intellect and application, and publicly acknowledged his better understanding of the detail; Portillo, in turn, appeared to learn much from Heseltine on matters of personal style. He improved the quality of the suits he wore, and the dramatic new quiff Portillo adopted in the autumn of 1991, in place of his former page-boy cut, was the handiwork of Heseltine's hairdresser.

Inevitably, when Heseltine carried responsibilities that were so politically sensitive, Downing Street took a close interest in their progress. Major had taken some risk in assigning the government's biggest problem to a potential rival with far greater ministerial experience. There was a mutual wariness, especially during the early months of 1991. 'I think he was puzzled by John Major at that time,' says Heseltine's PPS, William Powell. 'He didn't seem to confirm Michael Heseltine's view of how to be Prime Minister.'[12] But the Environment Secretary knew he had to make a success of the relationship: after the events of 1990, he couldn't afford to be seen as the slightest bit disloyal to his new leader.

The Prime Minister chaired the Cabinet committee dealing with the poll tax, though day-to-day monitoring was undertaken by Sarah Hogg, the financial journalist who had just become head of the Number Ten Policy Unit. Almost the first thing Hogg did was to ask for a note on how the tax might be abolished; for the next six months the poll tax was her principal concern.

Hogg herself says that initially Heseltine 'simply wanted to get back as quickly and smoothly as possible to the rates'.[13] Politically, that was impossible: most Tories would never have accepted it. Moreover, Heseltine was far from popular with party activists (some of whom, despite pleas by John Major for tolerance, were trying to deselect MPs who had backed him).

Michael Heseltine's problem was that, while he'd consistently opposed the poll tax, he had never once suggested an alternative of his own. Even his famous *Times* article of May 1990 had conceded that the poll tax would stay, and merely suggested ways in which it might be modified. Initially, the DoE review team trotted through all the options the department had considered twice before – local sales taxes, a local income tax, and other forms of property tax. Partly because he was a close associate of Heseltine's, they also took a look at Michael Mates's scheme to band the poll tax according to income, but quickly decided it was impracticable.

At regular intervals during the first four months of 1991, seemingly well-informed leaks emerged in the press, in what is described in one account as 'a deliberate strategy of policy-making by "leak and reaction" '.[14] Members of the DoE review team often found that the newspapers were the only way to get a 'steer' on what Downing Street and the Treasury were thinking.

'Sources close to Michael Heseltine' were used to leaking, of course, especially from the days of Westland. Now the tactic was an attempt both to test the water and also to soften up those who still believed in the poll tax. While Michael Heseltine was convinced it had to be abolished and replaced by a new measure, it was not clear if this was politically feasible. He had to bring round his Cabinet colleagues, and in particular John Major, who was at first cagey about what he'd accept, and even seemed at one point to rule out abolition. Many of the strongest supporters of the tax were from the Tory right, of course, but by no means all. Two Cabinet colleagues once considered on the left, Kenneth Baker and William Waldegrave, had been the main ministerial architects of the poll tax. Perhaps its fiercest defender was Ian Lang, the new Scottish Secretary, who believed the measure had now bedded down in Scotland, and didn't want further upheaval.

In January 1991 Heseltine announced an extra £1.2 billion of relief to lessen the poll-tax burden, but it was soon obvious that it wouldn't be enough. It would require major action in the March Budget if the impact of poll-tax bills due in April was to be reduced – an option Chris Patten dubbed 'Big Bertha'. At the last minute, John Major persuaded – if not ordered – the new Chancellor, Norman Lamont, to subsidize the tax by £140 a head, bringing it down to an average of around £250. The £4½ billion cost would be met by increasing VAT by 2½ per cent, to 17½ per cent. The decision was so late that the Treasury had to cover the costs of dozens of councils who had already sent out poll-tax bills and now had to issue revised ones. Heseltine took little part in the VAT decision, but it was this huge subsidy, rather than his own measures, which did most to resolve the problem. Indeed, some Thatcherites argued that, once Lamont had announced the subsidy, the poll tax could easily have been retained.

Two days after the Budget, the Environment Secretary confirmed to MPs what had been heavily trailed: the poll tax would be abolished. From 'the earliest possible moment' it would be 'replaced by a new system of local taxation'. The statement was vague, however, about what this would entail. Heseltine merely revealed that the new tax would consist of two elements for each household – 'the number of adults living there and the value of the property' – but the weight to be attached to each was not specified.[15] The next day, when Heseltine addressed the Conservative Central Council in Southport, he received what was probably his worst ever reception from party activists. For once he was denied a standing ovation. Some were angry that the tax was being abolished, while others were still upset over the way he had deposed Margaret Thatcher. It was an indication of the problems he might have faced if he'd been Prime Minister.

Initially the DoE review team had devised a quite complicated measure. As Heseltine's Commons statement had suggested, it was really two taxes in one. At first it was proposed there should be a banded property tax, but based on regional variations. The second element involved payment according to the number living in the property, which would have obliged councils to maintain their old poll-tax registers, showing who lived where. In some respects, this dual tax – for which the review team toyed with names such as 'local tax' or 'household tax' – would have been more complicated than either the rates or the poll tax, since authorities would now have to keep records of both people and property. 'The Prime Minister was not happy,' say Major's two political advisers, Sarah Hogg and Jonathan Hill. 'He asked the [Number Ten] Policy Unit to drop everything else, to engage the Treasury, and to try to help Environment come up with better answers.'[16]

At a time when the new Prime Minister was being accused of 'dithering', he was exasperated both at how slowly the DoE review was proceeding and at all the leaks. On one occasion, just before the Budget-week announcements, and after Heseltine's PPS, William Powell, had leaked details to Westminster reporters, Major delivered a strong reprimand to his Environment Secretary. Hogg and Hill's account suggests that Downing Street had to take a firm grip on Heseltine's ministry; they write of Number Ten at one point 'going into the Department of the Environment like rats into cheese'.[17]

The solution eventually reached was remarkably simple. First, the new council tax, as it was finally called, would be based on seven bands, according to property valuations. (Later Heseltine introduced an eighth band for properties worth more than £320,000 – largely on the grounds of fairness rather than to raise significantly more money, and at some personal cost in respect of his own homes.) Second, the only 'poll' aspect, allowing for numbers of residents, was a 25 per cent discount for households with only one adult. The far more complex initial scheme for payment directly according to the exact numbers in a property was dropped after Number Ten discovered there were relatively few households with more than two adults anyway.

The result was a compromise. Heseltine and the Treasury had achieved the property tax they had always preferred, yet it also involved a genuflection towards the poll tax through the single-person discount. The idea was so neat that it prompts the question of why nobody had thought of it before. Both the main features were familiar. The Treasury had first devised a banded property scheme in the mid-1980s, but nobody else would support it, while Heseltine himself had advocated a 'single-person discount' in his December 1987 Commons speech against the poll tax.[18]

If the Treasury had been more closely involved in the processes which had produced the poll tax in the mid-1980s, what turned out to be Mrs Thatcher's greatest blunder might not have happened. Now, in contrast, Treasury ministers and officials had played a significant part in deciding how the tax should be replaced. Indeed, the Treasury worked so closely with Downing Street that the DoE felt excluded at times. The precise levels of council-tax property bandings, for instance, were actually worked out by the Treasury's incoming Permanent Secretary, Sir Terry Burns, in his Welsh cottage during the Easter weekend.

After three months' consultation, the necessary legislation was rushed through Parliament in time for the April 1992 election, when the council tax was not a major issue. Despite Labour's commitment to abolish the new measure and introduce its own system of 'fair taxes', the tax aroused remarkably little opposition from the public, or from local authorities. After more than a decade of turmoil, ministers had at last found a successful way to replace the rates.

As with council-house sales, Heseltine often gets the credit for the council tax because it was introduced during his spell at the DoE. It should really be shared. Sarah Hogg and Michael Portillo, together with Treasury and DoE officials, were jointly responsible for the details. Most important, it was John Major who pressed Norman Lamont for the £140-a-head poll-tax relief in the 1991 Budget, which did most to defuse public hostility and gave the government breathing-space to implement an alternative. In accepting this subsidy, Heseltine had to swallow what was effectively universal government capping of local poll-tax levels – to stop councils simply using the money to spend more. Yet, in the past, Heseltine had always been a fierce critic of capping, especially if it was to be applied universally.

Although the poll tax was the hot potato, and Heseltine kept a close eye on developments, he saw it very much as the negative side of his brief. 'He was bored with the subject,' says William Powell. 'It didn't engage his attentions, except on the political level, and that's why he was happy to delegate it to Michael Portillo.'[19] A far more exciting prospect for Heseltine was the chance to rethink local-government organization and structure, which again illustrates his fascination with management systems. Significantly, whenever Heseltine addressed the Commons on his local-government review, he mentioned these areas first, rather than what was happening to the poll tax.[20] But in pursuing these other ideas – the fruits of his reflections out of office – his record was far from successful.

The prospect of yet more upheaval in local authorities was greeted with general horror, and Heseltine's predecessor at the DoE, Chris Patten, had opposed the wider review in Cabinet. Ministers were particularly unimpressed with Heseltine's much-trailed proposal for directly elected full-time mayors, although it was a sign of his new stature that his colleagues at least let him explore the idea, and did not dismiss it immediately. During his previous spell in office, Heseltine had carried limited weight in government, especially with the Prime Minister. Now he enjoyed a new authority. Heseltine was the only remaining survivor from Margaret Thatcher's first Cabinet in 1979, and he had even served in Ted Heath's Shadow Cabinet. Nor could it be ignored that in 1990 he had won the backing of more than a third of all Tory MPs.

Heseltine's belief in full-time elected mayors stemmed partly from his inner-city experiences of the early 1980s. He thought that strong figures with local mandates might reinvigorate areas such as Liverpool. And he liked the idea of a Secretary of State dealing directly with a city boss rather than with council leaders encumbered by committees. Heseltine saw his elected mayors as chief executives who would operate with mini-Cabinets in the same way as a British Prime Minister does, or an American city mayor. He also proposed that the leading members of each council should be properly paid for their work.

Heseltine had equally become convinced of the case for elected mayors through his own personal experience during five years on the back benches. He realized that the British system had no sources of power other than ministerial office. In America, politicians enjoy several possibilities – a place in the federal administration in Washington, or in Congress, or in state or city government. In France, many national politicians also serve as mayor of their home town. But in Britain there are no real alternative roles for politicians who want to exercise power. William Powell recalls Heseltine saying that, 'in opposition, if the choice was to be mayor of London or environment spokesman, he'd prefer to be mayor of London'.[21] Just as Heseltine felt that too much economic power was concentrated on the City and the South-East, he disliked the monopoly of political power in Westminster and Whitehall.

But the Cabinet quietly killed his idea. Their principal fear was that it would simply unleash a new generation of troublesome Labour city bosses, carrying much greater authority than past bogeymen such as Derek Hatton in Liverpool and Ken Livingstone in London. There seemed scant prospect of Tory mayors being elected in many places, especially in the big northern cities. The idea was discussed several times in Cabinet committee, but the disapproval from Heseltine's colleagues is thought to have been unanimous. 'I don't know of anybody else who was speaking for it,' says one DoE official. 'There was no enthusiasm for it.' The opposition from the Home Office and the Department of Education, which both had regular dealings with local government, was particularly strong. There was also a danger of deadlock between mayors and councils claiming separate mandates from the same electorate. At Westminster, Tories were worried, too, that the advent of elected mayors with their own local mandates would lessen the standing of MPs. The Chief Whip, Richard Ryder, told Heseltine the idea would never get through the House.

The Cabinet allowed Heseltine to save face by including his pet scheme in a consultative paper – along with his plan for local spending referendums – but the document made it plain that these proposals would go no further.

Heseltine did secure support, however, for pursuing the idea of unitary authorities – though many of his colleagues would come to regret it. This was a far lower priority on the Heseltine agenda, and something he'd adopted quite late in the day – it doesn't feature in his 1987 testament *Where There's a Will*, for instance. To a large extent, single-tier councils were a logical extension of his earlier initiatives in abolishing the GLC, the metropolitan counties and the ILEA, while the concentration of power complemented his plan for elected mayors. Heseltine envisaged the major English towns and cities, like Derby and Oxford, regaining the county-borough status which he and Peter Walker had deprived them of in 1972 (the problem that had caused him so much trouble with local Tories in Plymouth). The case for unitary councils had now gained significant support in Conservative circles – especially within the Association of District Councils, which the party then controlled.

In April 1991 Heseltine announced he was setting up a commission to examine England county by county, to see how unitary councils might be introduced, though he accepted they might not happen everywhere. The Local Government Commission quickly became known as the Banham Commission, after its first chairman, John Banham, who eight years before had been the initial controller of Heseltine's other major local-government quango, the Audit Commission (and had been one of the many helpers on *Where There's a Will*). While Banham's earlier work is highly regarded, he perhaps lacked the diplomatic touch for a body which had to mediate between competing local claims.

In theory, the Banham Commission should have been popular. It was an opportunity not just to reduce council bureaucracy but also to correct the mistakes of the early-1970s local-government reorganization, though Heseltine would never admit that he and Peter Walker had made mistakes. It could spell the end of the unpopular council areas like Humberside, Cleveland and Avon, which the two men had introduced. And Rutland, which they had abolished, could now make a comeback, along with the lamented Ridings of Yorkshire.

In practice, the structural review was a disaster. One academic study describes it as 'a policy fiasco, which had it been allowed to continue, could have had a discreditory impact comparable to that of the introduction of the poll tax'.[22] Like the poll tax, the review was rushed, and the Banham Commission therefore had no time to reflect on guiding principles for its work. 'We should have spent six months to take general stock about the general issues from people who knew their stuff before rushing off to individual counties,' says one commissioner, David Thomas. 'If we'd had time to assess all that, it would have given something for ministers to ponder a bit more.'[23] John Banham now feels the same way.

Most of the problems emerged only after Heseltine had left the DoE in 1992, and landed on the desks of his successors. Just as the Audit Commission is an achievement for which he has been given too little credit, the Local Government Commission was a failure for which Michael Heseltine has received too little blame. In retrospect, it was one of the worst mistakes he has ever made as a minister.

Heseltine's enthusiasm for unitary authorities was not shared by the Environment Secretaries who followed him. In April 1992, less than a year after Heseltine had set up the Local Government Commission, his successor, Michael Howard (who was no admirer personally), considered scrapping it altogether, on cost grounds, and imposing county boroughs in a few places instead. The commission survived only because abolition would have looked like another U-turn at a time when the government seemed to be falling into a habit of reversing previous policies. The subsequent Environment Secretary, John Gummer, later rejected many of Banham's proposals for unitary solutions in favour of the status quo.

The commission's work was to cause ministers, MPs and the Conservative Party considerable grief for four years. The prospect of unitary authorities threatened thousands of councillors with extinction, at a time when the party's unpopularity was already making Conservative council members an endangered species. Across the country, Tories squabbled with Tories, and shires struggled with districts. Heseltine warned Conservative councillors against 'expensive public-relations exercises' which would annoy the public, but many ignored him.[24] Tens of millions of pounds were spent by local authorities on consultants' reports, legal advice and court challenges (and even radio advertising), to promote their particular causes.

Many MPs were deeply unhappy with the changes recommended by Banham. One junior minister, David Heathcoat-Amory, is said to have threatened to resign over the proposals in Somerset. In Oxfordshire, the Foreign Secretary, Douglas Hurd, made public his strong preference for the status quo, rather than the kind of unitary system envisaged by his Cabinet colleague. Heseltine was the only local MP not to deliver an official submission to Banham's Oxfordshire review, though it is thought he wasn't too distressed when the existing arrangements were eventually preserved. Even government departments like the Home Office and Health made plain their dismay at the prospect that activities they supported on a county basis – such as police and social services – might be broken up. In 1995 John Banham was eased out by John Gummer, who then went to the extraordinary length of reconstituting the whole commission and scaling down its activity.

The government was lucky, perhaps, that the Banham Commission never became a national issue, and the enormous discontent was confined to the local level. One reason is that the opposition parties were as divided about it as the Conservatives.

Five years after it started work, the map of English local government looks a hotchpotch, though much of it actually remains unchanged from before. A mere four counties have been abolished – the unpopular Humberside, Avon and Cleveland, as well as the ancient and Royal County of Berkshire – and some form of two-tier system survives in thirty-four of the thirty-nine previous counties. Only forty-six unitary authorities have been established, mostly in cities such as Derby, Leicester, Blackpool and Plymouth. This is not a bad outcome in itself, but the controversy and expenditure involved in getting there were wholly disproportionate. (In Scotland and Wales, ministers simply imposed new unitary councils, though in England that might have caused even more trouble.)

One Heseltine proposal from the wilderness period that *did* succeed was his idea that local authorities should compete with each other for central funds for major capital projects. In the summer of 1991 he unveiled the City Challenge process. Urban councils were asked to devise exciting regeneration schemes which would involve community and voluntary groups and which, above all, would also attract investment from the private sector. Twenty-one authorities applied in the first contest, and eleven were awarded grants worth almost £40 million each over the next five years; the following year the scheme was expanded. The principle of competition was also extended to two-thirds of the housing investment programme, and even covered traditional grants to refurbish council estates.

'It obliged local authorities to talk to the private sector,' says the then junior environment minister, Tony Baldry, who admits that civil servants were 'sceptical' about whether holding contests for funds would work.[25] Politically it was astute, since the strong dose of market competition served to temper Heseltine's reputation on the Tory right as a public spender. Yet it was also another act of centralization. Instead of funds being granted automatically, according to established criteria, further power was placed in the hands of ministers in Whitehall – and civil servants in regional offices.

Within days of returning to the DoE, Michael Heseltine played a key role in John Major's decision to back Manchester's bid to stage the 1996 Olympics. It marked a radical departure from the Thatcher years, when ministers kept their distance from cities bidding for the Games, but the Environment Secretary saw it as a means to help to revitalize run-down parts of Manchester (though the bid ultimately failed). A far more visionary urban regeneration project adopted eagerly by Heseltine was the so-called East Thames Corridor – a linear city stretching eastwards from London's Docklands as far as Tilbury in Essex and the Medway towns in Kent. 'Hezzaville', as the tabloids called it, had been inspired by Professor Peter Hall, a former Labour Party member who had once been chairman of the Fabian Society and was later a leading light of the SDP. Hall suggested the potential of the area at a conference in the spring of 1991, and it dovetailed neatly with several of Heseltine's existing passions. First, of course, was his long-standing concern to redevelop Docklands, where local prospects were about to be improved by new transport links, including the extension of the Jubilee underground line, the expanded City Airport and the Dartford Bridge. Equally important, it was envisaged that the East Thames Corridor would ease development pressure to the west of London, in which, as MP for Henley, Heseltine had a particular interest. (It ran counter to his long-held view that activity should be enticed away from the overcrowded South-East, however, but by 1991 the region was suffering most from the recession).

On a wider plane, the East Thames Corridor could also be linked with the advent of the single European market in 1992. It was portrayed as the opening for trade with the Continent – hence the corridor's other name: the Thames Gateway. Heseltine and Hall saw London

as the end of a belt of industrial and economic activity stretching
down through Europe to northern Italy.

'Heseltine thinks of himself as the master builder, a great planner
like Napoleon III,' says Peter Hall, who agreed to become a DoE
special adviser on planning matters. 'The East Thames Corridor was
one of these rare political decisions that had everybody salivating.
It took pressure off the Oxfordshire–Berkshire area, and Labour
boroughs were offered development they thought they'd been cheated
of.'[26]

A key aspect of his *grand projet* was the route of the Channel
Tunnel Rail Link, over which Heseltine fought a bitter battle with
the Department of Transport. The Transport Secretary, Malcolm
Rifkind, supported British Rail's preference for a route through
south-east London, but Heseltine cleverly exploited the local resistance in places like Orpington and Hither Green. 'It was unbelievable,'
says an official who attended the showdown with the Transport
Secretary. 'Heseltine just ran the whole meeting, and ran roughshod
over Rifkind, and had this mania over the East Thames Corridor and
regeneration. Rifkind just let him run it.' As a result, the southern
route was jettisoned and the rail link was given the course on which
it is currently being constructed: along the north-Kent coast, over
the Thames near the Dartford Bridge, and into King's Cross via
Stratford and the East End.

But Michael Heseltine's grand designs for London in the twenty-
first century were not always appreciated by his colleagues. They
'tended to arouse instant suspicion in the Treasury', write Sarah Hogg
and Jonathan Hill:

The Prime Minister agreed to let the Environment Secretary make a presentation in the Cabinet Room of his vision of the regeneration of London and
points east. There was a ripple of unease when Canary Wharf, then very
definitely in trouble, suddenly featured in the slide-show. Michael, never
one to lose his nerve, stormed boldly on. But on learning that the whole of
east London and part of Kent would become part of a 'hot banana' curving
through Europe to Milan, some ministers evinced signs of alarm.[27]

Despite such scepticism, Heseltine was allowed to pursue the idea.
He also announced plans to move the Department of the Environment

itself down the Thames to new premises in Docklands, after securing approval for the DoE's ugly headquarters in Marsham Street to be demolished (even though the building had opened only in 1971). The move faced strong resistance from staff, and was subsequently abandoned by Michael Howard when it was shown to be too expensive. (Heseltine was no more successful when he took Lindsay Masters on a boat trip to persuade Haymarket to move to Docklands.)

Heseltine had hoped that the East Thames Corridor would be pursued by a body whose creation he had touted during his years out of office – an English development agency, similar to the Scottish and Welsh development agencies set up by Labour in the late 1970s. When the idea came up for consideration for the 1992 manifesto, colleagues – particularly Peter Lilley at the DTI and Norman Lamont at the Treasury – felt it would simply become an instrument of what they perceived as Heseltine-style interventionism. John Major was concerned that it might also increase the pressure for devolution. Ministers eventually accepted a much watered-down version of the Heseltine agency, and he appointed Peter Walker as the first chairman of what was called English Partnerships.

Michael Heseltine's other big responsibility, of course, was the environment itself. Green questions had been much less politically sensitive during his previous spells in the department, but were now a hot issue. For the first six months, while he grappled with the local-government review, Heseltine was happy to delegate environmental matters to his deputy, David Trippier, one of his few ministerial supporters in 1990, who had already acted as green minister under Chris Patten. And Tom Burke, the environmentalist who had advised Heseltine during the wilderness years and was a frequent critic of past government policies, became another special adviser. Burke, whose entry to the DoE would have been unthinkable under Nicholas Ridley, acted as a useful bridge to the green movement, and remained there under both Heseltine's successors.

The previous Environment Secretary, Chris Patten, had been highly receptive to environmental concerns, though the political climate was pushing in that direction anyway. Patten's 1990 White Paper had set out more than 350 green objectives for government action by the year 2000. Michael Heseltine now tried to impose management discipline and public accountability on the whole process, by setting target dates for each objective; a progress report was issued a year after the White Paper, explaining what had been done in each case – or, in eighteen instances, not done. Despite misgivings by David Trippier and many civil servants, Heseltine promised similar reports every year.

The setting of targets, and 'auditing' whether they'd been met or not, was typical Heseltine: it was similar to MINIS and the activities of the Audit Commission, though in this case adapted to external policy. Another personal feature was his determination to overcome Whitehall protocol and extend the DoE's green activity into other ministries. Every department was expected to appoint a minister to look after environmental issues in its field, with coordination being handled through a committee chaired by Heseltine. He also pressed for the all-embracing Environment Agency which was introduced after the 1992 election.

Michael Heseltine's rehabilitation as an accepted member of the Conservative high command was confirmed when John Major appointed him to the ministerial 'A team' to prepare for the election. (The other team members were Douglas Hurd, Norman Lamont, Kenneth Clarke and Chris Patten.) From an early position of mutual suspicion, Heseltine's relationship with the Prime Minister had greatly strengthened as the two had got to know each other. Major gradually came to rely on Heseltine's advice and experience, and soon trusted him enough to allow him to pronounce publicly across all areas of government policy. Some DoE officials noticed that their boss was already acquiring some of the characteristics of a Deputy Prime Minister.

When Heseltine's speech at the 1991 party conference revived his customary standing ovation, it was a sign that most Tory activists had now forgiven his ousting of Thatcher. And he re-emerged as a formidable front-bench performer with some bruising Commons assaults on Labour. In an economic debate in early 1992, for instance, he adopted Churchillian tones and mocked attempts by the Shadow Chancellor, John Smith, to woo the City – Labour's 'prawn-cocktail offensive', as it was called. 'All those prawn cocktails for nothing,' he cried. 'Never have so many crustaceans died in vain. With all the authority that I can command as Secretary of State for the Environment, let me say to the Right Honourable and learned Member for Monklands East, "Save the prawns." '[28]

Although the April 1992 election will always be seen as John Major's personal triumph, Heseltine was the Tories' star performer – not that the competition was stiff. Central Office and Downing Street seemed reluctant to employ his electioneering skills at first, through fear that he might upstage the Prime Minister. But, out on the hustings, Heseltine was happy to praise his leader in a way that would have been inconceivable with Margaret Thatcher. As the campaign developed and the Conservatives' chances looked more precarious, Heseltine was given a larger role, especially when the Chancellor, Norman Lamont, was deliberately shielded from the main economic debates.

Though he himself is no great intellectual, Heseltine did not hesitate to suggest that Neil Kinnock lacked brainpower. More brazenly, he even mocked the Labour leader's working-class origins and Welsh accent (again showing his ambivalence about his own South Wales roots). 'The Labour high command,' he claimed, 'shuddered at the sight of Neil Kinnock run riot, off the leash, telling it like it would be, boyo. Taxes up, interest rates up, inflation up.'[29]

One particular Heseltine turn, repeated night after night at Tory rallies, resulted from a session listening to a tape of the musical *Oliver*. Neil Kinnock was portrayed as the Artful Dodger – 'dodging the press who want answers, dodging the questions about his past which have got no answers, dodging the answers which he gave yesterday . . . a dodgy leader of a dodgy party – not quite 100p to the pound'. The Shadow Chancellor was inevitably cast as Fagin – 'You gotta pick a pocket or two.'[30]

Michael Heseltine loves campaigning, but in 1992 he seemed ebulli-ent. Many Tories thought they would lose, though he himself was always confident. But then Heseltine was likely to gain whatever the outcome. If the party was defeated, as many expected, there would be a new leadership contest, and he would be well-placed to succeed John Major – and certainly hold a much stronger position than in 1990. If the Tories won, it was widely thought that Heseltine would get the only other ministerial post he had always coveted.

20. *Hezza the Prezza*

Rarely can a politician have prepared so much for a particular ministry as Michael Heseltine had for the Department of Trade and Industry. It was eighteen years since he had first shadowed the DTI in opposition under Ted Heath. In the intervening period there had been eleven different Secretaries of State at the department, nine of them fellow Conservatives. Now, after the Conservatives' surprise election victory, when they secured a majority of twenty-one seats, he finally had his turn. Yet, if Heseltine's most recent spell at Environment was a disappointment, his period at Trade and Industry verged on the disastrous.

It started with high hopes. Not only did Heseltine take responsibility for Trade and Industry, which had once merited two separate Cabinet ministers, but now Energy was also subsumed into the DTI. His first decision was to abandon the cumbersome title of 'Secretary of State for Trade and Industry' in favour of the more old-fashioned, if grandiose, 'President of the Board of Trade'. The title had lain dormant since 1970, and its readoption provoked much ridicule; some suggested it was a case of if Heseltine couldn't be Prime Minister he'd go one better and be President instead. Rather than the usual 'Secretary of State', officials were now expected to refer to him in minutes as 'the President', and to address him as plain 'President'. ('Mr President' was considered a step too far.)

Heseltine was quick to familiarize himself with the 300-year history of his new responsibility, though, as he acknowledged, the Board of Trade hadn't actually met since 1850. Its members included the First Lord of the Admiralty, the Master of the Mint, and the Archbishop of Canterbury, though the current Archbishop, George Carey, seemed happily unaware of his responsibility for the nation's trading fortunes. The President could in any case operate without them: the quorum for board meetings was just one.

Previous Presidents included some distinguished figures: three

Heseltine heroes – Joseph Chamberlain, Lloyd George and Churchill – and three other twentieth-century Prime Ministers – Stanley Baldwin, Harold Wilson and Edward Heath. In contrast, the numerous Secretaries of State for Trade and Industry had a dismal record: none had progressed even to the so-called 'great offices of state', the trinity of Home Office, Foreign Office and Exchequer (though neither, of course, had Heseltine).

His new title was also emblematic. Heseltine wanted to remind people that 'We are a trading nation. If we don't trade, we won't survive.'[1] Production was not to be regarded by government as an end in itself: instead, emphasis would be placed on the market-place, where British firms had to sell and compete. The name change would also mark a new approach to trade and industry. Under Margaret Thatcher the DTI's role had been limited, reflecting her belief that government should keep out of industrial matters. One Industry Secretary, Nicholas Ridley, had even wondered why his department existed at all; he did so little in the post that Labour's Gordon Brown once joked that Ridley, a heavy smoker, had neither an in-tray nor an out-tray, just an ash-tray.

In contrast, much of Michael Heseltine's activity as Defence Secretary – particularly the episodes which caused so much controversy – had stemmed from his conviction that the government should do much more to help British business. Out of office, Heseltine had expounded the view that the DTI should be as influential in government as the Treasury, and preferably more powerful. His model was Japan's Ministry for International Trade and Industry (MITI), which is widely credited with the country's postwar economic success. MITI enjoys a close relationship with Japanese companies and takes a central role in developing their export markets. Indeed, before his return to government in 1990, the Heseltine team was planning a book about the Japanese economy, which he saw as 'a brilliantly orchestrated and managed partnership between the industrial and governmental worlds'.[2] Politically, considering the hostages it might have offered, it was probably just as well he didn't write it.

Many right-wing Conservatives, and some people in the Treasury, expected Heseltine to embark on the type of interventionist policies that Margaret Thatcher had so decried in 1990. 'Interventionism', like 'federalism', is a word much used in political debate – often pejoratively – though it is rarely defined. To Thatcherites, 'intervention' meant the industrial policies of the Wilson and Heath era, when the DTI had spent hundreds of millions of pounds supporting 'lame ducks', reorganizing and subsidizing state industries, and attempting to 'pick winners' – investing in high-tech projects that might one day flourish.

Yet there was scant evidence from Heseltine's past that he was likely to be an old-fashioned high-spending interventionist. Even with Concorde, most of the funds had been committed long before Heseltine took responsibility. He had been involved in launch aid for various aerospace projects, but that had been standard practice for years. There were also the award of a frigate to Cammell Laird to keep the company open, at a direct cost of £7 million; his initial suggestion of a £30 million grant to help Westland; and, of course, the urban development corporations. It didn't add up to much.

Moreover, even if the new President of the Board of Trade had wanted to be a high-spending interventionist, he didn't have the resources. The DTI's budget was now tiny; having shrunk from more than £3 billion in the early 1980s to just over £1 billion in 1992–93, it was due to fall further during the next two years. The Welsh Office, in comparison, spent five times as much.

In reality, Heseltine's interventionism has always been more about using power rather than money – and preferably his own power. He believed the whole Whitehall machinery had to be directed towards supporting British business. His book *Where There's a Will* had argued that the DTI Secretary should head the Cabinet committee on industry, backing national champions and doing everything within the government's ability to help British companies compete successfully overseas.

Where There's a Will had been a prescription for Heseltine as Prime Minister, of course; with John Major in charge, there was no question of quite such a radical adjustment of government priorities. Although a new Cabinet committee on industrial, commercial and consumer affairs was created, the job of chairing it went to the recently ennobled John Wakeham, who believed in a much more hands-off approach towards business.

Barely two months after taking office, Heseltine appeared to suffer another blow to his past strategy. *Where There's a Will* had trumpeted the role of the National Economic Development Office (NEDO, or 'Neddy'), the body set up by Harold Macmillan in 1962 to provide a forum for government to discuss economic issues with employers and unions. During the Thatcher years, ministers increasingly treated Neddy as a waste of time, and as a relic of old-style corporatism. Michael Heseltine, however, had written that 'NEDO's potential value is high,' and suggested that its regular meetings should be chaired by the Industry Secretary rather than the Chancellor: 'The organization needs more of the language of the factory floor and less of that of the Treasury.'[3] Now, in 1992, the Chancellor of the Exchequer, Norman Lamont, did indeed give up his chairmanship, but only by abolishing Neddy altogether. 'The age of corporatism must be put firmly behind us,' Lamont pointedly told MPs.[4]

Despite his previous utterances, Heseltine made no attempt to preserve Neddy. 'He didn't fight anything remotely like a rearguard action,' says his private secretary, Peter Smith. 'He was supportive of getting rid of it.'[5] The President had come to share the prevailing view that Neddy was now an irrelevance which the unions exploited to confront ministers and employers. He also reckoned that much of its work – and some of its staff – could be transferred to the DTI (and, in doing so, he could then neatly exclude the union element).

Neddy's director, Walter Eltis, became Heseltine's chief economic adviser. A respected former Oxford don, Eltis gave the President much-needed extra support in economic debates both with the Treasury and with Sarah Hogg in the Number Ten Policy Unit. It was a rare example of Heseltine turning rightwards for advice: Eltis is drier than Heseltine on economics, and more sceptical about European integration.

The transfer of Neddy's work also helped Heseltine carry out the internal reorganization he traditionally initiated on arrival in any new ministry. Several new DTI divisions were created to 'sponsor' particular industries, and these took on much of the responsibilities of the former industry working-parties run by Neddy. He also set up two new units to encourage greater competitiveness and more deregulation. And once again he instituted his MINIS management system.

At the same time, Heseltine volunteered a budget cut to the Treasury – a highly unusual action for a spending minister. It was part of his continuing effort to portray himself as a team player after the dramas of 1986 and 1990, and also served to distance himself from Cabinet colleagues by taking the high ground and setting them an example. The impact of the gesture was far greater than the small sums involved, but it deflected suspicions that he was a high-spending interventionist.

To the outside world, Michael Heseltine now looked like a beast that had been caged. At last he was responsible for industrial policy, but he appeared to have neither the tools he required nor the funds to implement it, while two arch-Thatcherites, Neil Hamilton and Edward Leigh, kept guard as his junior ministers. Heseltine had 'absolute power over a department which had become absolutely powerless', taunted Labour's trade and industry spokesman, Gordon Brown, in the summer of 1992:

The interventionist tiger of the rubber-chicken circuit has been brought low, reduced to trophy status. The tiger that was once the king of the jungle is now just the fireside rug – decorative and ostentatious, but essentially there to be walked all over.[6]

Yet the 'big beast' who stalked the Conservative conference in Brighton that October appeared neither caged nor walked upon. Still sounding very much like the Heseltine of the late 1980s, his speech made a point of stressing his role as an intervener:

If I have to intervene to help British companies, like the French government intervenes to help French companies, or the German government intervenes to help German companies, or the Japanese government intervenes to help Japanese companies, then I tell you . . . I *will* intervene, before breakfast, before lunch, before tea and before dinner.[7]

By 'intervention', Heseltine essentially meant involvement and activity, and working far more closely with industry than had his recent predecessors. This could be done by reducing obstacles to business – by cutting red tape, for instance – and ensuring that

35. Heseltine uses every foreign trip to indulge his passion for birds and trees. On a 1984 visit to inspect Falklands defences, he focused on these Gentoo penguins.

36. The Heseltines with goslings at Martin Mere wildfowl reserve on Merseyside in 1986.

37. Tending trees at Thenford. Heseltine says his arboretum is the thing for which he would most like to be remembered.

38. Heseltine prepares labels for the arboretum. He meticulously catalogues each tree.

39. As minister and gardener, Heseltine has never been afraid to make cuts. During his financial troubles of the early 1960s, he says he only kept sane by chopping down the undergrowth around his borrowed country cottage.

40. Serving a stirrup-cup to Anne and Alexandra. Heseltine himself takes no interest in horses, and Anne's involvement with the local 'horsy set' in the mid-1970s caused severe strains on their marriage.

41. Annabel clearly inherited her father's flamboyance. An occasional model in her early twenties, she has never been shy of publicity.

42. With his mother, Eileen, who was born in 1907, the daughter of a Swansea coal merchant. 'Michael was such an easy boy,' she says.

43. 1987 election: Alexandra, Rupert, Anne, Michael and Annabel. All three children are close to their parents.

44. Heseltine spent his five years in the wilderness carefully preparing for a leadership bid, but he never intended to challenge Margaret Thatcher in 1990. The rush of events that autumn forced his hand.

45. Fingers crossed as Heseltine announces his 1990 leadership bid on the doorstep of his London home.

46. Thirteen days later, conceding defeat to John Major.

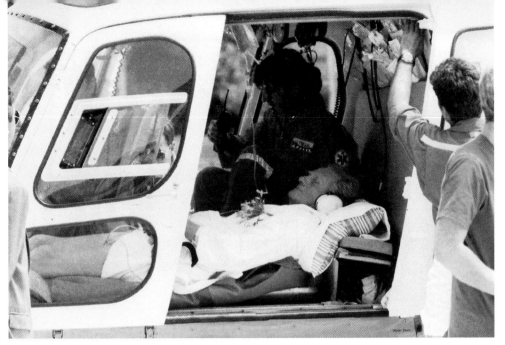

47. Leaving Venice in June 1993 after suffering a heart attack during a brief holiday.

48. A cartoonist's view: the biggest beast of the Tory jungle is denied the crown.

49. If John Major had faltered in the 1995 leadership election, Heseltine had a campaign team ready. Instead, he now wields more power than any Deputy Prime Minister since the war.

government departments were more aware of how they should help the wealth-creating parts of the economy. Equally, the DTI could play a much more active role in helping companies seize opportunities abroad, through government-led trade missions and improved export credit guarantees and by indicating untapped overseas markets. In short, the Heseltine approach was 'backing winners rather than picking them'. This could be done relatively inexpensively.

Coming just three weeks after the government's humiliating withdrawal from the European Exchange Rate Mechanism, Heseltine's confident oration in Brighton had been just what demoralized Tory activists required. While the chairman's claim that it was 'the greatest conference speech of our time' was an obvious overstatement, it was nonetheless a dazzling performance: Michael Heseltine at his very best.[8] But it was deceptive. Politics is a mercurial trade, and within six days of his euphoric reception Heseltine was plunged into the darkest, most miserable period of his entire political career: the crisis over pit closures.

The episode went to the heart of the contradictions which make up Heseltine's political philosophy. On the one hand there was his belief that governments could and should intervene in industrial matters for strategic reasons (the Heseltine of the European Fighter Aircraft consortium and Westland). On the other hand there was the Heseltine who advocated privatization and competitive tendering. In truth, these differing views did not sit comfortably together; the coal crisis brought them into sharp conflict.

Throughout the spring and summer of 1992, severe problems had been looming for the mining industry. The newly privatized electricity companies had insisted that in future they would require no more than 40 million tons of British coal every year, compared with 65 million in the current year. It was an inevitable consequence of their new freedom under privatization to invest in gas-fired power stations – the so-called 'dash for gas' – and sign contracts with the gas generators that were guaranteed for fifteen years. They were also importing more cheap foreign coal. Issues which would previously have been a matter of energy policy were now left to the individual electricity companies, who needed to satisfy their newly acquired shareholders. Indeed, the government was legally prohibited from intervening in the electricity market. But, without demand from Britain's coal-fired power stations, dozens of pits were doomed.

Despite its amalgamation with the DTI, Energy remained a semi-independent fiefdom within Heseltine's new empire, and its affairs were largely delegated to his minister of state, Tim Eggar. Although Eggar had never served in the former Department of Energy, he had a long-standing interest in the industry and was an experienced minister, considered to be future Cabinet material. It was Eggar – and to a lesser extent his colleague Tim Sainsbury – who initially had to resolve the problem of coal closures and negotiate with the Treasury over redundancy payments. 'Heseltine's style by this time was very detached, consistent with his management philosophy,' says a senior civil servant on the Energy side of the DTI. Although Heseltine later spoke of spending 'much time' sharing 'the agony of that decision', the official recalls the President having very little involvement with the impending closures during the months before his boss's first announcement.[9] 'Eggar was very much in charge of this process, and it was up to Eggar to decide when he needed to involve Heseltine.' The wider goal was not to keep redundant miners happy, but to prepare coal for privatization.

On 13 October 1992 both Michael Heseltine and British Coal held separate press conferences. The shock waves would reverberate for weeks. Thirty-one of the industry's remaining fifty mines would close, they announced, with the loss of up to 30,000 jobs – many of them through compulsory redundancy.

In terms of actual numbers the cuts were not exceptional, given the contraction since the early 1980s when the industry had involved almost 200 pits and more than 200,000 men. There had also been individual years in the 1960s when coal had lost many more pits and jobs, albeit from a far larger base. Nevertheless, there was public outcry. Nor did it come just from the government's political opponents, or simply from people in the mining areas. Conservative voters, and Conservative MPs, were appalled, and on two counts. First, the scale of the shutdown: almost two-thirds of the industry was being closed, leaving just nineteen collieries. Second, the abruptness of it all: six pits were to close at the end of that week – with the loss of 6,000 jobs – and another thirteen by Christmas, only eleven weeks away. Mining would cease altogether in several areas – Lancashire, north Staffordshire, North Wales and Derbyshire. (And only one pit would remain in South Wales, the coalfield that had generated the Pridmore family wealth, and indirectly paid for Heseltine's own start as an entrepreneur.)

Michael Heseltine was completely unprepared for the response. He was partly wrong-footed by the fact that an early leak of the proposals had produced only a muted reaction. Furthermore, according to Tim Eggar, 'the advice we received from the party managers was that concern would be limited to the mining areas', but when Heseltine visited the North-East shortly after the leak he was surprised by how little concern there was.[10] British Coal had been so successful in closing more than 100 pits since the end of the 1984–5 strike that ministers assumed they'd have no trouble continuing the process. But the government was warned the latest plans might meet strong resistance. In June, the industrial-relations director of British Coal, Kevan Hunt, had written three times to the DTI alerting them to the possibility of serious public disorder in mining areas and to a feeling of betrayal in Nottinghamshire, where most men had continued working during the miners' strike (Hunt even kept one memo deliberately short because he knew Heseltine didn't like reading). The DTI Deputy Secretary for Energy, Robert Priddle, had expressed similar concerns. When the British Coal board reiterated their anxieties at a dinner with Heseltine and Eggar in early October, 'they were dismissive of us', says one director.

To cushion the blow, Heseltine had also announced that £1 billion had been secured for miners' redundancy payments. The money followed prolonged wrangling with the Treasury – principally with his former deputy, Michael Portillo, recently promoted to Chief Secretary. It had been an immensely frustrating negotiation: for months the Treasury refused to renew the generous coal-industry redundancy terms which had just expired, and argued for the lowest possible payouts. Some DTI people felt that Treasury officials regarded the negotiations almost as an intellectual exercise. Why, the Treasury queried, should miners be treated any different from workers in private industry?

In the end the Treasury backed down only under pressure from

John Major, but then insisted that the additional money would be available only in the current financial year, 1992–93. This explains why the closures had to be rushed over fewer than six months. Equally, the closure programme could have been phased over a longer period if agreement on redundancy terms had been reached earlier. Nor did it help that the timetable was squeezed still further by a deliberate decision to delay the bad news until after the Conservative conference.

Heseltine's other big mistake was to hold a press conference on the same day as British Coal. Ministers didn't normally announce pit closures: during the 1984–5 miners' strike, for instance, such matters had always been dismissed as a question for the Coal Board. His announcement perhaps stemmed from a natural instinct to take credit for what he regarded as a minor triumph in extracting generous redundancy terms from the Treasury, but it meant that public hostility was directed not so much towards British Coal as the government, and him in particular. 'This is the toughest decision I have ever had to take,' he told journalists, 'but that does not make it the wrong decision . . . This is a dreadful thing to have to do, but it's the right thing to do.'[11] He was mauled by the labour and energy correspondents, many of whom knew far more about the coal industry than he did. 'He hadn't been briefed properly,' says one witness, 'and it showed.'

Politically, the closures had come at completely the wrong time – just four weeks after the débâcle of Britain's withdrawal from the Exchange Rate Mechanism. 'The government was pretty shell-shocked over the ERM,' admits Tim Eggar. 'We didn't realize how the political landscape had changed.'[12] Ministers faced difficulties from all sides. As Britain fulfilled its turn in the European presidency for six months, there were continuing problems over whether it and other states would ratify the Maastricht Treaty; moreover, the National Heritage Secretary, David Mellor, a close ally of John Major, had just been forced to resign over a scandal – partly about his sex life but also involving questions about his judgement. Nor did ministers yet appreciate how difficult it was to govern with a majority of only twenty-one: not since the early 1950s had the Tories coped with such a precarious parliamentary position. It meant the government could be rebuffed by what Heseltine privately called 'a dozen nutcases'.

The coal announcement had hit a sudden mood of intense disillusionment with the government; many people who'd voted Conservative the previous April now felt they'd made a mistake. To throw 30,000 miners out of work, and tens of thousands more in supporting industries, seemed crazy in the face of the prolonged recession and when unemployment had reached 2.8 million. To do so because of the government's privatization of electricity looked even worse.

In one move Michael Heseltine had transformed the miners' leader, Arthur Scargill, from a busted flush into a popular hero. The *Sun* newspaper, bishops and middle-class Tory voters across the English shires united in support of Scargill's cause. Despite his South Wales roots, Heseltine seemed not to understand the special place of coal in the national psyche, nor to appreciate the respect and sentimental affection the public has for men who do such an unpleasant job that was once so vital. And by closing the pits, people felt, the government was abandoning a national resource: there is still more coal underground than has ever been mined.

What ministers expected least was the fury from their own ranks. Sir Marcus Fox, the chairman of the 1922 Committee of Tory backbenchers, described the closures as 'unacceptable'.[13] Despite the free-market arguments for shutting pits, most Tory critics came from the right, including James Pawsey, Rhodes Boyson, Nicholas Winterton and William Cash. David Evans, one of his campaign team in the second leadership ballot in 1990, even called for Heseltine's dismissal over the way he had handled matters. 'Michael Heseltine has done what he has done and left the Prime Minister to take the flak,' he said. 'Now Mr Major should be strong enough to wield the axe.'[14] Evans's intervention led to a ferocious argument with Heseltine in the Members' Lobby.

The episode had again illustrated Heseltine's high-handedness and his tendency simply to press ahead without sufficient consultation. Two months later the High Court condemned both the government and British Coal for acting 'unlawfully and irrationally' in closing the mines so quickly, and without going through the necessary colliery review procedure instituted at the end of the miners' strike. Heseltine would be forced to concede 'we got it wrong'.[15]

It was also notable how little Heseltine had prepared his Cabinet colleagues for the news. The first time many senior ministers heard of the closure plans was as a postscript to a meeting of their Overseas and Defence Committee, when John Major said that the President of the Board of Trade wanted to brief them about a statement he was making that day. This lack of consultation was naturally seized upon by those who recalled Heseltine's past. John Watts, the chairman of the Commons Treasury Committee, echoed many in saying that 'one of the greatest ironies of the whole bungle' was that Heseltine had 'resigned from Margaret Thatcher's government claiming that Cabinet government had broken down, with too many decisions taken in committees'.[16] In fact the coal decision had not even been taken by a formal committee, but an ad-hoc group of ministers.

'The ground was not laid with his Cabinet colleagues as well as it should have been,' admits an official close to Heseltine. 'It was partly a failure on his part not to appreciate how his colleagues would react.' Had the plan actually gone to Cabinet, it would probably have been endorsed. But because they weren't involved it was easier for fellow ministers to blame the furore on the President, and he became the victim of hostile briefings to journalists. Heseltine had no more natural allies in John Major's Cabinet than he had had in Margaret Thatcher's: indeed, he probably had even fewer ministerial friends. Colleagues eyed him with a wary detachment, as if he were not quite one of them. His age, experience, reputation, personal wealth and style marked him as a minister apart.

The new Employment Secretary, Gillian Shephard, was particularly upset. She had been told a week beforehand that thirty-one pits would close, but didn't know which collieries or the precise timetable until she heard the announcement. This was especially odd given that she would be in charge of the measures to reskill miners; the Commons Employment Committee later criticized Heseltine for not involving her more closely. When pressed by the committee, Heseltine spoke of having had a one-on-one discussion with Shephard on the 'amelioration measures' a month before the details were announced, but he couldn't recall how long it had lasted.[17] It was primarily a cock-up: there was subsequent consultation at junior ministerial level, but the detail was never relayed upwards to the Employment Secretary.

Nor had Heseltine's sole Cabinet supporter in 1990, the Welsh

Secretary, David Hunt, been warned about the closure of Point of Ayr, the last pit in North Wales. Yet Hunt later had to defend Heseltine's actions in a Commons debate. Equally, MPs were unimpressed that Heseltine had called a press conference, rather than make a Commons statement when the House reassembled a week later. The timing had other tactical disadvantages: had the closures been announced while the House was sitting, the whips might have been much better placed to contain the dissent.

The government now faced the prospect of defeat when Parliament returned, as more than a dozen Tories threatened to enter the opposition lobbies. On the Sunday night beforehand, an angry John Major summoned more than twenty officials and ministers – including a large part of the Cabinet – to an emergency session in Downing Street. 'Everybody, but everybody, was downcast,' says an official who was there, 'and the Prime Minister was demanding answers to questions which officials were simply unable to give.' The gathering quickly planned Heseltine's retreat.

The next day, six days after his first announcement, Michael Heseltine told the Commons that no pits would now close immediately. Instead, ten collieries were being given the usual ninety-day notice period, and there would be a moratorium on closing the others while British Coal tried to pursue contracts with the power generators and the government held 'consultations'. Peter (now Lord) Walker had also agreed to take charge of economic regeneration in the affected mining communities, for which an extra £165 million had been allocated. And Heseltine himself promised to seek new markets for coal. It was one of the fastest and most spectacular U-turns by any minister in modern times. 'I regret this discourtesy to the House,' Heseltine told MPs. 'I accept full responsibility for that decision, as I do for the consequent events.'[18] The pressure of the last few days had clearly got to him. 'Stop being so plain bloody stupid,' he shouted at a Labour MP who heckled him at one point.[19]

Yet even these concessions were not enough, and Heseltine suffered a hostile response when he met angry Tory back-benchers, who had been chastened by the strength of constituency feeling. Extras quickly had to be tacked on to the U-turn package bit by bit as events seemed to slip beyond Heseltine's control. In a full Commons debate two days later, Heseltine conceded that all thirty-one collieries would now be reviewed, including the ten that had been due for immediate closure, and he insisted that British Coal would keep them in working condition pending the outcome. 'No miner must be disadvantaged by the announcements that have been made in the past few days,' he conceded. 'No miner,' he emphasized again.[20] Despite even these commitments, and the further promise of a White Paper on energy, five Tories still voted with Labour, though the government scraped through with a majority of thirteen.

What astonished most observers about the whole affair was that Michael Heseltine had a reputation as the most astute operator in the Cabinet, and as a politician who could scent trouble from afar. How had he completely failed to foresee either the public reaction or the likely response of Tory MPs?

In part, Heseltine's reputation was based on a misapprehension. He may have the rare political knack of inspiring an audience, but he can easily misjudge people's mood, and has never been one to care much about the opinions of Conservative back-benchers. The pit closure programme wasn't his first embarrassing retreat – nor the last. Council referendums in 1981, elected mayors and, later, the privatization of the Post Office were all important issues over which Tory MPs and ministerial colleagues forced him to back down. Heseltine's regular failure to gauge back-bench sentiment is, in fact, just what one would expect from a politician who spends so little time socializing with fellow Tories, and shows so little attachment to the House of Commons.

It took five months for the DTI to carry out its review. Much of the argument revolved around the complex economics of electricity supply – whether coal generation was really cheaper than gas or heavily subsidized nuclear power. From having taken little interest before his original announcement, Heseltine now expended most of his own energy on coal. Behind the scenes he was fighting both with the Treasury and with Cabinet colleagues for subsidies to help the industry. However, his failure to consult in the previous autumn didn't make ministers any more sympathetic: Gillian Shephard and Michael Howard were particularly hostile to the idea of using tax-payers' money to keep pits open.

For almost the first time in his long ministerial career, Heseltine had to negotiate with individual rebel MPs, such as Winston Churchill and Elizabeth Peacock in the newly formed Conservative Coal Group. He knew that a Commons defeat on his package would almost certainly force his resignation. An important part of the operation was trying to ensure a favourable report from the Trade and Industry Committee, where his efforts were assisted by the membership of Keith Hampson. In the end it came down to a numbers game, balancing dissident MPs with pits: how many collieries had to be saved to buy off enough rebels? It was exactly the kind of short-term thinking Heseltine had so often decried in the past.

Having initially been promised for January, the results of his review didn't appear until late March. As with Concorde twenty years before, Heseltine failed in his quest for new markets that might offset the extra £700 million in assistance he finally secured from the Treasury. Some funds paid for new measures for the coal communities, and up to £500 million was available for subsidies to keep thirteen of the original thirty-one pits open during the two years before privatization. A further six mines would be mothballed. In the long-term, however, the outcome was barely different to that announced in October. This was hardly surprising so long as electricity companies refused to order more coal. At the start of 1997 the deep-mined coal industry had been reduced to twenty-eight privatized pits – and the long-term future of many of those looked very uncertain.

But the process of Heseltine's coal review had had the effect of slowly defusing the political crisis. By the time he had reworked his original conclusions, in March 1993, the sense of outrage had dissipated. During the intervening months, both miners and the public had become resigned to a large-scale contraction of the industry. Only four Tory MPs voted with Labour (though three more abstained), and the government again secured a relatively comfortable majority of thirteen, having persuaded the Ulster Unionists not to vote with Labour with the promise of £10 million in subsidies to major electricity users in Northern Ireland.

After his conference declaration about intervening in the same way that overseas governments did, it was all the more ironic that coal should have been one of the British industries which suffered most from subsidized foreign competition. Indeed the three governments he had cited as interveners at the Tory conference in Brighton – Germany, France and Japan – all gave considerable assistance to their coal producers. In Britain, however, Heseltine was restricted by the law forbidding him from intervening in the electricity market. 'If I had had the power to negotiate with the electricity industry collectively,' he admitted to MPs, 'I might have been able to make more progress.'[21]

The inconsistency in Heseltine's stance was pointed up sharply in the Commons when he mocked the Labour-controlled Leeds City Council for buying cheap foreign coal rather than supplies from local Yorkshire pits. Opposition MPs reminded him that local authorities were obliged to buy the cheapest fuel, under efficiency measures he himself had instigated at the Department of the Environment.[22]

The crisis had seen a rather different Michael Heseltine from the man who had insisted that Merseyside's fortunes could not simply be left to the free market, and who had been willing to resign over the survival of Cammell Laird. He had been obliged to adopt the Thatcherite position on mining communities, and conclude that the market should prevail. 'We were aware that there would be consequences,' he said of the pit closures, 'but we came to a view, which is the view I am having to take all the time, that it is for the private sector to adjust to the changes in the market-place.'[23]

In February 1993 Heseltine's commitment to intervene like foreign governments was again found wanting with the collapse of the Anglo-Dutch lorry-maker DAF, whose subsidiary Leyland DAF was the former British Leyland truck division. Whereas both the Dutch and Belgian governments funded large rescue operations for parts of DAF's operations within their borders, Heseltine said Britain was not willing to join the multinational rescue.

People were beginning to ask whether Michael Heseltine was now a spent force who was being frozen out by his colleagues. Other misfortunes seemed to confirm that impression. Earlier, in January, when the Chancellor, Norman Lamont, cut interest rates to 6 per cent – their lowest level for fifteen years – nobody thought to tell the minister whose department had the greatest concern about lower borrowing costs. Three hours afterwards, when he turned up at the BBC Westminster studios to do another interview on coal, a reporter asked him for his reaction to the interest–rate cut. Heseltine expressed disbelief that it had occurred, and agreed to answer questions only on the understanding that they would be scrubbed if it later emerged that borrowing rates hadn't been lowered. Unfortunately for Heseltine, this exchange was seen by a Labour Party press officer on one of the BBC's internal monitors. Heseltine had merely been the victim of an unfortunate series of oversights within the DTI, but it was bad for his reputation when his astonishing ignorance soon became public knowledge.

The first year of Michael Heseltine's stint at the DTI had been the worst, and certainly the most stressful, period of his entire government career. And beneath the surface lay other troubles that were set to emerge.

It must have been with some relief that in June 1993 Heseltine and his wife took a rare weekend break. Their destination was Venice, where Anne wanted to visit the Biennale arts festival, and they stayed at the exclusive Cipriani Hotel.

21. *Up with This I Will Not Put*

The plan was to leave Venice on the Monday and return to London via a meeting Michael Heseltine had to attend in Germany that day. But around 2.30 that morning he suddenly got out of bed with bad pains in his arms and chest. According to Anne, 'He actually woke me up by crashing around in the bathroom, looking for Alka-Seltzer. I was rather cross. At that point he thought he had indigestion.' When his wife rang the hotel reception to ask for a doctor, they immediately recognized Heseltine's troubles were similar to the case of another recent guest. Instead of waiting for a doctor, says Anne, they were rushed off by water ambulance.

We went bump, bump, bump through the canals to the hospital. Thank God it happened at night when the canals were clear; otherwise it would have taken twice as long to get there. It wasn't *that* frightening. He wasn't unconscious at any stage and it wasn't as though he was screaming in agony, either.[1]

Heseltine's pains were not acute, and had actually gone by the time he reached hospital. 'That's why I wasn't that worried. It didn't last that long,' he said later.[2] The Venetian doctors soon diagnosed that he'd suffered a coronary thrombosis – a sudden blockage in a main artery to the heart. In short, he'd had a heart attack.

In some ways it wasn't surprising that it had happened. His father had died of a heart attack at fifty-five; Michael Heseltine was now sixty, and took no serious exercise while leading a frenetic lifestyle. People had also begun remarking how he had 'aged so suddenly' since returning to government.[3] On the other hand, unlike many politicians – Kenneth Clarke, for example – Heseltine doesn't drink much or smoke, and he has always stayed slim – one advantage, perhaps, of not spending much time in the notorious watering-holes of the Palace of Westminster.

After his recent political troubles, most observers assumed that this spelt the end of Michael Heseltine's lifelong ambition to become Prime Minister. Although he would probably return to his old ministerial job, could a man with heart problems ever hold the top office? There were some favourable precedents: Lyndon Johnson had suffered a heart attack and gone on to serve five years as US President, while the Labour politician John Smith (who sent Heseltine a 'get well' letter) had had a heart attack in 1988 and was now leader of his party.

A more interesting question was why Heseltine had gone to Venice. Anne had been helped in rushing her husband to hospital by the former Conservative Party treasurer Alistair McAlpine and his wife, Romilly, who live part-time in the city and had bumped into the Heseltines at the Cipriani over the weekend. Had this 'chance' meeting with Lord McAlpine had anything to do with recent problems over Conservative Party funding? It seemed too much of a coincidence, especially when Heseltine was due to speak in the Commons the following Tuesday in a debate about political donations.

In particular, speculation linked Heseltine's heart attack to the Conservatives' increasing embarrassment over money they had received from foreign sources, and in particular from the Turkish Cypriot businessman Asil Nadir. During the late 1980s the Tories had been given at least £440,000 by Nadir – he himself said more than £1 million – before the collapse of his Polly Peck empire in 1991 and his arrest on theft and fraud charges. In May 1993, only a few weeks before Heseltine's trip to Venice, Nadir had jumped bail of £3.5 million and fled to Northern Cyprus. There were several apparent links between Heseltine and Nadir which were simply too intriguing for journalists to ignore.

Foremost was the role that had recently been played by Heseltine's 1990 chief of staff, Michael Mates. Despite holding one of the most pressurized ministerial jobs - in charge of security in Ulster – Mates had gone to extraordinary lengths to help Nadir pursue complaints about his treatment by the British authorities. Mates resigned as Northern Ireland minister only three days after Heseltine's heart attack, when his efforts on Nadir's behalf became too embarrassing to the government.

The businessman's grievances had been brought to Mates's attention by Mark Rogerson, a friend who lived in the MP's Hampshire constituency and who was acting as Nadir's public-relations adviser. Rogerson's business partner, Christopher Morgan, was also close to the Heseltine camp, having worked for Lloyd's Merchant Bank and the European consortium during the Westland crisis. After Westland, Morgan had become a personal friend of Heseltine, and even arranged back-up research for him during the 1987 election.

Michael Mates's activity went well beyond what one might normally expect of an MP pursuing a constituent's problems – and Asil Nadir was not even a constituent, only the client of one. The MP wrote three letters to the Attorney-General's office suggesting that the Serious Fraud Office (SFO) was treating Nadir unfairly – and also went to see the Attorney, Sir Nicholas Lyell, personally. The Nadir case soon became something of an obsession for Mates. Journalists on the BBC's *Panorama*, for instance, were astonished at how he was so willing to drop ministerial business to talk to them about the businessman, whom Mates had obviously come to regard as a friend. In May 1993 he even presented Nadir with a watch on which he had famously engraved the words 'Don't Let the Buggers Get You Down'. To the MP's intense embarrassment – and subsequent condemnation – Nadir fled the country only three days later. Mates finally resigned when it was revealed that he had also borrowed a car from Nadir's PR man.

Michael Heseltine, too, had spoken to Sir Nicholas Lyell about the SFO's handling of the Nadir case, after it had been mentioned to him at what Heseltine later described as a 'purely personal lunch with a friend of mine'. The friend was Christopher Morgan:

I saw the Attorney in the division lobby very soon after this and mentioned to him the things I had been told. He said if there was anything that anybody wanted to say to him he would like to see it in writing and be able to consider it properly. I passed that message on to Christopher Morgan. We have heard nothing since. My own view is absolutely clear. What I did was right, and if I had done anything less, it would have been wrong.[4]

Quite apart from Michael Mates and Christopher Morgan, there were also smaller coincidences which seemed to link Nadir with the President of the Board of Trade, though Heseltine said he didn't think he had ever met him. There was a connection, for instance, through the accountants Rawlinson & Hunter, who had acted as Nadir's personal accountants and as auditors to his private property firm, South Audley Management, before it went into liquidation. Rawlinson & Hunter also managed a Jersey nominee company, R & H Trust Co. (Jersey) Ltd, which held a small holding – less than 1 per cent – of the Haymarket Group, though on whose behalf it was not clear.

But the most intriguing link between Nadir and Heseltine came through a leading tax inspector called Michael Allcock, who was head of the Inland Revenue's Special Office 2, which covered activities in the City. Between 1987 and 1992 Allcock had established a fearsome reputation for pursuing tax owed on dubious City share-dealings. In particular, he investigated the way people used offshore companies to avoid tax on such transactions. It was a tip from the Inland Revenue man, according to both Nadir and Allcock himself, which had prompted the SFO to carry out its 1990 raid on South Audley Management which led in turn to the collapse of Polly Peck. In his Commons resignation statement, Michael Mates alleged that there was 'evidence of improper collusion' between Allcock and the SFO.[5]

Michael Allcock's investigations had also led him to a former City stockbroker called Jonathan Bekhor, who had fled Britain owing millions of pounds. The broker's firm, A. J. Bekhor, had specialized in share transactions for offshore companies, and Allcock used legal powers to obtain from the company, and from Stock Exchange records, the names of the overseas firms for which Bekhor had dealt. At one point the stockbroker handed Allcock a handwritten list of about seventy individuals who he claimed were behind the offshore companies. One of the names on Bekhor's list was Michael Heseltine. Michael Allcock was keen to pursue this Heseltine lead, but his superiors reportedly stopped him even seeing the minister's tax files, on the grounds that the evidence was too flimsy.

It must be stressed that Jonathan Bekhor never produced any hard evidence about Heseltine, and Heseltine himself has always denied having anything to do with Bekhor or any of the other people whose names have publicly emerged as being on the list given to Allcock. Heseltine has also insisted, on more than one occasion, that none of his family investments are offshore. 'I have no overseas trusts,' he told the *Sunday Times* in 1990, 'no interest in them, no benefits of them and have always refused to do so.' And he specifically denied that either R & H Trust or another Jersey firm which held Haymarket shares represented any of his own investment in the company. 'They've nothing to do with me at all. I must tell you that those trusts do not have any part to play in my shareholding, never have had.'[6]

In 1992, Allcock was suspended from duty and subsequently charged with corruption and theft offences arising from other aspects of his work. He went on trial at the Old Bailey in October 1996.

Several journalists have spent months, if not years, investigating the possible Heseltine connections in the complex Asil Nadir affair, and nobody has ever produced any damaging evidence. It seems that Heseltine may simply have been the victim of mischief-making and smears. But Heseltine has encouraged suspicions about his finances by the complicated and secretive way in which his investments in Haymarket are organized. Though he was the government minister who at the DTI held overall responsibility for openness and public access to company records, Heseltine's own businesses set an atrocious example of how easy it is to confuse inquirers by concealing the identities of the real owners who benefit from a shareholding.

Since the early 1960s Heseltine's businesses have consisted of a patchwork of several dozen companies in a group structure; over the years, six different holding companies have successively acted as an umbrella for the whole group. The confusion is also increased by regular name changes – not just of the holding company but of many of the subsidiaries – and it's quite common for one of the Haymarket companies to adopt a name which has previously been held by another within the group. Although Heseltine and his family have long been the majority owners of the Haymarket business, their names rarely appear anywhere in the records. Instead, nearly all shares in the business are held by 'nominee companies'; in some cases, such as R & H Trust, these are located offshore.

In May 1996 Asil Nadir stirred the pot even more. Speaking from Northern Cyprus, he threatened further revelations about his links with the Conservatives. Only two senior Tories had stood by him, he said. 'Michael Heseltine was very supportive; he was told about the difficulties I was experiencing by Michael Mates and he appeared to do all he could to support me.'[7] Nadir also made astonishing claims about what had happened when Heseltine met Alistair McAlpine in Venice just before his heart attack. 'They had a terrible row,' Nadir claimed:

I know this because my ex-wife Ayşegül was a guest of Lord McAlpine's at the time, and she heard raised voices from an adjoining room. Lord McAlpine had just told the press I was a sleazy little crook and Michael wanted him to stop attacking me . . . I believe Michael knew that the Conservative Party felt vulnerable as to the way they raised their funds.[8]

'What Nadir has been saying is a complete load of baloney,' says McAlpine. 'It's fantasy of the wildest order.' The former Tory treasurer admits knowing Ayşegül Nadir, but denies that she was staying with him in Venice at the time, or that Heseltine had come to Italy to see him, or that they had a row when they met. 'The truth of the matter was I asked him, "Why did you come to Venice?" He said, "Oh God, you're the last person in the world I want to see, because I've got to answer a question on Tuesday on Asil Nadir."'[9] His account is corroborated by Min Hogg, the editor of *World of Interiors*, who was a guest of Lord McAlpine's that weekend. 'Asil Nadir's wife was certainly not staying with the McAlpines at the time,' she says. Nor does Hogg recall the two men having any serious discussions about Nadir and Tory funding on the brief occasions when they saw each other.[10]

The Commons debate on party finance took place while Heseltine was still recovering in hospital in Venice, whereupon the speculation about Heseltine took on a new dimension apparently unconnected with Nadir. Under the cover of parliamentary privilege, the Labour MP Clive Soley added to recent allegations in *The Guardian* that the Conservative Party had received £7 million from Saudi Arabia. Soley quoted from a letter, written to him by a Saudi he would not name, which alleged that before the 1992 election Heseltine had attended a meeting in The Boltons in Kensington with Prince Bandar of Saudi Arabia and the country's ambassador to the USA, at which they discussed financial aid for the Conservatives.[11] Central Office strenuously denied the claims; two years later Soley withdrew his charge.

Four days after his heart attack, Michael Heseltine was flown back to London. As he left the Venice hospital, dressed in surgical clothes and being pushed in a wheelchair, he looked gravely ill. In fact his wretched appearance was largely the result of gout in his foot, caused by the pills he was taking.

As Heseltine recovered that summer, his family inevitably discussed whether he should continue in politics. Friends say Anne would have been quite happy had he called it a day. But Heseltine claimed that a specialist had told him he'd got the 'arteries of a man of thirty or forty' and 'the heart of an average sixty-year-old who hasn't had a heart attack'.[12] For four months he avoided ministerial duties, and he cancelled his traditional speech to the Conservative conference. Nevertheless, he appeared on the platform in Blackpool and flexed his arms in a mock exercise to assure people he was well. During the autumn he gradually resumed his ministerial commitments, first attending Cabinet meetings and then making speeches again. Heseltine always says his heart attack wasn't serious, but he didn't resume full-time work until the New Year.

Even then he tried to lead an easier lifestyle. Anne insisted he get to bed early, and he was more careful with his diet: he substituted margarine for butter, for example (just as he supposedly once had for guests at the New Court Hotel). Instead of returning to London on Sunday evening, Heseltine's new routine was to come back from Northamptonshire on Monday morning. His ministerial office tried to put fewer papers in his red boxes, while the BBC programme *Newsnight* was deemed too late in the evening for live interviews; instead, they had to be recorded earlier.

Inevitably, many of these initial resolutions soon slipped, especially as the political pressures mounted again. At the end of February 1994 it was Michael Heseltine's turn to appear before the Scott Inquiry, which was investigating British arms sales to Iraq.

Sir Richard Scott's official investigation resulted from the trial of three executives of the firm Matrix Churchill on charges of supplying weapons-making equipment to Saddam Hussein. The case had collapsed in November 1992 after the former trade minister Alan Clark revealed that he had given the company 'a nod and a wink' to sell the equipment. It now looked as if the government had conspired to ensure that businessmen who had acted in good faith went to jail. Two months before the trial Heseltine had been one of four ministers who were asked to sign what are known as public-interest immunity certificates – or PIIs – to prevent official papers being made available to the defence, on the grounds of confidentiality and security.

It is a sign of the frantic, pressurized nature of ministerial life that Michael Heseltine should have taken his crucial decision over Matrix Churchill in September 1992, just before making his dreadful misjudgement over the pit closures. This time Heseltine's political instincts proved to be much more sound than they were over coal, and surer than those of his three colleagues – the Home Secretary, Kenneth Clarke; the Defence Secretary, Malcolm Rifkind; and the Foreign Office minister, Tristan Garel-Jones – who all agreed their PIIs without fuss. When the Attorney-General insisted that ministers had no option but to sign such certificates, it caused Heseltine considerable anxiety.

Sir Nicholas Lyell had asked him to sign his draft PII overnight. 'This is potentially troublesome,' his private secretary, Peter Smith, had warned Heseltine. 'In the short term,' Smith jotted on a briefing note, 'it appears we have no choice but to claim immunity, but, if it comes to court, the press will have a field day.'[13] Heseltine concurred. He had long arguments, dragging on for more than a week, with Lyell, who cited the recent Makanjuola police-complaint case as obliging ministers to sign PIIs in such circumstances. 'Something unheard of in a ministerial office,' says Smith, 'was he wanted to get hold of the *All England Law Reports* and read what Lord Justice Bingham had said in the Makanjuola case. There must have been half a dozen meetings lasting an hour or so each, with large quantities of paper going backwards and forwards. It was taken very seriously.'[14]

Heseltine realized that the case against the Matrix Churchill men was extremely shaky. DTI officials had told him that the government had been warned in 1988 that Matrix Churchill equipment was going to make Iraqi mortar shells, and also that the security service MI6 had been in regular contact with the firm. As with the *Belgrano* affair nine years before, his instincts were to be much more open than other ministers. 'It became apparent to me,' he told the Scott Inquiry, 'that, if this series of events unfolded at any stage, I would have to go and try to indulge in the process of – what is the word? – "incommunicative"' answers . . . and I was not prepared to do that . . . I said, "Up with this I will not put." '[15]

According to one DTI minute, Heseltine felt that 'no rational person, who had looked at the files, could have said that the documents should not have been disclosed. It would have been terrible if a defendant had gone to jail as a result of non-disclosure.'[16] While he accepted the principle that certain government papers should be withheld from court cases, in this instance the needs of justice overrode the public interest in suppression. 'I am not signing it,' Heseltine claims to have said.[17]

It is clear, however, that Michael Heseltine was concerned with the implications not just for the defendants but also for himself. If the judge subsequently allowed the papers to be disclosed, another DTI minute suggested, 'was he [Heseltine] not setting himself up? It would look as though he had been engaged in an attempt at cover-up and had been overruled by the judge.'[18] If the papers were disclosed, Heseltine admitted to Scott, 'I was certainly preoccupied to ensure . . . that the position I was in was defensible.'[19]

Heseltine was eventually persuaded by Lord Justice Bingham's ruling in the Makanjuola case: what especially impressed him was that Bingham was now Master of the Rolls. But his PII was carefully rewritten and watered down so as to be substantially different from those of other ministers, in the expectation that this would be spotted by the judge and interpreted as a sign that he had grave reservations. Heseltine was also careful to ensure that his ministerial colleagues knew that his PII was different from theirs. But, as Sir Richard Scott later pointed out, Heseltine's concern could have been stated much more explicitly. Lyell also assured Heseltine that he would get the prosecution counsel to inform the judge at the Matrix Churchill trial of Heseltine's view that some of the DTI papers concerned would indeed be helpful to the defence.

Sir Nicholas Lyell, however, failed to ask the prosecution QC, Alan Moses, to communicate Heseltine's concern to the trial judge. In the event, neither Moses nor the judge noticed that Heseltine's PII was any weaker than the others, and, despite what Heseltine had said, Moses even argued that all four ministers thought that each of their departments' documents were irrelevant to the defence. The episode reflected badly on Lyell, who admitted to Scott that a series of errors meant that Heseltine's wishes weren't passed on.

Michael Heseltine's appearance before the Scott Inquiry in February 1994 was treated as a big event – by himself as much as by the media. As he and his elegantly dressed wife turned up at the proceedings, they were mobbed by cameramen as if they were a couple of movie stars. Relaxed and looking confident that he had a good story to tell, the President then related what had happened when the Attorney-General had asked him to sign his PII. In an obvious attack on Lyell, he said he found it 'difficult to explain the way in which events worked out', or why the trial judge was never told of his views.[20]

Heseltine also revealed that in 1992 he had advised John Major to use the Scott Inquiry to be frank about how the guidelines on exports to Iraq had been altered without telling Parliament. They should all 'rely on the truth as the inquiry will reveal', he argued, rather than try to devise some new, implausible explanation as to what had happened to the guidelines. 'It would be extremely disingenuous for us now to say that there had been no change in their operation,' he wrote to Major.[21] It was, of course, an easier issue for Michael Heseltine than for some of his colleagues, since he hadn't been a minister when the guidelines had been secretly changed in 1988.

Heseltine was probably the most devastating of more than sixty witnesses to appear at Scott's public hearings. Politically, his testimony exposed serious differences within government ranks and was highly damaging to ministerial colleagues. In explaining why, in the interests of a fair trial, he had been reluctant to sign a PII certificate, he was implying that Clarke, Rifkind and Garel-Jones had been less than vigilant to ensure that the Matrix Churchill defendants didn't go to jail unfairly. And he couldn't help but show his annoyance at the way Sir Nicholas Lyell had behaved.

Michael Heseltine looked set to be the one minister who would emerge from the Scott affair almost untainted, while at the same time having delivered a carefully aimed kick at his leadership rival, Kenneth Clarke. Several Cabinet ministers – and not just those implicated by his evidence – were furious with the way he had attacked colleagues so openly. It was less than nine months after his heart attack, but Heseltine's performance before Scott suddenly reignited speculation about his long-term ambitions.

Heseltine had managed to paint himself as a minister with integrity – and rather more convincingly than he had over Westland – at a time when the government was beset by allegations of sleaze and poor ministerial conduct. His 'squeaky-clean' image would be reinforced by other episodes. The first came in July 1994, when it emerged that he had ordered a DTI inquiry into suspected insider-trading in shares by the former Conservative deputy chairman Jeffrey Archer, who had long been lobbying for a top political job. Heseltine and Archer are similar figures in many ways: intensely ambitious, self-made millionaires, they can both send Tory activists into rapture, but also infuriate the old-style grandees. Although Heseltine had occasionally attended Archer's parties, he had little time for the novelist. When *The Times* received a tip-off about the share investigation, Heseltine took the highly unusual decision to confirm the story. Again, it seems he feared accusations of a cover-up if the DTI stonewalled reporters' questions. In the end, the department's inspectors concluded there was insufficient evidence to prosecute Archer.

A year later Heseltine got up in the House of Commons and astonished MPs by announcing a DTI inquiry into whether the weapons manufacturer BMARC had broken government guidelines on arms sales to Iran in the late 1980s. Again it was politically embarrassing, for his Cabinet colleague Jonathan Aitken, the Chief Secretary, had been a director of BMARC during the period in question. What particularly surprised MPs was how Heseltine chose to break the news of his inquiry so ostentatiously, by making an oral statement rather than the more usual method of a written answer.

One of Heseltine's most important statutory responsibilities at the DTI was competition policy. In this he took a notably different tack from his predecessors, and was generally far less inclined to refer big company takeovers to the Monopolies Commission. When Lloyds Bank launched a bid for the Midland in 1992, the Office of Fair Trading (OFT) had considerable difficulty in persuading Heseltine to refer it to a Monopolies inquiry, even though a successful bid would have reduced the number of high-street clearing banks from four to three. 'Heseltine didn't help competition policy,' says a senior OFT source. 'He seemed to have a blind spot, seemed to believe that it didn't matter what happened to competition. "Let the market prevail" included for him "Let competition be stifled."' Whereas the more Thatcherite past Secretaries of State, such as Peter Lilley and Norman Tebbit, had been keen to ensure there was rigorous competition in domestic markets, Heseltine seemed more concerned about Britain having strong national champions to compete on the world stage.

Indeed, Heseltine's tenure saw a significant shift in DTI emphasis away from small and medium-sized business towards big companies. 'We live in a world not of rival toffee shops competing from either end of the same street,' he had once written, 'but, in certain key industrial sectors, of giant, taxpayer-financed, government-backed enterprises, all out to triumph over us.'[22] That was particularly reflected in Heseltine's beefed-up work for exports, and his concern that even 'Footsie 500' companies were surprisingly poor at finding new markets overseas.

During the Thatcher era, DTI efforts to help British exports had been treated with suspicion – as a hidden subsidy to business – and Peter Lilley, Heseltine's predecessor, had never been very active in trade promotion. Heseltine, in contrast, considered it a major part of his job and was keen to lead trade missions overseas. According to Peter Smith, 'Peter Walker once told him that Mitterrand had gone to Vietnam and flown in with three plane-loads of businessmen and their kit, and I remember Heseltine was taken quite vividly by that – the concept that if you want to be taken seriously in these markets you've got to go on this scale.'[23] So the President led far larger British delegations than ever before, taking jet-loads of businessmen to visit markets that had been neglected hitherto, such as South Africa, South America, Russia and China. In another move – an obvious variation on the DoE Financial Institutions Group resulting from the Liverpool bus trip – he started the Export Promoters initiative, whereby a hundred managers were seconded from private firms to help the DTI and British embassies overseas identify and pursue potential new markets.

At the end of 1992 Heseltine presided over the official advent of the Single European Market, but what surprised DTI officials – and people in the Foreign Office – especially given his past commitment – was how little he did to promote British interests in Europe. 'His pro-Europeanism is just vision,' says one of his DTI deputy secretaries. 'He's not interested in the nuts and bolts of relationships . . . He does not like going to Europe, especially Brussels, even when asked by his civil servants. He does not like *real* Continentals. He only went a few times at the DTI. It was very odd – this *great European*.'

At home, the two biggest moves to help British business were new units within the DTI to encourage deregulation and international competitiveness. Both areas were trumpeted with a great fanfare as examples of what Heseltine really meant by intervention, though neither was likely to produce exciting results or grab many headlines. Both initiatives involved Heseltine applying leverage right across government. The competitiveness unit obliged all ministries to state what they were doing to help the wealth-creating part of the economy, which then made it easier for outside business organizations, such as the CBI, to point out where they were falling down. 'It had quite an effect, actually,' says the former CBI director-general Howard Davies, 'because it forced people in Whitehall to look at their policy through the prism of what it was doing to British industry.'[24]

In 1994 John Major launched Heseltine's first White Paper on competitiveness, setting out a whole range of comparisons between Britain and rival economies and numerous ways in which the British record might be improved in its attempt to become the 'enterprise centre of Europe'. As with MINIS and Environment White Papers, Heseltine promised the document would be an annual event: a kind of yearly audit of the performance of the British economy and of government measures to improve competitiveness. Many observers were deeply sceptical about the process. 'The specific policies didn't live up to the vision,' one DTI official admits. If the process does make a difference, it will become apparent only after many years.

On deregulation, Heseltine had been ordered by the Prime Minister to cut through 'this burgeoning maze of regulations. Who better for hacking back the jungle?' Major asked the 1992 Tory conference.

'Come on, Michael, out with your club, on with your loincloth, swing into action!'[25] Another White Paper proposed hundreds of areas in which red tape might be cut – ranging from rules about froth on pints of beer to allowing Scottish barbers to open on Sundays. Overall, however, the impact has been less than promised: many reforms have been trivial, with negligible benefit to business. And serious constitutional issues were raised by the 1994 Deregulation Act, which gave ministers powers to alter numerous laws without coming before Parliament.

As a concept, deregulation, like privatization, was always popular with Tory MPs and party activists, as part of the continuing fight to reduce the role of government. Heseltine (along with Michael Portillo) was also among the keenest Cabinet advocates of speeding up the drive to privatize more Civil Service activity, or to hive it off into semi-independent agencies. Ever since leading the government drive to sell council houses in the early 1980s, he had always presented himself as a great pioneer of privatization, though the remaining possibilities were increasingly limited.

After the 1992 election the Post Office was among the few state industries left to sell – along with coal and the railways. Margaret Thatcher had always treated the postal service as 'different' from other privatization candidates, partly through fear that the Queen might object to interference with her Royal Mail. At the DTI, Peter Lilley had been equally cautious, and concentrated instead on measures for greater postal competition. Heseltine was far less interested in competition, but keen to examine full privatization again – not least, a former DTI official suggests, because it would allow him to appear more Thatcherite than the Thatcherites.

Privatization of the Post Office was to be the centre-piece of the 1994 Queen's Speech, but once more Heseltine was forced into an embarrassing climbdown. By that autumn the government majority had dropped to just fourteen, and the likelihood of a successful ambush by Tory rebels was even greater than it had been over coal. As with the pits crisis, his critics came from both wings of the party. Most were Tory left-wingers (and natural Heseltine supporters), such as Hugh Dykes and Robert Hicks. But there were also several populist right-wingers, such as Sir Rhodes Boyson and Nicholas Winterton, some of whom had also opposed him over pit closures. Most of the rebels were senior MPs, now too old to hope for ministerial office and therefore immune to the whips' bribes or threats. Their primary concern was the threat to postal services, especially in rural areas. As with coal, the sense of community had come into conflict with free-market economics.

Heseltine was slow to tackle the dissenters; indeed there was a long gap during the summer of 1994 when he didn't contact them at all. He did eventually meet them, individually and collectively, but failed to convince them to accept a compromise plan which involved selling just 40 per cent of the Post Office and placing another 20 per cent in trust. Instead of being painstaking and patient when he met the rebels, he was imperious and intolerant. The climax was a session with fourteen of them late one night at the Commons. 'He seemed to have lost touch,' says one who attended. 'He seemed to be amazed that anybody could possibly disagree with him. I had been a Heseltine supporter till then. This disillusioned me.'

At a three-hour Cabinet meeting, Heseltine even threatened to 'go down with the ship' and resign if his proposal failed – a prospect which might have won over personal allies like Dykes and Hicks.[26] But, despite Michael Portillo and Peter Lilley backing Heseltine, most ministers concurred with Michael Howard's view that, politically, it was too dangerous to go ahead. The measure's withdrawal left John Major's legislative programme looking pathetically threadbare; it was seen as the point where the government lost its working majority. 'I am disappointed,' Heseltine admitted. 'I don't like it. It isn't good news for democracy, but if you can't get a majority you can't proceed.'[27] He promised to pursue the matter for the rest of his career.

Heseltine had illustrated once again his weakness at building political support through personal contact and persuasion. He should also have realized earlier that the legislation would never get through the Commons (or, trickier still, the Lords). 'Michael insisted on ploughing on,' says a Downing Street adviser. 'It was a misjudgement of back-bench opinion. In the end the Prime Minister laid a restraining hand on him, and if he hadn't Michael might well have taken it to the House, and he wouldn't have survived it.' Yet, on a personal level, the Cabinet retreat did Heseltine no harm. In fact it contributed to a surprising groundswell of support for him from the Tory right. Many right-wingers saw the episode not as an example of poor judgement by Heseltine but instead as another example of John Major's weak leadership and lack of nerve.

Indeed, during 1994 and 1995 Michael Heseltine seemed to be going out of his way to court the Tory right. In Cabinet battles between those who wanted to consolidate and those who wanted to continue with radical change, Heseltine made no secret of where he stood. 'The need to consolidate is a familiar cry,' he told the Conservative Central Council in the spring of 1994. 'It speaks of comfort, of balmy days, of punts drifting in late summer along the backwaters of university cities.' This seemed a deliberate parody of a famous speech John Major had delivered a year before, nostalgically extolling warm beer, shadows over cricket pitches, and George Orwell's old maids cycling to holy communion. 'It will not do!' Heseltine thundered:

Change is gathering pace, not slowing down! Change is not an option. We will either change fast enough to keep ahead or keep abreast. Or change will be forced on us – in lost jobs and lower living standards – by nations who have seized from us that most intoxicating of Tory battle cries – 'Change is our ally!'[28]

Ironically, this echoed much of what Margaret Thatcher had said in the past – notably her 1987 conference speech mocking the idea of Tory banners proclaiming 'Consolidate'. Nor did Heseltine do himself any harm with the more authoritarian element in the party when he voted against lowering the homosexual age of consent from twenty-one to eighteen or sixteen. That genuinely reflected the more puritanical streak in the Heseltine character. Much less convincing, and more opportunistic, seemed to be his sudden attack on the Single European Market as 'overregulated, overprotected and overcentralized', and on what he termed 'Euro-sclerosis'.[29]

As MPs on the right grew increasingly disappointed and exasperated with John Major, some came to see Michael Heseltine as a means to undermine the Prime Minister, and in some cases as a preferable, strong-willed alternative. If Heseltine did become leader, many right-wingers calculated, his age and health meant it would probably be for only a short period, which would then pave the way for the right's then heir apparent, Michael Portillo, who was still considered too inexperienced. To some, Heseltine might also stop the more Euro-enthusiastic Kenneth Clarke, though the Chancellor's leadership prospects had already fallen with his recent tax increases and his unwillingness to hide his belief in a single currency.

'There are no circumstances in which I would stand against John Major,' Heseltine insisted when challenged by journalists. 'John Major is going to lead us into the next election, and people know that my forecast is that we shall win with a majority of sixty.'[30] The trouble was, of course, that the wording sounded all too similar to the formulaic protestations of 1990.

That Michael Heseltine should still remain a contender for the ultimate prize after three tempestuous years at the DTI was in some ways an even more remarkable feat than his survival on the back benches after Westland. Few politicians could have overcome the run of set-backs he had endured. Three times in three years commentators had written him off – over coal, after his heart attack, and then over the Post Office – and each time he had bounced back. After the death of the Labour leader John Smith in May 1994 – from his second heart attack – it was said that the Tories could never resort to a leader who had had similar health problems. But that consideration, too, was quickly forgotten.

More than ever, Michael Heseltine was 'the biggest beast in the Tory jungle'. To a large extent his continued stature was a reflection of the inadequacies of so many of his Cabinet colleagues. Despite his persistent troubles, the President of the Board of Trade still towered above most other ministers.

In the summer of 1995 it looked as if his moment might have come.

22. Deputy Prime Minister

Fellow MPs were most amused. Michael Mates was regaling them with how he'd recently called Michael Heseltine 'a bastard' to his face. His story was told at a lunch of the Macleod Group of Tory left-wingers in July 1995, when the Chancellor, Kenneth Clarke, was the guest speaker. But what Heseltine's former campaign organizer failed to explain to his colleagues was *why* he'd addressed his hero in such an abusive way.

It all stemmed, in fact, from John Major's surprise decision, two weeks earlier, to put his own job on the line. After months of public carping about his leadership – especially from Euro-sceptic right-wingers – and speculation about a probable challenge to his position that autumn, the Tory leader chose to 'lance the boil' by putting himself up for re-election. Michael Heseltine later related how the premier had advised him of his decision a couple of days beforehand. 'I said, after a moment's reflection, that I thought it was a very sensible thing to do.'[1] It was a highly risky strategy, based on the expectation that Major would probably see off a challenge, which was thought most likely to come from his former Chancellor, Norman Lamont, whom he'd sacked two years before. What Major hadn't predicted was that a current member of his Cabinet, the right-winger John Redwood, would resign as Welsh Secretary and oppose him instead.

The contest presented Michael Heseltine and his supporters with all sorts of fascinating possibilities. There was never any question of Heseltine challenging Major himself: after 1990, he could not survive a second charge of regicide. But what if Major was sufficiently wounded by a high number of Redwood votes and abstentions, and, like Margaret Thatcher five years before, was obliged to throw in the towel? Heseltine would certainly join any contest that followed, though others, including Michael Portillo, would probably stand as well.

Heseltine's most ardent supporters – including Keith Hampson, Peter Temple-Morris and Michael Mates – wondered what were the best tactics to advance his cause. They found it distasteful to think of voting for John Redwood, but the more MPs who failed to back John Major, the greater would be the pressure for him to step down. The calculation then was whether Heseltine was strong enough to defeat Portillo and Redwood in the second ballot. There was always the risk that the Heselteenies would succeed in ditching John Major only to be left with a right-wing successor whose views were far less congenial and more anti-European.

Michael Heseltine's public stance was one of total loyalty to his boss. He clearly stated that he would vote for the Prime Minister and wanted every other MP to do so. And his supporters knew they couldn't make the slightest move which might suggest otherwise to the Major camp. 'A lot of pro-Hezza MPs came up to me for advice on what they should do,' says one of his supporters. 'And I had to play it totally straight and say, "That's totally a matter for you." I could never be sure they weren't Major spies. It was awful, trying to do your best for Hezza, but not campaigning.' One Heselteenie found himself forced to tell television viewers he was voting for his leader, when he actually planned to abstain. (To vote for Redwood was too much to stomach.) 'I hated it – lying on TV,' he says. 'I knew that to do anything else would ruin it for Michael.'

Publicly, the President of the Board of Trade had no option but to continue with his ministerial duties as if everything were normal. Even privately, he insisted that everyone should support John Major. The crucial point was not just that Heseltine couldn't afford to be disloyal to his leader for a second time, but that, if Major eventually did resign and he himself entered the fray, he would hope for his leader's endorsement and, above all, his votes. If anybody even *thought* that Heseltine or his supporters had made the slightest move against the Prime Minister he would suffer an almighty backlash from those who were close to Major, many of whom might then switch to another candidate.

Nevertheless, behind the scenes Michael Heseltine was eagerly receiving regular reports about the state of play, from Hampson, Mates and Temple-Morris. They would dictate a paragraph or two over the phone to Eileen Strathnaver, which she then typed up for her boss. At weekends Heseltine would ring his lieutenants personally to hear their latest assessments. As ever, they were largely one-way calls, with Heseltine just taking in what his informants had to say, giving barely any reaction and certainly making no suggestion that anybody should take any positive action on his behalf.

Some Heselteenies were particularly assiduous in their intelligence-gathering. The morning before polling, Monday 3 July, Keith Hampson held a breakfast-time meeting with David Evans, a Heseltine supporter from the 1990 second ballot, who was now acting as John Redwood's campaign manager. When Evans called him, Hampson suggested his Tory colleague should come round to his home, but instead they met in the lounge of the Cumberland Hotel, near Marble Arch. That was far enough away from Westminster, they hoped, for their bizarre encounter not to be noticed by anyone in the know.

More than a year later, in November 1996, the *Express on Sunday* claimed that the two MPs struck an extraordinary deal that morning – for Hampson to deliver an estimated thirty-five votes from the Heseltine camp to Redwood. The newspaper claimed that Keith Hampson then told Evans that he'd have to go and consult 'the boss', and rang the MP back that night to say the deal was on.[2]

It's hard to believe that Evans would have used such precious time, at a crucial point in the campaign, if he didn't have hopes of securing Heseltine supporters. Hampson confirms the meeting did take place, but denies there was any such deal. 'I was just interested to find out what he was up to. You don't often get a couple of calls from the boss of a campaign for a guy who is totally alien to you.'[3]

It was obvious what David Evans would achieve from that kind of arrangement, but why would Hampson want to discuss it? Perhaps he needed to know the strength of Redwood's existing support, so as to assess whether additional Heseltine votes would make a crucial difference. Nothing could have been more embarrassing than for Heseltine supporters to switch to Redwood, only for John Major nonetheless to survive.

Keith Hampson also insists that Michael Heseltine knew nothing about his meeting with David Evans, either before or afterwards, and that Heseltine wouldn't have sanctioned any such pact. It must also be doubtful how many votes could ever have been delivered even if a deal had been agreed. The Heseltine camp was never a monolithic, unified force. Many of his strongest supporters were experienced MPs of long standing, and not the sort to do as they were told.

Another potential leadership candidate in 1995, Michael Portillo, got into deep trouble during the contest when a close friend jumped the gun and ordered telephone lines for a proposed Portillo campaign headquarters in Westminster. Michael Heseltine did nothing quite so blatant, but he certainly did prepare for the possibility that John Major might be forced out. The detailed planning was done by Richard Ottaway, the MP for Croydon South, who had served as Heseltine's PPS since the 1992 election. Ottaway, a solicitor who is inevitably called 'Rotterway' by friends, is a middle-of-the-road Conservative whose views are, if anything, slightly to the right of Heseltine's. Having lost his old Nottingham seat in 1987, he hadn't even been an MP at the time of the 1990 contest.

The contingency plans were approved by Heseltine the day before the ballot. The President of the Board of Trade told Michael Mates that if he contested the second round, then Mates would not be his chief of staff this time. It was a perfectly understandable decision by Heseltine. Mates had not been an ideal campaign manager in 1990, and the affair of Asil Nadir and the engraved watch had done nothing to improve his reputation with parliamentary colleagues. Heseltine decided that, instead, operations would be run by Ottaway, though it was hoped that a senior figure such as Tom King or Norman Fowler would fill the role of campaign chairman. Michael Mates was furious: he felt he was being treated badly after his years of loyal support. Hence the outburst in which he called Heseltine 'a bastard'. Mates should have known what he was by now, Heseltine responded, given how long they had been working together.

The following morning, as Tory MPs began voting, Richard Ottaway rang a few members of the putative Heseltine team to confirm their proposed roles if their man entered a second ballot. The personnel this time would be very different from that of the 1990 leadership challenge. Keith Hampson, like Mates, was also pencilled in for demotion, while more senior figures from 1990 would be absent altogether. Sir Neil Macfarlane and Sir Dennis Walters had both retired from the Commons, and Sir Peter Tapsell had made it clear he couldn't help. Heseltine was most upset when Tapsell wrote to say he wouldn't support him if he stood this time, as their views on Europe were incompatible (yet they were no more so than in 1990). The new line-up would also have reflected a very different strategy from the previous contest: then Heseltine had been the 'outsider', whereas now he would be presenting himself as the 'Establishment' candidate, preferably with John Major's backing.

Keith Hampson believes that Heseltine had a much better chance in 1995 than he ever did five years earlier, and the political editor of the *Financial Times*, Philip Stephens, is among several commentators who believe that Heseltine would have 'probably won'.[4] This must be doubtful. Heseltine would have needed to win over a vast new group of Tory MPs compared with the last occasion, since a large part of his previous vote had now disappeared. Many of his 1990 supporters had been from the older generation, and like Macfarlane and Walters, were no longer in the Commons. Philip Cowley of Hull University estimates that about forty-five of Heseltine's 131 votes in the second round in 1990 – more than a third – had left the House. Thirty or more had either retired or died, while a further ten had lost their seats in 1992.[5]

To have beaten Redwood and Portillo, Michael Heseltine would have needed to attract significant numbers of the 1992 entry of Tory MPs – who tended to be on the right – as well as many of those who had backed John Major and Douglas Hurd last time. Moreover, the experience in modern times of open leadership elections (i.e. where the incumbent is not standing), has been that the winner is usually the younger and more inexperienced candidate – a rule of thumb that applies to all parties. In this instance that would have meant almost anyone but Heseltine. One might argue that the dire conditions of 1995, when electoral defeat looked much more certain than it had in 1990, might have prompted MPs to go for an election-winner. But, compared with his challenge to Thatcher, there was much less compelling evidence that a Heseltine victory would have made a substantial difference to Conservative fortunes. Polls suggested that the party's problems went way beyond the leadership, and that replacing Major with Heseltine would make only a small impact.

Whatever some of his acolytes might have been hoping – or even planning – Michael Heseltine seems to have decided that the best he could do was to wait and see. Privately, he wondered whether the party would have been ungovernable anyway, having ousted two leaders in less than five years.

On the day, the Heselteenies split three ways: while most went for Major, quite a few abstained, and it seems that one or two did vote for John Redwood. John Major secured 218 votes to Redwood's 89, and there were 22 abstentions. One hundred and eleven MPs had failed to support the Prime Minister – more than a third of those entitled to vote, and well above the 100 mark which many commentators reckoned would be fatal. But Major's supporters seized the initiative and quickly presented the result as a triumph.

On the morning of the vote, Michael Heseltine received a summons to Downing Street which has aroused curiosity and speculation ever since. The mystery was fuelled by the fact that Heseltine spent more than two hours in Number Ten. The following day, when it emerged that Heseltine would be appointed Deputy Prime Minister, it was claimed that barely half of his Downing Street visit had been spent in discussion with John Major; the rest of the time he had been talking to the Cabinet Secretary, Sir Robin Butler, about what his proposed new job would entail. Nevertheless, people naturally wondered whether the two politicians had thrashed out a deal in which Heseltine got his new post in return for swinging his supporters behind a desperate Prime Minister.

If there was a deal as crude as that, one might have expected the two men to have started talking sooner, rather than meet when voting began at ten o'clock that morning. By the time Heseltine emerged from Number Ten, just before lunchtime, around half the parliamentary party had already cast their votes. The suggestion has often been made that many Heselteenies waited until the afternoon to vote, and once the word came about the 'deal' with Major, they then delivered their support for the Prime Minister. But even if Heseltine or his lieutenants had given the nod for his troops to vote one way or another, it is doubtful whether there were more than a dozen MPs who would have accepted such discipline. Some had already declared for the Prime Minister. Hugh Dykes, for example, had been seen in the Members' Lobby telling colleagues to back Major. Moreover, the fact that some leading Heselteenies still abstained, or went for Redwood, suggests that if there was an arrangement it was far from watertight.

The other alleged part of the Downing Street deal was that John Major would make way for his new deputy if the Tories' poll ratings hadn't picked up by the following spring. Indeed, rumours of such an understanding prompted intense speculation at the time of the May 1996 local elections, though Downing Street dismissed the claim as 'complete baloney'.[6] In any case, it would have been almost impossible for Major simply to deliver the Tory leadership to Heseltine. If he had stepped down, then under the party rules other contenders would have been entitled to stand, and Heseltine would almost certainly have faced opposition from John Redwood or Michael Portillo. In the event, the 1996 council results were barely less disastrous than those of 1995, but Major remained in place. If such a pact was struck in Downing Street, Major seems to have ratted on it.

After the announcement of Michael Heseltine's promotion, it was said that talks about his new role had been going on for three weeks. It seems that Major was initially eager for Heseltine to become party chairman, a job he might have enjoyed at one stage, and an idea which had been touted a lot during the past two years. But Heseltine had publicly made it plain that he wasn't interested in the chairmanship and would much prefer to stay at the DTI rather than move to Central Office. The idea of his being Deputy Prime Minister appears to have evolved from this suggestion, in an effort to make the chairman's post more palatable. (Major had actually offered the post to Douglas Hurd the year before, in an effort to prevent his intended retirement from the Cabinet, but Hurd had turned it down.) Heseltine, however, was naturally attracted to the thought of being Major's official deputy, but wanted to ensure the title would carry genuine substance and authority – unlike when Sir Geoffrey Howe occupied the post. Heseltine concluded the job would enable him to pursue many of the themes in which he'd taken an interest over the years.

Yet the outcome of the Downing Street meeting *was* an implicit 'deal' in as much as it meant that Michael Heseltine would be much less inclined to cause trouble if the leadership result looked at all inconclusive. And in the longer term he would be tied more closely in harness with John Major. For months now, the Prime Minister had come under attack from left and right, from supporters of both

Michael Heseltine and Michael Portillo who equally felt their man could do the job better. A firm alliance between Heseltine and the Prime Minister should at least silence the grumbling and grousing from Major's left flank.

Michael Heseltine emerged from Downing Street laden with goodies – a long list of influential jobs at the heart of government, and two titles that certainly sounded impressive. For, as well as Deputy Prime Minister, he got the additional post of First Secretary of State – a position which Rab Butler, George Brown, Michael Stewart and Barbara Castle had held in the 1960s, but which had since lain dormant. In fact the office is constitutionally futile, and eight months later Heseltine rather gave the game away when he admitted to MPs that when he first got the extra post, 'I was not aware that there was an office called First Secretary of State.'[7]

Even then, Michael Heseltine seems to have harboured doubts about taking the new job and leaving his beloved DTI – despite his difficulties there. The history of Deputy Prime Ministers was not an entirely happy one: the job tended to go to men who'd failed to become premier. Past holders included Rab Butler (1962–3) and, of course, Sir Geoffrey Howe (1989–90), while Willie Whitelaw had held the position unofficially from 1979 to 1987. Shortly after his appointment, Heseltine was heard asking anxiously whether 'Rab Butler had had enough to do' when he held the same two titles under Harold Macmillan.[8] When he turned up at Buckingham Palace, Heseltine was most upset to find that the seals of office the Queen presented were much smaller than those granted to his new Cabinet deputy, Roger Freeman, whose job as Chancellor of the Duchy of Lancaster had a much more distinguished pedigree.

Many of the right were furious about Heseltine's appointment, especially as it seemed to confirm what looked like a significant leftward drift in the new Cabinet. The Home Secretary, Michael Howard, who had backed Major and hoped to become Foreign Secretary, was particularly upset with the new powers that Heseltine had acquired, especially when the new Deputy Prime Minister invited Howard's Permanent Secretary to come and see him. One of the Home Secretary's friends says he was 'white and almost trembling' with fury.

At the time, much was made of the size of the new office Michael

Heseltine grabbed for himself within the Cabinet Office buildings at the back of Downing Street. In reality it was no bigger than the quarters inhabited by some of his senior colleagues, though Heseltine's deputy, Roger Freeman, liked telling people that the office was Mussolini-like in its grandeur.

Symbolically, Heseltine also acquired an electronic swipe card for instant access to Number Ten. Far more significant was the role he now acquired within the Whitehall power structure. The Deputy Prime Minister – or DPM as he became known within the system – was appointed to all the main Cabinet committees, and, like the Prime Minister, acquired *carte blanche* to attend any other committee that took his fancy. John Major was taking an immense risk in appointing Heseltine, as his new deputy conceded:

If I was advising the Prime Minister as to whether to create a deputy I would say, unless you have a very good personal relationship and you have absolute trust, don't do it . . . My job is an extension of his job. That is where my authority lies. If it was thought I was speaking a different language from the Prime Minister, I would rapidly cease to get decisions taken at Cabinet committees.[9]

Four permanent Cabinet committees, including those covering the environment and local government, were now chaired by Heseltine. He was also to preside over a new Competitiveness Committee, which carried a much wider remit than the name suggests, since it also covered the UK's 'other industrial, commercial, consumer, competition and regeneration policies; policy on science and technology; the pace of deregulation; and the handling of public sector pay'.[10] In effect, 'Competitiveness' was a diplomatic way of saying 'industrial strategy', and Heseltine had acquired the job of industrial overlord which he had prescribed in *Where There's a Will*. His new committee was almost a full Cabinet in itself, since all but four Cabinet ministers were appointed members.

Competitiveness was one of two areas of activity which John Major allowed Heseltine to plunder from his old job. It was the new DPM, rather than his successor at the DTI, Ian Lang (who retained the title of President of the Board of Trade), who launched the government's third White Paper on Competitiveness in June 1996. The other prize was the deregulation unit and the accompanying task force of outside advisers chaired by the former Treasury minister Francis Maude (who had lost his seat in 1992). There was some logic to the two transfers, in that Heseltine's approach to both competitiveness and deregulation had implications across the whole spectrum of government.

But the chairmanship which carried by far the greatest political clout was that of the new Cabinet Committee on the Coordination and Presentation of Government Policy. Code-named EDCP, it began meeting at 8.30 every morning, Monday to Friday, in Michael Heseltine's office. Its official members would include the Leaders of the Commons and the Lords, Tony Newton and Robert Cranborne; the new Conservative Party chairman, Brian Mawhinney; the Chief Whip, Alistair Goodlad; and Heseltine's deputy, Roger Freeman. Crucially, EDCP would operate as a sensitive interface between government and party, attended both by civil servants involved in policy presentation and by staff from Conservative Central Office.

EDCP had evolved from a daily gathering first established in 1991 under the then Chief Whip, Richard Ryder, which had been known internally as the Number Twelve Committee and externally as the 'Committee for Banana Skins'. Under Michael Heseltine's redirection, EDCP quickly became one of the most powerful bodies in government. The former Conservative communications director, Hugh Colver, who sat on both bodies, says the Number Twelve Committee was too negative and spent too much time whingeing about unfavourable press coverage. With EDCP, he says, Heseltine was keen to look ahead to issues during the coming forty-eight hours, and took firm control of the agenda. 'He has real presence,' says Colver. 'He never raises his voice. He always speaks quite softly, but he's in total command of the room. There's no doubt about who's running the meeting.'[11]

EDCP's task, of course, was to improve the government's image through news management: nipping troublesome issues in the bud, and coordinating activity so that any good news – or bad news for Labour – didn't get overshadowed. The daily thirty- to forty-five-minute meeting would be followed by heavy traffic around the Whitehall telephone system, much of it originating either from Heseltine himself or from one of his ministerial deputies. They would go to considerable efforts to tweak arrangements for imminent government events, often to the irritation of ministers and officials in the departments. In January 1996, for instance, the National Heritage Secretary, Virginia Bottomley, told morning radio listeners that she would be announcing new lottery grants later in the day. But then Heseltine suddenly insisted that she postpone her announcement so as not to detract from the opposition's embarrassment over the decision by the Labour shadow minister Harriet Harman to send her son to a selective school. Perhaps Heseltine's greatest presentational achievement was in coordinating the February 1996 response to the Scott Inquiry, when the government survived the judge's damning report without a single resignation.

Once a week EDCP would meet to explore more long-term presentation issues. If a minister planned to make some big policy announcement, for instance, he or she might be summoned before the committee and questioned about the timing, about likely reactions and whether back-bench opposition was expected. Heseltine's work with EDCP was also supported by the advent of a new cross-Whitehall computer network – Cab-e-net – which keeps a diary of all ministers' activities and other government events. To some it was evidence of Heseltine behaving as 'Big Brother', though the software had actually been ordered some months before he took the job. In fact, civil servants didn't find Cab-e-net very helpful. While it contained enormous detail about what the most junior ministers were doing, it often omitted details of Major and Heseltine's engagements.

The involvement of Conservative and Whitehall officials in the same body carried a serious danger of blurring the distinction between government and party. The precedent had been set with the previous Number Twelve Committee, but a year after taking over as DPM Heseltine himself attempted to bring civil servants much more closely into political propaganda. In the summer of 1996 he won the approval of both EDCP and John Major to ask officials to suggest 'cheerleaders' – people within the public service who might be identified to the media as 'vigorous and attractive proponents of government policies'. These might include headteachers, GP fund-holders, prison governors, and even people who had been awarded government contracts. A minute asking for names was circulated to ministers' private offices and was subsequently leaked.[12]

It was a naïve thing for Heseltine to suggest, especially with his long Whitehall experience. But the Cabinet Secretary, Sir Robin Butler, put a stop to his scheme, describing it as 'inappropriate', and insisted the job of finding 'cheerleaders' should be carried out by ministers' political advisers.[13] Heseltine skilfully escaped the episode by accusing Labour of 'dirty tricks', and by linking the leaked document to the recent elevation as an opposition peer of Liz Symons, the general-secretary of the mandarins' union, the First Division Association, though she and her organization denied any involvement in the disclosure.[14] Heseltine's proposals had striking echoes, of course, of DS19 before the 1983 election, when he had also pushed at the bounds of constitutional propriety by enlisting MoD civil servants in the propaganda war against CND.

The obvious question arose of how responsibilities were divided between Heseltine and the new Conservative chairman, Brian Mawhinney, who also sat on EDCP. Traditionally the party chairman has played a major role in coordinating presentation, and acts as an all-purpose spokesman in the media. The two men were very different characters who'd never had many dealings in the past and weren't obvious chums. Mawhinney inevitably had to cede much of the chairman's media role to Heseltine, especially after making a series of gaffes in his first few months and being over-aggressive in one or two interviews – notably with Sue MacGregor on the *Today* programme. During 1996 Mawhinney's broadcast appearances became less frequent, as Heseltine readily and regularly accepted invitations to appear on *Breakfast with Frost* or to spar with John Humphrys on *Today* or *On the Record*.

On one notorious occasion at Central Office the two presentation chiefs appeared together to launch an alternative version of Labour's new draft manifesto, pursuing the 'New Labour, New Danger' slogan dreamt up for the Tories by Heseltine's former assistant Maurice Saatchi (who was ennobled shortly afterwards). The format was a joint comedy act, with the two men exchanging lines as in *The Two Ronnies*. 'Michael, what struck you about it?' Mawhinney turned to ask his colleague. Although some of the material was quite witty and might have succeeded with a party audience, it was a disaster in front of sceptical journalists. And the pair obviously hadn't agreed on their strategy. 'The issue is not whether Labour has changed. It is now clear that it has,' Brian Mawhinney announced. But Heseltine took another tack: 'You can change the name. But you can't change the instincts. The old policies are in many ways there under the new policies.'[15] Their differences reflected the Tories' wider difficulty over how to tackle Tony Blair's New Labour, of course, but also suggested that the coordination process had badly broken down.

Heseltine's new job gave him extraordinary licence to roam the corridors of Whitehall and the right to interfere in departmental business on a scale unknown in modern times for any minister other than a premier. 'There is virtually nothing in which I would not have a locus,' he told MPs. 'I am either a member of, or I have access to, all Cabinet committees. So it is very difficult to find something which is not something in which I am entitled to be involved.'[16] Despite a ministerial career which stretched over more than a quarter of a century, there were still significant policy areas in which Heseltine had never held responsibility or taken much interest before. He was pronouncing for the first time, for instance, on foreign affairs, law and order, and the complexities of the Northern Ireland peace process.

Members of the Cabinet quickly found the new Deputy Prime Minister calling the shots. The Health Secretary, Stephen Dorrell, was dragged out of the opera one evening to take a call from the DPM announcing that Dorrell would be making a statement in the Commons the next day on the new-found link between BSE – mad-cow disease – and the human Creutzfeldt-Jakob disease (CJD). And when the Agriculture Minister, Douglas Hogg, was thought to have mishandled the BSE crisis, responsibility was transferred to Heseltine's deputy, Roger Freeman. There could be no doubt where Freeman stood in the Whitehall hierarchy: he explained to people that his job was simply to do what John Major and Michael Heseltine told him to do at the start of each week.

Most domestic ministers soon experienced Heseltine treading on their toes and invading their territory. Ian Lang, having already lost part of his DTI empire to the new DPM, put up strong resistance to his radical proposals to abolish employment laws for small businesses. The Transport Secretary, Sir George Young, opposed his efforts to commit the Tories to privatizing the London Underground; and the Education Secretary, Gillian Shephard, found the Deputy Prime Minister questioning education and training standards through a skills audit for his 1996 White Paper on Competitiveness. Several ministers were also upset about Heseltine's scheme to hold City Challenge-style contests for larger capital projects – new roads and schools, for instance, would now have to compete with each other for new investment.

Heseltine won the Challenge argument, but he didn't always prevail. Ian Lang emerged victorious from his tussle over employment rights. And when Michael Heseltine proposed new league tables to compare the performance of government agencies, the Cabinet resisted the suggestion almost unanimously; the Home Secretary, Michael Howard, was particularly contemptuous. Heseltine seemed to have taken to deploying the government levers like a trainspotter let loose in a signal-box, but his colleagues could often outmanoeuvre or outnumber him. Moreover, the DPM carefully steered clear of mainstream economic policy. By any objective assessment of the Whitehall power-game, the Chancellor, Kenneth Clarke, remained the more influential figure.

Despite his responsibility for better presentation, the Deputy Prime Minister had also become surprisingly gaffe-prone. In January 1996 Heseltine blurted out the latest fall in unemployment figures almost twenty-four hours before it was due to be announced officially. And, while ministers argued over the merits of new laws to make firms pay their bills on time, Heseltine told a private dinner how, when he was in business, he had been 'quite skilful at stringing along creditors'.[17] He had said it all before, but it was a foolish thing to repeat when he held such a responsible position and slow payment was such a sensitive issue.

Heseltine's intense partisanship and eagerness to score political points can also get him into trouble. In December 1996 he made front-page headlines by telling the Commons Public Service Committee that Labour candidates were to blame for recent leaks from the Treasury. Heseltine promised to expound on his complaint in a memo, but later asked the committee to 'disregard this part of my evidence'

and explained that he'd 'misread the original press report'.[18] Fortunately for the DPM, this withdrawal got little coverage in the press,
though Heseltine didn't bother to apologize to Helen Goodman, the
Treasury official he had implicated – though quite unjustly. It showed
a growing tendency for Heseltine to speak before he thinks. At the
DTI this had proved expensive when in 1995 the department had to
pay £55,000 costs and damages to a television journalist, Martyn
Gregory, after Heseltine had wrongly claimed his allegations on
the British export of torture equipment had been 'contrived' and
'scaremongering'.

Nor was Michael Heseltine of much help to John Major in pre-
venting the defection of Conservative MPs. Alan Howarth – who
joined Labour – and Peter Thurnham – who became a Liberal
Democrat – had never been close to him, so there was probably little
he could do to avert their departures. But Heseltine must bear some
responsibility for Emma Nicholson's decision in December 1995 to
join the Liberal Democrats. Nicholson, whose constituency covered
much of Heseltine's old Tavistock seat, had been one of his most
prominent supporters in 1990. When she announced her defection,
Heseltine was vituperative in saying the MP had left because she
hadn't been given a government job – though Nicholson claimed not
to have made such a request since her failed bid to become his PPS
shortly after the 1990 leadership battle.[19] Why hadn't Heseltine done
anything to deal with her frustration, especially if he knew she felt
overlooked? Nicholson is an able politician, and John Major's ministerial benches weren't exactly teeming with talent.

As well as standing in at Question Time when John Major was
away – on top of his own oral questions – Heseltine became a reserve
choice for big ceremonial occasions, notably at the 1995 Remembrance
Day service at the Cenotaph, the first time ever that a Prime Minister
hadn't attended (Major was abroad). It must also have given him
especial satisfaction to open the Farnborough Air Show in September
1996, when pictures appeared in almost every newspaper of a grinning
Heseltine in the cockpit of a model of the Eurofighter 2000 aircraft –
the long-awaited result of the European collaborative deal he had
brokered at the MoD in 1985. The Defence Secretary, Michael
Portillo, simultaneously announced orders for 232 planes at a cost of

£15 billion, though many defence analysts felt it was both a ridiculously expensive and an increasingly unnecessary plane.

The beauty of Heseltine's new job was how it enabled him to put his finger into almost any pie he wanted. He could both pull together strands from his past ministerial career and initiate new *grands projets*. When a gigantic 3,300 lb IRA bomb destroyed a large part of the centre of Manchester and caused £500 million of damage, the government was surprisingly slow to respond; eleven days later Michael Heseltine was sent to the city. The Deputy Prime Minister spent a day viewing the bomb damage and talking to local councillors, businessmen and traders, and quickly focused on Manchester's plight as if it were another Liverpool.

Over the next few months Heseltine made regular visits to Manchester. Just as with Merseyside in 1981, his immediate response was a task force, comprising local businessmen, council officials and civil servants. It was charged not just with rebuilding the damaged area, but also with thinking more deeply about the role of cities and how their centres might be better developed. Pursuing his love of competitions, Heseltine quickly launched an architectural contest to redesign the area that had been destroyed.

Yet, when the Deputy Prime Minister spent ninety minutes talking to local owners of small shops, they were far from impressed with his apparent lack of sympathy. 'We wanted to tell him how we felt, but it wasn't like that at all,' says one of their representatives, Audrey Brookes, who ran a business selling antique jewellery. 'He asked, "Were you insured against terrorism? If you weren't, that's your own fault and you can't expect this government to bail you out." It was rather cruel, because although people had public liability insurance they hadn't got terrorism insurance.'[20] The problem was that many shopkeepers hadn't bothered with such cover because of the recent IRA cease-fire, but the government has long compensated businesses hit by terrorism in Northern Ireland. Local traders felt Heseltine was much more worried about the major chain stores than about them. Such an attitude is surprising, perhaps, given that he is one of the few ministers ever to have run his own small business. Yet it also reflected Heseltine's wider outlook, and his emphasis – shown while at the DTI – on big companies rather than small enterprises. (In

Henley, local traders had been equally furious when he wouldn't help them fight the building of a new Tesco store.)

Michael Heseltine the Deputy Prime Minister seemed to have lost the charm that had won over the people of Liverpool. 'He hasn't got the common touch,' concludes Audrey Brookes. 'He has this superior arrogance, and I don't know why he chose politics.' When the Irish President Mary Robinson visited Manchester, she expressed specific concern for small businesses, and they found her a welcome contrast to the DPM. 'I can't believe someone could be so uncompassionate,' says another trader, Rik Lomas, who recalls how Heseltine kept looking at his watch during the meeting to make sure he wasn't late for the European Championship football semi-final at Old Trafford.[21] His match hosts spent much of the game explaining the offside law.

Yet, ironically, opposition politicians in Manchester were impressed with Heseltine's efforts. The local MP, Tony Lloyd, a front-bench spokesman in the Commons, says he 'can't really fault him on this. I think most of us felt that Heseltine was the one who began to cut through the red tape . . . Once the Deputy Prime Minister takes an interest, then others follow in his wake.'[22]

Michael Heseltine's other *grand projet* was the proposed exhibition to celebrate the millennium. He had originally been appointed to the Millennium Commission when it was set up in 1994 – when still at the DTI – and specifically asked to remain a member after becoming DPM. Heseltine was particularly eager for the proposed big national exhibition to be held on the site of an old gasworks on the Greenwich peninsula near the southern end of the Blackwall Tunnel. Like the site of the Liverpool Garden Festival, it was a derelict landscape that required serious decontamination work. When the Mersey shore was chosen for the 1984 event, it had been at the expense of a much stronger bid from Stoke; in the case of the Greenwich exhibition, the main rival was Birmingham, which proposed holding it at the National Exhibition Centre (NEC) and was left feeling even more badly bruised than Stoke over the unfair way it thought its bid had been treated.

The consultants appointed to create the exhibition, Imagination Design, actually preferred the Birmingham scheme, which also had better financial backing. Yet the Millennium Commission, with Heseltine playing a leading role, went for Greenwich instead. A telling argument was that people would never be attracted by the idea of a trip to Birmingham, whereas Greenwich was already a historic site: tourists from both home and abroad were likely to include it as part of a wider visit to London. Yet Heseltine's firm preference for the Thameside location seemed to contradict the belief he had once professed, with equal passion, that new projects should be dispersed away from the South-East. But the Greenwich location had the particular attraction of supporting his continued vision for the East Thames Corridor, though the 'hot banana' had cooled a little since his departure from the DoE – largely through lack of private investment.

By the summer of 1996 the Greenwich scheme was in such financial difficulty that it looked as if the exhibition might have to be abandoned altogether, to ministers' obvious embarrassment. Instead, Michael Heseltine took a firm grip on the problem. With the entrepreneurial zeal of the *Management Today* coup and the Liverpool bus trip, Heseltine set up a Cabinet subcommittee, brought in his old friend Sir Peter Levene, and began summoning bankers and businessmen to hear his sales-pitch as to why they should give financial support. Many, however, were put off by Heseltine's heavy arm-twisting, and were offended at being told it was their patriotic duty to help. Some companies employed the very self-interest factor that Michael Heseltine believes motivates society, and questioned how it would benefit their shareholders.

The snags were bureaucratic as much as financial. In the autumn of 1996 the Deputy Prime Minister summoned Virginia Bottomley and all the other leading players to his office at eight o'clock one morning and announced they would meet at the same time every day for as long as it took to resolve the difficulties. Exerting the heavy clout of his office, Heseltine tried to hack through the Whitehall jungle, bludgeoning departments such as the DoE, Transport and the Treasury to sort out problems such as higher external finance limits. It took breakfast meetings on three days in succession before the schedule could be eased down to weekly gatherings. 'When Michael is pointed in a direction and when you put blinkers on him and give him a bit of back-up, he's a very impressive operator,' says one participant. 'He knows Whitehall, the ropes, and if the exhibition happens he will deserve a very large plaque.'

The Millennium Exhibition would probably have collapsed had Heseltine not taken command, but he trampled over individuals in the process. He not only ignored the Labour-controlled Greenwich Council and Sir Robert Scott, the highly regarded 'Mr Fixit' impresario whom the authority originally hired to mount their bid, but also pushed aside his Cabinet colleague Virginia Bottomley. 'Frankly,' says a Labour MP who was close to events, 'without the Deputy Prime Minister using the influence of his office, which is clearly more influential than hers, it could well have foundered. That's been very important – using his rank, influence and contacts.'

Nevertheless, the struggle was long and fraught. Business was still reluctant to invest when it was so uncertain whether the exhibition would ever happen. Even after ministers scaled down its budget, the project came very close to being abandoned in January 1997. At the last moment Heseltine went to see the opposition leader, Tony Blair, and eventually hammered out an agreement by which Labour would guarantee the future of the Millennium Exhibition when and if it came to power. It was a humbling move for Heseltine, since the very act of talking to Blair acknowledged that a Labour government was a real possibility.

Michael Heseltine's most decisive contribution as Deputy Prime Minister was to the Conservatives' continuing war over Europe, in which the question of the single currency threatened to tear the party apart. Throughout most of 1996 the DPM seemed to be emitting mixed signals; some pro-European Tories feared he had lost his past enthusiasm for economic and monetary union. In April Heseltine was instrumental in the Cabinet's decision to adopt the policy of holding a referendum before Britain joined a single currency. In particular he persuaded Kenneth Clarke, an enthusiast for EMU, and who was threatening to resign, to accept the idea of a plebiscite, even though Heseltine had firmly dismissed the proposal himself when Margaret Thatcher had suggested it during the 1990 leadership contest. The price of Clarke's agreement was a commitment that the government would not decide either way on the single currency until after the next election – what became known as the 'wait-and-see' policy.

Conservative Euro-enthusiasts were also dismayed at how Heseltine appeared to leave it to Kenneth Clarke to take all the public flak on

Europe. In the interests of being loyal to John Major, he seemed to be neglecting the pro-European cause. They were surprised, for instance, when Heseltine was initially among the most hard-line of ministers in urging non-cooperation with Europe over the ban on British beef during the BSE crisis, though he later became more conciliatory. Many MPs equally felt that, if it came to the crunch, the Deputy Prime Minister might be willing to abandon 'wait-and-see' if he thought doing so might win an election. 'His European instincts wouldn't get in the way of a knockout blow to Labour,' said one prominent Heselteenie.

Early in December 1996 the *Daily Telegraph* took the same view, arguing that Heseltine might be 'persuadable' to accept plans report-edly held by John Major to drop 'wait-and-see'.[23] The article re-opened party divisions on Europe, and Kenneth Clarke immediately said it was 'quite preposterous' to suggest the policy would be changed and 'senseless' to do so. As he surveyed the divisive headlines at the EDCP meeting the next morning, Michael Heseltine was in furious mood and decided he himself would have to take action by doing some broadcast interviews. On the radio that lunchtime he insisted that 'wait-and-see' would not be ditched. 'We are not going to change our position in the election campaign or this Parliament,' Heseltine asserted.[24]

It looked as if Michael Heseltine and Kenneth Clarke had cleverly ambushed John Major. When challenged by Tony Blair at Question Time that Tuesday afternoon, the Prime Minister had no option but to endorse Heseltine's words. 'My Right Honourable friend said that; that is our position.'[25] Afterwards a foul-tempered John Major told Tory back-benchers in the tea-room that there was no way he could have wrong-footed his deputy in public. Heseltine had played a crucial role in keeping the 'wait-and-see' policy in place, much to the dismay of most of the Cabinet. Many Conservative MPs were even more furious; many of them saw the rejection of a single currency as the one remaining weapon to defeat Labour.

For three or four days that week Michael Heseltine seemed to appear on virtually every radio and TV programme, reiterating almost ad nauseam that 'wait-and-see' would remain. He handled the issue brilliantly. In this case, for example, he was asked if he'd consulted John Major before his Tuesday lunchtime intervention.

I'm part of a Cabinet that took a collective decision last April which hasn't changed. I didn't double-check to see if the Prime Minister had still got the same policy, because I knew he had the same policy. I've heard him discuss it many times, and I obviously, as a person who speaks for the Conservative Party, like many colleagues, I know what the party policy is, and I don't need to go back to the Prime Minister to ask if he still believes in it. Of course he still believes in it . . . The idea that I should sort of, when asked, should say, 'Well, excuse me, I know what the policy was yesterday, but I'd better ring up and see if that's the policy today, before I answer your question,' is preposterous . . . The Prime Minister is adamant that it will not change and therefore I have confidence in repeating what I know to be his view.[26]

Clarke and Heseltine denied any collaboration in their interventions, but they appeared to have boxed the Tories in for the 1997 election. Heseltine was set to play his traditional swashbuckling role in the campaign, but as time ran out for the government, his attacks on Labour grew increasingly desperate and histrionic. In January 1997, the man who had stormed his opponent's meeting in Gower back in 1959 gatecrashed a business conference held by the Institute for Public Policy Research (IPPR), a think-tank sympathetic to Labour. Heseltine was obviously rattled by Labour's growing appeal to the business community, and must have felt Tony Blair was intruding on his own personal patch. In truth, of course, the policies of a Blair government would be almost identical to what Heseltine was advocating in the late 1980s. Indeed, it's hard to think of anything in Heseltine's two books with which Blair would seriously disagree. (It was especially rich for Heseltine to denounce businessmen for associating with a 'Labour front organization' when throughout his own career he himself has happily sought the advice of socialists and Labour supporters.)

Heseltine's prediction of a Tory majority of sixty seats looks increasingly improbable, but should they pull off a surprise victory Heseltine will happily remain Deputy Prime Minister until he sees in the millennium in the middle of the next Parliament. He will reach the age of sixty-seven in the year 2000. That, surely, would then be too old to succeed John Major, though his age is only a problem by modern British standards. Neville Chamberlain was sixty-eight when he entered Downing Street, while Churchill was eighty when he left office, and Gladstone was eighty-four. America, France and Russia in recent times have all been led by men in their late seventies. Heseltine would be a victim of two ageist fashions in British politics: first, the tendency for parties to select younger and younger leaders; and second, the increasing confinement of the political class to the thirty-five to sixty-five age-range. Neither trend augurs well for Heseltine, especially with his history of heart trouble.

His leadership chances might be slightly greater – though still slim – if the Conservatives go into opposition in 1997. Some of his supporters moot the possibility of Heseltine emerging as a compromise, caretaker, leader at a time when the party looks like having no obvious successor to John Major. One MP close to Heseltine suggests he might be the immediate beneficiary of John Major's apparent preference for Chris Patten eventually to take over the party. Until Patten returns from his term as governor of Hong Kong, the theory goes, then Major might back his deputy as the man to keep his seat warm. But it's hard to see Tory MPs choosing Michael Heseltine – even as a caretaker – at a time when they seem to be growing increasingly Euro-sceptic, and the new Conservative intake in 1997 is expected to be much more so. MPs will be even less enamoured of Heseltine after his crucial role in maintaining the 'wait-and-see' stance over EMU.

After the 1997 election Michael Heseltine is likely to follow his own personal 'wait-and-see' policy. So long as there is the slightest chance of him becoming Tory leader or Prime Minister, he will probably stick around. But even once that possibility has evaporated, Heseltine may be tempted to stay in the Commons. A close friend consoled him after the 1990 defeat with the suggestion that he could always go back to business or concentrate on his trees. 'You don't understand, do you?' Heseltine responded. 'Politics is everything to me.' He has never understood Cabinet colleagues who have given up politics to go into business. Cecil Parkinson tells of a time during his own ministerial career when he asked Heseltine's advice on whether to take a top company chairmanship. 'He asked me whether the biggest decision taken over the previous year by any company in which I was involved would have been important enough to be included in the agenda for Cabinet. He then said, "The big decisions are taken here, and if you want to influence them, you have to be here." [27]

Michael Heseltine could, of course, return to Haymarket. Lindsay Masters will reach retirement age in 1997, and he and Heseltine have long been preparing for his departure through an operation known as 'Post Mortem', whereby Masters's shares are gradually being bought back by the company. This inevitably raises Heseltine's own stake in Haymarket, which declared a profit before tax of almost £11 million pounds for the latest financial year ending in December 1995 – more than 50 per cent up on the previous figure of almost £7 million. The first buy-back of Masters's shares implied a value for the business of £150 million, but the latest results suggest Haymarket's total worth may now be in the region of £200 million or more, of which the Heseltines owned just over 50 per cent before Post Mortem got under way. (Together with their other assets, the Heseltine family must be worth at least £150 million.)

Close observers say Haymarket is badly in need of new leadership. Maurice Saatchi once suggested that if Michael Heseltine had stayed, the business might have become a 'Murdoch-sized company', a multi-media conglomerate on a global scale.[28] But it is hard to believe that resuming the reins of his own enterprise would appeal much to the Deputy Prime Minister.

In 1995, when the former Cabinet minister David Howell announced his retirement from Parliament, Heseltine told him it would mean one fewer obstacle to his becoming Father of the House, the longest-serving MP with continuous service. His remark was probably made half in jest, but after the 1997 election only seven MPs will be ahead of Heseltine in the queue for the Fathership – including only one other Conservative, the current Father, Sir Edward Heath, who was elected in 1950.[29] In all probability, however, Heseltine would have to wait until Heath goes and for two or three more Parliaments before becoming Father himself.

The real pressure on Michael Heseltine to retire from politics will almost certainly come from his wife, Anne, who fears for his health. The most obvious option, of course, is to follow most of his Cabinet colleagues, don the ermine, and take his final grand title – Baron

Heseltine of Thenford, perhaps, or of Henley-on-Thames. Company boards will scramble for his name on their notepaper, and publishing houses will bid for his long-promised book on his arboretum, and for what is likely to be a pretty discreet autobiography, if he writes one at all. 'I'm unhappy about this memoir business,' he said in 1993. 'They're self-serving, self-pleading, self-justifying,' though he admits nevertheless that he 'might be tempted one day'.[30]

Though never a zealous, ideologically sworn cadre in the Thatcher revolution, Michael Heseltine has undeniably made an impact as one of the most radical, reforming ministers of the last twenty years. During his most fertile spell in government – at Environment and Defence in the early 1980s – he shook up the attitudes, organization and finances not just of his two vast ministries but also of the powerful vested interests of local government and the British armed forces. In his inner-cities and Liverpool period, he pioneered examples of cooperation between the public and private sectors that are now the presumed norm.

But for a few tactical misjudgements during the month of November 1990, Michael Heseltine might well have achieved the office for which he has always longed. Had he not challenged Margaret Thatcher, he would have stood a much greater chance of succeeding her when the Prime Minister fell for other reasons, or finally retired of her own accord. Even so, Heseltine very nearly pulled it off. Had Thatcher stuck to her pledge to 'fight on', he would almost certainly have beaten her on the second ballot.

On the wider level, Michael Heseltine was handicapped by his obvious disdain for ordinary back-benchers, an attitude which the former minister Steven Norris describes as 'the most extraordinary I've seen in a politician. He is utterly indifferent to their presence.'[31] Had Heseltine had a better empathy with Tory colleagues, he would much more easily have shed the reputation for unreliability and unsound judgement established by the two notorious outbursts of his career – the mace and Westland.

Whether Heseltine could have done better than John Major is hard to say. The great irony, given his Westland resignation, is that the Heseltine style of government would have been more Thatcher than Major: he would have been less tolerant of dissent, less conciliatory, less consensual. Whether he would have been any more successful in tackling the Euro-sceptics must be highly doubtful, though much would have depended on the size of his majority from an election he almost certainly would have called in the spring of 1991, and on whether he would have achieved a similar settlement at Maastricht later that year along the lines of John Major's two famous opt-outs.

A Heseltine premiership would certainly have been a bumpy ride, marked with as many bust-ups and showdowns as the six years of John Major, but certainly exciting. It would have been peppered with new projects and many more radical initiatives, and decorated with Heseltine 'monuments' on a scale to make even a French president envious. And, if he survived in office that long, it would have been topped in grand style with an extravaganza in the year 2000 to mark the new Hezzaville along the Thames estuary, ten years of his premiership – and the millennium.

Michael Heseltine is the one politician in modern times who tried to transplant entrepreneurship into government. As Prime Minister, he would have operated as the chairman of UK plc, conducting government as if it were a big business, and largely in the interests of big business. The great tragedy of Michael Heseltine's life could be that he goes down in history as the man who toppled Margaret Thatcher. It will be an inadequate way to remember one of the most fascinating and genuinely innovative careers of modern times.

Notes

MLC – Michael Crick
MSC – Margaret Crick
SM – Sean McDougall
TDFF – Tom Fairbrother
TEH – Tom Happold

Chapter 1: Family Furniture

1. Letter from Hubert Chesshyre to Elizabeth Wharton, 8 December 1983
2. Alan Clark, *Diaries* (Weidenfeld & Nicolson, London, 1993), p. 162 (17 June 1987)
3. *GQ*, February 1988
4. Viscount Devonport (H. E. Kearley), *The Travelled Road* (private publication, Rochester, 1935), p. 20
5. Ibid., p. 2
6. Ibid., p. 24 and pp. 12–14
7. Christopher Quinton, interview with MLC and TEH
8. *Hampstead and Highgate Express*, 6 December 1890
9. Ibid.
10. For example, marriage certificate of R. Heseltine and E. Pridmore, 16 February 1932
11. Charles Dibdin, *The Professional Life of Mr Dibdin* (Charles Dibdin, London, 1803), Vol. I, p. 11
12. *Gentleman's Magazine*, January 1836
13. Dibdin, op. cit., p. 8
14. Stanley Sadie (ed.), *New Grove Dictionary of Music and Musicians* (Macmillan, London, 1980), Vol. V, p. 426
15. Thomas Dibdin, *The Reminiscences of Thomas Dibdin* (Henry Colburn, London, 1827), p. 25
16. Anthony Heseltine, interview with MLC
17. *Daily Mail*, 26 November 1990
18. Heseltine interview

19. *Daily Telegraph*, 6 December 1882
20. See *Structural Engineer*, November 1933
21. Mansel Thomas, interview with MLC
22. Reg Pike, interview with MLC
23. See Heseltine–Pridmore marriage certificate, February 1932
24. *Register of Members' Interests*, HoC Paper 345, London, 1995–96, p. 66

Chapter 2: Swansea Boy

1. *Desert Island Discs*, BBC Radio 4, 17 January 1988
2. Betty Martin, briefing notes for journalists, November 1990
3. *The Guardian*, 22 May 1994
4. Martin notes
5. *Sunday Times*, 1 May 1983
6. James Cellan Jones, interview with MLC
7. *Sunday Times*, 1 May 1983
8. Susan Hampshire, *Every Letter Counts: Winning in Life Despite Dyslexia* (Bantam, London, 1990), p. 219
9. Martin notes
10. Ibid.
11. Belfast Public Record Office, SCH 644/1/3
12. Tom McShane, interview with MSC
13. Gertie Barnes interview and letter to MLC
14. See D. J. Walters, *Bromsgrove In Exile* (Bromsgrove School, Bromsgrove, 1971)
15. Mike Rees, interview with MSC
16. Ibid.
17. Peter Fielden, interview with MSC
18. Rees interview
19. Judgement, *Thompson* v. *Park*, Stafford Assizes, 10 March 1947
20. Court of Appeal judgement, *Thompson* v. *Park*, 28 February 1944. See also *All England Law Reports*, Vol. 2, 25 November 1944.
21. Ibid.
22. Julian Critchley, *A Bag of Boiled Sweets* (Faber and Faber, London, 1994), pp. 17–18
23. Stafford Assizes judgement, p. 18
24. Ibid., p. 22
25. Ibid., p. 23
26. Peter Hancock, interview with MSC
27. Rosemary Fleming (née Park), interview with MSC

28. Stafford judgement, p. 23
29. Hancock interview
30. Robert Gilchrist, interview with MSC
31. *The Times*, 8 October 1996
32. Sheilagh Mundle, interview with MLC
33. Peter Jenkins, *Mrs Thatcher's Revolution* (Jonathan Cape, London, 1987), p. 193
34. Geoffrey Hayes, interview with MLC
35. Ibid.
36. Critchley, op. cit., p. 55
37. Hayes interview
38. Patricia Owen (née Mort), interview with MSC
39. *Desert Island Discs*, 17 January 1988
40. *Who's Who* (A. & C. Black, London, 1996), p. 890 (and previous editions)
41. *Sunday Telegraph*, 15 July 1984
42. *Sunday Telegraph Magazine*, 1 May 1983
43. Michael Heseltine, *The Challenge of Europe: Can Britain Win?* (Weidenfeld & Nicolson, London, 1989), pp. 155–6
44. Hayes interview
45. Heseltine, op. cit., p. 155
46. Roger Lidstone, fax to MLC
47. *The Times*, 12 September 1992
48. Mike Evans, interview with MLC
49. Owen (née Mort) interview

Chapter 3: Learning to Come Second

1. Susan Hampshire, *Every Letter Counts: Winning in Life Despite Dyslexia* (Bantam, London, 1990), p. 221
2. Lord Wolfenden, *Turning Points* (Bodley Head, London, 1976), p. 107
3. Colin Leach, *A School at Shrewsbury* (James & James, London, 1990), p. 95
4. Brian Jenkins, interview with MLC
5. Wolfenden, op. cit., p. 89
6. Roger Shakeshaft, notes prepared for author
7. Julian Critchley, *Heseltine: The Unauthorized Biography* (André Deutsch, London, 1987), p. 2
8. *Shrewsbury School Lists*, 1947–8
9. Michael Charlesworth, interview with MLC
10. Shakeshaft notes

11. Robert Wild, interview with MLC
12. Michael Heseltine, *The Challenge of Europe: Can Britain Win?* (Weidenfeld & Nicolson, London, 1989), p. 155
13. Critchley, op. cit., p. 2
14. *Sunday Express*, 10 June 1984
15. Wild interview
16. *Shrewsbury School Lists*, 1948–9
17. Michael Charlesworth, *Behind the Headlines: An Autobiography* (Greenbank Press, Wells, 1994), p. 169
18. *The Salopian*, November 1950
19. Charlesworth interview
20. Wild interview
21. *Desert Island Discs*, BBC Radio 4, 17 January 1988
22. School report, Michaelmas 1950
23. *Tavistock Gazette*, 12 March 1965
24. School report, Michaelmas 1949
25. Ibid., Lent 1950
26. Jenkins interview
27. Wild interview
28. *The Salopian*, 3 June 1951
29. School report, Summer 1951
30. *Desert Island Discs*, 17 January 1988
31. *The Salopian*, 14 December 1952
32. Ibid.
33. Ian Josephs, interview with MLC
34. Ibid.
35. Michael Hoban interview with MLC
36. Josephs interview
37. *The Salopian*, 14 December 1952
38. Josephs interview
39. *Daily Express* and *News Chronicle*, 24 November 1952
40. Richard Sachs, interview with MLC
41. Hoban interview

Chapter 4: The Cellar of the Oxford Union

1. Bryan Magee, conversation with MLC
2. *The Times*, 12 September 1992
3. *Isis*, 20 October 1954
4. *Western Mail*, 2 May 1990

5. *World In Action*, Granada TV, 19 November 1990
6. Tyrrell Burgess, interview with MLC
7. Ian Josephs, interview with MLC
8. *Oxford Magazine*, 28 February 1952
9. Josephs interview
10. Julian Critchley, *Heseltine: The Unauthorized Biography* (André Deutsch, London, 1987), p. 18
11. Josephs interview
12. *Cherwell*, 16 June 1953
13. *Isis*, 20 October 1954
14. Margaret Thatcher, *The Path To Power* (HarperCollins, London, 1995), p. 45
15. Josephs interview
16. Guy Arnold, interview with MLC
17. Magee conversation
18. *Oxford Magazine*, 4 December 1952
19. Ibid., 19 February 1953
20. Ibid., 22 October 1953
21. *Isis*, 10 June 1953
22. Ibid., 21 October 1953
23. *Oxford Magazine*, 7 May 1953
24. *Isis*, 6 May 1953
25. *Cherwell*, 17 February 1953
26. Ibid., 16 February 1954
27. David Walter, *The Oxford Union: Playground of Power* (Macdonald, London, 1984), p. 214
28. Ibid.
29. Ibid.
30. *Isis*, 20 October 1954
31. Josephs interview
32. Julian Critchley, *A Bag of Boiled Sweets* (Faber and Faber, London, 1994), p. 56
33. Michael Tombs, letter to MLC
34. Sir Michael Pike, interview with MLC
35. Josephs interview
36. Critchley, op. cit. (1987), p. 15
37. Ibid.
38. Ibid.
39. *Isis*, 20 May 1953
40. *Oxford Mail*, 22 July 1954

41. George Richardson, interview with MLC
42. *Isis*, 26 May and 28 April 1954
43. Ibid., 20 October 1954
44. *Cherwell*, 4 May 1954
45. Letter from Bryan Ellis to his parents, 2 May 1954
46. *Cherwell*, 4 May 1954
47. Fred Newman, interview with *Cherwell* historian Robert Unsworth
48. *Oxford Magazine*, 6 May 1954
49. Jeremy Isaacs, interview with MLC
50. *Cherwell*, 4 May 1954
51. Ibid., 11 May 1954
52. Ibid., 9 June 1954
53. *Isis*, 20 October 1954
54. Letter, Heseltine to Geoffrey Hayes, June 1954
55. *Sunday Express*, 10 June 1984
56. John Stewart, interview with MLC
57. *Oxford Mail*, 22 July 1954
58. *Isis*, 27 October 1954
59. *Oxford Mail*, 1 November 1954
60. Pike interview
61. *Cherwell*, 2 November 1954
62. *Northern Whig* (Belfast), 6 November 1954
63. *Cherwell*, 30 November 1954
64. *Isis*, 20 October 1954
65. Philip Swindells, letter to MLC
66. Union Members' Payments Register, 1951–55; Standing Committee minutes, 17 January 1955
67. Magee conversation
68. Burgess interview
69. Paul Winner, interview with MSC
70. Josephs interview

Chapter 5: Opportunities for Graduates

1. *The Times*, 12 September 1992
2. Derek Budden, interview with MLC
3. *Sunday Express*, 5 October 1986
4. Jeremy Isaacs, interview with MLC
5. Jean Taverner, interview with MLC
6. Ian Josephs, interview with MLC

7. Ibid.
8. Ibid.
9. *Sunday Mirror*, 30 April 1995
10. *Sunday Express*, 5 October 1986
11. *Woman's Own*, 10 May 1986
12. *Evening Standard*, 11 October 1977
13. *Sunday Times*, 5 January 1986
14. Josephs interview
15. Taverner interview
16. *World In Action*, Granada TV, 19 November 1990
17. Heseltine interview with Peter Gillman for *Harpers & Queen*, conducted 2 July 1990
18. *GQ*, February 1988
19. Geoffrey Hayes, interview with MLC
20. Alan Watkins, *A Conservative Coup* (Duckworth, London, 1991), p. 80
21. Michael Heseltine, *Where There's a Will* (Hutchinson, London, 1987), p. 179
22. Josephs interview
23. Taverner interview
24. Josephs interview
25. Leigh Davies, interview with MSC
26. Taverner interview
27. Ibid.
28. Josephs interview
29. *Daily Telegraph*, 5 February 1996
30. Taverner interview
31. Josephs interview
32. Heseltine–Gillman interview
33. Taverner interview
34. Josephs interview
35. Ibid.
36. Heseltine–Gillman interview
37. Raymond Nash, conversation with TEH
38. *GQ*, February 1988
39. *Daily Mail*, 12 January 1986
40. *Jewish Chronicle*, 10 February 1956
41. Heseltine–Gillman interview
42. *GQ*, February 1988
43. Robert Myers, interview with MLC
44. Agreement between R. Myers and C. Labovitch, 15 March 1956

45. Myers interview
46. *Evening Standard*, 6 December 1961
47. Thomas Ackland, interview with MLC
48. Ibid.
49. *Profile*, BBC Radio 4, 31 October 1981
50. Gail Godwin, *Mr Bedford and the Muses* (Heinemann, London, 1984), p. 7
51. Nigel Dempster, interview with MLC
52. Thomas Stuttaford, interview with MLC
53. John Box, interview with MSC
54. *Daily Express*, 9 January 1959

Chapter 6: Sixty-One Days in the Guards

1. Johnny Rickett, interview with MSC
2. *Cherwell*, 1 March 1955
3. Public Record Office, DEFE 7/1048
4. Queen's Regulations 1955, para 672, sub-paras (e) and (g)
5. Ian Josephs, interview with MLC
6. Rickett interview
7. Lord Massereene, interview with MSC
8. George Rees, interview with MSC
9. Peter Horsfall, interview with MSC
10. Ibid.
11. Ibid.
12. Rees interview
13. Rickett interview
14. Tom Wills, interview with MSC
15. Rickett interview
16. Horsfall interview
17. Wills interview
18. Horsfall interview
19. Christopher Madden, interview with MSC
20. Desmond Lynch, interview with MSC
21. Rickett interview
22. Hugh Myddelton, interview with MSC
23. Madden interview
24. Ibid.
25. Peter Mitchell, letter to MSC
26. Madden interview
27. Ibid.

28. Ibid.
29. Mitchell letter
30. Ivor Ramsden, interview with MSC
31. Sir Charles Guthrie, letter to MSC
32. Rickett interview
33. David Lloyd, interview with MSC
34. *London Gazette*, 6 October 1959
35. Sir John Miller, interview with MSC
36. Ibid.
37. Ron Rumble, interview with MLC
38. Hugh Rees, interview with MLC
39. *Daily Telegraph*, 5 June 1987
40. Geoffrey Hayes, interview with MLC
41. *South Wales Evening Post*, 2 October 1959
42. Ibid., 5 October 1959
43. Ibid., 7 October 1959
44. *Sunday Pictorial*, 20 September 1959
45. Guthrie letter

Chapter 7: Man About Town

1. *Sunday Times*, 1 May 1983
2. *Man About Town*, Spring 1953
3. Tailor and Cutter press release, 21 December 1959
4. *Evening Standard*, 6 December 1961
5. *About Town*, April 1961
6. *Private Eye*, 9 March 1963
7. *About Town*, June 1961
8. Ibid.
9. *About Town*, April 1961
10. David Hughes, interview with MLC
11. Brendan Lehane, interview with MLC
12. Hughes interview
13. Jeanette Collins, interview with MSC
14. Prudence Fay (née Butcher), interview with MLC
15. Corinna Adam, interview with MSC
16. Felicity Solesbury, interview with SM
17. *Varsity*, 18 February 1967
18. Lord Beaumont, interview with MLC
19. Clive Irving, interview with MLC

20. Ibid.
21. Jeremy Wallington, interview with MLC
22. Adam interview
23. Irving interview
24. Ron Hall, interview with MLC
25. Wallington interview
26. Irving interview
27. *Topic*, 22 December 1962
28. Alan Brien, interview with MSC
29. Michael Heseltine, *Where There's a Will* (Hutchinson, London, 1987), p. 33
30. Ibid.
31. *Talking Politics*, BBC Radio 4, 19 September 1977
32. *Sunday Times*, 1 May 1983
33. Beaumont interview
34. Irving interview
35. Albert Dollimore, interview with MLC
36. Ibid.
37. Ibid.
38. Anthony Heseltine, interview with MLC
39. Minutes of Works and Planning Committee, Tenterden Borough Council, 2 June 1964
40. *Sunday Telegraph Magazine*, 1 May 1983
41. Alexander Hutchison, interview with MLC
42. Valerie Hutchison, interview with MLC
43. Bryan Collins, interview with MLC
44. A. Hutchison interview
45. Ibid.
46. V. Hutchison interview
47. Letter, Tenterden borough surveyor to Bastion, 24 August 1967
48. Rhys Morgan, interview with MLC
49. Milton Shulman, interview with MLC
50. Bryan Magee, interview with MLC
51. Jeremy Isaacs, interview with MLC
52. Unidentified review, March 1963
53. Michael Weigall, interview with MLC
54. *People in London*, ITN, 21 November 1963
55. Diana Edwards-Jones, interview with MLC
56. Sir Geoffrey Cox, interview with MLC
57. Ibid.

58. Ibid.
59. *Evening Standard*, 26 October 1960
60. *The Observer*, 30 October 1960
61. Letter, Heseltine to Coventry North activists, November 1964
62. Doug Mann, interview with SM and MLC
63. Ibid.
64. Ibid.
65. Marisa Masters, interview with MLC
66. *The Times*, 8 October 1968
67. Masters interview
68. *Daily Mirror*, 17 November 1990
69. Julian Critchley, *A Bag of Boiled Sweets* (Faber and Faber, London, 1994), p. 71
70. Ian Josephs, interview with MLC
71. Ibid.
72. *Coventry Evening Telegraph*, 2 December 1961
73. Cynthia Hubbard, interview with SM
74. Sonia Greenwood (née Edelman), interview with MSC
75. Tilli Edelman, interview with MSC

Chapter 8: The Last Member for Tavistock

1. See Dermot Englefield, Janet Seaton and Isobel White, *Facts About British Prime Ministers* (Mansell, London, 1995)
2. Gerard Woodcock, *History of the Tavistock Constituency* (unpublished manuscript, 1996)
3. Jim Cobley, interview with MLC
4. Archie Jack, conversation with MLC
5. James Taylor, interview with MLC
6. Cobley interview
7. *The Times*, 8 October 1968
8. *Tavistock Gazette*, 2 April 1965
9. Dick Broad, interview with MLC
10. Hilda Collinssplatt, interview with MLC
11. *Town*, February, March and April 1965
12. Cobley interview
13. *Tavistock Gazette*, 2 April 1965
14. Ibid.
15. *Tavistock Times* and *Tavistock Gazette*, 2 April 1965 (Reports of the exact words differ, but not significantly)

449

16. *Tavistock Gazette* and *Tavistock Times*, 2 April 1965
17. Cobley interview
18. *Tavistock Gazette* and *Tavistock Times*, 2 April 1965
19. *Tavistock Times*, 2 April 1965
20. *Tavistock Gazette*, 2 April 1965
21. Ibid.
22. James Mildren, interview with MLC
23. *Tavistock Gazette*, 2 April 1965
24. Broad interview
25. *Tavistock Times*, 2 April 1965
26. *South Devon Times*, 2 April 1965
27. Cobley interview
28. Ibid.
29. *Tavistock Times*, 11 March 1966
30. John Hart, interview with MLC
31. *The Economist*, 19 March 1966
32. *Daily Mirror*, 31 March 1966
33. Michael Heseltine, *Where There's a Will* (Hutchinson, London, 1987), p. 9. The true figure should be ten.
34. *Hansard*, 14 July 1966, cols. 1773–9
35. Peter Walker, *Staying Power* (Bloomsbury, London, 1991), p. 95; *Town*, November 1961
36. *Town*, March 1962
37. Barbara Castle, *The Castle Diaries 1964–70* (Weidenfeld & Nicolson, London, 1984), p. 374 (15 February 1968)
38. Margaret Thatcher, *The Path to Power* (HarperCollins, London, 1995), p. 143
39. Heseltine election address, Tavistock, 1966
40. *Tavistock Times*, 8 January 1968
41. Heseltine, op. cit. (1987), p. 180
42. *Hansard*, 16 July 1981, col. 1500
43. *Daily Telegraph*, 22 April 1968
44. *Tavistock Times*, 26 April and 3 May 1968
45. Ibid., 24 December 1969
46. Mildren interview
47. John Finnegan, interview with MLC
48. Betsy Gallup, interview with MLC
49. Harold Luscombe, interview with MLC
50. Heseltine interview with Peter Gillman for *Harpers & Queen*, conducted 2 July 1990

Chapter 9: Campaign *Strategies*

1. Julian Critchley, *A Bag of Boiled Sweets* (Faber and Faber, 1994), p. 101; *Heseltine: The Unauthorized Biography* (André Deutsch, London, 1987), p. 34
2. Brian Moynahan, interview with MLC
3. Ibid.
4. Adrian Bridgewater, interview with MLC
5. Ibid.
6. Ibid.
7. Paul Buckley, interview with MLC
8. Robert Heller, interview with MLC
9. Lindsay Masters, interview with Ivan Fallon, *c.* 1987, for *The Brothers: The Rise of Saatchi and Saatchi* (Hutchinson, London, 1988)
10. Neil Crichton-Miller, interview with MLC
11. Heseltine interview with Peter Gillman for *Harpers & Queen*, conducted 2 July 1990
12. Heseltine interview with Ivan Fallon, *c.* 1987, for *The Brothers*
13. Fallon, op. cit., p. 37
14. Heseltine–Gillman interview
15. *The Observer*, 17 October 1965
16. Heller interview
17. Ibid.
18. Ibid.
19. *Evening Standard*, 31 August 1966
20. Labovitch interview with Peter Gillman for *Harpers & Queen* magazine, conducted 1990
21. *GQ*, February 1988
22. Ibid.
23. Buckley interview
24. Crichton-Miller interview
25. *Talking Politics*, BBC Radio 4, 19 September 1977
26. Crichton-Miller interview
27. Heseltine–Gillman interview
28. Gordon Swanborough, interview with MSC
29. Buckley interview
30. Michael Jackson, interview with MLC
31. Roland Schenk, interview with MLC
32. Ibid.
33. Philip Kleinman, interview with MLC

34. *Campaign*, 12 September 1968

35. Jackson interview

36. Ibid.

37. Ibid.

38. Heller interview

39. Ibid.

40. Tariq Ali, *Street Fighting Years* (Fontana, London, 1988), p. 76

41. Heller interview

42. Fallon, op. cit., p. 262

43. Ibid.

44. Crichton-Miller interview

45. *Today*, 7 November 1990

46. Fallon, op. cit., p. 36

47. Heseltine–Fallon interview

48. Ibid.

49. Heller interview

50. Ibid.

51. Buckley interview

Chapter 10: High Flyer

1. *Sunday Times*, 1 May 1983

2. Ibid.

3. Michael Heseltine, *Where There's a Will* (Hutchinson, London, 1987), pp. 11–12

4. *Sunday Times*, 1 May 1983

5. John Steele, interview with TDFF

6. *Sunday Times*, 9 April 1972

7. Susan Hampshire, *Every Letter Counts: Winning in Life Despite Dyslexia* (Bantam, London, 1990), p. 220

8. Peter Walker, *Staying Power* (Bloomsbury, London, 1991), p. 95

9. Kenneth Baker, *The Turbulent Years* (Faber and Faber, London, 1993), p. 301

10. Lord Blaker, interview with MLC

11. *Hansard*, 19 May 1971, col. 1398

12. Bruce Wood, *The Process of Local Government Reform, 1966–74* (Allen & Unwin, London, 1976), p. 146

13. John Macmillan, interview with MLC

14. *Western Morning News*, 7 January 1971

15. Betsy Gallup, interview with MLC

16. Macmillan interview
17. Gallup interview
18. *Sunday Express*, 9 July 1972
19. *Daily Telegraph*, 16 June 1972
20. John Hay, interview with MLC
21. Heseltine, op. cit., p. 13
22. Cecil Parkinson, interview with MLC
23. Ibid.
24. Cecil Parkinson, *Right at the Centre* (Weidenfeld & Nicolson, London, 1992), p. 115
25. Geoffrey Knight, interview with TDFF
26. Parkinson, op. cit., p. 117
27. Parkinson interview
28. Brian Trubshaw, interview with TDFF
29. Ken Binning, interview with TDFF
30. John Campbell, *Edward Heath* (Jonathan Cape, London, 1993), pp. 321–2
31. Michael Heseltine, op. cit. and *The Challenge of Europe: Can Britain Win?* (Weidenfeld & Nicolson, London, 1989)
32. Heseltine, op. cit. (1989), p. 118
33. *The Times*, 29 September 1972
34. Parkinson interview
35. Cecil King, *The Cecil King Diary, 1970–74* (Jonathan Cape, London, 1975), p. 284 (1 May 1973)
36. *Hansard*, 12 February 1973, col. 222
37. Commons Science and Technology Committee Report, September 1973, p. xii
38. *The Guardian*, 7 September 1973
39. *Hansard*, 16 October 1973, col. 43
40. *Daily Telegraph*, 7 September 1973
41. *Sunday Times*, 9 September 1973
42. Campbell, op. cit., p. 101
43. Parkinson interview
44. Tony Lane, interview with MLC
45. *Daily Mail* and *Daily Express*, 8 September 1973
46. Parkinson interview
47. Science and Technology Committee Report, p. xxxii
48. *The Guardian*, 29 January 1977
49. Lane interview
50. Parkinson interview

51. *Daily Mail*, 22 November 1972
52. Parkinson interview

Chapter 11: Oh My Darling Heseltine

1. *The Times*, 21 October 1974
2. Norman Tebbit, *Upwardly Mobile* (Weidenfeld & Nicolson, London, 1988), p. 141
3. Margaret Thatcher, *The Path to Power* (HarperCollins, London, 1995), p. 287
4. Michael Jones, interview with MLC
5. Thatcher, op. cit., p. 287
6. Sir Bernard Ingham, interview with TDFF
7. Jones interview
8. Thatcher, op. cit., p. 300
9. *Independent on Sunday*, 11 November 1990
10. Jones interview
11. *News of the World*, 26 October 1975
12. *Sun*, 16 January 1975; *The Times*, 6 March 1975
13. *Daily Telegraph*, 7 May 1975
14. *Hansard*, 12 May 1975, col. 20
15. Tony Benn, unpublished diary, 12 May 1975
16. Tony Benn, *Against the Tide: Diaries, 1973–76* (Hutchinson, London, 1989), p. 516 (12 February 1976)
17. *Talking Politics*, BBC Radio 4, 19 September 1977
18. Michael Heseltine, *Where There's a Will* (Hutchinson, London, 1987), pp. 61–2
19. Conservative conference report 1975, pp. 45–6
20. Sarah Hogg and Jonathan Hill, *Too Close to Call* (Little, Brown, London, 1995), p. 128
21. Dermot Gleeson, interview with MLC
22. Jones interview
23. Gleeson interview
24. *The Guardian*, 13 October 1977
25. Bruce Anderson, *John Major* (Fourth Estate, London, 1991), p. 32
26. Conservative conference report 1976, pp. 117–19
27. Ibid.
28. Thatcher, op. cit., p. 319
29. *Sunday Times*, 11 January 1976
30. Thatcher, op. cit., p. 319

31. James Prior, *A Balance of Power* (Hamish Hamilton, London, 1986), p. 151

32. *Hansard*, 28 May 1976, col. 771

33. The earliest reference to 'Tarzan' I have found is in the London *Evening Standard*, 9 March 1972

34. *Daily Telegraph*, 28 May 1976

35. Norman Shrapnel, *The Performers: Politics as Theatre* (Constable, London, 1978), p. 195n.

36. Prior, op. cit., p. 151

37. George Thomas, *Mr Speaker* (Century, London, 1985), p. 152

38. Tom King, interview with MLC

39. *Daily Express*, 23 July 1976

40. *The Guardian*, 29 January 1977

41. *Hansard*, 28 May 1976, col. 769

42. *South Wales Evening Post*, 28 May 1976

43. Kenneth Baker, *The Turbulent Years* (Faber and Faber, London, 1993), p. 305

44. Thatcher, op. cit., p. 320

45. *The Times*, 15 February 1977

46. *The Guardian*, 11 November 1977

47. Pamela Collison, interview with TEH; *News of the World*, 8 December 1981

48. Robert Heller, interview with MLC

49. Heseltine interview with Peter Gillman for *Harpers & Queen*, conducted 2 July 1990

50. Ivan Fallon, *The Brothers: The Rise of Saatchi and Saatchi* (Hutchinson, London, 1988), p. 106

51. Ibid.

52. Ibid., p. 107

53. Heseltine–Gillman interview

Chapter 12: A Model Thatcherite

1. Margaret Thatcher, *The Path to Power* (HarperCollins, London, 1995), p. 446

2. Margaret Thatcher, *The Downing Street Years* (HarperCollins, London, 1993), pp. 423–4

3. *Sunday Telegraph*, 6 May 1979

4. *Hansard*, 15 January 1980, col. 1470

5. Labour Party manifesto, 1987

6. Michael Heseltine, *Where There's a Will* (Hutchinson, London, 1987), p. 79

7. Quoted in Paul McQuail, *A View from the Bridge* (DoE, London, 1995), p. 17

8. Heseltine, op. cit., p. 15

9. Peter Hennessy, *Whitehall* (Secker & Warburg, London, 1989), p. 607

10. Quoted in McQuail, op. cit., p. 19

11. Heseltine, op. cit., p. 18

12. Quoted in McQuail, op. cit., p. 18

13. Michael Heseltine, 'Ministers and Management in Whitehall', *Management Services in Government* (London, 1980)

14. Hennessy, op. cit., p. 440

15. David Edmonds, interview with MLC

16. Heseltine, op. cit. (1987), p. 21

17. Treasury and Civil Service Select Committee Minutes, 28 October 1981, pp. 158 and 165

18. Heseltine, op. cit. (1987), p. 22

19. Edmonds interview

20. Heseltine, op. cit. (1987), pp. 40–41

21. *The Guardian*, 29 December 1980

22. *Daily Mail*, 11 November 1981

23. David Howell, interview with MLC

24. David Butler, Andrew Adonis and Tony Travers, *Failure in British Government* (OUP, Oxford, 1994), p. 61

25. Tom King, interview with MLC

26. Butler et al., op. cit., p. 32

27. *Alternatives to Domestic Rates*, Cmnd 8449 (HMSO, London, 1981)

28. Butler et al., op. cit., p. 35

29. *Hansard*, 16 December 1987, cols. 1138–9

30. James Prior, *A Balance of Power* (Hamish Hamilton, London, 1986), pp. 150–51

31. Conservative conference press release, 1978

32. Heseltine speech, 18 July 1979, quoted in *Local Government Studies*, March/April 1980

33. Lord Finsberg, interview with MLC

34. Simon Jenkins, *Accountable to None* (Penguin, London, 1996), pp. 42–3

35. *Profile*, BBC Radio 4, 31 October 1981

36. Nigel Lawson, *The View From Number Eleven* (Bantam, London, 1992), pp. 122 and 312

37. Hugo Young, *One of Us* (Macmillan, London, 1989), pp. 199–200

38. Cecil Parkinson, interview with MLC

39. Lawson, op. cit., p. 40

40. Thatcher, op. cit. (1993), pp. 148–9
41. Young, op. cit., p. 218

Chapter 13: It Took a Riot

1. Paul McQuail, interview with MLC
2. *The Times*, 27 July 1981
3. David Edmonds, interview with MLC
4. Michael Heseltine, *Where There's a Will* (Hutchinson, London, 1987), p. 136
5. Heseltine speech, 23 May 1991
6. Heseltine, op. cit., p. 139
7. Eric Sorensen, interview with MLC
8. Edmonds interview
9. *John Dunn Show*, BBC Radio 2, 9 March 1987
10. *Sunday Times*, 26 July 1981
11. *Liverpool Echo*, 5 August 1981
12. Edmonds interview
13. *Daily Express*, 24 July 1981
14. *Daily Telegraph*, 21 July 1981
15. Lord Kingsdown, interview with MLC
16. Sir Brian Corby, interview with MLC
17. Peter Hennessy, *Whitehall* (Secker & Warburg, London, 1989), p. 699
18. Ibid.
19. Ibid., p. 690
20. *Sunday Times*, 18 March 1990
21. Conservative conference press release, 15 October 1981
22. Ibid.
23. Ibid.
24. *Panorama*, BBC1, 9 October 1989
25. *The Times*, 16 October 1981
26. Roger Bright, interview with MLC
27. Colette Bowe, interview with MLC
28. Sir Trevor Jones, interview with MLC
29. Jones interview
30. *The Guardian*, 12 April 1982
31. Jones interview
32. Heseltine, op. cit., p. 158
33. John Hamilton, interview with MLC
34. *Liverpool Daily Post*, 22 October 1979

35. Ibid.
36. Peter Walker, *Staying Power* (Bloomsbury, London, 1991), p. 86
37. John Silkin, *Changing Battlefields* (Hamish Hamilton, London, 1987), p. 133
38. *Something To Be Remembered By*, Central TV, 17 November 1986
39. Sir Nigel Broackes, interview with SM
40. Ibid.
41. *Evening Standard*, 2 December 1986
42. Bright interview
43. Ed Berman, interview with MLC and SM
44. Ibid.
45. Heseltine, op. cit., p. 14
46. George Bundred, interview with MLC
47. Margaret Thatcher, *The Downing Street Years* (HarperCollins, London, 1993), p. 424
48. Michael Parkinson, interview with MLC
49. Jones interview
50. John Hamilton, interview with MLC

Chapter 14: Defence Battles

1. *The Observer* and *Sunday Telegraph*, 19 December 1982
2. Sir William Jackson and Lord Bramall, *The Chiefs* (Brassey's, London, 1992), p. 425
3. Margaret Thatcher, *The Downing Street Years* (HarperCollins, London, 1993), p. 424
4. *The Guardian*, 21 January 1983
5. *John Dunn Show*, BBC Radio 2, 9 March 1987
6. John Ledlie, interview with SM
7. *Sun*, *The Times* and *Daily Mail*, 8 February 1983
8. *The Guardian*, 24 September 1983
9. Henry Porter, *Lies, Damned Lies and Some Exclusives* (Chatto & Windus, London, 1984), p. 77; *Daily Telegraph*, 14 December 1983
10. Ledlie interview
11. Michael Cockerell et al., *Sources Close to the Prime Minister* (Macmillan, London, 1984), p. 230
12. *Daily Telegraph*, 23 April 1983
13. *The Guardian*, 25 April 1983
14. Cathy Massiter affidavit, 12 July 1985
15. *Twenty-Twenty Vision*, Channel 4, 1985

16. *The Observer*, 17 May 1987
17. Thatcher, op. cit., pp. 296–7
18. *The Whitehall Warrior*, BBC2, 15 January 1986
19. *The Guardian*, 24 September 1983
20. *Oratory*, BBC Radio 4, May 1988
21. *The People*, 9 October 1983
22. *Daily Mail*, 11 July 1983
23. Michael Heseltine, *Where There's a Will* (Hutchinson, London, 1987), p. 24
24. Lord Bramall, interview with SM
25. Heseltine interview with David Taylor, for BBC *MoD* series, 1985
26. Ibid.
27. Heseltine, op. cit., p. 31
28. Ibid.
29. Bramall interview
30. *On The Record*, BBC2, 18 November 1990
31. Jackson and Bramall, op. cit., p. 446
32. *The Times*, 7 May 1984
33. *Daily Telegraph*, 19 July 1984
34. Bramall interview
35. Ibid.
36. Ibid.
37. Cassidi confirms the story as related in John Junor, *Memoirs: Listening for a Midnight Tram* (Pan, London, 1991), p. 321
38. Letter to SM
39. Sir Geoffrey Howe, *Conflict of Loyalty* (Pan, London, 1995), p. 468
40. Peter Jenkins, *Mrs Thatcher's Revolution* (Jonathan Cape, London, 1987), p. 194
41. *The Guardian*, 31 October 1983
42. Arthur Gavshon and Desmond Rice, *The Sinking of the Belgrano* (Secker & Warburg, London, 1984)
43. *The Observer*, 17 February 1985
44. *Hansard*, 18 February 1985, col. 737
45. *The Observer*, 17 February 1985
46. Clive Ponting, *The Right to Know* (Sphere, London, 1985), p. 138
47. Richard Norton-Taylor, *The Ponting Affair* (Cecil Woolf, London, 1985), p. 45
48. Ponting, op. cit., p. 138
49. *Hansard*, 18 February 1985, col. 744
50. *The Observer*, 17 February 1985

51. *Hansard*, 18 February 1985, col. 733
52. *The Observer*, 22 March 1987
53. *Washington Post*, 23 June 1985
54. *Hansard*, 26 November 1985, col. 740
55. *Panorama*, BBC1, 13 January 1986
56. Clive Ponting, *Whitehall: Tragedy and Farce* (Hamish Hamilton, London, 1986), p. 184
57. *Financial Times*, 28 September 1983
58. Nigel Lawson, *The View from Number Eleven* (Bantam, London, 1992), p. 283
59. Heseltine–Taylor interview
60. Bramall interview
61. Margaret Thatcher, op. cit., p. 424
62. Commons Defence Select Committee Report, June 1985, pp. xv and xli
63. *The Guardian*, 4 July 1985

Chapter 15: No Place for Me with Honour

1. Geoffrey Howe, *Conflict of Loyalty* (Pan, London, 1995), p. 471
2. Peter Hennessy, *Whitehall* (Secker & Warburg, London, 1989), p. 371
3. Ibid., p. 372
4. Michael Heseltine, *Where There's a Will* (Hutchinson, London, 1987), p. 46
5. *The Guardian*, 14 February 1989
6. Heseltine, op. cit., p. 46
7. *Analysis*, BBC Radio 4, 27 May 1987
8. Alan Clark, *Diaries* (Weidenfeld & Nicolson, London, 1993), p. 344 (11 November 1990)
9. Nigel Lawson, *The View from Number Eleven* (Bantam, London, 1992), p. 674
10. Clark, op. cit., pp. 74–6 (13 and 24 April 1984)
11. Lord Bramall, interview with SM
12. Howe, op. cit., pp. 461–2
13. Norman Tebbit, *Upwardly Mobile* (Weidenfeld & Nicolson, London, 1988), p. 247
14. Sir Colin Chandler, interview with SM
15. Ibid.
16. *The Times*, 27 September 1985
17. Tebbit, op. cit., p. 238
18. Commons Defence Select Committee Report, July 1986, p. 13

19. Margaret Thatcher, *The Downing Street Years* (HarperCollins, London, 1993), p. 426
20. Magnus Linklater and David Leigh, *Not With Honour* (Sphere, London, 1986), p. 63
21. Howe, op. cit., p. 461
22. Thatcher, op. cit., p. 419
23. Linklater and Leigh, op. cit., p. 199
24. *Hansard*, 15 January 1986, col. 1165
25. Thatcher, op. cit., p. 427
26. Defence Select Committee Report, p. 22
27. Ibid., p. 25
28. Linklater and Leigh, op. cit., p. 82
29. *The Times*, 10 January 1986
30. *Daily Mail*, 3 January 1986
31. Commons Defence Committee Minutes, 6 February 1986, p. 210
32. *Panorama*, BBC1, 13 January 1986
33. *On The Record*, BBC1, 18 November 1990
34. Kenneth Baker, *The Turbulent Years* (Faber and Faber, London, 1993), pp. 302–3
35. Thatcher, op. cit., p. 430
36. *The Times*, 10 January 1986
37. *The Economist*, 4 January 1986
38. *The Times*, 4 January 1986
39. Defence Select Committee Report, p. 40
40. Thatcher, op. cit., p. 436
41. *Daily Telegraph*, 28 January 1986
42. *The Thatcher Factor*, Channel 4, 7 April 1989
43. *Sun*, 7 January 1986
44. Thatcher, op. cit., p. 431
45. Lawson, op. cit., p. 678
46. Howe, op. cit., p. 467
47. Lawson, op. cit., p. 678
48. Baker, op. cit., p. 303
49. Norman Fowler, *Ministers Decide* (Chapmans, London, 1991), p. 231
50. Thatcher, op. cit., p. 432
51. Nicholas Ridley, *My Style of Government* (Hutchinson, London, 1991), pp. 48–9
52. Lawson, op. cit., p. 678
53. Baker, op. cit., p. 303
54. Lord Young, *The Enterprise Years* (Headline, London, 1991), p. 179

55. *Daily Telegraph*, *Daily Express* and *Daily Star*, 10 January 1986
56. Peter Walker, *Staying Power* (Bloomsbury, London, 1991), p. 187
57. Clark, op. cit., p. 131 (9 January 1986)
58. Walker, op. cit., p. 187
59. *The Times*, 10 January 1986
60. *Dispatches*, Channel 4, 21 November 1990
61. Richard Mottram, interview with MLC and SM
62. *Sunday Times*, 13 October 1985
63. Linklater and Leigh, op. cit., p. 3
64. Ridley, op. cit., pp. 47–8
65. *Panorama*, 13 January 1986
66. Defence Select Committee Report, p. 17
67. Lord Whitelaw, interview with MLC and SM
68. *Panorama*, 13 January 1986

Chapter 16: Where There's a Wilderness

1. *Hansard*, 13 January 1986, cols. 780–86
2. Ibid., 17 January 1986, col. 870
3. *The Downing Street Years*, Prog. 2, BBC1, 27 October 1993
4. *Hansard*, 27 January 1986, col. 662
5. Commons Trade and Industry Select Committee Report, 3 February 1987, pp. 9–10
6. See *Close Up West*, BBC West, 4 March 1993
7. *Financial Times*, 11 January 1986
8. *Hansard*, 13 November 1990, cols. 461–5
9. John Lee, interview with TEH
10. *Daily Telegraph*, 13 January 1986
11. Ibid., 15 January 1986
12. *World In Action*, ITV, 13 January 1986
13. Heseltine, *The Challenge of Europe: Can Britain Win?* (Weidenfeld & Nicolson, London, 1989), pp. 208–9
14. Margaret Thatcher, *The Downing Street Years* (HarperCollins, London, 1993), p. 440
15. *Daily Telegraph*, 10 February 1986
16. *New Society*, 14 February 1986
17. *Sunday Times*, 1 May 1983
18. *Daily Telegraph*, 21 July 1986
19. Steven Norris, *Changing Trains* (Hutchinson, London, 1996), pp. 57–8
20. *Sunday Express*, 5 October 1986

21. *The Independent*, 10 October 1989
22. *Sunday Telegraph*, 27 September 1987
23. *New Society*, 14 February 1986
24. *The Independent*, 7 October 1986
25. *New Society*, 14 February 1986
26. *Daily Telegraph*, 20 November 1986
27. Richard Cohen, interview with MLC
28. Ibid.
29. Michael Heseltine, *Where There's a Will* (Hutchinson, London, 1987), p. 5
30. Ibid., p. 101
31. *The Guardian*, 28 April 1987
32. *Hansard*, 16 December 1987, col. 1141
33. David Butler, Andrew Adonis and Tony Travers, *Failure in British Government* (OUP, Oxford, 1994), p. 241
34. William Powell, interview with MLC
35. *Daily Mail*, 17 January 1986
36. *Oxford Mail*, 14 March 1988
37. *The Spectator*, 16 September 1989
38. Tom Burke, interview with MLC
39. Ibid.
40. Richard Jameson, letter to MLC
41. Michael Heseltine, op. cit. (1989), pp. 126–54
42. Ibid., p. 77
43. Ibid., p. 213
44. Ibid., pp. 73–4
45. Ibid., p. 91
46. Ibid., p. 94
47. *The Times*, 19 November 1989
48. *Hansard*, 18 May 1989, col. 532
49. Heseltine, op. cit. (1989), p. 214
50. *The Times*, 27 June 1990
51. Speech reproduced as a pamphlet: Michael Heseltine, *Unemployment: No Time for Ostriches* (Employment Institute, London, 1988), p. 5
52. Heseltine, op. cit. (1987), p. 252
53. Christopher Johnson, interview with MLC
54. Kenneth Baker, *The Turbulent Years* (Faber and Faber, London, 1993), p. 274
55. Sir Anthony Meyer, interview with TEH
56. *The Downing Street Years*, Prog. 4, BBC1, 10 November 1993
57. Ibid.

58. *The Guardian*, 13 March 1990
59. *Daily Express*, 15 March 1990
60. *Sunday Telegraph*, 10 December 1989
61. *Tribune*, 22 December 1995
62. *Panorama*, BBC1, 9 October 1989

Chapter 17: Country Life

1. *Talking Politics*, BBC Radio 4, 19 September 1977
2. *Profile*, BBC Radio 4, 31 October 1981
3. *Harpers & Queen*, June 1985
4. Elizabeth Hayes, interview with MSC
5. *Evening News*, 13 October 1980
6. Ibid.
7. *Harpers & Queen*, June 1985
8. Sonia Greenwood (née Edelman), interview with MSC
9. Hilary Rubinstein, interview with MSC
10. *Mail on Sunday*, 18 November 1990
11. *Daily Mail*, 23 October 1993
12. Baroness Mallalieu, conversation with MLC
13. *Talking Politics*, 19 September 1977
14. *Daily Express*, 7 December 1976
15. *The Guardian*, 17 January 1984
16. The letter was reported in *The Times*, 30 January 1976, and later reproduced in full in the *Daily Mirror*, 12 December 1979. Mysteriously, it doesn't appear in the stated issue of *Country Life*, or any edition nearby. Anne Heseltine confirmed the story to a BBC journalist in 1996
17. Nikolaus Pevsner, *The Buildings of England: Northamptonshire* (Penguin, London, 1973 edn), pp. 425–6
18. *Country Life*, 4 October 1946
19. Martin Summers, interview with MSC
20. *The Times*, 13 May 1987
21. *Desert Island Discs*, BBC Radio 4, 17 January 1988
22. *Evening News*, 13 October 1980
23. *Talking Politics*, 19 September 1977
24. *Sunday Telegraph*, 27 March 1994
25. Roy Lancaster, interview with MSC
26. Ibid.
27. Ibid.
28. *Business Life*, July/August 1996

29. Letter from John Simmons to MSC
30. Lancaster interview
31. Alan Borg, interview with MSC
32. Christopher White, interview with MSC
33. Quinlan Terry, interview with MSC
34. Hugh Colvin, interview with MSC
35. *Daily Mail*, 19 October 1983
36. Ibid., 23 October 1993
37. White interview
38. *Sunday Express*, 11 February 1990
39. Kenneth Eckersley, interview with MSC
40. *Profile*, 31 October 1981
41. *The Times*, 15 July 1996
42. Ibid.
43. *Daily Mail*, 2 April 1986
44. Ibid.
45. Ibid., 29 March 1996
46. Lady Wardington, interview with MSC
47. *Talking Politics*, 19 September 1977

Chapter 18: Stop Heseltine

1. *The Times*, 10 May 1990
2. *Question Time*, BBC1, 10 May 1990
3. Andrew Neil, *Full Disclosure* (Macmillan, London, 1996), p. 245
4. Alan Watkins, *A Conservative Coup* (Duckworth, London, 1991), p. 95
5. *The Observer*, 4 November 1990
6. Raymond Monbiot, interview with TEH
7. Ibid.
8. Kenneth Baker, *The Turbulent Years* (Faber and Faber, London, 1993), p. 382
9. *Daily Mail*, 7 November 1990
10. *The Times*, 12 November 1990
11. Nigel Lawson, *The View From Number Eleven* (Bantam, London, 1992), p. 999
12. Bernard Ingham, *Kill The Messenger* (HarperCollins, London, 1991), p. 380
13. *Daily Mail*, 5 November 1990
14. *The Times*, 12 November 1990
15. *Daily Mirror*, 7 November 1990

16. *Daily Mail*, 7 November 1990
17. *The Downing Street Years*, Prog. 4, BBC1, 10 November 1993
18. *Hansard*, 13 November 1990, col. 465
19. *The Economist*, 9 March 1991
20. Cecil Parkinson, *Right at the Centre* (Weidenfeld & Nicolson, London, 1992), p. 25
21. *Financial Times*, 15 November 1990
22. Steven Norris, *Changing Trains* (Hutchinson, London, 1996), p. 154
23. *Financial Times*, 15 November 1990
24. *Daily Telegraph*, 19 November 1990
25. *Daily Mail*, 31 October 1990
26. *Daily Telegraph*, 19 November 1990
27. *The Times*, 19 November 1990
28. Baker, op. cit., p. 391
29. Alan Clark, *Diaries* (Weidenfeld & Nicolson, London, 1993), pp. 352–3 (19 November 1990)
30. Parkinson, op. cit., p. 25
31. *The Times*, 22 November 1990
32. Clark, op. cit., p. 364 (21 November 1990)
33. *The Downing Street Years*, Prog. 4, BBC1, 10 November 1993
34. *Sun*, 21 November 1990
35. *Financial Times*, 22 November 1990
36. Margaret Thatcher, *The Downing Street Years* (HarperCollins, London, 1993), p. 853
37. Baker, op. cit., p. 410
38. Quoted in Malcolm Balen, *Kenneth Clarke* (Fourth Estate, London, 1994), p. 209
39. Tom King, interview with MLC
40. Clark, op. cit., p. 359 (20 November 1990)
41. Thatcher, op. cit., p. 854
42. *Wogan*, BBC1, 19 May 1986
43. Philip Cowley, 'How Did He Do That?', in *British Elections and Parties Yearbook* (Frank Cass, London, 1996), p. 211
44. Robert Hayward, interview with MLC
45. William Powell, interview with MLC
46. Ibid.
47. Cowley, op. cit., pp. 208–9 and 204
48. Philip Cowley and John Garry, 'From Handbag to Underpants', draft article yet to be published
49. Quoted in Teresa Gorman, *The Bastards* (Pan, London, 1993), p. 9

50. Clark, op. cit., p. 369 (22 November 1990)
51. Philip Norton, in Anthony King (ed.), *Britain at the Polls, 1992* (Chatham House, Chatham, N.J., 1993), p. 59

Chapter 19: Here We Go Again

1. *Daily Telegraph*, 28 November 1990
2. *The Economist*, 24 November 1990
3. Emma Nicholson, *Secret Society* (Indigo, London, 1996), p. 152
4. Cecil Parkinson, *Right at the Centre* (Weidenfeld & Nicolson, London, 1992), p. 49
5. Kenneth Baker, *The Turbulent Years* (Faber and Faber, London, 1993), p. 423
6. *Hansard*, 5 December 1990, col. 318
7. Ibid., col. 324
8. Ibid., col. 316
9. David Butler, Andrew Adonis and Tony Travers, *Failure in British Government* (OUP, Oxford, 1994), p. 167
10. Michael Gove, *Michael Portillo: The Future of the Right* (Fourth Estate, London, 1995), pp. 195–6
11. Ibid., p. 200
12. William Powell, interview with MLC
13. Sarah Hogg and Jonathan Hill, *Too Close To Call* (Little, Brown, London, 1995), p. 57
14. Butler, et al., op. cit., p. 172
15. *Hansard*, 21 March 1990, col. 404
16. Hogg and Hill, op. cit., p. 68
17. Ibid., p. 69
18. *Hansard*, 16 December 1987, col. 1140
19. Powell interview
20. See, for instance, *Hansard*, 21 March 1991, cols. 401–5, and 23 April 1991, cols. 901–3
21. Powell interview
22. Steve Leach, 'The Local Government Review: From Vision to Damage Limitation', *Politics Review*, February 1996
23. David Thomas, interview with MLC
24. Conservative conference press release, October 1991
25. Tony Baldry, interview with MLC
26. Peter Hall, interview with MLC
27. Hogg and Hill, op. cit., p. 179

28. *Hansard*, 19 February 1992, col. 363
29. *Daily Mail*, 14 March 1992
30. *Daily Mail* and *The Times*, 28 March 1992

Chapter 20: Hezza the Prezza

1. *Mail on Sunday*, 24 May 1992
2. *The Spectator*, 31 March 1990
3. Michael Heseltine, *Where There's a Will* (Hutchinson, London, 1987), p. 119
4. *Hansard*, 16 June 1992, col. 778
5. Peter Smith, interview with MLC
6. *Hansard*, 6 July 1992, col. 36
7. *On The Record*, BBC1, 8 November 1992
8. *Daily Mail*, 8 October 1992
9. *Hansard*, 19 October 1992, col. 211
10. Tim Eggar, interview with TEH
11. *The Times*, 14 October 1992
12. Eggar interview
13. *Daily Express*, 17 October 1992
14. *Mail on Sunday*, 18 October 1992
15. *The Times*, 22 December 1992
16. *Daily Mail*, 19 October 1992
17. Commons Employment Select Committee Minutes, 16 December 1992, pp. 275–6
18. *Hansard*, 19 October 1992, col. 205
19. Ibid., col. 215
20. Ibid., 21 October 1992, col. 463
21. *The Times*, 28 October 1992
22. *Hansard*, 21 October 1992, cols. 456–8
23. Employment Select Committee Minutes, p. 265

Chapter 21: Up with This I Will Not Put

1. *Daily Mail*, 23 October 1993
2. *On The Record*, BBC1, 10 October 1993
3. *The Independent*, 27 February 1993
4. Ibid., 8 June 1993
5. *Hansard*, 29 June 1993, col. 825
6. *Sunday Times*, 21 October 1990

7. *Independent on Sunday*, 5 May 1996
8. Ibid.
9. Lord McAlpine, interview with MLC
10. Min Hogg, interview with MLC
11. *Hansard*, 22 June 1993, col. 253
12. *On The Record*, 10 October 1993
13. Scott Inquiry transcript, day 69, 28 February 1994, p. 42
14. Peter Smith, interview with MLC
15. Scott Inquiry transcript, p. 47
16. Ibid., p. 114
17. Ibid., p. 53
18. Ibid., p. 61
19. Ibid., p. 113
20. Ibid., p. 141
21. Ibid., p. 9
22. Michael Heseltine, *The Challenge of Europe: Can Britain Win?* (Weidenfeld & Nicolson, London, 1989), p. 119
23. Smith interview
24. Howard Davies, interview with MLC
25. *Six o'clock News*, BBC1, 9 October 1992
26. *The Times*, 5 November 1994
27. *The Guardian*, 4 November 1994
28. *The Guardian*, 11 April 1994
29. *The Times*, 8 March 1994
30. *Independent on Sunday*, 13 March 1994

Chapter 22: Deputy Prime Minister

1. *The Times*, 2 December 1995
2. *Express on Sunday*, 17 November 1996
3. Keith Hampson, interview with MLC
4. Philip Stephens, *Politics and the Pound*, Macmillan, London, 1996, p. 326
5. Unpublished analysis by Philip Cowley
6. *Daily Telegraph*, 1 May 1996
7. Commons Public Service Committee Minutes, 28 February 1996, p. 2
8. Quoted in Peter Hennessy, *The Hidden Wiring* (Victor Gollancz, London, 1995), p. 22
9. *The Times*, 2 December 1995
10. *Ministerial Committees of the Cabinet* (Cabinet Office, October 1995)
11. Hugh Colver, interview with MLC

12. Heseltine Minute, 24 July 1996
13. *The Times*, 11 November 1996
14. *Daily Telegraph*, 11 November 1996
15. *The Times*, 3 July 1996
16. Public Service Committee Minutes, p. 4
17. *Daily Telegraph*, 3 February 1996
18. Letter from Heseltine to Public Service Committee, 16 December 1996
19. Emma Nicholson, *Secret Society* (Indigo, London, 1996), pp. 218–19
20. Audrey Brookes, interview with MSC
21. Rik Lomas, interview with MSC
22. Tony Lloyd, interview with MSC
23. *Daily Telegraph*, 2 December 1996
24. *The Times*, 4 December 1996
25. *Hansard*, 3 December 1996, col. 791
26. *World at One*, BBC Radio 4, 6 December 1996
27. Cecil Parkinson, *Right at the Centre* (Weidenfeld & Nicolson, London), 1992, p. 255
28. Ivan Fallon, *The Brothers: The Rise of Saatchi and Saatchi* (Hutchinson, London, 1988), p. 36
29. The order ahead of Heseltine is Heath (1950); John Morris (1959); Tam Dalyell (1962); Alan Williams and Robert Sheldon (both 1964); and Kevin McNamara and Roy Hughes (both sworn in ahead of Heseltine in 1966)
30. *On the Record*, BBC1, 10 October 1993
31. Steven Norris, interview with TDFF

Index